D0154492

Producing Fashion

HAGLEY PERSPECTIVES ON BUSINESS AND CULTURE

SERIES EDITORS

Roger Horowitz, Philip Scranton, Susan Strasser

A complete list of books in the series is available from the publisher.

391
B613

Producing Fashion

Commerce, Culture, and Consumers

Edited by Regina Lee Blaszczyk

WITHDRAWN

PENN

University of Pennsylvania Press

Philadelphia

LIBRARY ST. MARY'S COLLEGE

Copyright © 2008 University of Pennsylvania Press

All rights reserved. Except for brief quotations used for purposes of review or scholarly citation, none of this book may be reproduced in any form by any means without written permission from the publisher.

Published by
University of Pennsylvania Press
Philadelphia, Pennsylvania 19104-4112

Printed in the United States of America on acid-free paper

10   9   8   7   6   5   4   3   2   1

A Cataloging-in-Publication Record is available from the Library of Congress

ISBN-13: 978-0-8122-4037-5
ISBN-10: 0-8122-4037-5

YBP $46.48   7/11/08   reprint

WITHDRAWN

LIBRARY ST. MARY'S COLLEGE

CONTENTS

PART II

Inventing Fashions, Promoting Styles

PART III

Shaping Bodies, Building Brands

PART IV
Customer Reactions, Consumer Adaptations

CHAPTER ONE

Rethinking Fashion

Regina Lee Blaszczyk

"WHAT IS FASHION?" In November 1993, marketing consultant Estelle Ellis posed this "deceivingly simple question" in a speech at the Fashion Institute of Technology (FIT) in New York. Ellis had spent more than five decades in the fashion business, launching her career during the late 1940s and early 1950s at *Seventeen* and *Charm* magazines, before establishing Business Image Inc., a creative marketing firm that helped companies to understand how social change affected business trends. Founded in 1958, Business Image Inc. had an impressive roster of clients, such as FIT, Carter Hawley Hale Stores, Condé Nast Publications (including *Glamour, House and Garden*, and *Vogue*), Evan-Picone, Joseph Schlitz Brewing Company, Kimberly-Clark, and Yves Saint Laurent Fragrances. With more than fifty years of marketing experience, Ellis was well qualified to speak about the nature of fashion and to define it for educators, students, and industry professionals. At FIT, founded as the "MIT for the fashion industries" in 1944, Ellis faced an expert audience, but she spoke her mind, undaunted.[1]

How *did* Ellis define fashion? Her FIT address is worth examining at length because it provides a fitting launchpad for this book on how fashion is produced through the interactions of commerce, culture, and consumers. Ellis had a broad view of fashion that touched almost everything in the material world. She perceived fashion in anthropological terms, that is, as a cultural force that drew sustenance from social customs, group psychology, material life, economic institutions, and other types of human interaction and, in turn, influenced them. In her eyes, fashion found its fullest expression in four areas of culture: "*mode*—the way we dress; *manners*—the way we express ourselves; *mores*—the way we live; and *markets*—the way we are defined demographically and psychologically." Looking at the world through the lenses of these Four M's, Ellis understood fashion simply and directly, that is, as a causal agent that constantly reshaped all material things, from "the fabric environments which surround our bodies" to "the nature of design and architecture." Fashion, Ellis persuasively argued, was like a perpetual motion machine, always busy, always moving, and always recontouring "daily living, whether in the home, office, institution, or community."[2]

Ellis's definition of fashion, which emphasizes creativity and innovation, has important ramifications for scholars seeking to understand how fashion is produced. At first glance, her ideas may seem too inclusive or evanescent to be useful in historical analysis, but Ellis's clarifying remarks about the knottiness of the question "What is fashion?" get to the core of this book's themes. Speaking at FIT, Ellis hoped to open her audience's eyes to the material world at large, and to highlight the creative possibilities inherent in all aspects of design, production, marketing, and merchandising. She understood the fertile fields that waited to be plowed, the benefits of cross-fertilization, and the wonderful fruit that could be borne by expansive thinking and careful looking.

The students, teacher-practitioners, and others who may have listened to Ellis speak at FIT became the future and current *producers* of fashion. Many probably aspired to join New York's thriving "creative economy," to become members of the "creative classes" who generate the sketches, color palettes, style forecasts, fabric combinations, and design innovations used by manufacturers to sew or knit apparel for American consumers and, increasingly, for global markets.[3] We may never know if anyone who heard "What is fashion?" graduated from FIT to begin the long journey to design celebrity, following in the footsteps of sensational Seventh Avenue success stories such as Ralph Lauren and Donna Karan.[4] Most students listening to Ellis as she lectured at FIT, however, probably found entry-level jobs behind the scenes in the apparel, beauty, design, publishing, and retailing industries. In these positions, few would leave their personal imprint on the look and feel of American style, but collectively they would help to shape and reshape fashion through their everyday duties and assignments in advertising agencies, apparel companies, accessories and fragrance licensing, beauty salons, newspapers and publishing houses, public-relations firms, and television studios.

With this situation in mind, Ellis sought to encourage and inspire creativity among the rank and file who would soon help the gears of the fashion business to mesh. As a highly successful creative professional, Ellis took her cues from anywhere in the culture where ideas, values, emotions, and meanings percolated. She reminded students that it was important not to lose sight of the big picture, eschewing the Marxist and postmodern analyses of fashion that dominated academic discourse at the time. Ellis spoke at a moment when the theories of French semiotician Roland Barthes, who had interrogated the "fashion system" as an expression of bourgeois values, generated and sustained by the media, enjoyed wide currency in American universities. Put simply, Barthes had argued that the mass media constructed certain visual priorities as "truth," advancing representations that furthered the bourgeoisie's social position. The media helped invent bourgeois tastes and to define them as "tradition," even though these tropes had no foundation in nature and few precedents in history. In Barthes's interpretation, which was ideologically sympathetic to the Marxist belief in the irreconcilable differences between capital and labor, everything was about the struggle for power.[5] In contrast, Ellis took a more pragmatic and far less sinister position on fashion, its meaning, and its production. Her straightforward understanding has ramifications for this historical study of how fashion has been created.

As a former fashion editor, Ellis certainly understood the persuasive power of the mass media, acknowledging the emotive sway that photographs of sexy young models in glamorous settings could have on human desire and shoppers' motivations. Visual seduction was the stock-in-trade of fashion photography; verbal enticement, the forte of fashion editors. But Ellis knew that the media hype was only part of the story, and that something more important needed to be emphasized in her talk that day at FIT.

Ellis saw fashion as something other than a media extravaganza that celebrated big-name designers, anorexic supermodels, and trendy wardrobes in *Vogue* or *Esquire*. For her, fashion reached beyond apparel, clothing, and dress. She had long understood it to be a visual and material system of symbols and meanings that extended to all things produced by people, from hats to goods for the home. All these artifacts were suspended in and connected by the gel popularly known as "culture," so that changes to one family of objects might reverberate and have an impact on other types. When innovations bubbled up among an object group such as shoes or housewares, a chain reaction could occur *if* the visual or material shift resonated in the culture, that is, if it touched the emotions and stirred the imaginations of other creators, retailers, publishers, and consumers. New products that struck a chord in popular culture or that found fans in a niche market could initiate a sea change across the board, affecting a range of goods, materials, applications, and settings.[6]

There was no predetermined pattern to this process of producing fashion, but those in the business could learn to discern the ebb and flow; some could even anticipate the most likely future scenarios.[7] Everything was subject to changes in style: architecture and automobiles, kitchen gadgets and kids' clothing, furniture and personal grooming products. In *mode* and *mores*, fashion could be fickle, like the 1960s fad for the miniskirt fed by the decade's rebellious but ephemeral youth culture; but it also could be enduring, like the *manners* that dictated silverware, white table linen, and fine china for wedding banquets and somber black clothes for funerals and mourning. Depending on the *market* segment, fashion in apparel might be elite and expensive like Parisian haute couture, or democratic and affordable like the ready-to-wear that made Seventh Avenue world famous. Sometimes, it could be both high and low, integrating highbrow elements in mass-market designs. Some styles fed on elite culture, some on popular culture; some trickled down, while some bubbled up from below, as ordinary people sought to express their individuality in dress or to personalize their surroundings.

This multidirectional flow had consequences for those who worked or hoped to work in the business of fashion. Everything was fair game for the people who designed the goods, ran the manufacturing companies, worked as retail buyers for chain stores, modeled the clothes, designed the photo shoots, published the glamour magazines, surveyed consumers for marketing studies, waited on customers in the shoe department, and so forth. All products—appliances, cars, clothes, jewelry, houses, home furnishings, and movies—were subject to the cultural force known as *changing fashion*. Those whose livelihoods depended on the design, production, marketing, advertising, and sale of goods would be wise to heed the vagaries of style and taste, in whatever form these elements materialized.

Ellis's catholic viewpoint, which valued fashion writ large, opens the doors to the analysis of fashion as form of cultural production, as the richly textured interplay between economic institutions and private individuals, social trends and belief systems, entrepreneurs and tastemakers, marketers and consumers. Historical analysis that pivots on the fundamental premise that fashion affects all types of products has the potential to be remarkably illuminating.[8] It can show how fashion—styles, trends, *modes*, and other manifestations of beliefs, values, ideas, *manners*, and *mores*—took hold in all aspects of material life. Most important for this book, Ellis knew that business played a foundational role in creating, establishing, and maintaining fashion. Just as it would be folly to overlook *modes*, *manners*, and *mores*, it would be foolish to ignore *markets*.

Business History Meets the Fashion System

Ellis offered an amazingly open-minded view of fashion, one that challenged her audience—and subsequent scholars who might read her lecture notes—to "think big" when contemplating fashion. Yet, the voices of businesspeople like Ellis are largely, but not exclusively, missing from the annals of fashion history. Over the past thirty years, fashion history pioneers have broached territory often dismissed as "frivolous" by the academy, establishing the study of apparel and dress as a serious scholarly discipline. Much of this bold new work has focused on haute couture designers, clothing as material culture, and the role of sexuality and sensuality in sartorial expression. Less is known about the commercial institutions of the fashion and beauty businesses, or the interface between enterprise, culture, and consumers in producing fashion. This book pursues a new line of inquiry by primarily, but not exclusively, examining how economic institutions shaped Western fashion from the early nineteenth century to our own time.

To do so, this volume draws on new work in business history that seeks to understand connections among enterprise, society, and culture. Rooted in the Business History Conference, the largest international organization of business historians, and the Hagley Center for the History of Business, Technology, and Society, this scholarship on American enterprise posits alternatives to the powerful institutional paradigms that dominated business history until the 1990s.[9] Particularly relevant to this book is scholarship on innovation. A new group of business historians have drawn on models and theories in economics, design history, cultural studies, and other disciplines to examine the creative process that leads to innovation and the mechanisms for the dissemination of novelty. They have examined the ways in which firms innovate, looking at the paths that feed data into companies, how corporate actors sift through new ideas, the interactions that result in new goods, and the strategies for promoting them.[10]

In my contributions to this literature, I have focused on consumer product innovation for the American mass market, looking at the micro-level process of design through a magnifying lens to understand macro-level relationships among business enterprise and consumer society. Specifically, my work on the politics of the design and the process of creativity has shown how networks of business professionals that I call "fashion intermediaries" studied the marketplace, collected data about consumer taste, created products to meet public expectations, and promoted them. Their efforts often succeeded, but failed when the design antennae pointed away from the market channel.[11] In this model, the high-profile industrial-design consultants celebrated in museum exhibitions are less important than the thousands of corporate professionals—art directors, retail buyers, home economists, and magazine editors—who worked behind the scenes to produce and reproduce cultural forms. Fashion intermediaries often coexisted side by side with these tastemakers, their horns often locked over whether it was best to reshape taste or to respond to it. Tastemakers such as industrial designer Raymond Loewy wanted to uplift mass taste and sometimes to remake consumers in their own image, while fashion intermediaries like Lucy M. Maltby, a home economist who helped Corning Glass Works create Pyrex, were more accepting of ordinary people's preferences. Put simply, *tastemakers* sought to reform consumer taste, *fashion intermediaries* to mediate the relationship between producers and consumers and help companies better understand demand.[12] Using the concept of the "fashion intermediary," my approach homes in on the experiences, practices, and ideas of businesspeople like Estelle Ellis—folks often on the corporate front line, who were charged with the tasks of scoping out consumer tastes and determining the likely direction of change.

How did innovative networks foster creativity in the apparel trade, the industry most often associated with fashion per se? By thinking expansively, we can find compelling evidence in seemingly unlikely places. The histories of New York's Seventh Avenue fashion district and the American synthetic fibers industry, particularly in the post-World War II era, shed some light on the puzzle. During the golden age of American capitalism, large corporations wrestled with the conundrum of fashion in a major way when industrial chemists generated new polymers that promised to revolutionize the look and feel of fabrics and clothing. To perfect these synthetic fibers, chemical companies not only had to overcome technical hurdles in the laboratory and the factory, but also had to determine what consumers liked and disliked about their everyday apparel. Fiber giants like E. I. du Pont de Nemours & Company added complex marketing packages, complete with staff knowledgeable about menswear and women's wear to help guide the way. By the 1960s, DuPont had a sophisticated marketing department, with major offices in New York and Geneva. DuPont's in-house fashion intermediaries conducted market-research surveys, talked regularly with retail buyers from all around the United States (who routinely visited New York's garment district to purchase stock for their stores), and networked with garment manufacturers, all with the goal of fathoming consumer expectations. Back in Wilmington, DuPont scientists used this feedback to improve fiber performance and the aesthetic appeal of the new synthetics. Meanwhile, DuPont marketers forged new contacts in the fashion world, hiring French haute couturiers—tastemakers par excellence—to give synthetics high-style appeal and collaborating with Seventh Avenue garment makers to translate those Parisian designs into mass-market apparel (Figure 1.1). This example shows how tastemakers and fashion intermediaries coexisted and sometimes collaborated in the quest to find new markets and expand existing ones. When technology and style met, everything was fair game.[13]

This brief DuPont story presents a model of networked innovation, business-culture interaction, and consumer mediation that has important implications for the study of fashion history. Just as businesses making household goods had to "imagine their consumers," so, too, companies in the fashion trades had to be in constant touch with the marketplace. Whether the product was chain-store house dresses, synthetic fibers that went into everyday fabrics, or haute couture for an elite clientele, creators who were *successful* kept tabs on their customers. In turn, a matrix of cultural institutions informed consumers, from factory workers to Wall Street brokers, political wives, and jet-setters. Just as interactions between organizations, objects, ideas, and individuals meshed to create stylish consumer durables, parallel occurrences produced the cultural value known as fashion, and the goods that were fashionable.

On the Shoulders of Fashion-History Giants

In recent decades, fashion history has blossomed into a thriving field, attracting scholars from anthropology, sociology, history, home economics, cultural

Figure 1.1. In fashion, high culture can mesh with mass culture. In 1954, French couturier Hubert de Givenchy designed this prêt-à-porter dress using fabrics made from DuPont's synthetic fibers. Courtesy Hagley Museum and Library.

studies, and fashion design. Building on insights from earlier studies by curators and connoisseurs of dress and costume, a new generation of scholars has
situated fashion within broader historical and cultural frameworks. But few
have examined the economic and institutional practices of the fashion system.
The fashion-history literature is vast, and this summary focuses on studies
relevant to the project at hand.

Historians and curators who study fashion have often focused on aesthetics, meaning, and use. Along these lines, major historians include Valerie
Steele, Kathy Peiss, and Christopher Breward, who have adapted methods
and theories from cultural studies to study clothing fashions in relation to
sexuality, gender, beauty, and culture.[14] A sophisticated material-culture approach is taken by Dilys E. Blum, Alexandra Palmer, and Lou Taylor, whose
scholarship on the cultural significance of clothing blends archival research
with the careful analysis of costume collections.[15] More recently, cultural
studies has energetically contributed to the mix, particularly with the 1997
introduction of the scholarly journal *Fashion Theory* and the expansion of
Berg's "Dress, Body, Culture" list. Historians now know a good deal about
French and Italian haute couture; fads like mod, hip-hop, and other bubble-
up street styles; the impact of Nazism and Fascism on sartorial trends; and
the various ways consumers used, adapted, or rejected all of this.[16]

Sociologists of culture have also produced insightful studies, blending
rigorous research with theoretical analysis. For example, Diana Crane and
Yuniya Kawamura have studied the social nature of fashion, examining the
people, networks, and institutions that make up the "fashion system."[17] They
have shown how fashion professionals, including designers and magazine editors, and dissemination mechanisms, such as advertising, operated in this
milieu to generate the concept and practice of fashion. Both scholars debunk
the myth of the fashion designer as a creative genius. They instead emphasize
fashion as a collective activity—the output of deliberation, conflict, and ne-
gotiation within a complex network of institutions and individuals—and as
a symbolic product that anchors cultural dreams and social aspirations. This
work is most sympathetic to my approach to the business history of design
and innovation.

In addition, costume curators, fashion-industry practitioners, and business journalists have examined some economic aspects of the fashion industry. Claudia Kidwell and Margaret B. Christman's landmark Smithsonian
Institution exhibition, "Suiting Everyone," set the stage by surveying the
mass-market clothing trade from colonial times through the 1970s. In Yeshiva

University's 2005 exhibition, "A Perfect Fit," curators Gabriel M. Goldstein and Phyllis Dillon built on this tradition to examine the role of Jewish entrepreneurs in America's mass-market garment industry.[18] For contemporary history, Nicola White and Ian Griffiths's *The Fashion Business* is often cited as a seminal work. In this book, scholars and fashion experts, many comparable to Estelle Ellis, offer different perspectives on the trade, focusing primarily, but not exclusively, on the recent past. Finally, Teri Agins's masterful *The End of Fashion* provides insight into the contemporary global fashion business from the perspective of the *Wall Street Journal*.[19]

This Book

Like other books in the Hagley Perspectives Series, this volume examines the subject at hand—in this case, the history of fashion—as a topic linking business enterprise and economic culture to broader historical trends. It is driven by a set of intertwined questions about the relationships among people, styles, and things: What is fashion? Who determines what is "in" and what is "out"? How do the interactions among commerce, culture, and consumers produce different fashions and help to disseminate them, sustain them, and contribute to their "going out of fashion"? Taking a historical perspective, this volume contains more than a dozen original essays about the creation of fashion in the West from the nineteenth century to the present. It looks at the organizational frameworks that buttressed the fashion business and the style industries over the longue durée; considers how various types of producers, from magazine editors to multinational corporations, interacted with the marketplace; and examines how consumers welcomed new styles created for them or, alternatively, reshaped fashion to suit themselves.

Much like other volumes in the series, the book builds on an extant body of literature while offering new viewpoints rooted in the study of economic culture. It does this by blending models of business innovation as a social and cultural practice with paradigms in fashion history, design history, and anthropology that emphasize meaning and aesthetics. The presence of contributors from history, anthropology, fashion studies, and other fields diversifies the perspective. Fashion is a cultural phenomenon growing out of the interactions of individuals and institutions. Business has long played an important role in fashion—shaping the look of artifacts and helping to define the parameters for what is generally considered to be fashionable—and enterprise often takes cues from the marketplace, where ideas about style percolate from different sites and circulate through the culture. Fashion producers have to "imagine the consumer." Trickle-down theories about fashion emulation, which long dominated the literature, can only partly explain change. Although much depends on the time, place, and product, fashion is far more complicated than emulation theories postulate. Business history has shown that successful firms, particularly those in the style industries, can shape taste, but they must also heed customs and emerging practices in target markets.

All the essays in this book deal with the themes of "producing fashion" and "imagining consumers." They have been grouped in ways that will facilitate classroom discussion about how different disciplinary approaches and research techniques can shed light on various themes and shape scholarly conclusions.

Organizing the Fashion Trades

Part I examines some of the business institutions that have historically underpinned the fashion system, and considers how these organizations helped produce the cultural value known as fashion. The chapters acknowledge the centrality of Paris, the capital of high-end dressmaking, or haute couture, but also consider how fashion was created in other places and through other means. Drawing on cases from Russia, Italy, Belgium, and France, they consider fashion magazines as business enterprise, department stores as style merchandisers, trade associations as fashion intermediaries and regulating agencies, and marketing practices by late twentieth-century couture houses that struggled to beat the odds in an era that democratized fashion. In "Spreading the Word: The Development of the Russian Fashion Press," Christine Ruane traces the evolution of women's fashion magazines as a business enterprise in tsarist Russia. Concerned with modernization, the tsar dictated that a fashionable appearance, based on European prototypes, was the duty of Russian citizens. Fashion magazines emerged in response to the demand for information about European manners and style, forging a commercial link between Russian readers and the cosmos of continental fashion. Using evidence from Russian archives, Ruane looks at editors, publishers, and government censors to consider how changes in the organization of production affected the content of the magazines and definitions of what was fashionable.

The next three essays shift to Western Europe, exploring the business strategies of fashion makers in Milan, Paris, and Brussels. In "Accessorizing, Italian Style: Creating a Market for Milan's Fashion Merchandise," fashion scholar Elisabetta Merlo and business historian Francesca Polese examine accessories marketing in Milan during the 1880s, when this commercial center had the highest per capita income in Italy. Using mail-order catalogs published by the Grandi Magazzini "Alle Città d'Italia," the authors examine the modalities that created the market for Italian fashion accessories and critique the standard interpretation of the department store as the "democratizer of consumption."

Véronique Pouillard's "In the Shadow of Paris? French Haute Couture and Belgian Fashion Between the Wars" examines the exportation of Paris fashion to Brussels and its emulation by Belgian dressmakers. A major player in this effort was the Chambre Syndicale de Haute Couture Belge (Belgian Syndicate Chamber of Haute Couture), a trade association for retailers and artisans from Brussels and the Belgian provinces. Member firms performed as fashion intermediaries, importing models of French dresses, displaying them in Brussels, and stimulating the demand for copies among the Belgian bourgeoisie and foreign visitors. Drawing on records from this trade association, Pouillard's study complements Ruane's essay by exploring how commercial channels disseminated Parisian fashion in Western Europe.

Tomoko Okawa's essay, "Licensing Practices at Maison Christian Dior," considers a little-examined aspect of French fashion's recent history: brand licensing. Established in 1946, Maison Dior helped to rebuild the French fashion business after World War II. After Christian Dior's 1957 death, the maison prospered, garnering its profits primarily from licensing activities in accessories, such as stockings, scarves, handbags, and neckties. Okawa uses untapped material from French national collections and the Christian Dior Couture S.A. Archives, augmenting the essay on Milan by extending the discussion of accessories into the late twentieth century.

Inventing Fashions, Promoting Styles

Historians of fashion, advertising, and consumerism often use published primary sources to study how tastemakers created and circulated styles. Part II examines advertisements, magazine and newspaper articles, and other promotional material to probe unexplored niches in the history of apparel and other consumer goods. Often these primary sources, created as propaganda, can illuminate highly public topics such as nationalism, a major theme in two of the chapters in this section.

In the first essay, "The Wiener Werkstätte and the Reform Impulse," art historian Heather Hess considers the efforts among Austrian tastemakers to find a style that embodied the state's ethnic identity. In Vienna, design reformers at the Weiner Werkstätte (Viennese Workshop and Production Cooperative of Art Works) created a new international style in textiles, clothing, and furnishings by engaging a modern Germanic vocabulary of ornament. Hess shows how Austrian tastemakers created a new style that epitomized Vienna, and examines how they used magazines, newspapers, stores, and exhibitions to publicize the new international look.

Marlis Schweitzer's "American Fashions for American Women: The Rise and Fall of Fashion Nationalism," examines the ill-fated efforts to establish a native fashion industry in America during the 1910s. Edward Bok used his editorship at the *Ladies' Home Journal* to advocate a break from the dictates of Paris fashion, which had long dominated the American scene. Schweitzer considers how Bok and like-minded reformers broke from the dictates of Paris fashion and promoted their vision of a distinctive American aesthetic through magazines, dress patterns, and newspapers. The campaign foundered, but presaged more successful mid-century developments as the ready-to-wear trade expanded.

Ariel Beaujot in "Coiffing Vanity: Advertising the Celluloid Toilet Sets in Twenties America," probes the corporate records of E. I. du Pont de Nemours Company at the Hagley Museum and Library to analyze the symbolic meanings of a ubiquitous fashion accessory: the celluloid boudoir set. The multifaceted history of these artifacts shows how tastemakers' ideas about womanly self-presentation influenced design, development, and promotion of fashion accessories. Her judicious analysis of trade advertisements DuPont circulated to retailers highlights an underused resource in business and cultural history. She also provides a connection to a marvelous Web site, sponsored by the University of Toronto, on the material culture of dress and grooming, which can be used by instructors in conjunction with her essay.[20]

Shaping Bodies, Building Brands

Scholars acknowledge the importance of gender, sexuality, and bodies to the construction of consumer identity and the iconography of fashion. Building on this foundation, Part III examines how cultural ideas about the body influenced corporate decision makers and how tactics for building brands produced new prescriptions for gender behavior that were inexorably linked to fashion. The chapters focus on sites of cultural production that have not been examined by many fashion historians: the Los Angeles menswear trade, the post-World War II advertising and modeling businesses, and the textile fibers department of the nation's leading chemical company. At these sites, people concerned with building markets for leisurewear, cigarettes, and synthetic fibers redefined the dimensions of masculinity and femininity in ways that reflected athleticism, flexibility, and modernity. For the most part, these essays draw on company records, institutional archives, and oral-history interviews to provide readers with different viewpoints on bodies, gender, and the production of fashion.

William R. Scott's "California Casual: Lifestyle Marketing and Men's Leisurewear, 1930–1960" discusses how a regional style—California casual—was transformed into a national brand by manufacturers who promoted a definition of masculinity developed on the West Coast. Drawing on industry journals and trade association records from the Men's Apparel Guild in California (MAGIC), Scott shows how promotions and merchandising techniques capitalized on men's disenchantment with sartorial drabness and helped make resort wear de rigueur. New ideas about men's bodies, masculinity, and leisure lay at the root of these changes.

In "Marlboro Men: Outsider Masculinities and Commercial Modeling in Postwar America," Elspeth H. Brown offers an American studies analysis of heteronormative fashion and the male body, focusing on the Leo Burnett advertising agency, which in 1954 launched a campaign to make Marlboro "the cigarette with balls." Using oral history interviews conducted in the 1980s by the Archives Center at the Smithsonian National Museum of American History, Brown examines how the Marlboro Man advertising campaign presented a vision of hypermasculinity that capitalized on and fed into the segmented market that drew corporate attention in the postwar era. Through this process, the butch idea of masculinity was linked to the mythical American West and became part of fashion's established iconology.

Finally, anthropologist Kaori O'Connor in "The Body and the Brand: How Lycra Shaped America" combines materials in the Hagley archives and oral-history interviews with female consumers to trace Lycra's history from stretchable elastic for women's girdles to exercise wear. O'Connor's chapter shows how consumer-driven new uses for spandex redirected the marketing efforts at a major American corporation. The novel applications were conditioned by feminist ideas about women's bodies and the athletic craze that surfaced in the Me Decade. The essay provides an excellent lead-in to the book's next section on consumer agency.

Customer Reactions, Consumer Adaptations

Audience response is a major theme in recent fashion and consumer histories. Did the public accept, reject, or adapt ideas about fashions that were advocated by producers? How, if at all, did customer reactions redirect the public discourse about what was "in" and "out"? Earlier essays in this book show that successful fashion brokers necessarily paid attention to consumer taste, but the role of consumer choice in shaping fashion is sometimes less apparent. The type of historical source has much to do with whether scholars can explore the dynamic relationship between consumers and producers, and how much "power" the consumer appears to exert in the marketplace. The essays in Part IV use evidence about markets, following customers as they pushed the style industries to expand the parameters of what was fashionable. In the classroom, instructors can compare and contrast the consumer-focused approach here with earlier essays from the viewpoint of the producers.

"French Hairstyles and the Elusive Consumer," by historian Steve Zdatny, steps into an important site of beauty production—the hair salon—to scrutinize the testy relationship between Parisian women and their stylists. By the early 1900s, bottom-up fashions, such as the Marcel wave and the bob, challenged the hegemony of haute coiffeurs over the hairdo. During the 1930s, Hollywood exerted powerful sway over stylish Parisiennes; in the 1960s, the youth movement's anti-fashion posture stimulated consumer interest in shorter haircuts. Hairdressers found public taste to be enigmatic, and consumers difficult, if not impossible, to manipulate.

In "Ripping Up the Uniform Approach: Hungarian Women Piece Together a New Communist Fashion," feminist scholar Katalin Medvedev pulls back the Iron Curtain to peek at clothing consumers in a totalitarian regime. The communists in Hungary who saw Western styles as a threat to the new order created a mode of dress that was nondescript, practical, and comfortable. Medvedev shows how women's demands challenged and then reshaped the state's position on fashion, a powerful example of consumer agency. Aesthetics and subversion were weapons in the Hungarian consumers' battle against cultural repression.

The last essay, "Why the Old-Fashioned Is in Fashion in American Houses" by historian Susan J. Matt, extends the definition of fashion to the home. Matt compares the consumer demand for houses in two periods of major cultural and economic change: the early nineteenth and late twentieth centuries. She skillfully unpacks public exposés and private confidences, including today's blogs, chat rooms, and e-mails, to show how tastemakers and consumers negotiated the look of American houses and home fashions, both in the antebellum era and in our own time.

What Next

This book hopes to provide readers with a deeper understanding of how economic institutions have historically helped to shape the world of fashion around us. Far from the last word on the subject, it instead seeks to serve as a springboard, as a source of inspiration for scholars wanting to know more. If we are to understand how the fashion system works, scholars need to build on the research presented here to examine fashion's relationship to commercial enterprise, looking more closely at connections among firms, individuals, ethnic groups, trade associations, and industries. For the United States, for example, it is astounding that we know so little about New York's history as a garment manufacturing hub and a fashion center, or about the city's role in creating that distinctive American look: casual dressing.[21] Similarly, our knowledge about how ideas about what has been stylish (or not) circulated among individuals, companies, and industries is still limited. In this book, Heather Hess shows how design reformers created a new Viennese aesthetic that encompassed everything from apparel to home furnishings, while Katalin Medvedev demonstrates how consumers living in a communist regime borrowed images from Western popular culture to create their own highly individualized dress styles. Elspeth H. Brown tells us how the Marlboro Man bubbled up from film and print culture to capture the imagination of organizational men, who modified this masculine ideal to meet their firm's needs—and their own vision of what was macho. As a whole, work like this is wonderfully suggestive, pointing to fashion as an inclusive cultural phenomenon with multidirectional flows. The observations of businesswoman Estelle Ellis, it seems, were remarkably insightful.

By looking at "dress codes" and "invented traditions," these essays turn conventional ideas about fashion inside out in another way. Innovation, creativity, and constant change are only one side of fashion's Janus face. On the other side are continuity, stability, and collective identity. Christine Ruane shows how Peter the Great, anxious to augment his imperial image, required European dress for his subjects, and how Russian fashion journalists responded by promoting a sartorial code that honored transcontinental uniformity rather than individual expression. Looking at the other side of the globe, Susan J. Matt demonstrates the enduring allure of the country cottage, which for two centuries has appealed to Americans as the ideal embodiment of "Home, Sweet Home." These cases, along with the work of Beaujot, Zdatny, O'Connor, and others, show that the old and new persisted and coexisted in the realm of style, fashion, and taste. Perhaps what engaged the wheels of the fashion system, then, was not the incessant quest for novelty and the concomitant media hype, but the dynamic interaction between change and stasis, differentiation and uniformity, which could vary with time and place.[22]

Finally, these essays suggest the tremendously rich territory awaiting those who want to augment theory with in-depth empirical research. While cultural theorists have speculated on the media's role in manipulating words and images to stimulate excitement over changing fashions, contributors in this book have taken another approach, stepping inside the offices of mass-market magazines, advertising agencies, retail stores, trade associations, and manufacturing firms to watch the agents of change and continuity at work. Marlis Schweitzer's analysis of Edward Bok's editorial role at the *Ladies' Home Journal*—the nation's largest women's magazine—and his vision for an American aesthetic in dress, along with William R. Scott's essay on the trade association for California menswear makers, use the lens of gender to show how corporate actors labored to define and lay their stamp on femininity and masculinity. In these essays, we actually hear the voices of historical actors, learn about their intentions in creating fashion, and see the final products. Bok's "American Fashions for American Women" were simultaneously cutting-edge and conservative, while the creators of the California look fed on Hollywood, the ultimate change machine, and helped popularize celebrity culture among middle-class Americans who saw themselves as weekend warriors. Both scholars dig into personal and professional networks among businessmen, and scrutinize the politics of design and the process of cultural production to show how the ideal American beauty and the postwar casual male were imagined and replicated.[23] These stories, along with the essays by

Merlo and Polese, Pouillard, and Okawa, are remarkable for revealing the vision and venerability of corporate actors, and for unpacking their motivations as the producers of fashion.

* * *

Fashion, like other forms of culture, is a great jigsaw puzzle. Digging through the archives, historians retrieve pieces of the puzzle without knowing where those parts actually fit. To date, cultural historians of fashion have collected many of the pieces and assembled them to reveal a portrait of an elegant couple attired in haute couture, poised to promenade through the luxurious shops of the Champs Elysées, New Bond Street, or Fifth Avenue. Yet much is missing from the picture: the people on the side streets, dressed in ready-to-wear apparel or home-sewn clothes they believed were stylish; the distant lofts where the clothing was designed; the garment factories where it was made; the stores where it was sold; and the advertising executives, retail managers, market researchers, design-school instructors, magazine editors, and other ingenious entrepreneurs who worked behind the scenes to produce fashion. As historians, we don't know what pieces of the fashion jigsaw puzzle we will find next, or how the fully assembled picture will look. We can, however, use the essays in this book to speculate on where the missing pieces might be found and to direct our new inquiries in fruitful ways.

Before we begin the hunt, we might remember Estelle Ellis's deceptively straightforward query—"What is fashion?"—and heed her call to think expansively about *modes, manners, mores,* and *markets* as we plan our research. Only then might we find pieces that help to complete the jigsaw puzzle, showing how fashion was produced through the interaction of commerce, culture, and consumers.

PART I

Organizing the Fashion Trades

CHAPTER TWO

Spreading the Word: The Development of the Russian Fashion Press

Christine Ruane

IMPERIAL RUSSIA (1682–1917) may seem an odd place to begin a book on the fashion industry. Modern-day Russia is not known for either its fashion sense or its business acumen. Except for a few athletes and fashion models, the American image of Russians remains one of heavyset, shabbily dressed peasants, oblivious to the latest clothing styles. Moreover, the American media are filled with stories about Russia's unhealthy business climate that thrives on cronyism, bribery, extortion, and sometimes murder. These contemporary stereotypes, however, conceal Russia's sustained engagement with both capitalism and fashion, beginning in the eighteenth century and ending with the 1917 Russian Revolution. Not only did imperial Russia develop a fashion industry in the nineteenth century, but it became one of the success stories of Russia's modernization drive.

One of the institutions central to that success was the fashion press. In Western Europe and the United States, magazines have been essential for the success of the fashion industry, providing detailed descriptions of clothing and accessories, and information on how to acquire the necessary items. But these magazines were more than simply an inventory of goods and stores. The fashion press created a fantasy world in which all women could participate, regardless of their financial circumstances. In fact, there is a growing scholarly consensus that magazines were largely responsible for creating the *desire* to wear fashionable dress, which, in turn, led to an increase in production of fashionable goods.[1] The purpose of this chapter is to explore how entrepreneurs created just such a fantasy world for Russian women by examining the introduction of Western European magazines and business practices into Russia, and how they evolved over the course of the nineteenth century. While Americans often think that capitalism works best in democratic societies, this chapter provides a better understanding of how capitalism and fashion functioned in an autocratic political system by exploring how Russian publishers combined a fashion sensibility and savvy entrepreneurial skills to secure a place for themselves in Russia's growing commercial sector. Working within the constraints of government censorship, these men and women created popular magazines that helped Russian women feel themselves a part of the world of high fashion even though they were thousands of miles away from Paris.

The Introduction of European Fashion into Russia

In 1700 Tsar Peter the Great (1682–1725) decreed that his subjects must abandon their traditional clothing and wear European dress. Prior to the tsar's decree, Muscovites wore long, flowing robes that covered their bodies, but Peter wanted women to bare their bosoms and men to wear tight-fitting breeches, revealing what had long been hidden. Having just returned from an extended stay in Western Europe, the tsar had become convinced that if Russia was going to be taken seriously as a full-fledged member of the European family of nations, he must make Russia more like Western Europe. Interestingly, his dress decree was one of the earliest of his Westernizing reforms. Peter understood that if Russians dressed like Europeans they would begin to behave like them as well. This transformation was essential if Europeans, who tended to view Russians as semi-Asiatic barbarians, were going to treat representatives of Peter's government with respect and dignity. And while Peter's decree is often viewed as impetuous, he was only doing what King Louis XIV of France had done several years earlier when he established a uniform for his courtiers at Versailles (Figure 2.1).

In the beginning, then, European clothing in Russia served as a kind of uniform for urban residents. Little is known about the attitudes of ordinary Russians to the tsar's sartorial decree, but if they worked in the city, they had

Figure 2.1. Early twentieth-century reproduction of seventeenth-century elite
Muscovite dress. Courtesy Library of Congress.

to don European clothing appropriate to their station in life. Aristocrats and government officials who supported the tsar's Westernization policies wore their new clothes with pride. Others wore European dress because they had to, preferring to wear Russian dress at home. Nevertheless this reluctance had virtually disappeared by the second half of the eighteenth century. No longer a uniform, elite Russians spent exorbitant sums to acquire the latest fashions. In fact both Empresses Elizabeth (1741–62) and Catherine the Great (1762–96) introduced sumptuary legislation to control Russian expenditures on fashions worn at court.

To help Russians acquire their new clothing, Peter the Great invited European artisans to Russia. The government granted tailors and dressmakers special tax incentives if they would set up shop and teach Russians the art of European fashion design and manufacture. These adventurous entrepreneurs faced a number of problems in their new homeland, chief among them the need for information about the latest styles. In Western Europe, fashion magazines had been developed to report on changes in *la mode*, but since Russia was located at the very edge of Europe, by the time they arrived the fashions were frequently out of date. Because elite Russians were trying to overcome feelings of inferiority and backwardness vis-à-vis Western Europe, this was unacceptable. Russian fashionistas wanted to participate directly in the world of Parisian haute couture. The only way to do that was to publish a domestic fashion magazine that would help eliminate the distance between Paris and Petersburg, and establish the Russian capital as a legitimate center of the European fashion industry.

The Beginnings of the Russian Fashion Press

Russian publishers faced some serious challenges in their attempts to establish a domestic fashion press. The Russian reading public was small in the eighteenth and early nineteenth centuries. During the eighteenth century, the most popular published works included religious tracts of all kinds, almanacs, and calendars, followed by stories and novels. No precise figures exist, but one scholar has calculated that in the 1790s, when the population of central Russia was about 28 million, publishers annually sold approximately 30,000 calendars, the most popular publication.[2] By comparison, the newly formed United States had almost 4 million residents in 1790 and almanac print runs of 10,000 copies; France had 26 million people and almanac print runs of

150,000 copies.[3] Because the French reading public was larger, it allowed publishers to expand their publication lists to include periodicals and newspapers, while Russian publishers had to stick to publications that had the widest possible appeal or face bankruptcy.

Only a few of Russia's 30,000 potential readers were women, and this created its own set of problems for publishers interested in producing a domestic fashion magazine. Designed exclusively for women readers, the fashion magazine offered illustrations and text describing the latest clothing styles, tips on the best fabrics and boutiques, and commentary on fashion's role in society. The magazine's purpose was to report on the "frivolous" world of fashion, far removed from the high politics and commercial transactions that constituted men's lives.[4] In Russia it was not until Catherine the Great, an author in her own right, established schools for young women of the elite that Russia began to develop a female reading public. Prior to 1830 this market was simply too small to sustain a periodical just for women. Since Russian elite women were bilingual in French and Russian, they read French fashion magazines to obtain information about the latest styles.

In addition to the problem of readership, Russian publishers faced technological problems in the late eighteenth and early nineteenth centuries. By the early nineteenth century, the one feature that defined the fashion magazine was the inclusion of hand-colored fashion plates. Because these lovely art forms were produced only in Paris, acquiring them was expensive and time-consuming.[5] By the 1820s, the plates had proved so popular that fashion magazines began to include more illustrated material such as needlework and embroidery patterns. The technical difficulties of printing these patterns, coupled with the expense of ordering the plates, proved insurmountable for Russian publishers. The few attempts to publish a Russian-language fashion magazine before the 1830s collapsed after a few issues.

Nevertheless some important changes began to reshape the Russian reading public in the first decades of the nineteenth century. After Napoleon's unsuccessful invasion of Russia in 1812, Russian Francophilia began to subside. The government and the reading public, under the spell of romantic nationalism, began to work toward the creation of a national literature written in Russian on Russian themes. Part of this new emphasis included the publication of periodicals called "thick" journals whose purpose was to discuss the serious political, social, and cultural issues of the day. These journals helped create a wider market for printed material by making it easier for individuals outside Moscow and Petersburg to read about and participate in Russian intellectual life.

There was one important feature to this new Russian literature. Under the powerful influence of early nineteenth-century Romanticism, Russians, like other Europeans, defined literary genius as male. According to this view, it was men's prerogative to write about the moral and philosophical issues of the day, while women's literary output was to be confined to the domestic realm. This domestic ideology had two outcomes. Women writers, discouraged from writing on "serious" topics, excelled at society tales. In these stories, women dominated the social scene, which, in turn, gave them an important role in determining what constituted good taste.[6] The cult of male genius helped reinforce women's sphere as domestic, but at the same time it allowed women to serve as the arbiters and chroniclers of their sphere. This, in turn, encouraged savvy entrepreneurs to contemplate the creation of a Russian fashion magazine that on its pages would privilege women's interests and their role as social arbiters.

In order to tap into this emerging market, however, Russian publishers needed government approval. Russia, like other continental European countries but unlike England or the United States, reviewed all texts and illustrations before publication.[7] In 1803, Tsar Alexander introduced a mild form of censorship into Russia. In 1828, his successor Nicholas I set up a Central Censorship Administration and placed these men in charge of Russian publishing. Their chief task was to prevent the circulation of any ideas that might undermine the government. As a result, Russian censorship had two complex and interrelated functions. The first function was editorial. A Russian publisher submitted a "program" to the Central Censorship Administration, outlining the format and price structure of the proposed periodical.[8] In the case of the fashion magazine, the interests of publishers and censors came together very nicely. Using the French press as their model, publishers wanted to take the features that made fashion magazines distinctive—fashion plates, tips on shopping and fabrics, and articles on other aspects of women's domestic life—and "Russify" them. The government, too, wanted to contain French cultural influences by encouraging the development of Russian taste and promoting a national literary culture. The goal of both government officials and publishers was to diminish the power of French culture over the female reading public by providing them with texts "appropriate" to their gender role.

At the same time, the government also wanted to maintain the status quo, and this created a second, distinctly commercial task for Russian censors. Government censors were supposed to sustain the social position of the court and aristocracy against the welfare of any other group in Russian society. This meant that the Central Censorship Administration had the unlikely task of serving as a kind of fashion police to make sure that the industry stayed in the "right" hands. Consequently, in the early years of the fashion press not all magazines received permission to publish. In 1841, a German woman was denied permission to publish a fashion magazine because the censors believed that Russia already had too many such magazines. In 1852, censors denied another woman permission to publish a magazine for seamstresses. The censors would not allow publishers to expand the fashion market beyond the elite, even though such a publication would have been enormously beneficial to Russian dressmakers.[9]

These two decisions show clearly how men who were government bureaucrats and not experienced businessmen helped shape the contours of the Russian fashion industry during the first half of the nineteenth century. For the censors, the bottom line was not the financial success of the fashion magazines, but the preservation of the government's autocratic power and the status of the Russian nobility. Perhaps paradoxically, it was the government itself that "politicized" the Russian fashion magazine by insisting that it maintain elite women's cultural and social power.

Having won permission to publish, Russian publishers next had to establish themselves as "experts." This was essential if they were going to woo subscribers away from French periodicals. They did this by reporting on fashions in both Paris and St. Petersburg, thereby legitimating the Russian capital as a center of European fashion. Editors often included stories that demonstrated the superior taste of St. Petersburg society women, who transformed French fashions into something suitable for Russian conditions. Most of this advice revolved around how to stay warm, dry, and fashionably dressed given Russia's unpredictable climate. In 1851, one fashion journalist admonished her readers to wear Russian fur hats, regardless of the latest Parisian hat styles. Given the chill of Russian winters, she warned her fellow countrywomen not to become so enslaved to fashion that they endangered their health.[10]

As more and more women followed the advice in the magazines, the fashion columnists helped to confirm the magazines as arbiters of good taste and judgment in large part by writing about women who violated the "laws of Fashion" laid down in the magazines. One example of this type of journalism appeared in *Fashion* (*Moda*) in July 1856. The anonymous article took up the issue of the relationship of dress and patriotism. At the time the article was written, Russia was fighting against France, Great Britain, and the Ottoman Empire in the Crimean War. Apparently some women had abandoned French fashions during the war, donning their native dress as a sign of patriotism. The reporter criticized this misplaced patriotism by comparing these women to children who dressed in ridiculous costumes to fight imaginary enemies. The journalist quoted Nikolai Grech, a well-known Russian conservative, who complained, "Jumping around during a polka or waltzing in the style of dress of Natal'ia Kirillovna [Peter the Great's mother, who lived during the seventeenth century] is absurd and funny." Grech begged the women of Russia to dress "like all the other well-bred women and girls in Europe. Wear sarafans [a Russian jumper] and ribbons only when they suit you and to please your husbands. But do not think that patriotism consists of this: a beautiful hat interferes with healthy thoughts and a French corset stifles a Russian heart." The magazine's advice, in turn, was "that the dress of women from educated society should be tasteful, conforming to the habits and customs of the modern epoch."[11]

It is difficult to know how many women actually read the advice columns, as no circulation figures survive from the early years of the fashion magazine. In 1864, however, the magazine *Fashionable Shop* (*Modnyi magazin*) had 4,500 subscribers while one of its rivals, *The Vase* (*Vaza*), had between 1,500 and 2,000.[12] There are other indicators that suggest that the market was beginning to expand as publishers began to introduce marketing strategies to increase their sales. This proved especially tricky for Russian publishers, who had to keep subscription prices down to attract readers, but pay for the expensive plates and other costs involved in production.

Once again Russian publishers looked to their European counterparts for a solution to this problem. The first remedy adopted was advertising. Advertisements were initially just a few lines, but beginning in the 1850s the ads became larger and provided information about goods and stores mentioned in the pages of the magazine, creating a mutually beneficial relationship for advertiser and publisher.[13] Second, Russian publishers began to include supplements that subscribers could receive for the price of the subscription. Magazines offered patterns and books on embroidery, knitting, and other forms of needlework. From the mailing instructions in the magazines themselves, we can see that the market for the magazines had moved beyond the confines of Petersburg and Moscow to the outlying provinces. Elites in these areas became subscribers so that they, too, could dress *comme il faut.*[14]

The Rise of the Female Publisher-Editor

The person most responsible for laying the foundations of a Russian fashion press was Elizaveta F. Safonova. Little is known about Safonova, but in 1830 she was the wife of a minor government official and lived in St. Petersburg. A few years later, she petitioned the Central Censorship Administration to publish and edit a magazine dedicated to sewing and embroidery. According to her proposal, *The Vase* would contain illustrations of fashionable items from Paris and explanations as to how to make them.[15] Safonova proclaimed that she was the perfect person to undertake this endeavor because, like publishers in Europe, she had excellent connections to the best embroiderers and shops in the Russian capital. The censors approved her petition. In 1838, she submitted another request, asking permission to publish a new magazine, *Fashion*, which would provide pictures of the latest fashions and articles on social events in St. Petersburg, Paris, London, Berlin, and Vienna. This time the censors allowed her to publish the fashion plates, but refused permission to publish articles of any kind. According to Elagin, the censor responsible for fashion magazines, "the purpose of the fashion magazine was to provide a description of the latest fashions, nothing more."[16] Elagin's decision provides another example of how Russian censors tried to limit the influence of the developing fashion industry.

Having established these two magazines, Safonova's publishing enterprise grew. She regularly petitioned the Censorship Administration to allow her to add new features to her magazines. Despite Elagin's continued objections, in 1850 the Central Censorship Administration gave permission to include an advice column for homemakers in *The Vase* and a column about the latest fashions in *Fashion*.[17] This shrewd businesswoman was ever so gently giving shape to the Russian fashion magazine.

In 1851 Safonova committed her one tactical error in her long career as a successful publisher. Apparently the task of publishing and editing two successful journals had grown burdensome for one woman alone. So in 1850 she ceded publication of *Fashion* to her daughter, Sofiia Lund. For unspecified reasons, however, Lund quickly turned the magazine over to Olimpiada Grigorevna Riumina, the wife of an officer in the Imperial Guards. Like Safonova before her, Riumina emphasized her excellent connections to the court, high society, and Petersburg's finest shopping establishments in her petitions to take control of the magazine.

For two years Riumina followed the publishing program that Safonova had developed for the magazine, but in 1854 she turned over her publishing and editing duties to her husband. Riumin wanted to transform the magazine into a literary publication that would report on the Petersburg cultural and social scene more broadly. His mistake was that he proceeded with his plans without getting permission from the Censorship Administration, which led to a major confrontation between government officials and the publishers.

The first salvo in the battle that developed between Safonova and Riumin came when he published a book on needlework, the first in a series. According to their respective publishing programs, only *The Vase* could produce sewing patterns. Safonova immediately petitioned the Censorship Administration, demanding that they look into the matter; as the former publisher of *Fashion*, she knew full well that Riumin's needlework handbook exceeded his authority.

The resulting conflict among publishers and censors reveals a great deal about the Russian fashion press at mid-century. In her petition, Safonova emphasized her obedience to government censorship, but she also used gendered language to place herself in an unassailable position. She wrote that in all her years in business, she had only once violated her publication program, when she placed an article about dancing in *The Vase*. Other than this minor mistake, she had done nothing to violate the trust that the censors had placed in her. Now Riumin's incursion into her area of the fashion market—sewing and embroidery—threatened her very livelihood, as his sewing handbook was clearly intended to lure away her subscribers. She emphasized in her petition that she was a "poor" widow with a young son in the Russian army, and her publishing business was her only means of support. Safonova cleverly used gendered language to present herself as on the verge of destitution, thereby masking her considerable skills as a savvy businesswoman with over twenty years of experience in publishing.

Riumin foolishly went over the heads of the Censorship Administration and wrote directly to the minister of education, whose job it was to oversee Russian censorship, to lay out his plans for a newly revised periodical. Riumin's actions, however, demonstrated that he did not understand the publishing business and its relationship to the government. As an officer and an administrator of a cadet school, Riumin tried to use his social and professional connections to present his side of the story. He clearly thought he could outmaneuver both Safonova and the government censor, Elagin; instead he underestimated the power of both to manipulate bureaucratic procedures in their favor.

When Elagin discovered what Riumin had done, he wrote a scathing report to the minister of education outlining the publisher's violations of government protocols. Elagin informed his superior that Riumin had not asked for permission to publish a series of sewing handbooks, a clear violation of the censorship laws. Second, Elagin had refused Riumin's request to publish an article on the Italian artist Benvenuto Cellini, but he went ahead and published it anyway. Elagin firmly believed that Cellini's checkered personal life should not grace the pages of a woman's magazine, and he restated his firm belief that a fashion magazine not be allowed to publish anything but descriptions of the clothing. Elagin urged his superiors to support the "poor" widow Safonova.

The outcome of this bureaucratic battle was as complex as the situation itself. Riumin ultimately failed to gain support for his position. In 1855, he petitioned the Censorship Administration to change the name and program of his magazine. The censors turned down his request, and he gave control of the magazine back to his wife. At the same time, however, the Censorship Administration removed Elagin as the person responsible for the fashion press. The result of that decision was that both Safonova and Riumina petitioned in 1856 for a change in their publication programs. Henceforth, *The Vase* added literary and fashion commentary and *Fashion* included articles about art, literature, and sewing. The magazines now became rivals.

The Censorship Administration's decision to abandon Elagin's narrow definition of the fashion magazine came at a critical moment in Russian history. In 1855, Tsar Nicholas I died during the Crimean War, which the Russians subsequently lost. That bitter defeat ushered in a new program of liberalization and industrialization, seeking to avoid any further military setbacks. These reforms included the abolition of serfdom, liberalization of censorship, educational reform, and incentives to improve economic productivity. This liberalization program had a powerful impact on the fashion press. Russia needed all of its subjects, male and female, to participate in the revitalization of the empire. Noblewomen were no longer part of a privileged class with the time and leisure to think about only their clothing. Russia needed citizen-mothers and thrifty household managers, and this redefinition of womanhood was extended to all Russian women, not just the elite. Raising the "woman question" allowed publishers like Safonova and Riumina to take advantage of the more liberal censorship regulations to create a magazine that they hoped would cater to all aspects of a woman's life; at the same time they sought to expand the market beyond the aristocracy to include women of the middle ranks. The government call to all subjects to participate in Russia's revitalization meant that the fashion market would of necessity expand as more and more Russians needed advice on what to wear, and the fashion press was only too happy to oblige.

The Rise of the Mass-Circulation Fashion Magazine

The second half of the nineteenth century marked the beginning of the "new journalism" in Europe and America. Technological innovations such as mechanized typesetting, steam-powered multi-cylindered presses, and chromolithography, to name just a few, allowed publishers to produce larger print runs. The larger print runs meant lower subscription costs for consumers as publishers sought out advertisers to help them defray the publication costs. At the same time, large publishing houses began to dominate the industry, in part because of the significant capital needed to purchase the expensive machinery. The changes in printing technologies occurred alongside the expansion of public education throughout Europe and America. There were now more potential readers of print materials, which further encouraged innovation and expansion in the publishing industry.[18]

Imperial Russia also experienced the "new journalism," but fitfully. A new censorship statute paved the way in 1865. Publishers still had to seek government permission for each new publication, but they had more independence over editorial content. With the easing of censorship, Russian publishing became more of a commercial enterprise than ever before.[19] While this greater freedom allowed publishers to contemplate the development of mass-circulation periodicals, problems remained on the technological side of the business. Overall the printing industry expanded in Russia in the second half of the nineteenth century. However, some firms mechanized, while others preferred more traditional publishing technologies, which limited opportunities to expand their print runs.[20]

Another vexing problem concerned the size of the reading public. Imperial Russia was Europe's most populous political entity by the end of the nineteenth century, with almost 170 million inhabitants, a truly vast market for any magazine or newspaper. The majority of Russia's burgeoning population, however, were illiterate or semiliterate peasants, wary of written documents and state-sponsored "enlightenment" programs. Furthermore, the population was scattered over the immense distances of the Eurasian continent. Publishers had to work very hard within Russia's incomplete transportation system to create a reliable distribution network for printed materials. These serious problems are reflected in the circulation figures. In 1895 the three most popular fashion magazines had between 9,000 and 12,500 subscribers. By contrast, the English women's magazine *Forget-Me-Not* had 141,000 readers in 1894, and the American *Ladies' Home Journal* exceeded a million subscribers in 1910.[21] While the Russian numbers appear small compared with the European and American markets, the Russian reading public and its interest in print matter continued to expand. Russia's most popular illustrated magazine, *Cornfield* (*Niva*), which reached more than 200,000 readers annually, had its own fashion supplement, *Paris Fashions* (*Parizheskie mody*).[22] Although the magazine was not technically part of the fashion press, it nevertheless worked very hard to provide female consumers with access to the world of high fashion. Furthermore, print runs do not tell the whole story. It is important to remember that women who could not afford a subscription would often borrow a magazine from a friend so that they could improve their clothing, obtain household hints, or simply indulge themselves in the fantasies fashion magazines created on their pages.

Despite the uneven development of Russia's new journalism, the market was growing sufficiently to encourage a new generation of publishers to reinvent the Russian fashion magazine. In large part, the need for a new magazine was due to the success of the earlier ones. Publications like *The Vase* and *Fashion* had given Russian women confidence in their fashion sense and taste. The magazines had drawn them into the world of Paris fashion, and they now felt at home there. Consequently, Russian fashionistas now wanted up-to-date information on the latest styles, unmediated by Petersburg journalists (Figure 2.2).

Publishers met their readers' desires with plans to translate French fashion magazines into Russian rather than continue with a distinctively Russian product. The advantage of a translated magazine was that publishers did not have to hire a large staff of writers, but could rely upon a few translators and a good editor to create a Russian edition of a foreign periodical. The visual materials would be identical to those in the foreign magazines. The new periodicals would look and read like European magazines, but also include some commentary on the Russian social scene. By 1870, two translated fashion magazines had established a niche in the Russian market. *New Russian Bazaar* (*Novyi russkii bazar*), was a translation of the German magazine *Der Bazaar*, and *Fashionable Society* (*Modnyi svet*) was a translation of *Die Moden-*

Дамскій Міръ

КОНТОРА И РЕДАКЦІЯ:
С.-ПЕТЕРБУРГЪ, НЕВСКІЙ, 88.

Контора проситъ гг. подписчиковъ, обращающихся за справками и заключающихъ выкройки, сообщать точный адресъ, письмо возможно яснѣе, и заказныя квитанціи и накладныя номера не возможно получения свѣдующаго.

При настоящемъ номерѣ подписчикамъ журнала «Д. М.» по трактамъ 31, 36, 38, 39, 40, 41, 42, 43, 44, 45, 47, 48, 53, 54, 55, 56, 57, 58 и 59 разсылаются прейсъ-куръ, фирмы Т. И. Соловьевъ.

За перемѣну адреса подписчики уплачивающіе. 25 к. (можно письм. почтов. марк.).
Журналъ выходитъ разъ въ мѣсяцъ—перваго числа.

Заграничныхъ подписчиковъ, для ихъ выгоды, просимъ подписываться чрезъ почтамтъ.

Въ этомъ номерѣ три безплатныхъ приложенія:
1) Альбомъ блузъ и юбокъ.
2) Листъ съ рисунками для рукодѣлій.
   (на оборотѣ выкроечнаго листа).
3) 2 выкроечныхъ листа.

Цѣна за объявленія строка нонпарели передъ текстомъ—60 к. послѣ текста—30 к. На 4-й стран. обложки—70 к. Въ стран. 3 столбца.

Хроника моды.

Письмо изъ Парижа.

Осенній сезонъ начинается... Появляются первыя модели, которыя несомнѣнно даютъ нѣкоторыя указанія касательно фасоновъ, модныхъ тканей и цвѣтовъ для предстоящаго сезона, но по началу трудно еще опредѣлить, что именно установится, такъ какъ не всѣ новинки моды одобряются и принимаются парижанками.

Новыя ткани отличаются большимъ разнообразіемъ выдѣлки и оттѣнковъ, причемъ всѣ шелковыя и шерстяныя матеріи, исключительно мягкія, какъ нельзя лучше подходятъ для драпированныхъ платьевъ, которыя предполагаются въ изобиліи. Новинкой для «тальеровъ» является особая ткань, «gabardine» («габардинъ»), напоминающая репсъ, но несравненно мягче послѣдняго. Для нарядныхъ визитныхъ костюмовъ остается неизмѣннымъ мягкій шелкъ, гладкій, или брошэ, а часто тотъ и другой вмѣстѣ, причемъ такое сочетаніе обѣщаетъ большой успѣхъ. Вообще слѣдуетъ отмѣтить, что современная мода допускаетъ самыя разнообразныя комбинаціи тканей и цвѣтовъ, что очень практично при передѣлкахъ старыхъ платьевъ на новые фасоны.

Преобладающими цвѣтами являются бѣлый и черный, или же сочетаніе ихъ. Нѣкоторыя первоклассныя заграничныя фирмы пропагандируютъ коричневый цвѣтъ, отъ самаго темнаго до ярко-рыжеватаго и золотистаго. Для костюмовъ и выходныхъ платьевъ преобладаютъ темные цвѣта, которые оживляются все болѣе и болѣе входящими въ моду жилетами, бѣлыми, или цвѣтными. Для послѣднихъ можно использо-

Модель дома Steinmann et Cᵒ. London. Piccadilly, 185-186.

5273. Модный кружевной воротникъ (берта), одѣваемый на любое вечернее платье.

вать сохранившіеся куски стариннаго шелка, гладкаго, или дамá; такіе жилеты чрезвычайно элегантны, изысканы и своеобразны, такъ какъ старый шелкъ представляетъ собою рѣдкость, которую нельзя пріобрѣсти даже въ самыхъ большихъ магазинахъ.

Блузы дѣлаются почти исключительно съ очень открытымъ воротомъ, причемъ вырѣзъ обрамляется рюшью изъ плиссированнаго батиста, или тюля. Прямымъ слѣдствіемъ этой моды является самое широкое примѣненіе мѣха для защиты шеи отъ холода. Много блузъ и жакетовъ будетъ съ воротниками «Медичи», при которыхъ неизбѣжны высокія прически, открывающія затылокъ, и соотвѣтственныя шляпы.

Выборъ фасона, ткани и оттѣнка для вечернихъ туалетовъ предоставляется личному вкусу; преобладаютъ мягкія драпировки, очень много кружевъ и тюля. При выборѣ цвѣта слѣдуетъ считаться съ цвѣтомъ волосъ, такъ напримѣръ: блондинкѣ ярко оттѣняетъ вишневый цвѣтъ («cerise»), а брюнеткамъ очень идетъ свѣтло-зеленый тонъ и т. д.

Слѣдуетъ помнить, что слишкомъ смѣлыя и яркія сочетанія цвѣтовъ требуютъ очень много вкуса, поэтому сочиняющимся въ удачномъ выборѣ предпочтительнѣе придержаться темныхъ и спокойныхъ тоновъ, тѣмъ болѣе, что современная мода позволяетъ самымъ разнообразнымъ способомъ оживить ихъ отдѣлками изъ болѣе свѣтлыхъ тканей, тюля и кружевъ. Такъ напр., модный корсажъ можно составить изъ мягко задрапированныхъ, глубокихъ складокъ, образующихъ и рукава; передъ корсажа открывается изъ легкихъ бѣлыхъ, или свѣтлыхъ шемизеткахъ изъ тюля, кружевъ, шелковаго шифона и т. д.

Figure 2.2. Front page of the Russian fashion magazine *Women's World*, October 1913. Private collection.

welt.[23] These German magazines were selected because they themselves were translations of French magazines. Since Germany was geographically closer to Russia than France, this meant less time and money spent on bringing the fashion news to Russia. Ironically a third publication appeared in 1885 to challenge these German translations of French fashion magazines. Waving the flag of Russian nationalism, the publisher of *Fashion Herald* (*Vestnik mody*) declared that he was tired of the "German domination" of the fashion press and promised his readers that he would provide "real" French fashion plates as soon as they appeared in Paris, a promise earlier magazines had not dared to make.[24] Despite the purple prose, all three magazines promised their readers a timely discussion of *Paris* fashions, and for this reason, *New Russian Bazaar*, *Fashionable Society*, and *Fashion Herald* dominated the Russian fashion press in the second half of the nineteenth century.

This new generation of fashion magazines was the handiwork of men, especially Herman Goppe and Nikolai Alovert. Goppe had come to Russia from Westphalia in the mid-nineteenth century and began a successful business publishing guidebooks, directories, and calendars. In 1867 Goppe's firm created *Fashions and News* (*Mody i novosti*), the predecessor to *Fashionable Society*. As business improved, Goppe hired Nikolai Alovert in 1869 to work on his new magazine, *Illustration of the World* (*Vsemirnaia illiustratsiia*). In 1878, having received an excellent education in publishing, Alovert set up his own firm and began to compete with his former employer for business.[25]

In spite of this intense rivalry that developed between these two men, they had one feature in common—they had established themselves as publishers of technical publications. By the second half of the nineteenth century, chromolithography and then halftones had transformed the print media. Fashion magazines no longer consisted of one or two fashion plates, but contained large numbers of dress designs, needlework patterns, and numerous advertisements. All this pictorial material required great technical skill and capital to reproduce in large quantities. One of Goppe's admirers wrote that "the publisher of *illustrated* magazines must give all his attention to the *outward appearance* of the publication. The paper, print, plates, drawings, and then the business part of the firm—all these demand the very organizational and administrative talents that Goppe possessed."[26]

This emphasis on the technical and business aspects of publishing brought about an important change in the magazines themselves. Although the news from Paris might reach Russia more quickly due to the technical prowess of Goppe and Alovert, neither man ever wrote a fashion column.

Foreign correspondents who were French or adopted French pseudonyms, like *Parisian Woman* (*Parizhanka*), now wrote the articles. This change affected the tone of the magazines. The direct and intimate link between Russian publishers, editors, and readers was lost in favor of a more modern, "European" tone. Instead of editor and publisher Olympiada Riumina writing about changes in fashion, Goppe and Alovert confined their editorial presence in the magazines to occasional notices concerning subscriptions, publication delays, and other technical matters. For these men the fashion press served as a vehicle to make money for themselves and their firms—the fashion magazines were only one part of their growing publishing empires.

Despite their lack of interest in the actual content of the magazines, these men bore a tremendous responsibility for influencing not only how men and women dressed but also in shaping the gender order in imperial Russia. More was being imported than merely news about clothing styles. Domesticity, which had taken shape in Western Europe, came to Russia through the medium of the fashion magazine. Articles about clothes, cooking, and childrearing became blueprints for how Russian women should conduct themselves. As more women began to consult these magazines for advice, their role as social arbiters grew stronger.

Furthermore, while women continued to play important roles in the fashion industry as editors, writers, and translators, men now dominated publishing. The reasons for this are not hard to find. First, women were not given the opportunity to acquire the technical skills as printers like Goppe and Alovert; most women who worked in the printing industry before 1906 served as proofreaders or binders. Second, to set up all the machinery and to hire a well-trained workforce necessary to publish an illustrated magazine required large amounts of capital. It was no longer a question of simply paying for a fashion plate or two from Paris, expensive as that was; the new generation of publishers needed to mechanize the workplace, at least partially, if they were going to be able to provide high-quality illustrations. Most Russian women did not have access to the money necessary for such capital investment, nor the technical expertise to establish successful publishing houses. Given the advantages which Goppe and Alovert had when they began their fashion magazines, it is no surprise that women publishers had difficulty competing with them. These male publishing ventures drove the earlier magazines out of business.[27]

Government Censorship and the Fashion Magazine, 1865–1906

In addition to the intense rivalry that developed among publishers, they still had to contend with the scrutiny of government censors. In 1874, the editor of *New Russian Bazaar* wanted to include in the magazine a short story titled "Mest' ksendza" ("The Revenge of a Polish Catholic Priest").[28] The tale incorporated themes that were to become typical of women's Gothic romances: A beautiful young Russian countess is married off by her family to a man many years her senior. She is deeply unhappy, dreaming of a better life, when she meets and falls madly in love with a young Russian gentleman named Dorin. Their affair culminates in the birth of a male child who is then given to a Polish Catholic priest to raise. The priest takes the child to Poland, where he raises him to hate all things Russian. In 1863, during the Polish uprising, the Russian father and his now-Polish son meet on the battlefield. Taken prisoner and sentenced to hard labor, the son fractures his skull in prison and dies. The priest then reveals to Dorin that he is the father of the dead prisoner and Dorin promptly goes mad.

According to Amaliia Andreevna Lishke, editor of *New Russian Bazaar*, the story concerned daily life in Russia and Poland, and did not constitute a threat to the government or involve any actual participants in the uprising. Furthermore, she claimed that the description of the uprising was taken from a book the censors had approved in 1868. The censor Smirnov took issue with Lishke's assertions, claiming that the story was not about "daily life" but very much about the Polish uprising, a topic that all Russian publications were forbidden to discuss. Moreover, this kind of story was inappropriate for a fashion magazine with such a large audience. The Censorship Administration upheld the censor's decision to deny permission to publish the story.[29]

To modern readers, "The Polish Catholic Priest's Revenge" is a typical melodrama aimed at a female audience and therefore what one might expect in a fashion magazine. Government censors, however, saw it as politically subversive, no matter how melodramatic. The government did not want any story publicizing Russia's ignominious role in the Polish uprising to grace the pages of a woman's magazine and encourage sympathy for the Polish cause. For this reason alone, the censor Smirnov rejected the story and knew he would have the support of his superiors. Nevertheless he must have had additional concerns about a story that condoned a woman's flight from an unhappy marriage into an extramarital affair, undermining the Russian government's view of family life. If this was a story about "daily life," as Lishke claimed, what did that say about marital relations in imperial Russia? For both reasons, the government was determined that this story and others like it should never be published.

Fiction was not the only part of the fashion magazine that drew the wrath of government authorities. Ecclesiastical authorities sometimes objected to the reproductions found in the fashion journals. The Russian Orthodox Church placed strict limits on the reproduction of well-known icons. So in 1882, when *Fashionable Society* published a picture of the Kazan Mother of God icon, Konstantin Pobedonotsev, the Ober-Procurator of the Holy Synod, wrote an indignant letter to the Censorship Administration. He stated that the magazine was only allowed to publish drawings of dress and needlework. Furthermore, he argued, the Ecclesiastical Censorship Committee had the right to oversee the publication of all religious images, including the image of the Kazan Mother of God. The minister of internal affairs himself replied to Pobedonotsev. He justified his censor's decision to allow publication of the holy image by arguing that the magazine was allowed to publish sacred images in its needlework section, as many women readers used them to create liturgical articles for Orthodox services. The Kazan Mother of God had been approved for just such a purpose, and it was published separately from the fashion plates. Nevertheless the minister agreed that from now on such images would not appear without prior approval from the ecclesiastical authorities.[30] There were at least three other occasions when the religious authorities criticized the reproduction of religious works in fashion magazines.[31] In contrast to Western Europe, where religious images were used to support a traditional view of family life, in Russia the religious authorities forbade the mixing of secular and holy images. The Orthodox Church was determined to maintain a strict division between the sacred and the profane.

Despite these interventions, the instances when government censors refused permission for publication were rather rare. Most of the time, government censors arbitrated petty squabbles between publishers rather than exercising editorial control. One such moment occurred in 1885, when Goppe wrote to the Censorship Administration to complain about his rival, Alovert. Alovert claimed that *Fashion Herald* was the only Parisian fashion magazine in Russia. Goppe insisted that the censors intervene and force Alovert to change his advertising campaign. In rather sharp contrast to what would have happened forty years earlier, the censors refused to get involved.[32] Thus by the 1890s the censors had essentially ceded their editorial and commercial authority to the publishers themselves. Consequently, when the Revolution of 1905 ended censorship of all Russian publications, there was very little change in the magazines themselves. Publishers had copied the successful Western European formula of mixing fashion and fiction, illustration and text that appealed to women readers no matter where they lived. Apparently Russian women felt so completely integrated into that European fashion world that they did not need their "own" magazine.

Conclusion

Despite the great distances between Paris and Petersburg, imperial Russia developed a vital and fiercely competitive fashion press during the nineteenth century. The creation of such a dynamic market for fashion news was due to the remarkable entrepreneurial skills of those who worked in Russian publishing. The men and women who created Russia's fashion magazines believed that they were serving their autocratic government by ensuring that Russians had the information they needed to dress properly. As Russia's modernization drive took hold and expanded in the nineteenth century, the need for this kind of sartorial information intensified, allowing for a spirit of cooperation to develop between the government and the publishing industry as they worked together to ensure that Russians knew how to dress.

At the same time, it is also clear that the relationship between government censors and publishers was a complex one. The censors were supposed to ensure that the fashion press did not discuss politics or any other controversial issue, and they performed this function well, as the few cases that were brought before the Censorship Administration demonstrate. After 1865 the Central Censorship Administration became more of an arbitration board as it attempted to settle the squabbles among publishers, a role that the courts often assume in democratic societies.

Perhaps the most remarkable feature of the early years of the fashion magazine was the role of women in its development. Unlike English and American women, Russian women were allowed to own property. Usually in the form of landed estates, women could and did sell their estates to go into business, a phenomenon that historians are only now beginning to study.[33] In the case of the fashion magazine, it was Elizaveta Safonova, Olimpiada Riumina, and other female publishers whose marketing strategies, fashion sense, and business acumen succeeded in creating profitable magazines during the first half of the nineteenth century. Their motivations for undertaking this work are as varied as the women themselves. Safonova was the sole bread-winner for her family after her husband's death. Riumina was married and, with her husband's support, sought to improve their financial status through publishing. For ambitious, educated women who lived in St. Petersburg, the fashion press offered a rare opportunity to have a meaningful professional life.[34]

At a time when Russian women could not have their own passports or live separately from their husbands, women's success in the fashion press is all the more remarkable. Safonova began her publishing house in the 1830s well before anyone had raised the "woman question" in Russia. What un-doubtedly made her success possible was the nature of the fashion magazine itself. Its purpose was to provide women with practical advice and support for their role as wife, mother, and household manager. Because the fashion magazine was for women only, who better to run such a venture than women themselves? The irony was that at the same time that these women publishers were touting the importance of women's domestic role, they were creating a counter-role for women outside the home.

Despite the success of the Russian fashion press, it is important to stress that from the very beginning it was completely dependent on European mag-azines—there was very little that was original in these magazines. The fashion plates and lithographs came from Paris directly or via Berlin. The editorial features—light fiction and poetry, articles on cosmetics, housework, and hy-giene—and even the layout of the advertisements and supplements appeared first in French magazines. Indeed, the direct copying of European magazines presented publishers with their greatest challenge—why should any woman read an inferior copy of a French fashion magazine? The early generation of Russian fashion magazines worked hard to establish their expertise as re-spected interpreters of the laws of fashion. They acted as intermediaries be-tween Paris, the capital of fickle fashion, and their fellow Russians. In the process they made St. Petersburg a legitimate and respected branch of the European fashion industry. Russia was no longer on the periphery, but a full and equal member of the empire of fashion.

The next step in the development of the Russian fashion magazine ap-pears paradoxical, given the success of the early magazines. Why would trans-lations take the place of well-established and well-regarded domestic periodicals? The answer to this question gets to the heart of what Russian readers got out of the magazines. Having come late to the fashion world and being far away from Paris, both spatially and spiritually, Russians had to overcome feelings of inferiority. The best way to do this was to make St. Petersburg a center of fashion just as London, Berlin, and Vienna had done. The fashion magazines worked really hard to develop the sense among Russian women that they could become a part of that world through the simple act of buying a magazine. Every woman who sewed a skirt, baked a cake, or fashioned a hat based on information acquired through the fashion press could feel herself part of a modern, cosmopolitan community of women with the same interests and tastes.

Thus, the Russian fashion press made an important contribution to the world of fashion. First, it helped to bring haute couture to the European periphery by keeping Russian society informed of the latest fashions in European modes of dress. At the same time, publishers introduced Western European business culture and practices into Russia. Russian entrepreneurs learned how to utilize advertising, new technologies, and marketing strategies to create a lively and competitive publishing industry and business culture in which fashion could flourish. Just as important, the Russian fashion press helped to create an international community of women consumers. Feelings of inferiority gave way to a growing self-confidence and pride in themselves and Russia's role in the fashion industry. In less than a hundred years, the lighthearted and "frivolous" fashion magazine had played a profound role in transforming Russians from semi-Asiatic barbarians into cosmopolitan Europeans.

CHAPTER THREE

Accessorizing, Italian Style: Creating a Market for Milan's Fashion Merchandise

Elisabetta Merlo and Francesca Polese

THIS CHAPTER INVESTIGATES the early development of the Italian fashion industry by considering the specific case of Milan at the end of the nineteenth century. In those years, Milan was one of Italy's most advanced industrial centers, with a diversified economy and an advanced clothing and textile industry. With almost 322,000 people in 1881 (491,460 in 1901), Milan was the second largest Italian city after Naples, with a population of 494,314. In Milan's traditional clothing industry, the artisans making the garments and accessories sold them to small stores or directly to consumers. After mid-century, Milan's highly productive clothing and fashion industries were enriched by the addition of large department stores, which began to modernize distribution. The most important was the Grandi Magazzini "Alle Città d'Italia," founded by the Bocconi brothers in 1865 and renamed La Rinascente in 1921 under new ownership and management.[1]

Department stores helped to create a wide market for the products of the emerging fashion industry. Not only did these palaces of consumption lure customers with attractive window displays and opulent buildings, but they also introduced innovative selling methods, including mail-order catalogs. These mail-order catalogs were important vehicles for producing and consuming fashion. For consumers, they advertised fashion goods and acces-

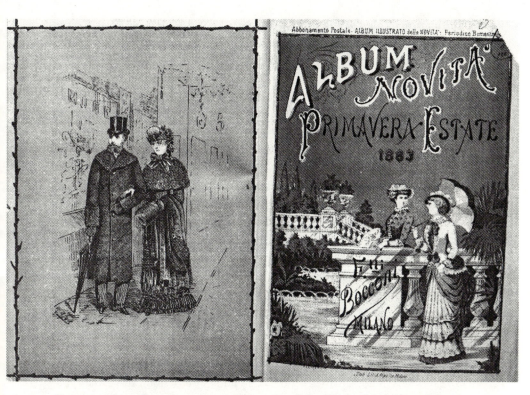

Figure 3.1. Cover from the spring–summer 1883 mail-order catalog (*Album delle Novità*) of the Bocconi department store, showing the latest fashions. Courtesy Biblioteca Nazionale Braidense, Milan.

sories, spread the latest style trends, and diffused information about etiquette. For the garment trade, they disseminated information about sewing, cutting, and other techniques essential to the process of manufacturing clothing.

This chapter analyzes the emergence of a market for accessories in Milan, drawing on mail-order catalogs published by the Grandi Magazzini "Alle Città d'Italia" in the 1880s (Figure 3.1).[2] A comparison of these catalogs and other sources gives insight into important historical issues in the fashion business. Our analysis provides data about the prices of fashion accessories and pairs this information with data on wages and family income to define the characteristics of Milan's fashion market. In terms of prices and styles, we also compare the fashion accessories listed in the department store's catalog with information found in the period's major fashion magazines. For sure, catalogs were a powerful means of advertising for the department store, which printed colorful images to attract potential customers. The glossy pages of the mail-order catalogs, however, also allow economic and business historians to assess and define better the department store's role in the development of the modern fashion industry.

From a stylistic point of view, in the 1880s the Milanese population was surely fashion conscious. Interest in fashion had far-reaching historical roots that produced a highly specific Italian style. Traditionally Milan's local aristocracy, later joined by the bourgeoisie, had distinguished itself from noble elites in other Italian states through its rather pronounced interest in industrial activities. In addition, the distance of Milan from the Italian peninsula's two major courts—the royal and the papal, both in Rome by the 1880s—also contributed to the formation of a distinctive Milanese fashion. The Milanese choice of clothing had several hallmarks. Most notable was the attention to quality fabrics and fine tailoring, combined in moderation with elements of ornament and splendor. Over time, soberness and severity emerged as the distinctive qualities of Milanese fashion. One must not forget, however, that in the 1880s France still provided the dominant stylistic model. Yet, when imitating Parisian styles, the Milanese adapted the French designs to suit local taste, often simplifying or toning down frivolities and novelties.[3] The attention devoted to fashion by the Milanese, and their interest in French novelties, is well documented by the large number of fashion magazines published in the city.

Although the Milanese of the 1880s were quick to follow the newest fashion trends, the market for fashion in Milan was much more traditional. For sure the most common channel through which garments circulated among the lower social classes was through itinerant peddlers of second-hand clothing and textiles. Domestic production of clothing was widely diffused among all social classes, but sewing machines were still uncommon, limited to the wealthiest households. Upper-class women sewed, making dresses for their own wardrobes. They generally copied the models and styles published in fashion magazines after purchasing fabrics, lace, and trimmings.

If not produced at home, clothing for both men and women would be custom-made by tailors or seamstresses. These professions were widely diffused in the city and represent the majority of the fashion-related activities included in the Savallo guides, the nineteenth-century version of our city directories. Indeed, throughout the 1880s, the number of tailors and seamstresses was increasing. In 1881, only 249 of these artisans were listed in the guides, but by 1886 there were 383. These figures suggest that having clothing custom-made was not limited to Milan's wealthiest social classes. As a matter of fact, ready-to-wear garments were still rare in Italy as late as the mid-1950s, when a survey by Doxa, the most important Italian statistical research and poll analysis agency, showed that most Italians still predominantly wore homemade, used, or custom-made garments.[4] In the 1880s the industrial production of ready-to-wear was limited, and most firms working in this mode generally supplied outfits to the army or the government.

We believe that mail-order catalogs not only show the extent to which department stores departed from traditional retailing, but also shed further light on their alleged "democratizing" power. Since the 1980s, historians have made powerful arguments for department stores as innovative retailers whose novel business practices, including fixed prices, open stock, and easy-return policies, transformed European and American consumer society, opening its doors to people of modest incomes. Our mail-order study, which examines both the assortment and prices of goods, redefines the extent of standardization achieved by early department stores. In this respect, we believe that the comparison between the prices of catalog goods and average incomes is an important analytical tool. The comparison makes it possible to test the common notion that department stores created a mass market for fashion and clothing products by the late 1880s. Our analysis of mail-order catalogs suggests that, in late nineteenth-century Italy, department stores had not yet singled out a specific market segment. Instead, they sold to customers from a variety of classes. Although their reach was broad, Italian department stores of the 1880s were most likely too expensive for lower-middle-class shoppers.

Milan in the Age of the First Italian Department Store

Although there is a lack of accurate statistical data, historians generally agree that Italy began to industrialize in the second half of the nineteenth century.[5] A "first coat of paint" of industrial activity was laid between the 1860s and 1880s, a foundation built on at the turn of the century. [6] In the period following the country's political unification (1861), Italy saw a growth in the major economic indicators, such as industrial output and exports. Italian modernization exhibited strong regional differences, with industry concentrated in the northern regions, especially the "industrial triangle" of Piedmont, Liguria, and Lombardy.

Although significant, especially in the years 1896 to 1914, the modernization of Italian industry before World War I must not be overemphasized, even when taking into account the most developed regions. Most firms were still active in largely traditional (although rapidly and deeply evolving) sectors, particularly textiles, often maintaining strong links with agricultural activities. The silk industry is a case in point. Concentrated in the northern regions, the cultivation of silk cocoons and the manufacturing of silk fabrics thrived, thanks to the seasonal employment of an abundant agricultural workforce, while the exported products (raw, semifinished or, more seldom, finished goods) assured Italy a place in international markets.[7] As far as organization is concerned, industrial activities remained largely of an artisan type, with a few large companies limited to the most modern industrial sectors, such as engineering and rubber.

Lombardy, especially the city of Milan, was one of the chief beneficiaries of industrialization, which almost completely transformed the city into a modern industrial center by the beginning of World War I. The most obvious effect of the industrial upsurge was demographic. Between 1859 and 1915, the city's population nearly tripled, from 232,000 to 658,000, with a particularly strong increase between 1879 and 1889, from 299,008 to 408,294. This impressive trend was largely fueled by immigrants who were attracted to the prosperity that made Milan unique in the Italian economy.[8] Although the most rapid modernization occurred in various branches of engineering, Milanese industrialization did not significantly alter the traditional urban economy, comprised of a miscellany of tiny, labor-intensive artisan sweatshops. When businessman-engineer Giuseppe Colombo addressed public opinion at the Italian National Industrial Exhibition in 1881, he famously noted that Milan was still more similar to Paris than to Manchester.[9]

The comparison between Milan and Paris was especially true for the clothing and "fashion" sectors. Both cities had large numbers of very small workshops producing clothes and fashion accessories, such as gloves, hats, scarves, umbrellas, and walking canes. Like Paris, Milan boasted a well-developed, diversified fashion economy, as documented by different kinds of historical sources. Among them, commercial guides such as the above-mentioned Savallo guides, published yearly from the 1840s onward, provide a comprehensive picture of a productive urban environment in which all elements of the clothing and textile industry were largely present.[10]

A more detailed picture of Milan's clothing and fashion trades is provided by Italy's first national industrial census, taken in 1881. The census shows an industrializing city primarily characterized not by large factories, but by a dense network of small and tiny workshops and a productive organization closely resembling a highly developed "putting out" system. The total number of industrial workers was 92,087, of which a large share—29,754— were active in the production of clothing. Among the latter, the number of women was especially high, 84.6 percent. Like their counterparts in New York City's garment district, these household workers produced items at home on account for commercial firms. Together, artisan workshops and domestic workers made a wide assortment of consumer goods designed to satisfy the demand for fashion and luxury products: silk textiles, velvets, ribbons, voiles, knitwear, trimmings and braids, elastic fibers, wool shawls, embroideries and laces, hats, leather gloves, fur coats, linens and lingerie, clothing, and shoes. This productive organization was not merely the heritage of preindustrial times. On the contrary, domestic work and the prevalence of female labor signaled the beginning of a modernization process that took advantage of decentralized production and mechanization. Instead of being wiped away by the factory system, this domestic system had been reinforced by the diffusion of the sewing machine.[11] Data from the 1911 national industrial census show that, of the 175,871 Milanese industrial workers, 42,711 were active in the production of clothing. The high number of women remained consistent, 84.2 percent.

Grandi Magazzini "Alle Città d'Italia": The First Italian Department Store

These economic transformations were prerequisite to the emergence of innovative retailing forms that appeared in the textile, clothing, and fashion sectors in the mid-nineteenth century. The first Italian department store was created in 1865, when the brothers Ferdinando and Luigi Bocconi acquired a shop on one of Milan's major shopping streets. Previously the Bocconis worked alongside their father as itinerant peddlers, selling textiles and clothing.[12] The Bocconi store marked the beginning of the brothers' rise within the city's prominent business community.[13] The store was a true novelty for Italian retailing, and its growing popularity explains the move to a larger building in 1870. Although somewhat remote from the city center, the new location provided spacious quarters, making it possible to exhibit a larger variety of items. The Bocconis stocked not only textiles and clothes, but also linens, hats, shoes, drapes, and some furniture. Well aware that a department store must be situated in the urban core, in 1877 the Bocconi brothers moved back to one of Milan's central areas, opening a *grand magasin* inspired by Parisian models like the Bon Marché. The French influx was echoed clearly in the choice of the name, Aux Villes d'Italie, showing that the Bocconis knew that all activities connected to fashion needed some kind of relationship with Paris, the undisputed world fashion capital of those days. In 1880 the store became Alle Città d'Italia, adopting the Italian version of the French name, only because of the strong anti-French trend of Italian foreign policy in those years.

By the early twentieth century, Alle Città d'Italia was undoubtedly the largest department store in the country. It had branches centrally located in all major Italian cities, including Milan, Rome, Genoa, Turin, Palermo, Naples, Venice, Florence, and Bologna.[14] The flagship store, however, was located in the heart of Milan, occupying a main square in front of the stupendous Gothic cathedral, the Duomo. As far as architectural style is concerned, the Bocconi brothers created a store that resembled the "typical" department store that had become a specific feature of the boulevards in the late nineteenth-century *ville lumière*. It was an imposing, three-story building with window displays overlooking the square. The interior featured vast series of shelves facing monumental staircases. Inaugurated in 1889, the building, designed by leading architect Giovanni Giachi, was the first edifice in Italy to be constructed with the specific purpose of hosting a department store. The Bocconi firm also resembled the more advanced European counterparts in its internal organization. As is well known, one of the major revolutionary ideas behind the department store was the concept of low profit per unit compensated by a high stock turnover.[15]

Comparing department stores to traditional shops, historians have talked about the new retailers as major vehicles in the "democratization of fashion."[16] But the case of Alle Città d'Italia does not fully confirm such a hypothesis. More specifically, our analysis of prices for accessories and clothing sold through the Bocconis' mail-order catalogs suggest a more mixed picture. Average prices for clothing seem altogether unaffordable, or barely affordable, by lower-income groups. In the case of accessories, only the most basic models, and therefore less fashionable items, were within reach of families of modest means.

Another characteristic of the department store adopted by the Bocconi firm was the large variety of products offered for sale. The scope of the stock was especially striking when compared to traditional shops, which generally specialized in a limited variety of items. A 1879 article in Milan's *L'Illustrazi-*

one Italiana focused on Aux Villes d'Italie, enthusiastically describing the enormous stock, which included perfumes, toys, matches, rugs, furniture, clothing, and fashion accessories.[17] Due to the relative backwardness of Italian industry, some of the goods sold by the Bocconis were imported from Paris. In this regard, the importance of French origins to the marketing of style goods led the Bocconi brothers in the 1870s to establish a buying office in Paris.

The *Illustrazione Italiana* article also gives some information concerning the productive organization of the Milanese department store during the late 1870s, evoking similarities with the more famous French counterpart.[18] As a matter of fact, in the initial phases of their business, the Bocconi brothers had relied on domestic producers. As we have already seen, this organization enabled capitalists to exploit the abundant domestic workers active in Milan. By 1879, however, the firm ran two production workshops, one in Turin and a second in Milan, employing 900 workers to make ready-to-wear for both men and women. At the same time, each of the five branches of the store, including the one in Turin, employed some 150 artisans to produce custom-made garments, showing that domestic industry still represented a large part of the department store's activity.[19]

Evidence of this wide assortment of goods is also found in Alle Città d'Italia's mail-order catalogs, which helped disseminate the department store's merchandise throughout the country. This sales instrument was a common feature of the nineteenth-century department store. The French precursor to the department store, the *magasin de nouveautés*, introduced mail-order service during the early nineteenth century.[20] The Bon Marché, the most important of the "true" French department stores, featured mail-order service by 1871; at the century's end, its "mailings were massive," not only to customers in Paris and French provinces, but also to foreign markets, thanks to catalogs translated into a variety of languages.[21] In 1902, packages were mailed virtually all over the world, from South America to Russia.[22] Mail-order sales were remarkably important to the overall business of the Bon Marché in the last decades of the nineteenth century. In 1871–72, orders sent by mail accounted for almost 15 percent of total sales; by the beginning of the 1900s they had increased to more than 17 percent.[23]

Organization of such a wide-reaching business was clearly a complex matter, involving hundreds of employees and workers, each with specific tasks. French novelist Emile Zola, who published *Au bonheur des dames* (*The Ladies' Paradise*) in 1883, collected firsthand material on the Bon Marché in

1881–82. His notes allow us to fill in a gap in our knowledge of mail-order catalogs and to compare Alle Città d'Italia with its more famous counterpart. According to Zola, the Bon Marché had thirty-six departments and 2,500 employees in 1881–82; its mail-order department employed 226 persons.[24] The volume of letters received in a year could reach 5,000.

Unfortunately we lack similar data for the Bocconi store. We do know, however, that in the last decades of the nineteenth century, the catalog of the Milanese store was published every two months. In 1880, each issue had 120 pages and more than 300 illustrations, and was mailed to some 40,000 customers. By 1879, the firm had established its own typography shop, with the capacity to print some 30,000 catalogs. By the beginning of the 1890s, Alle Città d'Italia's mail-order department received 38,000 letters and shipped some 100,000 parcels.[25]

It is important to stress that the sales volume suggested by these figures does not mean that the department store became a retailer specializing in ready-to-wear garments. On the contrary, detailed analysis of the apparel offered by the 1880s catalogs shows that most of the clothing and accessories for sale by Alle Città d'Italia was not standardized. The clothing featured in the catalog generally suggested instead that significant intervention by tailors and seamstresses was needed to fit individual measurements and customer specifications, such as the requests for different types of fabrics.

Alle Città d'Italia's Mail-Order Catalogs

This section analyzes the major fashion accessories offered by the Bocconi brothers' department store, in terms of styles, assortments, and prices. Our analysis is based on four Alle Città d'Italia mail-order catalogs: 1880 autumn–winter, 1882 autumn–winter, 1883 spring–summer, and 1886 spring–summer.

Before proceeding, a caveat is in order. The origins of Italian mail-order catalogs are connected to radically different factors from those leading to specialized mail-order houses in the United States. In the mid-1800s, American dry-goods establishments like A. T. Stewart and department stores like John Wanamaker did a substantial wholesale mail-order trade, shipping fabrics and readymade clothing to faraway retailers. These early mail-order businesses have been overshadowed in the historical literature by the specialized mail-order firms that emerged in the late 1800s. Some of these mail-order giants, including Sears, Roebuck and Company, later opened retail stores. In

Italy, mail-order sales developed in a different manner, reflecting the distinctive socio-demographic, urban, and commercial characteristics of the country. The population density of the rural areas, the country's fragmented commercial structure, the overall low incomes, and the persistence of traveling street merchants or peddlers prohibited the emergence of specialized mail-order companies. The first attempts were made by manufacturers and retailers like the Bocconi brothers, who saw mail-order catalogs as part of their marketing and distribution systems.

The Bocconi brothers began issuing illustrated sales catalogs on a bimonthly basis in 1878. The most important issues appeared in April and October, showing fashion novelties for spring and summer and for autumn and winter respectively. The other numbers focused on specific lines or publicized sales special events: March was dedicated to underclothing, December to Christmas decorations and toys. The remaining issues were for "end of season special offers." Accessories appeared in all issues.

It must be emphasized that accessories and clothing were not the major feature of the Bocconi stores in the 1880s. The Alle Città d'Italia's catalogs suggest that the bulk of the stock consisted of dry goods such as laces, thread, and fabrics. Other items included linens, undergarments, furniture, toys, luggage, perfumes, and jewelry. Although it is difficult to establish what types of items represented the brothers' core business in the 1880s, it was probably not the sale of readymade garments. Indeed, in some of the catalogs, women's dresses and fabrics were presented on the same page, side by side, suggesting that perhaps the former represented a sort of marketing instrument or advertising device for sales of the latter.

Overall the layout of the Alle Città d'Italia's catalogs suggest that they functioned as a sort of virtual shop, reproducing the elegant atmosphere of the store in Milan's Piazza del Duomo. The publication's colored front cover brandished the latest trends in fashion; its more sober pages featured illustrations framed in stylized decorative motifs. The illustrations were generally preceded by a section explaining shipping, packing, and payment procedures, instructions on how to take body measurements, and the system for returning unsatisfactory goods. Following this practical information, the catalog featured a large section devoted to textiles, with several pages occupied by various types of cloth: silks, satins, velvets, cottons, and wool. The next section showed clothing, which included the entire range of apparel: woolen outerwear, male and female underwear, wedding dresses, men's and women's suits, hats, gloves, and ties. Household linens came next. The final section offered

Figure 3.2. Selection of female hats from *Album delle Novità*, spring–summer 1883. Each hat has a feminine name and is presented in two versions, with a price difference, determined by quality of material and the quantity of ornament. Courtesy Biblioteca Nazionale Braidense, Milan.

miscellaneous articles for the person and the home: sewing necessities, travel goods, umbrellas and parasols, perfumes, sewing machines, household objects, decorative articles, and artistic bronzes. Women's accessories were generally next to women's clothing, showing hats and gloves next to dresses, for example, to suggest the complete wardrobe (Figure 3.2).

It is important to note that the catalogs gave far less space to clothing and accessories for men and boys than to articles for women and girls. The men's and boys' section was generally restricted to the last few pages. At times, however, some gentlemen's accessories, such as gloves and umbrellas, were shown together with women's accessories. This comes as no surprise if we consider that nineteenth-century fashion was predominantly female fashion. After the "great renunciation" of flamboyant men's apparel by Britain's emerging industrial bourgeoisie in the first decades of the nineteenth century, women's wear occupied center stage in fashion, and it was in women's clothing and accessories that changes in style became more evident.[26]

Catalog Accessories: Style, Assortment, and Prices

The stylistic characteristics of the accessories sold by the Bocconi brothers show that Alle Città d'Italia was an up-to-date store offering the latest fashion novelties. The language used to describe the accessories was taken directly from the fashion glossaries of Paris and London. This revealed the store's desire to show strong links with the two European style capitals, which dictated the trends in male and especially female fashion. The accessories shown in the catalogs were in many ways similar to models in the most elegant fashion magazines, including *Margherita* and *Corriere delle Dame*, both published in Milan and read by Milanese ladies from the higher social classes.

Generally speaking, women's fashions in Italy during the 1880s mirrored those in Paris. This was not only due to a form of snobbery. The imitation of Parisian styles was rooted in the lack of Italian creativity, a factor closely linked to the country's economic backwardness. The tendency to lengthen the female figure, launched during the early 1880s by French haute couture, was gradually abandoned. Over the course of the decade, simple styles emerged that accentuated the curves of the body and the slender waist. Upper-class wealth was not made apparent by the amount of drapery, as had been the case in earlier periods. Rather, prosperity was displayed in the sumptuousness of the clothing, including heavily embroidered velvets, brocades, and satins, and through the variety of garments owned, each for a specific occasion.

Narrowing our focus to accessories, only a few accouterments gained undeniable importance in fashionable female dress during the 1880s. As for shoes and stockings, in these years their primary function was still more practical than decorative. The feet were almost always covered by a long skirt, sometimes shorter in summer. Hence the catalog offered a very small selection of socks and stockings.[27] Handbags and purses were not yet part of an elegant lady's apparel, so the catalog offered few of them. Typically, a lady's maid would accompany her mistress, handling the money on her account. Leather goods were largely confined to travel accessories such as luggage and trunks.

In the 1880s the major ladies' accessories advertised in the Alle Città d'Italia catalogs were hats, umbrellas, and gloves. During the 1880s the catalogs sold readymade decorated hats and plain hat shapes that could be decorated to suit the wearer's fancy. Hats had earned increasing importance as fashion accessories after wigs—and, more generally, the elaborate hairstyles of the seventeenth and eighteenth centuries—became outdated. For wigs, the undisputable trendsetter had been the French court. French noblemen were used to carrying hats under their arms, waving them while bowing in front of a woman. Female hairstyles were often embellished with jewels and adorned by trimmings such as ribbons, knots, and flowers. From the mid-eighteenth century onward, ladies started to prefer hats because of their greater practicality. Unlike elaborate hairstyles, hats could easily be changed depending on the circumstances and were much more responsive to fashion trends. Their shapes and decorations could quickly vary according to the latest novelties.

The number of readymade hat models featured in the catalogs grew steadily, from four in autumn-winter 1880–82 to about a dozen in later years. Most were particularly suitable for young ladies. More often than adults, young people wore ready-to-wear, which cost less than comparable premade clothing for adults. The price of ladies' readymade hats varied. Winter hats were made of velvet, plush, or felt, less expensive summer hats of straw. A plain hood that fastened under the chin with ribbons cost a mere 12 lire. In contrast, an elaborate, elegant model called Egle, made from two shades of felt, ornamented with ostrich feathers, and clasped with a patterned scarf, cost 42.75 lire. The prices of summer hats ranged from 10 to 50 lire. Another expensive model, Dolores, was described as "a bizarre hat made from fine plaited straw in new colors with ostrich feathers and long silk ribbons." As specified in the catalog, this was so enormous that it could not be wrapped in a parcel, but had to be purchased at the store.

The variety of hat shapes (which could be decorated with feathers, velvet bows, shiny buckles, silk ribbons, and imitation flowers and birds) sold in the catalog was much wider than the selection of readymade hats. There were about fifteen to twenty basic models, each with a different style of brim, rim, and cap, for ladies and girls of all ages. Winter shapes cost between 2.75 and 11.75 lire; summer ones were cheaper, from 0.95 to 7.25 lire. The decorations were sold separately and illustrated on subsequent pages. Ribbons could cost as much as 7.95 lire for a meter of damask 20 cm wide, as could velvet braid in various colors. Ten of the fourteen ribbon choices, however, cost less than

3.45 lire per meter. There were about fifteen different types of feathers, rang-ing from those resembling the most common birds, which cost less than 1 lira, to those resembling feathers of rare birds such as ostriches, at more than 30 lire. Similarly the catalog offered ample assortments of fake flower-and-fruit decorations; the most elegant example could be bought for less than 5 lire.[28]

A large number of decorative warm-weather umbrellas and parasols were represented in the mail-order catalogs. Umbrellas are generally credited as being invented in China roughly 1,700 years ago. They were considered status symbols, because very few people had the privilege to hold a parasol over the emperor's head. The Chinese invention was later brought to Japan via Korea and also introduced to Persia and the West by merchants traveling along the Silk Road. The use of the umbrella in Europe dates to about the mid-seventeenth century. At that time it was not employed as a protection from rain, but was primarily a fashion accessory. At the end of the nineteenth century, its main use was still ornamental. In men's nineteenth-century fash-ion, the umbrella was regarded as a sign of elegance and distinctiveness, along with top hats, perfectly polished shoes, starched collars, and carefully ironed suits. Moreover, the parasol was an important accessory in ladies' fashion, as a woman's skin had to be maintained perfectly pale according to the Roman-tic ideal of female beauty diffused in the 1800s.

The abundance of umbrellas and parasols in our catalogs testifies to the importance of holidays in the open air, which became more popular as a result of the fin de siècle enthusiasm for healthy living.[29] Indeed upper-class Milanese increasingly spent their holidays at exclusive resorts in the nearby lakes and hills. The long straight handle and long metal point that character-ized 1880s umbrella models produced a slimming effect on the figure. It was fashionable to carry the umbrellas closed, with the lining tightly wrapped-up and held in place by buttons. In the case of umbrellas, the assortment of models, and the corresponding variety of prices, was large. The most refined parasols were made from lace matching the color of the dress, from gauze hemmed in silk, or were covered with flowers and petals to imitate a large flower corolla. The handle, in contrast to the richness of the dome, did not catch the viewer's attention at first glance. A closer look, however, revealed the handles were very elegant and precious, made out of ivory, tortoiseshell, and rare woods.

The catalogs include about 25 to 35 different models of umbrellas with prices ranging from 2 to 28 lire. Models varied in terms of length, the kind of handle (which was the most important decorative feature), and the quality of the silk. Such a great assortment was probably a result of the department store's decision to open a workshop for the production of umbrellas, organized "along the lines of the best English factories." The Bocconi brothers told catalog customers: "The application of the division of work, the introduction of the latest machinery and the purchase of large amounts of raw materials allow us to produce top quality articles at very competitive prices." Among the production of fashion accessories, the manufacture of umbrellas was surely the most diffused in the Milanese urban context of the mid-1880s. The Savallo commercial guides of these years record more than a hundred laboratories and workshops active in the production and trade of umbrellas.

Gloves were worn by women of the 1880s for different purposes. Of course they were used to avoid exposing the hands to cold weather and unwanted outside contacts, they were also an important sign of social distinction. From the twelfth century onward, gloves—decorated, embroidered, perfumed, and adorned with gems and pearls—became an accessory of paramount importance in women's apparel. Since then, in male apparel gloves have been used as a sign of dignity and honor. Broadly speaking, gloves were regarded as a status symbol, since members of the working class did not wear them while attending to manual activities. In the nineteenth century, fashion dictated colored silk gloves in tone with evening dress, decorated with open work and embroidery or made of soft, white suede, elbow length, and always with three vertical seams on the back to make them more tapered. Summer gloves were made of silk or cotton and were always long. The assortment of gloves offered by the department store included a few dozen styles, which differed in length, number of buttons, material, and, obviously, season. Missing from the catalogs were the more elegant models of gloves for evening wear. On the contrary, short gloves were largely represented. Winter gloves were mainly made of ordinary wool or leather in suede or glacé finish.[30] Summer gloves were mainly woven with Scottish woolen, or cotton thread. The price ranged from 1.60 to 4 lire, but could sometimes cost as much as 6 lire, as for fur-lined leather gloves presented in the autumn-winter catalogs.

The Alle Città d'Italia's catalogs do not allow us to determine whether the store's accessories offerings were susceptible to frequent stylistic changes. Certainly the accessories stocked by the store were generally made using standardized production methods. A survey of Milan by the Società Umanitaria, an important institution founded in 1893 with the aim of improving the professional, economic, and cultural position of industrial workers, confirms that the city's glove manufacturing was organized on an industrial scale from the early nineteenth century. The survey stated that there were 1,352 workers in the industry, 482 men and 870 women. The men worked in the factories as glove makers and handled the refining and leather-tanning operations. The women embroidered, hemmed, sewed, and ironed the articles and nearly always worked from home.[31] The 1880s Milan Savallo guides record 69 activities involved in the production and distribution of gloves.

Various sources agree that Italian production of umbrellas by manually assembling various standardized parts grew during the second half of the century. Increase in umbrella production is indirectly supported by the fact that, in these same years, umbrellas started to be exported, although quantities and destinations are not known.[32] The hat industry, renowned abroad for high-quality gentlemen's headgear, did not come into direct competition with millineries that used craft techniques to produce decorated women's hats. Instead it supplied department stores with a wide range of shapes that female customers could personalize as they wished.

Buying Fashion

The analysis of the mail-order catalogs of Alle Città d'Italia raises important questions that we will try to answer in this section. Who were the customers for the fashion accessories? Who could afford to purchase the items? What was the potential market to which the Milanese department store was catering? In order to tackle these issues, we will undertake a comparison between prices of accessories and information on average incomes of Milanese families. We can anticipate here that such an analysis suggests that only few customers could afford to buy the fashion accessories sold in the mail-order catalogs. It must be stressed that answers to these queries are extremely provisional, as they are drawn from information that is by no means fully reliable. The inconsistency of historical data becomes especially evident with our analysis of incomes or household budgets, which we can only use as a very rough indicator of the purchasing power of Milanese households.

Literature on the social structure of Milan in the nineteenth century has focused mainly on the working classes in an attempt to define the professional features of industrial workers and has paid less attention to a broader analysis. As mentioned above, industrial workers surely were present in large numbers by the 1880s, although it is difficult to distinguish artisans or domestic workers from actual factory workers. An 1852 survey captures the city's social variety. During this period, the lower classes were made up of industrial workers, to which one should add a large number of individuals active in traditional artisan crafts; petty trades; service of various types, including domestics, cooks, maids, and nursemaids; and other "blue collar" jobs. There were middle classes, comprising civil servants (5,340), teachers (1,500), attorneys (630), and others in similar moderate-income "white-collar" jobs. At the upper level of the social hierarchy, we find "property owners" (16,500 individuals), physicians (almost 600), engineers (375), and lawyers and notaries (320). Of course the elite category also included the nobles, 3,400 in an 1837 survey.[33]

Bearing in mind this kind of composite and not always precisely definable social structure, we can attempt to assess the purchasing power of the Milanese population in the last decades of the nineteenth century. Except for an increase in the number of factory workers, the Milanese social structure and professional groups of the 1880s did not differ much from the above-described picture.

Unfortunately, income data for the 1880s are very patchy, and we must use information provided by household budgets. A household budget is a concise account that briefly summarizes a family's income and expenditures over a fixed period of time.[34] Generally the four main sources of income were: property owned by the family, subsidies received by the family, wages from employment, and earnings from self-employment.[35] Expenditures included money spent on food, housing (rent, furniture, heating, and lighting), clothing (apparel, repairs and cleaning, and household linens), and "others" (school, health, and leisure). These accounts, however, are far from being totally reliable. First, one must consider the source from which they have been taken. The household budgets we cite were compiled by the professional associations of the different workers featured in Table 3.1, generally with the purpose of advocating the need for an increase in wages or the provision of "social services" by the Milanese city council. As a matter of fact, the purpose for which the budgets were published might well undermine their objectivity.

Table 3.1 provides an example of household budgets calculated from a range of primary sources. Drawing on material from the 1880s and 1890s, we present data for four income groups, bearing in mind that the information is only partially comparable to that from the 1852 survey. The data describe the expenditures of a "typical" Italian household, consisting of two parents and four children. For the "working classes," we have a household budget for a "workman," which would have included a young man employed either in a

TABLE 3.1. ANNUAL ACCOUNTS OF A TYPICAL MILANESE FAMILY (LIRE)

	Workman (e.g., in factory or small artisan laboratory)	Man worker in clothing industry	Woman worker ' in clothing industry	Employee (e.g., accountant)
Total expenditures	1,613.30	748.25	638.75	1649.57
Clothing (total)	255.59	182.50	91.25	244
Clothing	109.50	73.00	54.75	116
Shoes	146.00			80
Laundry		36.50	36.50	48

"Family" means two parents and four children.
Sources: column 1, "Spese giornaliera della mi famiglia, la moglie con 4 figli," 1878; column 2, *Sarti e sarte*, in "La Lotta," 1880; column 3, *Come vive un impiegato milanese*, in "Il giornale degli impegati," 1893, all quoted in S. Zaninelli, *I consumi a Milano nell'Ottocento* (Rome: Edindustria, 1973), 108–17.

factory or working in a small artisan laboratory. In addition we have domestic budgets for male and female workers in the clothing industry, which could have included semiskilled tailors and seamstresses. Finally, there are budget data for the family of a civil servant or white-collar worker, such as an accountant.

Let us return to the comparison between the prices found in the catalog and the expenditures on clothing. As already discussed, prices for accessories varied widely: umbrellas cost from 3.15 to 17.50 lire in the early 1880s and from 3.95 to 25 lire in later years. The accessories that showed the smallest price variation were hat shapes, from 3.50 lire at the beginning of the decade to 7.50 lire in 1886. These figures reveal the wide price variation characteristic of fashion accessories.

Next, we describe shopping baskets of two hypothetical customers. The first belongs to the highest income group among the professional categories for which 1880s data are available: a white-collar, middle-class worker (such as an accountant). The second belongs to the lowest of our income groups: a female laborer in the clothing industry. For both we considered a household's potential purchases of female accessories from the mail-order catalogs. For the "middle-class" family, we constructed a shopping basket assuming that this "white-collar" employee would have bought the most expensive item among each type of female accessories. We assumed that the woman textile worker would have bought the cheapest items.

The results show that the family of the Milanese office worker could not afford the complete top-range assortment of female accessories featured in the 1880s catalogs. If this family were to buy one ladies' accessory from each of the two collections (one from the autumn-winter catalog for the cold season, one from the spring-summer catalog for warm weather), the household would spend 150 lire. This amount would not include the additional costs eventually spent to personalize the accessories. Given that the family's entire annual clothing budget was estimated at 116 lire, annual purchase of a full line of high-end ladies' accessories would have been impossible. Of course we can imagine that it would have been possible for a Milanese office worker to select one or two items from the catalog's top-range female accessories in the course of the year. This, however, would have dramatically reduced the possibility of purchasing other clothing items, or even the fabric to make garments. It thus seems that a Milanese office worker could shop from the mail-order catalog of the Bocconi brothers' department store only occasionally; even then, the household would have to be careful in balancing top- and entry-level products.

The picture is very different if we consider the less expensive, most basic, and less fashionable models of ladies' accessories sold through the mail-order catalogs. Again assuming the purchase of one item of each female accessory from each of the two collections (autumn–winter and spring–summer), the total expense would be 22 lire, excluding any personalizing of the accessories. For example, a 22-lire purchase could have included a hat shape without flowers or feathers, which were very fashionable but could also become very expensive. Such an expenditure could be easily afforded even by the families with the lowest incomes listed in Table 3.1. The 54.75 lire annually devoted to the purchase of apparel by a woman worker in Milan's clothing industry meant that she could easily afford more than one of the accessories in their simplest and most basic models. Of course nothing can be said about the accessories she would choose, and how much the embellishments would add to the cost. But if she were a skilled seamstress with an artistic flair, she would have been able to accent her new hat in a creative way with meager extra expenditure. And these items certainly fell within the reach of the middle-class office worker we discussed earlier.

Conclusions

Overall this analysis of the Bocconi brothers' 1880s mail-order catalogs suggests that the most elaborate, and thus the most fashionable, accessories remained out of reach to all but the wealthiest consumers. Undecorated hats, gloves, and umbrellas could be purchased by greater numbers of people. Given the low quality and the plainness of the basic models, consumers had to personalize these items to make them fashionable and up-to-date. Yet personalization added to the purchasing price. Middle-income people, such as physicians' and engineers' households, could perhaps indulge in some of these luxuries. Our analysis, however, casts doubt on the extent to which accessories were truly affordable for consumers from the lowest income groups.

Personalization was one of the main ingredients in the sales formula of the Alle Città d'Italia's mail-order catalogs. Its centrality suggests that increasing standardization in fashion accessories, as evidenced by the Bocconi brothers' investment in umbrella production, did not result in the homogenization of fashion. On the contrary, the store's marketing strategies put a strong emphasis on shoppers' individual tastes and discretion in fashion. In other words, standardization did not restrict consumer choice. Rather, it meant diversification of the stock, so the store could meet the requirements of a wide variety of tastes and economic means. Accessories played a very important role in this development, providing consumers with ways to personalize their outfits.

In the end, our research suggests that catalogs diffused fashion items to a wide audience of potential customers, but that most clothes and accessories had to be personalized. The costs associated with personalization were generally quite high. In the 1880s Alle Città d'Italia did not aim at selling to the lowest social classes, the widest market segment, even though one of the main principles of the department store was low unit prices and high sales volume. Except for specific events, such as the store's famous "white sales," which sold highly standardized household linens, the lower social classes could not afford to shop at Alle Città d'Italia. The doors of the department store were surely open to all, but most of the items it stocked were not affordable by all.

CHAPTER FOUR

In the Shadow of Paris? French Haute Couture and Belgian Fashion Between the Wars

Véronique Pouillard

IN THE INTERWAR years, the Belgian and French fashion industries entered a symbiotic relationship that extended haute couture's reach in Western Europe. Established in 1929, the Chambre Syndicale de Haute Couture Belge (Belgian Syndicate Chamber of Haute Couture), a trade association dedicated to the fashion industries, played an important role as a tastemaker and trendsetter. As a new intermediary in the European fashion scene, the Belgian Chamber responded to the demand for French styles by importing, promoting, and circulating Parisian haute couture. Its actions strengthened Belgian links to the European style capital, solidifying the hegemony of Paris fashion in major cities like Brussels and Antwerp and in neighboring countries such as Holland and Germany. The international political economy of the Great Depression accelerated this process, curtailing transatlantic trade and encouraging continental exchanges.

Leading fashion historians like Valerie Steele have acknowledged the longstanding dominance of French fashions, but few have examined the commercial networks by which Parisian styles circulated through North America and Western Europe in the early twentieth century. Exceptions include art historian Nancy Troy, who has examined Paul Poiret's licensing efforts in 1910s America, and historian Mary Lynn Stewart, who has studied the democratization of couture styles from the 1900s to the 1930s.[1] In this volume, Christine Ruane contributes to this debate by examining how the nineteenth-century Russian fashion press promoted Paris styles in Eurasia, while Tomoko Okawa considers the licensing practices of Maison Christian Dior, which extended French fashion's reach across the globe after World War II. The records of the Belgian Chamber, which have not been used by fashion scholars, provide a wonderful opportunity to study the mechanisms of fashion diffusion in Western Europe.

The formative years of the Belgian Chamber are especially important for understanding how Parisian couturiers controlled the European fashion scene in an era of great economic and cultural change. At the moment when Americans tried to break away from continental styles, the Belgian middle class seemed to be yearning for the conservative look embodied by haute couture. In the eyes of the Belgian bourgeoisie, French dress epitomized good taste, prestige, and luxury. Catering to this demand, the Belgian clothing industry and retailing trade devised tactics for obtaining French designs that could be legitimately copied for the home market. French couture was an exclusive industry that closely guarded its designs and maintained tight control over the dissemination of its models, or product prototypes. In the interwar period, the Belgian fashion business both accommodated and circumvented this system, experimenting with new ways for dealing with the conservative French couture industry. By examining how this was done, this chapter explores the production and reproduction of fashion.

Parisian Hegemony

Despite a strong textile manufacturing tradition, Belgium remained in the fashion shadow of France for many years. Two questions help us understand this situation. What cultural mechanisms established the hegemony of French fashion before the 1920s and 1930s? How did European commercial networks perpetuate the idea of French fashion supremacy between World War I and World War II?

The hegemony of Parisian fashion has long been beyond question.[2] French haute couture, or "high dressmaking," was an elite industry producing one-of-a-kind dresses and fashion accessories for wealthy consumers. In turn, the couture industry used the prestige associated with its elite clientele as a marketing tool to sell spin-off products to mass merchandisers, including

American pattern manufacturers and department stores. Haute couture has long promoted itself as a fashion leader, and many historians, curators, and journalists have buttressed this claim.[3] Indeed women's fashion has been studied mainly as the formal evolution of haute couture clothes.

In *Paris Fashion: A Cultural History*, Valerie Steele explains the rise of Paris as a capital of fashion, which today has become that of *primus inter pares*, its peers being London, New York, Milan, and Tokyo.[4] Ever since the Englishman Charles-Frédéric Worth founded haute couture during the Second Empire, high-end dressmakers in Paris claimed world superiority in fashion on the basis of exquisite craftsmanship and the cosmopolitanism associated with the French capital.[5] During the early twentieth century, Paris continued to act as a fashion magnet, attracting famous foreign dressmakers, such as England's John Redfern and Edward Molyneux and Italy's Elsa Schiaparelli. Although England assumed a leadership position in men's fashion and sportswear, France still dominated women's wear in the interwar years.

Asserting Paris as the world's fashion capital was the first step in establishing haute couture's cultural hegemony. To survive, the haute couture sector also had to be profitable. Foreign consumers became the couture houses' largest customers, and institutional fashion intermediaries played an important role in exporting models and transmitting the taste for French fashion to foreign countries.[6] Some of the organizations and processes responsible for the diffusion of Paris fashion have been the subject of scholarly study: pattern makers, department stores, and, more recently, copyists. Patterns were an important vehicle for the reproduction of models and the dissemination of French fashion to the mass market.[7] The technology for printing patterns was perfected during the nineteenth century, especially in the United States. As cutting methods evolved, the reproduction of models became easier. In 1925, *McCall's* magazine announced a new era when it introduced patterns by famous French dressmakers such as Gabrielle "Coco" Chanel, Baron Christoff von Drécoll, and Paul Poiret.[8] Department stores have not often been studied from the angle of reproduction and copy, but they were the main customers for and producers of copies. Finally, copying has been studied as a phenomenon in and of itself by Nancy Troy, drawing on the example of Paul Poiret, who sold copies and reproduction rights of his models to American customers in the 1910s. The question of fraudulent copy and the protection of models has also been the subject of a recent study by Mary Lynn Stewart, focusing on the creator's rights.[9]

Several Parisian trade organizations played important roles as fashion

intermediaries that promoted French fashion through exportation and reproduction. Despite their importance, these trade associations have only begun
to be studied by historians, who have in the past often focused on the couturiers, their designs, and their elite clientele. The French dressmaking business
evolved as a national industry from the late 1600s, when Jean-Baptist Colbert,
Louis XIV's finance minister, first encouraged the expansion of fashion as a
preferential sector of the economy. The institutionalization of the fashion
sector began two centuries later, with the 1868 creation of the Chambre Syndicale de la Couture et de la Confection pour Dames et Fillettes. This trade
association monitored three commercial activities in women's fashion: dressmaking, tailoring, and "confection."[10]

In 1911, this organization became the Chambre Syndicale de la Couture
Parisienne, an employers' syndicate whose goal was to guard the interests of
the high dressmaking profession.[11] The Parisian Chamber negotiated with
labor unions, arbitrated internal conflicts, standardized wages, organized
fashion education, and set professional standards.[12] Every year, the Parisian
Chamber also scheduled fashion shows. Each couturier had to present two
main collections—for summer and winter—and two smaller optional mid-
season collections. Each had to realize a minimum income to retain its membership in the organization. Today the Parisian Chamber not only plays an
important role in France but also helps to promote French fashion at the
international level.[13]

In the early twentieth century, a select circle of wealthy private clients
traveled to Paris from around the world and ordered custom-fit clothing
directly from the couture houses. Haute couture models were also transmit-
ted to foreign retailers and clothing manufacturers through the sale of patterns, fabrics (toiles), and dresses, along with the reproduction rights. Foreign
retailers had to acquire buyers' cards from the Parisian Chamber, which allowed them to attend the semi-annual fashion shows where new collections
were introduced. This privilege was denied to provincial dressmakers and
confectioners during the interwar years, when the Parisian Chamber expressed its will to guard the secrets of haute couture from French copyists,
and to maintain its elite aura. After World War II, haute couture finally
opened its salons to provincial French manufacturers. By paying for "droit
de vision" or "viewing rights," these provincial companies could finally see
the couture originals at the same time that the foreign buyers.[14]

Although foreign buyers had access to the salons, they were subject to
strict rules and regulations. In 1926, for example, a French salesman had to

open an account for the foreign buyer. The buyer's card was not transferable. The invoice for purchases had to be paid through a French bank. Finally, the buyer had to give the couture house a certificate proving that the merchandise was intended for resale out of France.[15] The foreign buyer could also work through a commissionaire, or agent, and often did both. The latter ensured the purchaser's representation in Paris, introduced him or her to suppliers, and oversaw the shipment and insurance of the goods.[16] The aim of the foreign buyers was to buy Parisian models they could reproduce and sell to their clients.

Several other associations helped to regulate French couture. The most important was the Association pour la Protection des Industries Artistiques Saisonnières (Association for the Protection of Seasonal Art Industries, PAIS). This organization was established in 1921 as the Association pour la Protection des Arts Plastiques et Appliqués (Association for the Protection of Plastic and Applied Arts) by dressmaker Madeleine Vionnet and the general director of her firm, lawyer Louis Dangel.[17] Ironically, Vionnet, who became a staunch advocate for the rights of creators, had launched her career by copying models for a London shop.[18] During the 1930s, the PAIS was headed by Maggy Rouff (Marguerite Besançon de Wagner), a dressmaker of Belgian origin. This highly influential and prestigious trade network included Parisian dressmakers, as well as suppliers and representatives in related industries.

The PAIS aimed to protect original designs from piracy.[19] It established a blacklist of buyers who made illegal copies and supported several couturiers in their lawsuits against counterfeiters, reinforcing case law in favor of the creators. The PAIS represented a more select and more prestigious circle than the Parisian Chamber.[20] But it was not accepted by all couturiers. Some obviously rejected its practices as too rigid. For instance, in 1934 Marcel Rochas decided to pursue his business independent from the PAIS. To protect his models, he seems to have adopted a very modern method, changing his collections at a rapid pace.[21] Today a similar but modernized technique, —called "fast fashion" by Simona Segre Reinach, is widely used by ready-made brands.[22]

Establishing the Chambre Syndicale de Haute Couture Belge

Although Parisian professionals were terribly anxious about copying, they depended on the widespread circulation of their models for their economic survival. The success of copying rested on a combination of efficient export practices and French cultural hegemony in fashion. To highlight some aspects of this process, we shall examine the importation and copying of French models in Belgium during the interwar years.

Belgium is a small country that has an open market. Brussels, its capital, is only 150 miles from Paris, a short distance by train. Before World War II, as noted above, customers from the French provinces were prohibited from the Parisian Chamber's fashion shows. Dressmakers in Brussels, however, as long as they possessed a buyer's card, were allowed to reproduce Parisian models and enjoyed a privileged position compared to their counterparts in the French provinces. Sharing a language with the French, Belgian couturiers could quickly interpret Parisian designs and adapt them to the tastes of clients from northern Europe. The Belgian dressmakers interacted with the Parisian couturiers on a regular basis. Let us look at this relationship to learn more about the role of the Belgians in spreading French fashion throughout Europe.

The Chambre Syndicale de Haute Couture Belge (Belgian Syndical Chamber of Haute Couture) was the primary institution that forged links between French dressmakers and Belgian copyists. Belgian businessmen contemplated this organization in 1919, when a small group met to set up a program of "general interest from a professional standpoint" with particular bearing on labor problems. These concerns are to be understood in the context of reconstruction following World War I. The list of participants at this first meeting is significant. Whereas the Parisian Chamber brought together people at the head of the haute couture sector, that is, creators, the Belgian organization also attracted noncreating dressmakers and department store owners.

Ten years after the first deliberations, the Belgian Chamber was officially founded on 8 November 1929. Its list of members was quite short; it included a dozen enterprises,[23] luxury businesses based in Brussels that often supplied goods by appointment to the Belgian Royal Court.[24] Most members were Belgian dressmakers with a national clientele and customers from neighboring countries. One exception was Hirsch & Cie (1869–1962), a Belgian couture company, which had an international network of branches in Amsterdam, Cologne, Dresden, and Hamburg. Hirsch also had strong ties to fashion enterprises in other countries, such as the Hermann Gerson department stores in Berlin and the couturier Baron Christoff von Drecoll in Vienna.

In a list dated 1936, the founding members of the Belgian syndicate were identified mostly as "industrialists," with some "company administrators" and one "retailer."[25] This is significant, suggesting that no members wanted to be identified as designers. Nine of the ten were men, the Belgian fashion profession being mostly masculine. This contrasted with the haute couture business in Paris, where several prominent dressmakers were women: Gabrielle Chanel, Madeleine Vionnet, Jeanne Lanvin, Maggy Rouff, Louise Boulanger, and Augusta Bernard, among others. All the founding companies were located in Brussels, most of them on the fashionable Avenue Louise; not one provincial firm appears in the 1936 list. At this time, Belgian couture was institutionally based in Brussels rather than Antwerp, a port city that became a center of creative and much alternative-minded fashion in the late 1980s. Beginning in 1929, Robert Hirsch and Léon Natan, president and secretary of the Belgian Chamber, actively encouraged their fellow dressmakers to join the association. Membership was based on an application that had to be approved by the Chamber's members;[26] it was refused to some firms that failed to meet the organization's standards for prestige and good name.

From the beginning, the Belgian Chamber was a restricted circle rooted in Brussels. As in France, membership was selective. But there was a fundamental difference between the Belgian and French chambers. Traditionally, French haute couture was considered to be a high-cultural activity and a Parisian enterprise.[27] Therefore the French association only admitted Parisian dressmakers. In December 1929, the Belgian Chamber decided at its second meeting to encourage membership applications from provincial dressmakers.[28] This decision points to an open-mindedness toward *nouveaux entrants*, or newcomers.[29] The Belgian syndicate adopted a commercial attitude totally different from its counterpart in France, where dressmakers and outfitters from the provinces were not admitted as either members or even as observers at fashion shows.[30]

At the December 1929 meeting, the Belgian Chamber discussed several major issues. The first concerned the workforce: the association planned to organize a special meeting to examine wages in the sector.[31] It made efforts to better define the required qualifications for these highly specialized workers: the profession would face several strikes, especially in the years 1928–29 and 1936. Although these strikes paled in comparison to the French conflicts, which carried along the whole business, especially in 1934–36, labor unrest was a major concern for the profession. Most Belgian couture houses were small-scale family businesses highly dependent on a specialized workforce. Managers saw union negotiations as a necessity and worked with trade-union representatives, aiming at creating a uniform wage scale. Beginning in the late 1920s, the employers met several times to examine workers' wages.[32] During the interwar years, the wages remained subject to variation from house to house. The labor question would resurface after World War II with the discussions of the Social Pact, which established the foreground of social security and the welfare state in the postwar years, the basis of Belgium's new social security system. Meanwhile, following the example of the Parisian Chamber, the Belgians visited the main professional training establishments and set up an apprenticeship school.[33]

A second concern of the Belgian Chamber was debt collection. Defending the common interests of haute couture firms meant that the organization had to take an interest in debit accounts. One of the main objectives of the firms represented by the Belgian Chamber was the creation of an information service about delinquent debtors. For security and legal reasons, the names of those credit risks remained confidential, available only to Chamber members. The evidence suggests that the Belgian Chamber kept tabs on contentious cases, but these records have been lost.[34]

The third aim of the Belgian Chamber was publicity. Although it did not claim the status of creator for each of its members, the Belgian fashion sector was nevertheless setting up a fashion system that recognized the added value of prestige.[35] From the beginning, a press secretary took charge of the Chamber's relationship to the media. The Chamber's publicity chief also worked as an advertising broker for both *Le Soir*, a major Brussels newspaper, and the Hirsch & Cie couture house.[36] From the association's beginnings, the Belgian press was provided with information on the Chamber's activities. More important, the association developed charitable activities. Beginning in 1929, companies that manufactured dressmaking supplies were asked to support a series of fashion balls.[37] From the start, the founders of the Belgian Chamber showed a keen understanding of both economic needs and symbolic imperatives. At the lower end of the production chain, close attention was paid to relations with suppliers and to the economic advantages that they could offer. At the upper end, advertisement, fashion journalism, and the organization of prestige events all numbered among the tasks of the Belgian Chamber.

Figure. 4.1. Parisian couturiers visit the Belgian Syndicate Chamber of Couture, Brussels, 1931. I288, Folder 2182. Courtesy Archives Générales du Royaume de Belgique.

French Fashion in Belgium

The aims of the Belgian Chamber were directly related to the interests of its members. Most Belgian fashion firms did not create their own dress designs. The act of "creation" remained the exclusive purview of Paris. Belgian companies purchased French models, or prototypes, along with the legal rights to reproduce them. Their directors and buyers went to Paris at least twice a year (Figure 4.1). In late August or early September, they viewed the winter collections; in late February or early March, the summer ones. Sometimes they traveled to Paris between these dates to see the mid-season collections. The Belgian firms abided by the terms set up by Parisian firms for foreign buyers, particularly when it came to that "passport" to Parisian fashion, the buyer's card. In all transactions, they were helped by Parisian commissionaires.

During the interwar years, several factors made Parisian haute couturiers uneasy about the future. Although some foreign retailers had maintained Paris buying offices as early as the 1870s and 1880s, ever more English and American department stores were opening these purchasing offices by the 1920s.[38] Americans in Paris sent fashion flashes to the United States, using the transatlantic cable for quick reports on the latest styles in shops, showrooms, and fashion shows. The concurrent expansion of the fashion press allowed retailers in San Francisco and St. Petersburg to keep abreast of Paris fashions from a distance. These developments, especially the increased circulation of Parisian models, made French haute couture wary of losing its monopoly on fashion.[39]

In this context, a Belgian firm like Hirsch & Cie imported French models, manufactured reproductions in its workshops, and sold them in its Brussels stores. Founder Leo Hirsch was Jewish migrant from Altena, Westphalia; his wife, Johanna Freudenberg, was a cousin to the Gerson family that ran the renowned Berlin department store. Initially, Hirsch ran a small confection shop, or accessories store, in the highly commercial Rue Neuve in Brussels. The business flourished, allowing Hirsch to reimburse his creditors within the short span of ten years. In the 1880s and 1890s, several of his employers bought the rights to found their own Hirsch branches in Amsterdam, Dresden, Köln, and Hamburg. Between the wars, Hirsch & Cie reached its golden age. It had a staff of 400 to 500 and a well-established reputation for good taste and high quality. Beginning in 1881, the house had supplied apparel and accessories to the queen of Belgium.

At first glance Hirsch & Cie might have looked like a department store, but it was a very different type of commercial institution. Unlike John Wanamaker in Philadelphia and Marshall Field in Chicago, Hirsch & Cie never diversified its retail stock beyond women's and girls' garments to departments dedicated to fabrics, furniture, radios, and pets. Instead, Hirsch focused on making and selling high-end apparel and accessories. The quality of its products defined the top scale of the Belgian couture business. It had several haute couture departments: *flou* for couture dresses, *tailleur* for women's tailored outfits, and *manteau* for coats. Hirsch & Cie also had a high-profile fur department, which offered maintenance and repair service during the summer months. Accordingly, its highly specialized staff of dressmakers, seamstresses, and salespeople, who were valued for their knowledge of Paris fashions and their familiarity with the Hirsch clientele, had very long careers with the store.[40] These employees got to know the customers, providing wealthy clients with the personalized service for which Hirsch & Cie was known. By the interwar years, the third generation of the Hirsch family—the brothers Lucien, Robert, and Jean-Paul—managed the house.[41] Robert, who specialized in haute couture and public relations, was active in several commercial and cultural associations and eventually became founder and president of the Belgian Chamber, the only association specialized in the couture. He often traveled to France to meet his French counterparts and to confirm the Belgian point of view in front of the Parisian Chamber.[42]

In this context, Hirsch & Cie was able to present its clients twice a year with a collection of around 300 numbers, half them "Parisian originals."[43] The provenance of the other half is unspecified in the company's records, but they were not designed by the firm, which did not act as a fashion creator and never pretended to be one. The other numbers could have been models made from paper patterns, illegal copies, or creations in the taste of Paris. All these possibilities interestingly show the difficulty of drawing a clear line between different forms of copy and, in some cases, identifying which processes were legal and which were not. As for the Parisian originals, at Hirsch & Cie they were presented at least three times: at a show for private clients, another for small-scale dressmakers, and a third for professional schools. The company also offered private showings to very distinguished customers, such as rich bourgeois customers, actresses, and members of the Belgian royal family. The firm's own collection, based on the French models, was shown a week or two afterward. Customers ordered their dresses, which Hirsch & Cie delivered within ten or fifteen days, depending on how difficult the copies were to make.[44] Other firms in the Belgian Chamber operated in the same way.

Robert Hirsch, acting as syndicate president, worked hard to build a strong relationship between Belgian and French dressmakers.[45] The commercial exchange was particularly intense during the early 1930s. Society events and meetings aimed at reinforcing commercial relations abounded in Paris and Brussels. Under Robert Hirsch's auspices, the Belgian syndicate sponsored official dinners, visits to the couture houses, and balls and galas.

All of this took place during the economically challenging interwar years, including the Great Depression of the 1930s. The Belgian and French fashion sectors had been in trouble during the 1920s, and the situation worsened dramatically after the 1929 stock market crash. Developments in the international political economy contributed to the problem. By imposing a 90 percent ad valorem tax on imported garments embellished with embroidery, tulle, spangles (*lamé*), or lace, the U.S. Smoot-Hawley Tariff Act, effective in

1931, accelerated the decline of French couture.[46] Designed to protect the American market, the tariff discouraged imports of French luxury garments to the United States. Smoot-Hawley, which epitomized the height of trade protectionism, launched a tariff war. European countries retaliated by raising their tariffs, which led to a freeze in the international garment trade.[47] In a domino effect, American clients might no longer come to Paris to buy luxury garments, and couturiers were more afraid than ever to lose cultural cachet. In the United States, retailers like New York's Lord & Taylor combated the hiatus in French imports by promoting fashions by American designers. As the Great Depression spread, middle- and low-level dressmaking was also affected. In general the decrease in spending power is believed to have led to the further simplification of clothing, which had been underway for several decades.[48]

Since the 1910s, French dressmakers had encouraged the commercialization of models and the sale of reproduction rights.[49] Although the growing simplicity of clothing and accessories made it easier to make copies, we must remember that the situation was far removed from contemporary mass marketing.[50] Couture remained an elite business. Entrepreneurs emphasized their high-culture image, even if they were forced to sell models to a wider range of customers. In the 1930s, the Parisian couturiers Chanel, Lanvin, Patou, and Poiret opened dressmaker's boutiques in an effort to combat the economic crisis. In Belgium, dressmakers like Hirsch & Cie followed suit with the opening of its boutique in 1937. For his part, the Parisian couturier Lucien Lelong launched the label Robes d'Edition. This line of high-quality premanufactured clothing requiring just one fitting and was far less expensive than Lelong's coveted haute couture line.[51]

Early in the Great Depression, the French and Belgian dressmakers worked out a commercial agreement for their mutual benefit. In September 1931, the Belgian syndicate explained: "Aware of the possibilities offered by Belgian firms, the famous French couturiers have decided to help Belgian firms to spread copies of their improvisations across the world." The Franco-Belgian agreement was supposed to give Belgium a competitive advantage over other countries, including Germany, Austria, Switzerland, and United States, which imported French models, copied them, and reexported the originals or the spin-offs. The commercial exchange between France, Belgium, and other Western countries benefited the Belgian trade balance, bringing tens of millions of Belgian francs into the country.[52]

Of course the goal of the Parisian couturiers in this protectionist era was not to help their Belgian counterparts but to exert control over the fashion business. From their perspective, collaborations with trusted business partners like the Belgians gave the French as much control as possible and allowed them to stay at the top of the cultural hierarchy. At the other end, the aim of the Belgian Chamber was to secure markets for itself, while maintaining its role of France's preferential intermediary.

Thanks to these agreements, in February 1931 Belgian dressmakers visited two Paris haute couturiers, Callot Sœurs and Dupouy Magnin,[53] whose directors were the president and the secretary respectively of the Parisian Chamber. In February 1932, the members of the Belgian Chamber, "after long and laboured negotiations," were allowed to visit Lanvin and Bernard & Cie without any obligation to make a purchase.[54] The Belgians had to pledge not to bring cutters or draftsmen along, and they were not allowed to take notes or sketches.[55] Obviously however, there was nothing to prevent them from doing so once they were back outside.[56]

Traveling to Paris was a traditional way of acquiring French models, but Parisian dressmakers also organized fashion shows in Brussels. But French fashion displays abroad were rare. Retailers and dressmakers in foreign countries, particularly in Europe, resisted them. Local intermediaries tried to prohibit French dressmakers from selling directly in their country.

One exception was the Gala de l'Élégance at the Palais des Beaux-Arts at Brussels on 26 March 1931, co-organized by the French and Belgian syndical chambers. The glamorous show included collections from Jeanne Lanvin, Agnès, Callot Sœurs, Philippe & Gaston, Lucien Lelong, Edward Molyneux, the House of Redfern, and Bernard & Cie (Figure 4.2). The technical organization was the responsibility of Jean Labusquière, director of Lanvin. The Belgian Chamber took care of the logistics. Through this effort, a network of transnational relations developed between some of the French designers and the Belgian firms, including Agnès-Drécoll, Philippe & Gaston, Bernard & Cie, O. Wolff & Cie and Hirsch & Cie.[57] Although the commercial ties were close, the firms' capital generally stayed distinct, a protective measure which was the general rule in this unstable economic sector.[58]

In 1931, a dozen French dressmakers showed off their spring models at this fashion parade at the Palais des Beaux-Arts. An impressive audience attended: Queen Elisabeth of Belgium, the Duchess of Brabant (the future Queen Astrid), and the French ambassador, Peretti de La Rocca. The national and regional press covered this high-society event.[59] It unveiled the latest seasonal trends, including the "pyjama," a woman's evening suit with

Figure. 4.2. Fashion show, Gala de l'Elégance, Brussels, 26 March 1931. I288, Folder 2182. Courtesy Archives Générales du Royaume de Belgique.

trousers, still a scandalous piece of feminine clothing in the eyes of provincial journalists.[60] The press made a lot of this fashion "à la garçonne" in satin and fur, a far cry from the chic pauper style of Chanel.[61] The aim was to export the essence of haute couture. The democratization of fashion was not on the agenda.[62]

Behind the scenes, the event required an important logistic deployment orchestrated by Ambassador de La Rocca and Jean Labusquière. Trains carried the clothes and models back and forth from Paris to Brussels in a single day. Belgian and French customs were forewarned, so as to avoid unnecessary taxation and to protect the models against any surreptitious attempts at copying. The dresses and coats arrived in enormous trunks. A Belgian customs officer accompanied the convoy to the Palais des Beaux-Arts. Although French and Belgian professionals collaborated to organize the event, the Brussels stores selected the fashions. The Belgian Chamber announced: "The clothes presented by the French models will be those chosen by the Belgian firms, as being most in accordance with the taste in our country."[63]

The distribution of French models was thus assured in Belgium thanks

Figure. 4.3. Les Clochettes, dress by the French House of Worth, in the spring collection of Belgian dressmaker Natan, 1931. I288, Folder 2268. Courtesy Archives Générales du Royaume de Belgique.

to bilateral agreements, but the monopoly of legal copy stayed strictly in the hands of the Belgian intermediaries. Just one month after the show, in April 1931, the collections of three Belgian firms—Natan, Profète, and Hirsch & Cie—included French creations signed by Worth, Agnès-Drécoll, Philippe & Gaston, and other Parisian couturiers (Figure 4.3).[64] The collaboration between French and Belgian dressmakers was now official, the Belgian Chamber having done everything in its power to make it flourish. On the French side, Pierre Gerber, president of the Parisian Chamber, spoke to the Belgian press. When asked for his opinion on the Franco-Belgian collaboration, Gerber acknowledged its necessity as a measure against the treacherous competition from some foreign firms—without further explanation on the nature of those supposedly delinquent firms. In this context, the Belgian couturiers would not be rivals or plagiarists but "honest collaborators" and "precious auxiliaries." Gerber thought that the French couture had to focus on creativity. It had no time to linger over reproduction issues and could best delegate that responsibility to auxiliaries able to disseminate the copies. Therefore, Gerber's conclusion to his Belgian interlocutors was the following: "The French and Belgian Haute Couture Syndical Chambers met in your capital to try to find ways in which to victoriously beat off the assault we withstand from all sides."[65] Gerber meant the fraudulent copyists, who were virtually everywhere.

Indeed, haute couture was feeling that its supremacy was threatened, especially in the economic sphere. The "honest collaborators" and the "precious auxiliaries" were indispensable intermediaries in a system that had to preserve its magic to survive.[66] French couture was in a difficult situation, due to the Great Depression and protectionist trade barriers. This crisis led to the democratization of fashion, which was not much to the taste of haute couture, even though some of couturiers were leaning in this direction with their boutique collections, or even with their own designs—Chanel's little black dress was nicknamed the "Model T Ford" of haute couture. It was imperative that the French secure the Belgian market. This was a logical choice because Belgium was entirely turned toward France when it came to clothing.

One may nevertheless wonder why Belgian dressmakers satisfied themselves with this position of "honest collaborators." At this time, Belgium had very few fashion creators, and those making original designs operated in separate spheres from the houses in the Belgian Chamber. The career of Norine (Honorine Deschrijver-Van Hecke), a Brussels designer from the 1920s to the early 1960s, is the exception that proves the rule.[67] Norine was married to Paul-Gustave Van Hecke, a man of letters, collector, and art critic, who ran Le Centaure, a gallery on the posh Avenue Louise. Sometime in the 1920s, Norine opened a dressmaking establishment in the space above her husband's art gallery, hiring the surrealist painter René Magritte to design some advertising. From the beginning, she presented original creations. One of the famous Belgian dressmaking firms of the interwar years, it survived despite the financial difficulties of the early 1930s.[68] Significantly, Norine's firm is not mentioned in the correspondence between the Belgian and French syndical chambers.[69] This suggests that firms importing Parisian models and Belgian creators belonged to entirely separate professional networks.

Indeed, the Belgian Chamber did not show any interest in the development of a distinctive national mode of high style or avant-garde fashion. It focused on economic priorities, which hinged on satisfying a bourgeois clientele. In Belgium the middle class was particularly important. Showing membership in the bourgeoisie by following Parisian fashion did not allow for much extravagance, but led rather to staunch conformity in dress. Middle-class notions of social and religious respectability dictated restraint in the adoption of foreign fashions.[70] From a cultural point of view, recent research has highlighted Belgian consumers' inferiority complex, which contemporary designers have come to acknowledge as an important factor in Belgian national taste.[71] Insecure about their own tastes, Belgian consumers expressed a preference for French, English, and Italian labels, even if they were imitations.[72]

The Belgian Chamber very rapidly showed its capacity to master the fashion system and to act as a pressure group. For instance, it opposed the luxury tax and devoted a lot of energy to organizing prestige events and to generating publicity. Its objectives were nevertheless very different from its French counterpart. The standpoints of the two organizations were completely different. The Belgian Chamber did not copy the French institution, even if, from a cultural point of view, the French model was a constant reference in the work of Belgian dressmakers.

To Copy or Not

The cooperative relationship between the Belgian and Parisian chambers facilitated the reproduction of French models meant for Belgium's domestic and foreign markets. It also aimed to resolve the sticky question of copying, which worried the Parisian Chamber, as was seen in the statement of its president, Pierre Gerber. Copying depended on the cooperation of specific types of intermediaries, including commission agents, retailers, trendsetters, and fashion journalists. Belgium occupied a strategic position in this network. Considered uncreative in the shadow of France, the country's couture industry nevertheless acted as a relay in the spread of French models not only in its own internal market, but also abroad.

Besides legal exports encouraged by the two chambers, frauds were very frequent. Belgian dressmakers did not hesitate to copy French designs they saw at fashion shows sponsored by the two chambers.[73] Some department stores openly copied at a grand scale, matching the speed of today's mass-market retailers like H&M and Zara, who reinterpret models presented at couture shows in less than a week. In 1939, the Belgian magazine *Reflets* published a well-illustrated article, "The Story of a 49 Franc Hat Bought in Paris for 1000 Francs." In just one week, a French hat signed by Molyneux, Agnès, or Renée Saint-Cyr was adapted for mass distribution by the fashion department of a Belgian department store. The store created 250 copies: 1 hat x 11 colors x 2 sizes x 12 shop branches. The store widely advertised the hat's launch, and proudly displayed the Paris spin-offs in the show windows of its main store in Brussels and its provincial branches.[74]

Seen from the viewpoint of fashion professionals, reproduction was a paradox. But the structure of the French system itself required numerous intermediaries; observers of the sector were aware, already in the 1930s, of the necessity to reproduce models created by designers and dressmakers of exceptional talent.[75] In this respect, the interwar years were, in a way, a laboratory of new ideas. The economic crisis of the Great Depression accentuated the difficulties in an emerging fashion system that balanced tradition and modernization.

Everybody did not consider, as Gabrielle Chanel famously said, that copying was proof of love, that imitation was the greatest form of flattery. Nor did most fashion professionals have the detachment of the theoretician René Bizet, who considered dresses destined for export to be *traductions libres*, or "free renderings" of the originals.[76] Overall, the attitude of French dressmakers toward copying varied. During the interwar years, the Parisian Chamber devised various tactics that did not forbid copying, but tried to establish economic controls over the process. The Parisian dressmakers came to understand that copying was inevitable, and they labored to benefit from it.

Geographically Brussels was favored by its proximity to Paris, especially because during these years purchasing conditions for Parisian models were a lot stricter for the French provinces than for Belgium. Compared to Marseille or Lyon, Brussels occupied a privileged position. Belgian firms tried to maintain, and where possible to reinforce, this advantage, which allowed them to sell French models in Germany or the Netherlands.[77] The aim was to create a distribution network in which Belgium was situated as high on the culture ladder as possible. For instance, Hirsch & Cie allowed firms belonging to its commercial network, including branches in Amsterdam, Hamburg, Cologne, and Dresden, to buy its French models only days after the Brussels buyers returned from Paris. In other words, Hirsch & Cie in Brussels, whose representatives systematically visited Chanel, Lanvin, Patou, Rochas, and other prominent couturiers during show time, enabled its branches to acquire models from Brussels, alleviating the long and expensive trip to Paris. Unfortunately the records do not allow us to estimate the volume of models exported by Hirsch & Cie through these channels.[78] Most likely some foreign buyers, such as those working for American department stores, traveled to Belgium to buy French models. By importing French dresses from Belgium, Americans could avoid part of the model's costs. They used commercial agents in Antwerp or Brussels as intermediaries, announcing their presence in Belgium by means of advertisements in the professional journals.[79]

The direction in which models traveled, which was so important during the interwar years, came once again to the fore after World War II. At that time, some French creators tried to reverse the flow and to reinstitute direct purchases from France by organizing their own shows in Belgium. The Belgian Chamber, renamed the Belgian Federation of Couture, took actions to make it illegal for French creators to organize shows and to sell their products anywhere in the Belgian kingdom.[80]

Why Belgium Mattered to French Fashion

Was there any Belgian fashion during the interwar years? Creation was rare in Belgium during that time. It was practiced only by a small number of dressmakers, who, like Norine, were often more closely related to avant-garde artists than to the textile industry. Even cutting-edge creators like Norine acknowledged the French as a source of inspiration. Norine and her husband Van Hecke wrote: "Our references? . . . Our claims to be creating a Belgian fashion? . . . We are so close to Paris, its industry and its way of thinking that we prefer to make do with Paris! Maybe too the proud Belgian simplicity—considering the attempts of the Americans and Viennese to go against Parisian fashion to be totally vain—prefers to be intelligently dependant rather than ridiculously personal."[81]

Most Belgian dressmakers and stores deliberately became copiers of Parisian models. Belgium followed Parisian creation, but the models were expressly selected by the Belgian dressmakers for their bourgeois customers. This was the case at the 1931 show at the Palais des Beaux-Arts. Belgian dressmakers and stores also played a relay role, disseminating Parisian models to other European countries, such as the Netherlands and Germany, and across the globe to South America. In several European countries, and especially France, attempts were made to put an end to the illegal copying of models.[82] The proliferation of French associations shows the difficulties faced by Parisian haute couture, a dilemma that continues to plague the international fashion industry today.

The relationship of dressmakers from Western Europe with Paris during the interwar years has been little studied until now. When looking at Belgian dressmaking, a distinction must be made between avant-garde dressmaking and organized copying. There was a legal form of reproduction based on the purchase of models at Parisian fashion shows, along with the rights to reproduce them. Alongside this legal practice, there were many fraudulent copies that French dressmakers attempted to stop by various means. Nonetheless copying was in fact an integral part of the fashion system. It was sometimes difficult to distinguish between lawful reproduction and illegal copies, or between reinterpretation and plagiarism. The label remained the only sign of authentication.

The records of the Belgian Chamber add to our understanding of these phenomena. While the Belgians valued copies, the French aimed to put an end to copying. The position of the French couturiers, bemoaning themselves as victims of plagiarism, looks quite different when seen through the eyes of the Belgian importers. The paradox of dressmaking is best understood from a commercial point of view that was as essential to French haute couture as to its purchasers. The Belgian dressmakers did not, in fact, copy indiscriminately. They actually intended to preserve French creation, while earning a maximum profit and maintaining their position of preferential intermediaries. This privileged commercial position profited from the geographic proximity of Brussels and Paris. It was reinforced by the activities of the Belgian Chamber, which defended its position as purchaser. In turn, the Parisian Chamber responded positively to Belgian firms, a fact that contradicts the idea that French couture was, as a general rule, opposed to copying.[83]

CHAPTER FIVE

Licensing Practices at Maison Christian Dior

Tomoko Okawa

ESTABLISHED IN 1946, Maison Christian Dior, or the house of Christian Dior, has reigned supreme in the world of fashion for more than sixty years.[1] Today, Maison Dior is still one of the few French couture houses in existence, its name familiar throughout the world. Due to the vicissitudes of the fashion industry, very few couture houses have managed to survive over the long term. Because of its scope, longevity, and size, it was compared to General Motors in the 1950s.[2] Maison Dior became the world's leading fashion company by fusing the French couturiers' tradition of craftsman with modern business practices. Specifically, Maison Dior's impressive record as a global company rests on the development of the Dior brand and its early aggressive licensing practices.

Maison Dior has exerted an extensive, wide-ranging influence on the fashion industry, much of which is beyond the scope of this study. This essay focuses on the company's history from its founding in 1946 through the licensing explosion of the 1970s. During this era, Maison Dior pioneered the use of brand licensing, developing the business strategy that came to be known as the "Christian Dior model."[3] Although licensing kept Maison Dior alive for much of its sixty-year history, the strategy was rejected in the mid-1990s to keep the Maison's prestige by Moët Hennessy-Louis Vuitton (the LVMH Group), whose top executive, Bernard Arnault, had acquired the venerated couture house in 1984. This chapter examines the nature of Maison

Dior's business expansion while clarifying what the licensing business meant to the fashion industry from the 1950s through the 1970s.

In 1975, Maison Dior asserted in its press releases that its business depended on licensing practices.[4] Indeed, this practice allowed "French manufacturers or manufacturers from other countries to make and distribute, under Maison Dior's control, products under the name of Christian Dior." In exchange for the right to use the prestigious Christian Dior name, manufacturers of fashion accessories, from textile-related goods (neckties, scarves, linens, etc.) to leather goods (bag, belts, purses, etc.), all over the world, paid royalties to the maison. From the manufacturers' perspective, licensing enabled them to produce and sell lines with the value added associated with the exclusive *maisons de couture*. From Maison Dior's perspective, licensing allowed the house to broaden its scope beyond garments, investing a small initial amount for the specialized production of glass and leather goods, and to make a profit during a challenging moment for haute couture. Because the contract was for a certain fixed period, licensing guaranteed Maison Dior steady revenues. The contract also gave the house quality control, specifying that it as the licensor could break the contract with the licensee if problems arose in production, marketing, or distribution.[5]

Before Maison Dior introduced its wide array of licensed lines, few French haute couture designers allowed manufacturers to use their names industrially. In 1911, Paul Poiret (1879–1944) was the first French couture designer to make this move. Poiret created a perfume with his daughter's name, Rosine, and sold it in his boutique. Commercially speaking, it didn't work well. After Poiret, however, the haute couture designers Gabrielle "Coco" Chanel (1883–1971), Jeanne Lanvin (1867–1946), and Jean Patou (1880–1936) sold perfumes under their names, augmenting the profits of their dressmaking empires. Introduced in 1921, the famous and best-selling perfume Chanel No. 5 assisted the designer in financing her maison, and the fragrance continues to be profitable today.[6] The modern practice of licensing, a way of managing intellectual property through branding, built on these developments. Global licensing has diversified the fashion marketplace, introducing new brands into licensee countries using an industrial format. Before Maison Dior in the 1930s, this business format existed in the form of "bonded lines" for garments, which French couture houses sold to foreign manufacturers and retailers to avoid the problems associated with currency exchange, tariffs and import restrictions, and illicit copying.[7]

With the United States as the forerunner, licensed products spread rapidly throughout the world as a result of the democratization and popularization of fashion in the 1960s. At the same time, licensing delivered planning, rational productivity, and sound profitability to an uncertain, labor-intensive industry. It was Maison Dior that established this business model that was to greatly influence the fashion industry and enable the global expansion of French fashion through marketing diverse products emblazoned with designers' names.

Talent Needs Entrepreneurship: Christian Dior and Groupe Boussac

What are the distinctive features of Maison Dior? Before Maison Dior, the exclusive Parisian highly skilled dressmaking establishments, which the Chambre Syndicale de la Couture Parisienne permitted to be called *maisons de couture*, or couture houses, were mostly family-run businesses, as represented by the workshops of Charles Frederick Worth and Jeanne Lanvin.[8] Like these couturiers, designer Christian Dior (1905–57) had a good deal of artistic talent and surrounded himself with a team of craftspeople who provided technical support. Quality and craftsmanship were its foundation, but Maison Dior was also financed by enormous amounts of capital for the era. This marked a total departure from the way French couture had been run in the past and established a new direction for the fashion industry after World War II.

Although it would take an entire book to do justice to Christian Dior's career and achievements, a brief look at the designer's background highlights his dedication to quality fashion. Dior was born in 1905 in Granville, Normandy, to a bourgeois family that had made its wealth in the production of sulfuric acid for phosphate fertilizer.[9] He studied at l'École Libre des Sciences Politiques (known as Sciences-Po), one of the best French *grandes écoles*, but left before completing his studies to open an art gallery in partnership with a friend in Paris. In 1931, Dior's family business, affected by the Great Depression, went bankrupt. His gallery closed soon afterward. Deeply disappointed, Dior gradually became involved in fashion by selling illustrations to support himself.[10] After working as a designer at Maison Robert Piguet and Maison Lucien Lelong, Dior was introduced by a friend to textile magnate Marcel Boussac (1889–1980). In 1946, when Dior was forty-one years old, Boussac financed the launching of Maison Dior.[11]

A leading French industrialist, Boussac had established a textile business in Paris in 1911, expanding his firm during both world wars to reign supreme as France's "Cotton King." His massive conglomerate, Groupe Boussac, managed about sixty companies, including Maison Dior. Groupe Boussac's primary arm, Comptoire de l'Industrie Cotonnière (CIC), actively acquired cotton textile factories and cotton textile printing plants in France. Between 1920 and 1940, CIC expanded into Poland (1923–34), North Africa, and the Far East, with the goal of procuring raw materials and selling textiles to North Africa. Boussac was also famous as the greatest French breeder of thoroughbred horses who ever lived. CIC provided the financial and operational backing to Maison Dior. Henri Fayol, who had worked for Boussac since 1943 and was one of CIC's general directors, served as the chief liaison between Dior and CIC.[12] Fayol's wife had admired Dior's designs at Maison Lelong, which led to friendship between the two men. Fayol was the most important person to help Dior set up his couture house.

On 12 February 1947, Maison Dior's first collection with about 96 models was described by Carmel Snow, editor of *Harper's Bazaar*, as a "New Look" for a new era.[13] The "New Look" became a sociological, aesthetic, and commercial phenomenon with enormous impact.[14] On the day following the collection, *Women's Wear Daily* reported the characteristics of Dior's presentation: Curved Silhouettes, Skirt Lengthened, Sloping Shoulders, Fabric Range Interesting.[15] The sophisticated models, feminine gentle curves in silhouettes like flowers, long skirts, and "slim" or "ultra-slim" waists reintroduced a touch of femininity to fashion. The diversity of luxury fabrics implied affluence after the austerity of war. Dior became an important figure in modern fashion and made an enormous contribution to France's postwar recovery. Maison Dior actively expanded as a result of the success of his first collection. The preparations for this business expansion were carried out by CIC, which envisaged international expansion for Maison Dior.[16]

Foothold in Licensing: Christian Dior-New York

On 8 October 1948, Maison Dior's foreign expansion began with the opening of a branch on 730 Fifth Avenue in New York. This new American branch, Christian Dior-New York, became a vital operational foothold in Dior's international growth and key platform for expanding the licensing business. Ellen Engel was the executive vice-president and general manager, handling technical and production departments, sales, publicity and public relations; she also oversaw perfumes and hosiery, in addition to various firms manufacturing and distributing Dior accessories.[17] A letter between CIC and the Office des Changes, dated 18 July 1946, discusses early plans for a branch in New York, and the Office des Changes gave its authorization 19 August 1946.[18] The Office des Changes was a government agency that monitored, assisted, and granted permission to French companies seeking to set up businesses abroad and kept tabs on the remittances. CIC's executives negotiated with the Office for Maison Dior's overseas expansion. According to its October 1946 application, CIC planned to "establish a branch with the aim of selling ready-to-wear clothing in the United States and Mexico" through a joint venture between CIC and local business partners. In reference to the establishment of the North American branches, CIC stated that "the product preferences of both the United States and Mexico are similar in form and color. In other words, there is a high likelihood of success despite the fact that they are two different markets. These overseas branches will contribute to the promotion of the exports of French cotton products and printed textiles." CIC's application also emphasized that "the new company selling 'ready-to-wear' clothing can contribute to the development of the French fashion industry above and beyond what the existing branches can contribute." Between July and October 1946, CIC executives thus demonstrated to the French authorities that they had a clear vision about the overseas expansion of Maison Dior's ready-to-wear business.[19]

CIC's aggressive business strategy meshed with Christian Dior's own ideas about the changing role of haute couture and its relationship to ready-made clothing. From 1941 to 1946, Dior had worked as a designer for Maison Lucien Lelong, the top couture house at the time with 1,200 employees. In 1935, the French Ministry of Industry commissioned Lelong to visit the United States and survey the American apparel industry. Lelong's exposure to the American market inspired him with ideas of how a couture house might sell its products to a broad class in society while retaining its prestige, particularly during the economic crisis of the war. Shortly after he returned to France, Lelong developed Robes d'Edition, a prestigious ready-to-wear line that was shown and sold separate from haute couture. The Robes d'Edition catalog explained the rationale: "For a modern lady, it is important that she can wear clothes at affordable prices. Now, by wearing Lelong's Robes d'Edition, women can express feminine elegance with class and personality, against the banality and fake luxury that has always being associated with ready-to-wear fashion."[20]

Devised as a business strategy to combat flagging sales during the Great Depression and the war, Robes d'Edition became the cornerstone of prêt-à-porter, or high-end ready-to-wear. The line was designed to sell large quantities of garments while maintaining Lelong's prestige.[21] Along with Pierre Balmain and Hubert de Givenchy, Dior had worked for Lelong just as prestigious prêt-à-porter emerged. This experience exposed them to the potential of luxury ready-to-wear. In the post-World War II era, Dior built on his observations of Lelong's high-end ready-to-wear as he developed his own vision for a new direction for the fashion industry.

Success in the United States mattered to CIC and Dior. Both recognized the importance of the American market, if for different reasons. CIC imagined the profitable, large-scale business operations that could be developed by this genius designer and his name "Christian Dior." This was apparent from Maison Dior's establishment, which CIC announced first in the United States. On 25 November 1946, the newspaper for America's fashion industry, *Women's Wear Daily*, issued the bold headline: "Dior Opens Paris Couture Establishment Shortly." In France, the fashion magazine *Elle* followed suit, announcing the opening of this new couture house in January 1947.[22]

In contrast, Dior saw the New York venture as an opportunity to reshape American taste. Dior acknowledged the importance of the vast American market to prestigious French prêt-à-porter in a backhanded way. In 1947, he received the Neiman Marcus Award for Distinguished Service in the Field of Fashion, the Oscar of fashion awarded by the eponymous Dallas department store. When visiting the United States for the awards ceremony, Dior noticed how American women dressed. "What alarmed me most in the course of my stay in the United States was the habit of spending enormous sums of money in order to archive so little real luxury," he wrote. "America . . . represents the triumph of quantity over quality."[23] By exporting French fashion, Dior hoped that his couture house could help uplift American tastes, remedying these deplorable conditions wrought by mass-produced fashion products.

The Licensing Business and Early Maison Dior

The licensing business that began with Dior's entry into the United States produced large profits for the maison. It should be noted, however, that behind Maison Dior's endeavors lay a change in the firm's business strategy that was triggered by personnel shifts within the company as well as a wider transformation of the market. Licensing did not emerge in isolation from the larger business environment or the broader social milieu. In fashion, executives who drive the business can play an important role in translating the instinctive work of the designer into profitable lines that help the company to grow. During the late 1940s and early 1950s, the symbiotic relationship between CIC executives, especially Fayol, and the creative genius of Dior pushed Maison Dior to the front of the international fashion business.

From its inception, Maison Dior was run on a scale unprecedented in the fashion industry. At its October 1946 launch, Maison Dior was capitalized at old F5 million (about $42,000), an enormous sum for a couture house at the time. The investment was influenced by Groupe Boussac's experience in overseas expansion prior to its partnership with Dior. Although Dior did not own a single share in Maison Dior, he was named chief designer and general manager.[24] Fayol recognized the importance of letting Dior have breathing space, and under his watchful eye CIC gave the couturier a good deal of artistic freedom. During his ten years as creative head, Dior created many unique designs, such as the "Corolla line" (baptized as the "New Look"), the "H-line,"—and the "Y-line," which made lasting contributions to fashion.[25] Fashionistas flocked to Dior's semiannual shows in Paris. Nearly 25,000 journalists, public figures, professional buyers, and individual clients visited Maison Dior to see each new collection.[26]

From its first collection in February 1947, Maison Dior attracted worldwide acclaim and found itself inundated with orders. Problems arose, however, in meeting retailers' delivery requirements. Maison Dior's headquarters at avenue Montaigne could not meet production demands, and the New York subsidiary could not fill the large American orders. In response, Maison Dior decided to separate the French and American operations. Although Maison Dior already used some American fabrics in the collection shown in New York on 1 November 1948, by the fall of 1949 the New York branch sourced approximately half its fabrics in the United States, with the rest being imported from France.[27] Dior himself spent several weeks in the United States with CIC's Fayol and Maison Dior's general director Jacques Rouët. They explored the wants and needs of the American consumer and concentrated on developing products that could be better integrated into the American market.[28]

Maison Dior's business expansion took two interrelated forms. One was the operation of overseas wholesaling offices in New York, London, and Caracas under the direct control of the Paris headquarters; the other was the licensing business. In 1952, Rouët appointed Christian Legrez as the director of licensing in Paris.[29] For the ready-to-wear "boutique" line, André Levasseur, who had been employed at Maison Dior since 1946, was the designer; beginning in 1955, Yves Saint Laurent was an assistant designer for Dior. Under the traditional couture system, customers traveled to Paris, where the maison's staff measured them for the custom-made garments. With prêt-à-porter, customers purchased items directly from retail stores without traveling to Europe for fittings. If Maison Dior garments were made in France and exported to the United States, they would be subject to heavy customs duties and restrictions on foreign commercial transactions. The best way to ensure price competitiveness was to manufacture prestigious products in the country where they were being marketed.[30]

Between 1946 and Dior's death in 1957, Maison Dior expanded the firm's core businesses by opening specialized branches and entering licensing agreements with manufacturers. In France, Maison Dior established subsidiaries to produce and market a wide variety of lines: perfumes and furs in 1947, ties and shoes in 1950, hosiery in 1951, and menswear in 1954. For the United States, in 1948 the firm created branches to oversee the production and marketing of ready-to-wear and accessories. The next year, Maison Dior created Christian Dior Perfumes-New York and contracted with Julius Kayser & Co., a prestigious American hosiery maker, to produce women's stockings under the label "Christian Dior Hosiery-New York." Maison Dior licensed other manufacturers to reproduce garments for Mexico and Cuba in 1950, and for Canada and Australia in 1951.[31] The firm's new licensing division began to oversee the production of hosiery, gloves, scarves, neckties, lingerie, and knitwear, while the export division coordinated relations between all subsidiaries and licensees starting in 1951. In 1952, Maison Dior established Christian Dior Models Limited in London, the antecedent to Christian Dior-London Limited, with Dior's acquaintances. In 1955, CIC restructured this branch and put Rouët in charge as president.[32]

Christian Dior-London Limited presented a prestigious ready-to-wear collection four times a year. Maison Dior also had two branches in Venezuela. One was for exploitation of the boutiques of Caracas; the other, "Christian Dior del Sur," handled the financial aspects of the North and South American business (the foreign remittance).

Licenses can differ depending on the characteristics of the products being made, their marketability, and the distribution channels. A company can have exclusive rights to manufacture and sell products in the country where it is based. In other instances, it will have exclusive rights to a particular continent, such as Europe, North America, or South America, or exclusive global rights to market a particular product line. In view of the broad range of products sold around the world, Maison Dior ensured that the organization generated statistical surveys on sales, monitored costs, and controlled the revenue flow by using business machines, and inaugurated a program designed to circumvent pirating by immediately identifying copycat dresses sold in France and overseas.[33] All the franchised firms handled the Dior lines as separate operations from their own lines. Most of their executives made periodic trips to work with Dior in Paris, from which the seasonal new designs evolved.[34] All manufacturers operating under franchise reproduced the same features at all times. Furthermore, each season all licensees received the same instructions for promotion and publicity, so the entire hosiery operation established a unified character throughout the world. Maison Dior established a uniform scale for retail prices, aimed at the highest market level. This policy was pursued with all franchised accessories.[35]

The Dior business was not one of a "Genius at Work," but a matter of creative artistic ability combined with concentrated study of changes in living and dressing.[36] To respond to the global market, Maison Dior introduced standardized proportions based on the measurements of private clients from all over the world. At Maison Dior in Paris, a designer and an assistant for each product prepared all the materials, designs, and samples needed by the licensees to execute their creations. Each licensee also had a team that prepared the Dior lines with the information sent from Paris; quality control was overseen by an itinerant stylist. When a licensing agreement was signed, the designers would come up with a new theme for the item once or twice a year. The division had its own lawyers to deal with intellectual property issues, while the staff in charge of each continent made frequent visits to production sites and retail outlets. The goal was to ensure that only products representing the spirit of Maison Dior were being made and sold.[37]

This rigorous approach to quality control was also evident in the way the products were sold. Two sales catalogs displayed at the 2006 exhibition, "Christian Dior et le Monde" at the Musée Christian Dior in Granville, France, contained annotations in French by a maison saleslady. In the catalog for the 1949 autumn-winter exhibition in New York, the handwriting next to the entry for Model No. 1828, a day dress named San Francisco, reads in

French: "This model will sell well. A good price. Would sell better with small sleeves. Lowering the armhole is a legitimate reworking of the model." Similar annotations appeared in a catalog for the spring-summer 1957 collection. A garment with the double-barreled name "Bullock Wilshire," designed for the American market, sold for $425. The staff member's remarks were incisive: "Stores would rarely purchase this type of dress at this price. Clients can have a made-to-order dress for the same price. This copy of a typical Paris model should have a lower price."[38]

Can a model be sold at this high price? The comments are rigorous, expressing the strict quality control requirements important to guaranteeing sales of prêt-à-porter. The house label was a weapon in maintaining those standards. Each label signed "Christian Dior" had a special number permitting instant identification of models sold in France and abroad.[39] Consumers dissatisfied with garments could return them to retailers, and the Christian Dior wholesaling operation could subsequently discipline the manufacturer.

During the very early years of Maison Dior, design and merchandising were carried out at the Paris headquarters. From around the world, high-end retailers and manufacturers seen as worthy of producing and selling Maison Dior's products were signed on as licensees beginning in 1949. After the establishment of the licensing division in 1951, the scope of Christian Dior's product line and the regions in which the goods were marketed grew substantially.

Dior's prêt-à-porter was important to Dior-New York because this boutique line was the same as haute couture.[40] The duality of these two completely different images and businesses, "grand couturier" in Paris and "ready-made garment manufacturer" in New York, lay at the basis of Christian Dior's expansion.[41] In the early years of Maison Dior, business was carried out by and grew around Dior, Rouët, Legrez, Levasseur, and Fayol.

Expanding the Business

In 1947, Maison Dior was launched at 30, avenue Montaigne with three workrooms and 85 staff. By 1954, the firm had five buildings, 28 workrooms, and 1,000 employees in Paris. More important, it was now a multinational corporation doing business on five continents, with 8 overseas branches and 16 associated companies.[42] In 1953, overseas sales represented two-thirds of Maison Dior's total sales revenue, with the remaining one-third from sales in

France. For the entire French fashion industry, 65 percent of output was made for export, of which 40 percent went to the United States.

Behind the rapid business expansion of Maison Dior was a conversation between Boussac and Dior that took place after the February 1948 collection. The two discussed the future of the business. Should Maison Dior continue with its haute couture business alone, or should it carry out a major expansion to capitalize on the success that would no doubt be achieved by Christian Dior as a designer? After much deliberation, the two chose "the continuity of the Maison" and decided to search for new markets outside France and the United States.[43] Christian Dior would have been satisfied to continue as the head of the elegant *maison de couture* named after him. As long as the business remained financially dependent on Groupe Boussac, however, it could not just be an "elegant maison." The key concern of Groupe Boussac was to maximize the profits that could be generated by the genius designer. In other words, it was clear that profits would hit a ceiling by only dealing in haute couture, whereas the licensing business would be able to fulfill the expectations of Maison Dior's investor.[44]

Although Dior did not own Maison Dior shares, Groupe Boussac paid him a fee for every licensing agreement that was signed.[45] This arrangement may have influenced Dior's attitude toward expanding the business. Rouët received operational instructions directly from Dior and made great efforts to secure agreements. The discussions between Dior and Boussac effectively led to the expansion of Maison Dior after 1950.

At first glance, the business appeared to be growing steadily. Dior, however, was beginning to feel a sense of disquiet, as expressed in his autobiography. In *Christian Dior et moi*, the designer reflected on Maison Dior's rapid expansion: "Since 1948, it had opened a house in New York, and concluded agreements with England, Canada, Cuba, Australia, Chile and Mexico. It was becoming obvious that the peaceful little business which I had at first envisaged was in the process of devouring me."[46]

The larger than anticipated and rapidly developing business continued to expand, much to the designer's chagrin. Yves Saint Laurent, who had worked as Dior's assistant since 1955, recalled the stress of the master couturier. On the day of his collection, Dior was "so distressed that he couldn't even go to the couture house."—After consulting with his fortune teller and driving around in his car, Dior finally agreed to attend the show. "He had no idea that his own maison would become so huge,"—Saint Laurent recalled. "In the end he was a little bewildered by his success."[47] The next year,

1957, Christian Dior died of a heart attack at age fifty-two, at the Hotel La Place in Montecatini, Italy, where he was recovering from his poor physical condition.[48] While funeral preparations were underway at the avenue Montaigne headquarters, the selection process of his successor was also being carried out.[49]

Dior's death was significant for the fashion industry for two reasons. First, Maison Dior's couture products represented half of France's haute couture exports at the time. It was therefore inevitable that the performance of the Maison would affect the direction of Parisian haute couture as a whole.[50] Second was the effect of Dior's death on the licensees, many of them in New York's Seventh Avenue garment district. The relationship between Christian Dior and Seventh Avenue was based on mutual need.[51] The American manufacturers who made Christian Dior products acknowledged that his designs had a tremendous influence on fashion, and recognized that his presence had an equally enormous influence on sales. The fashion industry all over the world suffered a great loss with the death of Dior, but it was a matter of crucial importance to American manufacturers doing business with the company.[52] Maison Dior had grown into an enormous business, with global sales totaling $17 million in 1956 and $22 million in 1957. This included the businesses in Paris and London, Christian Dior-New York, Christian Dior in Caracas, Venezuela, perfumes, and all licensees.[53]

At a press conference on 15 November 1957, Maison Dior announced that Saint Laurent, Dior's twenty-one-year-old protégé, would succeed his mentor as chief designer. Jacques Rouët, now Maison Dior's president, spoke about the organization's bright future.[54] Based on the 1948 discussions between Dior and Boussac, the continuity of the Maison was to be a priority. Rouët planned to perpetuate Maison Dior's unique creative activities in "style, sense, technique and organization" by harnessing the talent of four principal staff members—Saint Laurent, Raymonde Zehnacker, Marguerite Carré, and Mitzah Bricard—who had been trained in the "école Dior," or the Dior tradition. This plan collapsed, however, when Saint Laurent left the firm on 1 September 1960 to serve in the military.[55] After his departure, Maison Dior took its artistic direction from a new chief designer, Marc Bohan, who had joined the firm's London branch as a prêt-à-porter designer in 1958. Bohan had worked at Maisons Robert Piguet, Captain Molyneux, Madeleine de Rauch, and Jean Patou. In 1953, he ran his own maison associated with the company Raphaël. And just before he started at Maison Dior, Bohan also worked for some American manufacturers.[56]

By this time, Christian Dior-New York had built a solid business in America, which had increased Maison Dior's visibility in the United States. In 1961, the French journalist Lucien François recounted a trip to Manhattan, where he found Maison Dior products in the swankest stores. On the best shopping streets, he saw "the name of Christian Dior in the windows of luxury boutiques" and "felt more proud than seeing the same thing in the beautiful streets of Paris." Fifth Avenue's stylish stores were filled with "ready-to-wear models, hats, furs, clothing, men's ties, scarves,"—all with labels in "three syllables that are so French 'Christian Dior,' a symbol of the Parisian taste."[57]

In October 1961, the design operations of Maison Dior and Dior-New York were completely separated. Guy Douvier was appointed resident chief designer for Dior-New York. Douvier, like Bohan, also had experience in ready-to-wear.[58] Initially, there were some concerns that Dior designs created in Paris would sit uncomfortably with American women, who were growing more casual in their tastes. To cope with this concern, Douvier carefully adapted Parisian styles for America. Twice yearly, he traveled to Europe to see the couture collections at Paris headquarters. Taking the spirit of the Paris shows into account, he designed two collections, in June and November, geared to American tastes. In 1961, Douvier explained his approach to the *New York Times*: he appreciated having the "freedom to Americanize, to design for Americans." Yet he always kept "the Dior look in mind," with careful attention to detail, elegance, and luxury.[59]

Prêt-à-porter's importance was increasing. Of the approximately 250 ready-to-wear prototypes created by Maison Dior every season, 50 models were sold through the Paris headquarters, 110 through Christian Dior-New York, and 90 through Christian Dior-London.[60] In the United States, the New York branch distributed Dior ready-to-wear to 250 local retail outlets; in England, Christian Dior-London had 55 retail outlets.[61] In this context, Bohan and Douvier complemented each other. Bohan's tendency to design classical garments, combined with Douvier's American attitude, helped Maison Dior achieve the stability and acclaim that benefited the firm as it pursued licensing agreements. In 1963, Gaston Bethelot took Douvier's position as Dior-New York's designer. Bohan, as chief designer in Paris, continued to work in harmony with Bethelot and his New York successor, Dominic Toubeix.

These important developments in design were accompanied by shifts in top management. In 1962, Henri Fayol, who had acted as go-between for

Groupe Boussac and Christian Dior, receded from the front line of CIC. At one stage, Fayol was Marcel Boussac's right-hand man, but a conflict is said to have emerged between the two men.[62] Documents at the Centre des Archives du Monde du Travail include a letter that describes Fayol's struggles with an anti-Dior faction at CIC around the time of the maison's establishment.[63] Fayol had guarded Dior's creativity from the financial pressures of Groupe Boussac and had worked with the young Rouët to manage the maison. His resignation from CIC marked the end of Maison Dior's early period.

Expansion After the 1960s

A clear distinction was drawn between Maison Dior, seen as a symbol of elegance, chic style, and creativity since its establishment in 1946, and fashion in the 1960s, characterized by avant-garde materials and forms and a street look. This was a decade in which massive changes took place in social norms and values against the background of the emergence of the counterculture movement and resistance to authority among youth. The 1960s also arguably represented one of the most democratic periods in fashion. In 1977, Rouët reflected on the dramatic transformation of haute couture: "Now, of course, couture has changed. Do you realize that, in 1949, there were 250 different stores which bought couture? Today, couture exists as an expression for a creator to give his message to the press and to his private clientele."[64] In the 1960s and 1970s, from the point of view of sales, couture was coming to matter less to Maison Dior than prêt-à-porter and far, far less than licensed accessories. But couture activity was needed for keeping Maison Dior's prestige as a representative couture house in Paris.

During this period, Rouët assumed full responsibility for Maison Dior's operation without Fayol, while Geoffroy de Seynes followed Legrez as director of Maison Dior's licensing business.[65] After the death of Dior and the departures of Saint Laurent, Fayol, and Legrez, the licensing business continued to be promoted under the direction of Rouët, Bohan, and de Seynes.

Let us look at Maison Dior's expansion during this period. Between 1964 and 1975, the firm extended its retail operations by opening more than a dozen boutiques in Europe. Sites included glamorous vacation spots for jet-setters, such as Geneva, Lausanne, Berne, and Gstaad in Switzerland; Berlin, Munich, and Düsseldorf in Germany; Brussels, Belgium; Athens, Greece; and Monte Carlo, Monaco. The company created a ski collection, Miss Dior, for the younger generation, and Baby Dior for the offspring of fashionistas. It diversified into furs with a New York store, the creation of the *haute fourrure* division in Paris, and a ready-to-wear fur line. Men's accessories beyond neckties were added in 1970, and Christian Dior Monsieur, a licensed line, in 1973. Global expansion continued with Japanese connections in 1964, as we will see below.

By 1975, more than 130 licensed products were being sold in 80 countries. Stockings were sold in 18 countries; neckties in 10 countries; scarves, corsets, bras, ladies' shoes, and men's shirts in more than 5 countries; and suitcases, socks, men's shoes, gloves, lingerie, and sweaters in fewer than 5 countries. Licensed handbags and glasses in particular were being sold globally. Dior-New York controlled American ready-to-wear projects and managed licensees.

In this context, the classic designs that skyrocketed Maison Dior to international fame in the 1940s and 1950s were losing their appeal among shoppers. Reflecting on his 1960s designs in 1983, Marc Bohan commented on the continuity of his style. He told *Women's Wear Daily* that he was struck "by how much it looked like what I do today. I could see that I haven't changed at all that much."[66] In February 1967, for the summer collection, Bohan had announced his Safari Look for Maison Dior. Although media reported on the new style, Saint Laurent's Safari Look, introduced in 1968 by the young designer's own company, attracted greater response. In retrospect, Saint Laurent's Safari Look epitomized the new direction that emerged in the 1960s. Although Bohan's designs were certainly popular among a certain class of customers, this classic look, together with its clients, was slowly beginning to age. The two men's competing Safari Looks vividly exemplified this change.

As a way of responding to the new direction of the times, in 1967 Maison Dior announced the creation of Miss Dior, a line targeted at younger consumers who did not normally buy Christian Dior products.[67] Bohan's assistant Philippe Guibourgé, who eventually left Dior to become Maison Chanel's ready-to-wear designer, created Miss Dior. A boutique was opened at Maison Dior's headquarters at 11, bis rue François 1er, in Paris. Normally, products in the ready-to-wear line were priced at $150 and up, but the prices in the Miss Dior line were kept below $150.[68] Production began in the United States in October 1970.[69] In France, Miss Dior boutiques were also opened in the new distribution channel of shopping centers near Versailles in 1969, a strategy that responded to the increasing popular and younger market while still maintaining Dior's upmarket image.

In the same year, Maison Dior released a series of handbags in a jacquard weave into which was woven the name "Dior."[70] These became icons of Maison Dior's licensing program and were long-time best-sellers. In 1973, these products were still carried by the Saks Fifth Avenue department store in New York, where they were shown in window displays (Figure 5.1). Recently, Maison Dior put out the new version, Logo Diorissimo, a reinterpretation of this bag.

By around 1975, there was a growing tendency among American retail buyers visiting Paris to buy more ready-to-wear than haute couture. Many new talented designers of ready-to-wear began to appear. *Women's Wear Daily* reported on those who attracted the most attention in the Paris collections: Saint Laurent, Givenchy, Chloé, Courrèges, Issey Miyake, Thierry Mugler, Kenzo, Cacharel, and Dorothée Bis.[71]

Against this background, Dior's profits continued to grow around licensing. Since 1953, the prestigious department store Daimaru, headquartered in Osaka, had had an exclusive contract to sell Dior's couture line in Japan.[72] In May 1964, a licensing agreement was drawn up between Maison Dior and the Japanese firm Kanebo. Established in 1887 as Kanegafuchi Bōseki (Kanegafuchi Cotton Spinning Company), Kanebo by the postwar era was a major multinational in cosmetics, fibers, and food. From the vantage point of the couture house's Paris headquarters, Rouët saw Japan as Maison Dior's most important market after the United States. At a press conference on 8 May 1964, Rouët said Maison Dior had been interested in the Japanese market from the start. It had held fashion shows in principal Japanese cities in 1953. When the contract with Daimaru was complete, Maision Dior needed another Japanese partner, this time in licensing. Rouët and Henry Sherman, president of Dior-New York, both went to Japan for the signing of the agreement.[73]

At this conference, Rouët announced the plans for Christian Dior's future business with Kanebo. Although haute couture was still central to Maison Dior, he explained, fashion was constantly developing and changing. Maison Dior needed to be involved with other products. To introduce the firm's ready-to-wear garments and accessories to the Japanese market, all Maison Dior products were to be manufactured and sold in partnership with Kanebo. The models to be recreated by Kanebo would come from Dior's headquarters in Paris and its subsidiaries in London and New York. Within

Figure 5.1. Saks Fifth Avenue window display, showing handbags in a jacquard weave with the name "Dior." Photograph taken during Marc Bohan's visit to New York, 26 February 1976. Courtesy Christian Dior Couture S.A. Archives, Paris.

the year, chief designer Marc Bohan and fifteen staff members would arrive in Japan to stage an haute couture fashion show. The clothes presented in the show would not be available for purchase, but would serve to introduce Maison Dior to Japanese customers.[74]

Rouët's guidelines are a strong indication of Maison Dior's intention to promote its licensing business in Japan. The shipment to Japan of models from Paris, New York, and London was significant. In North America, the Canadian department store Holt Renfrew had secured exclusive rights to sell Christian Dior's New York and Paris lines.[75] Dior's expansion into Japan involved a combination of models from three cities, probably because the maison thought it would be necessary to adjust the sizes and styles to suit the Japanese market to ensure absolute success. As a commercial strategy, Maison Dior decided to hybridize French, American, and Japanese taste, rather than imposing one country's taste. In later years, Bohan also admitted that Japan, since its 1964 launch, had gradually become a more important market than the United States because of the diversity of its products.[76]

Maison Dior dispatched a permanent designer to Japan who would travel between Tokyo and Paris four times a year.[77] Kanebo had an important design team in Tokyo and also worked with Emile Ungemacht, who was based in Tokyo for Maison Dior.[78] Jean Marc Dubois, an executive director at Maison Dior, commended the licensing agreement with Kanebo, saying that it was the first example of licensing that succeeded in overcoming the many hurdles, in particular related to quality, that faced Maison Dior. The overseas expansion was highly lucrative. Of the total turnover disclosed for 1979, the United States represented 35 percent, followed by Japan at 22 percent, and France, Dior's homeland, at 21 percent.[79]

As for the Dior organization, Sherman, president of Dior-New York, who together with Rouët had developed the American side of Dior's business, resigned in June 1970.[80] Before he left, Rouët created two posts for vice-presidents in Dior-New York: Lou Cohen in charge of production, and Donald Fries in merchandising.[81] In September of the same year, Hubert Latimer was appointed the first American to Dior-New York resident designer, following Guy Douvier, Gaston Bethelot, and Dominic Toubeix. In 1975, however, Maison Dior decided that Dior-New York and then Dior-London[82] would be closed, and that Bohan would oversee all designs from Paris. The closings symbolized the end of an era against a background of growing market globalization. Meanwhile, however, Rouët continued to promote the licensing business.

In 1975, Christian Dior issued a press release exclaiming, "Thanks to the world's licensing activities."[83] Maison Dior had no hesitation in making this statement to the press. In France, haute couture and *haute fourrure* now represented only 20 percent of Maison Dior's business, while earnings from boutiques represented 30 percent, ready-to-wear 15 percent, and accessories 35 percent.[84] Dior's licensing business not only grew in Japan, but continued to expand throughout the world.

Despite this success, Boussac, Dior's investor since its inception, appeared to have reservations about the expansion of its licensing business. In 1979, Rouët made the following statement: "When I told Mr. Boussac that no store buyer would bother buying Dior haute couture, he could not accept what I was trying to tell him."[85] According to Rouët, Boussac tenaciously held onto the prestige of Dior's haute couture. More than two decades earlier, he and Christian Dior aspired first to maintain "an elegant Maison" and, second, to tend to "the expansion of the licensing business." After Dior's death, the aspiration was reversed. Product licensing represented a greater share of Maison Dior's business. Indeed, in 1981, it accounted for 90 percent of sales.[86]

Groupe Boussac, the parent company that had owned all the shares in Maison Dior's businesses from its inception, began to eat into the fashion house's profits in the 1960s when its own earnings began to decline.[87] Although Parfums Christian Dior was already a separate entity when Maison Dior was established in 1947, the sale of Parfums Christian Dior to Moët & Chandon in 1968 was a symbolic move that arguably represented an epitaph for Groupe Boussac as it spiraled downward.

Profits at Maison Christian Dior

In the past, haute couture had served as a symbol of a Parisian maison's glory, and few questioned its profitability. It was a "black box" in an industry comprised of private companies. Let us examine the documents held by the Centre des archives du monde du travail (CAMT) to study the nature of Maison Dior's business performance since its inception.[88] CAMT, in Roubaix, in northern France, is a national archive that principally preserves company records. When the Groupe Boussac was purchased by Ferret-Savinel (LVMH Group's antecedents), the Groupe's documents were deposited in this archive.[89]

TABLE 5.1. NET PROFITS AT CHRISTIAN DIOR S.A., 1947–1961

Year	Net profits (francs)[1]	Net profits ($)
1947	4,783,032.05	40,210.78
1948	3,101,076.25	10,047.49
1949	28,778,877.00	86,825.89
1950	40,679,221.00	116,261.22
1951	39,401,947.00	112,531.98
1952	47,271,180.00	135,006.51
1953	36,987,135.00	105,635.27
1954	6,466,781.00	18,469.13
1955	20,335,043.00	58,076.89
1956	7,651,479.00	21,844.95
1957	49,427,663.00	117,440.24
1958	45,841,954.00	108,828.80
1959	264,577,190.00	539,208.46
1960	488,144.67	99,519.81
1961	390,044.61	79,503.59

[1]Old francs, 1947–1959, francs, 1960–1961.
Source: *Bilan* (Balance Sheet), *Société Christian Dior*, 31 Dec. 1947–31 Mar. 1977, Ref. No. 1987–003–251, Centre des archives du monde du travail, Roubaix, France; Convergence: Economic History Services, Exchange Rates (http://eh.net).

Although the *répartition des bénéfices* documents, which show a firm's profits, end in 1955, the CAMT's holdings of the *bilan*, or balance sheets, dating from 1956 show more detail (Table 5.1). To judge from these documents, although Maison Dior attracted worldwide acclaim with its "New Look," we can see that the company did not show a profit until 1950. Groupe Boussac established the foundations for Maison Dior's licensing business in 1949, increasing capitalization sixfold, from F5 million to 30 million, to realize Dior's overseas expansion.[90] The licensing business venture proved effective, as evident from the significant growth in profits.

Judging from the records, it is clear that Maison Dior was not easily generating ever-increasing profits. In the early to mid-1950s, it began to acquire real estate for expansion and extensive renovations of its headquarters, enlarging the Paris facility to nearly its present size. After this, profits appear to have slowly recovered. The sudden drop in profits in 1954 was probably due to the reduction in the salesroom area caused by the 1953–55 renovations or the temporary closure of the Dior store. Ironically, it was 1959, during the three-year epoch when Saint Laurent worked as Christian Dior's chief designer, that the maison produced its highest profits. Although Rouët believed that there was no link between media recognition and sales, it is clear that Saint Laurent contributed to Maison Dior's business performance.

The CAMT documents also reveal details of Maison Dior's business performance for the five years from 1973 to 1978.[91] These include sales and profits from the couture and licensing businesses. This material enables us to understand the importance of the licensing business to Maison Dior fifteen to twenty years after Dior's death. I have extracted figures from three of these years: 1973, 1975, and 1977 (Table 5.2).

Table 5.2 reveals several important facts. First is the high earnings of accessories. In 1975, accessories (primarily neckties, bags, and scarves) were important licensed items, constituting a third of Maison Dior's earnings in France. It is evident from the table that income from accessories nearly tripled over a four-year period. Next is the downturn in the couture business between 1973 and 1977. Although the figures remain unchanged in terms of sales, a loss of more than double that of five years previously is revealed. Looking back on those years in an interview, designer Marc Bohan stated, "In 1980, I realized that couture was in decline."[92] In reality, haute couture had been on the skids for much longer, due to the industry's reliance on North American consumers, who were the best buyers for French couture.[93]

Factors such as the rise of casual dressing, the two oil shocks in 1973–74 and 1979, and the fall in the U.S. dollar meant that things were not easy for the couture business from the late 1960s through the 1970s. As a businessman, Rouët had a more realistic vision. "By the end of the 1950s," he commented in an interview for Didier Grumbach's 1993 book, *Histoires de la mode*, recalling this era to mind, "couture was no longer a viable activity."[94] Despite the fact that the couture business faced extremely tough conditions after Dior's death, Rouët maintained its image while simultaneously building the licensing business.

In 1973, one company, Kanebo, is mentioned as a separate item in the CAMT documents. As is evident from Table 5.2, not only the Maison Dior couture business but also the ready-to-wear business was in deficit. Maison Christian Dior's profits continued to rise was entirely due to the licensing business. Kanebo represented a 40.8 percent share of Christian Dior's licensing business; Japan, like the United States, was extremely important to the maison.

As shown in the previous section, the licensing business was carried out on a global scale. The CAMT documents also include records of Maison Dior's licensing royalties from 1965 to 1976, with estimates for 1977 through

TABLE 5.2. NET SALES AND PROFITS AT CHRISTIAN DIOR S.A., 1973–1977

Line	Currency	31 December 1973		31 December 1975		31 December 1977	
		Sales	Profits	Sales	Profits	Sales	Profits
Haute couture	Francs	9,634,669	(1,980,920)	8,839,865	(2,918,836)	10,000,776	(3,998,867)
	U.S.$	2,171,437	(446,455)	2,064,424	(681,652)	2,034,745	(813,604)
Fur	Francs	10,024,112	1,173,554	12,184,228	1,540,108	15,550,363	(933,728)
	U.S.$	2,259,209	264,493	2,845,452	359,670	3,623,526	(189,975)
Ready to wear (old line)	Francs	569,182	(401,985)	1,255,572	1,243,083		
	U.S.$	128,280	90,598	293,220	290,304		
Ready to wear[1]	Francs	7,827,794	(1,253,829)	4,029,650	4,519,888	12,561,240	(2,159,352)
	U.S.$	1,764,209	282,585	941,067	1,055,555	2,555,694	(439,339)
Accessories[2]	Francs	25,576,799	4,674,792	38,482,660	8,024,158	69,359,682	16,541,583
	US$	5,764,435	1,053,593	898,707	1,873,927	14,111,837	3,365,530
Licenses in Paris	Francs	5,602,356	3,482,398	11,313,023	3,669,370	22,249,850	10,634,614
	U.S.$	1,262,645	784,854	2,641,995	856,929	4,526,927	2,163,705
Kanebo[3]	Francs	2,283,907					
	U.S.$	514,741					
Boutiques	Francs	25,093,624	3,453,690	29,407,435	1,818,720	39,253,97	3,110,507
	U.S.$	5,655,538	778,384	6,867,686	424,736	798,656	632,860
Headquarters	Francs		257,753		255,266		304,129
	U.S.$		58,092		59,613		61,877
Total	Francs	86,612,443	9,405,453	105,512,433	18,151,757	169,065,818	23,498,886
	U.S.$	19,520,494	2,866,144	16,552,551	4,239,082	27,651,385	4,781,054

[1] Combined with undergarments and prêt-à-porter from 1977.

[2] "Accessories" refers to accessories, handbags, scarves, and gloves.

[3] Kanebo, the Japanese licensor, is mentioned in 1973, but after 1974 its earnings were included with "Licenses in Paris" in the line above.

Source: État comparatif des chiffres d'affaires et résultat (Comparative statement of the sales and the results), Christian Dior S.A., 31 Dec. 1977, Ref. No. 1994–020–112, Centre des archives du monde du travail, Roubaix, France. Convergence: Economic History Services, Exchange Rates [http://eh.net].

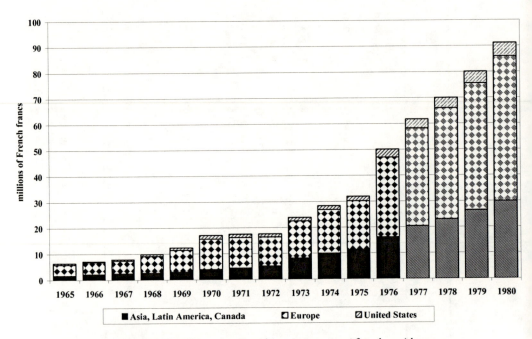

Figure 5.2 Christian Dior Licensing Royalties, 1965–1980. After the mid-1970s, royalties from the United States increased only slightly, while those from other continents increased significantly, due to growth of the European and Japanese markets. Royalties for 1977–1980 were estimated in March 1977. Source: Rendement Mondial des Licences Christian Dior (World Royalties from Licensing Christian Dior), 31 Mar. 1977, Ref. No. 1994–020–112, Centre des archives du monde du travail, Roubaix, France.

1980. An analysis of these figures shows the changing makeup of the world market for Christian Dior's licensed products. In this fifteen-year period, the U.S. market grew steadily, but the real gains came from licensing efforts in Europe, and in Asia, Latin America, and Canada (Figure 5.2). Furthermore, due to improved pretax profits, Maison Dior increased its royalties from 1 to 2 percent in 1979. At the same time, it planned for increased earnings in all regions of the world. The number of franchise boutiques was increased, and management was decentralized in various countries such as Brazil, while greater attention was paid to product diversification.[95]

As we have seen so far, economic conditions of the 1970s were not ideal for business expansion. In terms of the profitability of the maison, however, the licensing business, for which Maison Dior was the first couture house to be involved in a major way, laid the foundations for a system that was to become a model for the rest of the fashion industry.[96] Arguably, it was the tradition and the positive image of the individual named Christian Dior that assisted the expansion of licensed products bearing his name and that also contributed to Maison Dior's continuity.[97]

Significance of the Licensing Business to the Fashion Industry

As we have seen so far, Maison Dior's achievement in the history of the fashion industry lies in the creation of a format for producing profits while continuing to operate the maison as a viable business by licensing. For this to be realized, Maison Dior was based, from its inception, on an operating foundation designed to realize a vast expansion of the business. The reason the company was able to overcome a period of instability surrounding the selection of a successor after Dior's death was due to the fact that its licensing business, which represented its greatest source of profits, had continued to be actively promoted and developed.

Apparently, however, this did not always represent the sort of business that Christian Dior, the founding designer, had envisioned. In his autobiography, Dior referred to those affiliated with Groupe Boussac as "the Group," or the clique. In context, these words were not always positive. At the same time, although "Maison Dior" obviously referred to Dior himself, the designer openly and frequently stated that he was "playing the role" of "Christian Dior."[98]

The battles between Dior and Groupe Boussac do not necessarily represent a clear demarcation between "business expansion," on the one hand, and the desire "to continue to be an elegant Maison," on the other. Dior himself felt a sense of responsibility as the master of the couture house that bore his name. Not to be forgotten are the rewards paid to Dior. Although Dior did not possess a single share in the company, individuals such as Fayol at CIC defended the master couturier's creativity to the end. Similarly, even though Boussac never once visited the house while Dior was alive, the designer always conveyed his gratitude to his financier, even though he may have just been trying to be polite.[99] Moreover, Boussac in his final years expressed his reservations about Rouët, who actively promoted the licensing business. As a result, the issue was complex and more than simply a simple confrontation between two opposing views, those of Dior and Boussac.

In today's fashion business, the marketing of products based on a brand name is a highly emulated, up-to-date model. This approach matured in the 1970s and 1980s, which have been described as the "licensing flood era." In this period, the "emperor of license" was Maison Pierre Cardin, whose licensed products increased by almost 40 percent from 350 to 540 between 1977 and 1982. Cardin also worked for Maison Dior at the beginning for three years. His licensing efforts were big business; the house earned $50 million in royalties on $10 billion in annual sales in 1982.[100] As is evident from a comment by an American retailer, however, suspicion emerged over the quality of licensed products. "The times when product can be sold simply because of the name of a famous designer are over," Frank Droff, vice president of Macy's New York, told *Women's Wear Daily* in 1982. "Ultimately it is up to the quality of the product."[101] As a maison's licensed offerings increased, quality control of the products became less stringent, thus creating a negative view toward those products.

Like Christian Dior, the designer Pierre Balmain, who also had worked for Maison Lelong and who became a leader in French fashion after World War II, supported the licensing business. Similar to Dior, Balmain also stressed the importance of the licensee's skills and the ability of its designers to create adaptations faithful to the couturier's sample.[102] This statement arguably represented the perspective of a designer who aspired to business expansion through the licensing business. Maison Dior, with its quality standards and rigorous production controls, continued to supply the market with licensed products bearing the name of its founding designer, through which it realized the continuity of the maison as well as profits.[103]

Did the diverse products generated by the licensing agreements that were rapidly and actively promoted by Maison Dior after the 1960s represent the highest standards of design? Not necessarily, according to a statement by Sidney Toledano, who has been president of Maison Dior since 1998. "For a veritable luxury brand, licensed products can be damaging," Toledano told *Women's Wear Daily* in 2004.[104] Bernard Arnault, chairman at the LVMH Group and owner of Maison Christian Dior since 1984, has gradually been expanding the business in a way distinct from licensing. Arnault adopted a strategy of not renewing contracts with licensees, thereby eliminating licensed Christian Dior goods from the market.[105] The French newspaper *La Tribune* reported that the termination of Christian Dior's licensing business represented the death of everything the maison symbolized.[106] In Japan, the contract with Kanebo was ended in 1997. A dramatic change in direction was implemented, giving Paris headquarters of the maison total control over Christian Dior designs. With the end of licensed production of menswear in 2001, all Maison Dior licensed products have disappeared from the Japanese market.[107] For Maison Dior, licensing offered a viable tool for expansion when the business was young. Once this model was adopted by many designers, licensed lines began to lose their cultural cachet. If Maison Dior were to maintain its high-quality image, it had no choice but to drop licensing.

As though following the Maison Dior strategy, other French couture houses have been undergoing a dramatic shift to global expansion. In 2004, Toledano praised couture, even though it is not a profitable activity: "If Haute Couture activity exists only for the client, it doesn't work. However through the fashion show, it appeals to the public and it greatly affects ready-to-wear, perfume, etc. It's more than publicity. I feel the Haute Couture product is more important as a concept than as a product itself. And moreover, the Haute Couture is the place where the young talented designers can train. So I believe firmly we have to preserve it, even as a small business."[108]

In retrospect, is licensing something that should be rejected by brands? Licensed products, in fact, were not products that were indiscriminately supplied to the market. It is necessary to remember that there were members of the general public who loved and enjoyed these products. No business operates without customers. What the customers think of the business means success or failure.[109] The growing earnings from licensing are a testimony to this fact. The fact that today's designers continue to become involved in the licensing business and continue to release ever more moderately priced diffusion lines arguably proves the validity of this business.

PART II

Inventing Fashions,
Promoting Styles

CHAPTER SIX

The Wiener Werkstätte and the Reform Impulse

Heather Hess

THE WIENER WERKSTÄTTE (1903–1932), intent on reforming every aspect of daily life through excellent craftsmanship and even better design, produced furnishings, silverware, jewelry, metal objects, fashions, pottery, and entire interiors. This Austrian company encouraged its designers to follow their own vision of the modern home and modern life in late imperial Vienna. Unapologetically elitist, the firm refused to compromise on matters of quality or taste; buoyed by wealthy patrons, it did not need to bend to prevailing tastes or appeal to a mass audience. At every turn, the firm emphasized that it belonged more to the world of art than to the world of commerce. From its founding, critics and taste professionals promoted the Wiener Werkstätte as the epitome of new Austrian design, but the company's broad public success in its native land came only after the firm proved fashionable abroad.[1] Yet, at the highest levels of society, the Wiener Werkstätte quite literally courted acceptance, garnering patronage and praise from emperors, kings, and princesses in Austria-Hungary, England, Germany, and Italy. Rather than provoke the ruling and educated elites, Vienna's most forward-looking artists set out to decorate their homes.

Art-historical interest in the Wiener Werkstätte has focused primarily on the firm's transformations of style, and particularly on the radical designs of its early years. But the firm's founders never intended to retreat from industrial society or to break totally from the art of the past.[2] Instead, they repudiated the "boundless evil in the field of decorative art, which, on the one hand, was caused by poor mass production, and on the other, by the thoughtless imitation of old styles."[3] The Wiener Werkstätte's founders rejected the legacy of historicism and tackled the problems of industrialization. Their goal was to tap the lost traditions of preindustrial craftsmanship to raise the level of Austrian design.[4]

The Wiener Werkstätte and Its Critics

Josef Hoffmann and Koloman Moser, with the financial backing of the scion of a textile manufacturing family, Fritz Waerndorfer, founded the Wiener Werkstätte in May 1903. In a city that valued age and maturity, Hoffmann and Moser were both young, only thirty-two and thirty-five years old.[5] Yet neither needed to be introduced to the Viennese public or to subscribers to the German-language art and decorating journals of the time. As professors at Vienna's Kunstgewerbeschule, the Imperial-Royal School of Arts and Crafts, they educated and influenced an entire generation of Viennese designers, including many who later joined the Wiener Werkstätte's artistic staff.[6] More important, professional ties to the Vienna Secession linked them to the nascent modern art movement. Moser's graphic design gave the Secession's publication, *Ver Sacrum* (Sacred Spring), much of its distinctive flavor in its early years, and he used the magazine to experiment with geometric motifs that he later elaborated for the Wiener Werkstätte.[7] Hoffmann's exhibition designs for the Secession displayed his distinctive approach to the modern interior.[8]

The Secession gave Hoffmann and Moser a place to cultivate future patrons for the Wiener Werkstätte. Under the sheltering foliage of the Secession's golden cupola, the sacred spring of fin-de-siècle Viennese art and culture bloomed. Vienna experimented and innovated in all aspects of the visual arts, literature, and music. Sigmund Freud probed the recesses of the psyche. Hugo von Hofmannsthal penned his elegant, erudite poetry for Vienna's educated, culture-loving elites, while Karl Kraus exposed the hypocrisy of that society in his magazine *Die Fackel* (The Torch).

The Wiener Werkstätte did not solely produce the designs by Hoffmann and Moser. During its twenty-nine-years, the firm employed many of Austria's finest decorative artists, including Gustav Klimt, Oskar Kokoschka, Carl Otto Czeschka, Eduard Wimmer-Wisgrill, Dagobert Peche, and Vally

Wieselthier. Only Hoffmann stayed with the firm until its liquidation in 1932. Moser officially left in 1909 (rather than in 1907, as is usually reported), but his departure had little effect.[9] The Wiener Werkstätte still produced Moser's designs and contemporaries associated his work with the Werkstätte until his death in 1918. The same was true for other designers.

The firm's artists, many of whom graduated from Hoffmann and Moser's classes at the School of Arts and Crafts, designed objects but did not produce them. That task fell to company craftsmen, who were among the best in Vienna. Although the Wiener Werkstätte, like all producers of decorative art, used machines, the firm emphasized the individual qualities of its handcrafted products and the exceptional treatment of its workers. The maker's marks stamped onto every Wiener Werkstätte object produced gave credit to both the designer and the craftsman, manifesting two of the firm's tenets: the equality of artist and craftsman, and the unity of mind and hand. In addition, craftsmen enjoyed superior working conditions that earned praise from Vienna's leading socialist newspaper, the *Arbeiterzeitung*.[10] Art publications hailed the firm's efforts in tackling the problems of industrialization and urbanization. Writing for *Deutsche Kunst und Dekoration*, Joseph August Lux declared: "The social question has ceased to be an issue in this company."[11]

The financial support of a series of major patrons—first Waerndorfer, who provided the firm's initial capital, and later the Primavesis, a family of industrialists and bankers—made possible the accomplishments of the Wiener Werkstätte's designers and patrons. Without this support, the Wiener Werkstätte would have folded years earlier, as it never sold enough to cover its expenses.[12] The firm exhausted the private fortunes of its most generous patrons, including Waerndorfer, who immigrated to America in 1914.[13] The final auction of its holdings, held in Vienna in September 1932, revealed thousands of unsold objects that dated back years and showed that the firm still produced designs by long-departed colleagues like Moser.[14]

The firm included workshops capable of producing every kind of object for the home, including the home itself. The earliest workshops focused on gold- and silversmithing, metalworking, bookbinding, carpentry, leathertooling, and lacquering. Eventually the firm produced ceramics, textiles and upholstery, hats, and women's wear. The addition of the latter workshops decisively altered the character of the Wiener Werkstätte's operations by broadening its reach. Initially, however, the firm made few overtures toward casual clients who might only buy a cigarette case or a vase. Instead, it focused on customers wishing to have their entire lives outfitted by the Wiener Werkstätte.[15] In its early years, the firm built and furnished numerous villas for wealthy Viennese, particularly members of the *Bildungsbürgertum*, the professional and educated middle class. The firm's first major commission, for the Purkersdorf Sanatorium (1904–6), a convalescence hospital for wealthy patients with nervous disorders, demonstrated Hoffmann and company's talent for creating an entire environment in a unified style.[16] The next major project, the building and outfitting of the Palais Stoclet (1905–11), a private residence in Brussels for Baron Adolphe Stoclet—an exceptionally wealthy engineer, industrialist, and art collector—and his wife Suzanne, represented the full realization of what the firm might accomplish with unlimited artistic freedom *and* funds.[17]

Most consumers, of course, did not have unlimited resources. It was not just a question of money, however; Wiener Werkstätte designs did not appeal to the parvenu. Professing taste for the Wiener Werkstätte marked one as educated and refined, a supporter of the reform and design philosophies of John Ruskin, William Morris, and the English Arts and Crafts movement. German and Austrian theorists understood these ideas to be centered primarily on an overall improvement of life, rather than a simple move toward a new style.[18] The designers, critics, and writers who produced objects, advice manuals, and decorating guides correlated the home's architecture and interior decoration with the moral character of its inhabitants. Educating and refining the tastes of the growing middle classes—the fastest-growing segment of the Austrian population at the turn of the twentieth century— became a matter of serious public interest, power, and prestige.[19]

In Germany and Austria, concern with middle-class taste reflected the ambivalence toward the social changes wrought by industrialization, urbanization, and the growth in mass culture. These transformations undermined the power of ruling elites and the status of the aristocracy.[20] When Hermann Muthesius explained that the decorative arts had become "in the broadest sense of the word a cultural movement, which influences the ways in which we live, our behavior, our social relations," he expressed the central role ascribed to the minor arts in negotiating the trials of modernization.[21]

Hoffmann and Moser founded the Wiener Werkstätte as an institution for improving taste in Austria. As they explained in their "Working Program" in 1904, "Our middle-class has by far not fulfilled its artistic mission."[22] Drawing on the intellectual legacy of the English Arts and Crafts movement, the Working Program outlined the Wiener Werkstätte's commitment to the individualized production of objects and quality craftsmanship, design, and materials. It described the firm's various workshops and justified the cost of the firm's production as part of its social responsibility toward the craftsman who executed the designs. Throughout, the Working Program's authors stressed the social context and the ideas behind the designs, rather than aesthetic criteria or allegiance to a specific style.

In the emphasis on ethics and social responsibility, the Wiener Werkstätte's Working Program discursively paralleled the German reform dress movement in women's fashion. This early twentieth-century effort rejected the stylistic conventions of commercial fashions, prioritizing, as Henri van de Velde noted, morality and health over aesthetics.[23] Like the Wiener Werkstätte and other proponents of a new decorative art, advocates of German reform dress emphasized its "artistic" qualities. In the language of the time, "artistic" garments followed the nature of the material, clearly revealed their construction, and were handmade.[24] Not everyone hoping to refine taste appreciated this approach. Anna Muthesius and other supporters of dress reform doubted the artistic merits of *Gesundheitskleid*, or "health-dress," as it was commonly known in Germany.[25] As a later writer bluntly summarized, "It was simple, but it was not pretty."[26]

Reform dress marked the wearer as a member of a certain economic and social class, which overlapped with the initial clientele of the Wiener Werkstätte.[27] Berta Szeps-Zuckerkandl, who hosted a salon where the ideas of the Secession were born, continuously proselytized for the Wiener Werkstätte's modern designs in art journals and the newspaper *Wiener Allgemeine Zeitung*. She had worn reform dress, although she later derided these loose dresses as "shapeless flour sacks."[28] Photographs of Emilie Flöge, wearing reform clothes designed by the Secessionist painter Gustav Klimt, appeared in *Deutsche Kunst und Dekoration* in 1906.[29] The interior of the Schwestern Flöge fashion salon, run by Emilie and her sisters, was one of the Wiener Werkstätte's earliest commissions. In 1905, *Deutsche Kunst und Dekoration* published photographs of the salon interiors.[30] In home furnishings and interior design, the Wiener Werkstätte demonstrated how reform ideas could be yoked to stylistic innovation.

In the Working Program, the leaders of the Wiener Werkstätte described in words the meaning of their designs. In November 1904, the art journal *Hohe Warte* first published this program of aesthetic reform. Named for the leafy Viennese suburb where Hoffmann had built villas for Moser and fellow artists from the Vienna Secession, *Hohe Warte* reached precisely the audiences with the taste and financial resources to appreciate the Wiener Werkstätte.[31] Aimed at middle-class audiences as well as professionals such as curators, artists, salesmen, and gallery owners, these journals disseminated the ideas of reform institutions like the Wiener Werkstätte. Alexander Koch, publisher of the most important art journal of the era, *Deutsche Kunst und Dekoration*, realized that "Without our new art-periodicals [there would be] no new decorative art."[32]

The new art periodicals provided a forum for critics who aimed to help middle-class audiences refine their tastes and navigate the vagaries of fashion.[33] Writing for these journals were "taste professionals," scholars and museum professionals trained in the emerging field of art history as well as writers of advice manuals and decorating guides.[34] These "taste professionals" differed from the business-oriented "fashion intermediaries" who labored to read and interpret consumer desire on behalf of mass-market manufacturers.[35] The "taste professionals" served as "heralds" of the new art, not dispassionate chroniclers.[36] Critics and artists were allies in the fight for public taste and patronage.[37] In turn, the Wiener Werkstätte, as a design workshop, benefited from the publicity generated by Vienna's critics, taste professionals, and art journals.

Dedicated to promoting German art, the periodical *Deutsche Kunst und Dekoration* was the Wiener Werkstätte's most stalwart supporter. Between October 1904 and March 1911, it published twelve special issues dedicated to the Wiener Werkstätte. These issues were set apart from the journal's other issues by a distinctive checkerboard page border, and every illustration in these issues showed objects designed by Wiener Werkstätte. Next to each photograph, in the page's margin, a monogram identified the artist responsible for designing the object. These monograms functioned as much like an artist signature—or a couture label—by proclaiming the artistic quality and significance of the objects.[38] While maker's marks for both the designing artist and the craftsmen appeared on the objects, *Deutsche Kunst und Dekoration* did not publish the monograms of the executing craftsmen. A key objective of the decorative arts movement was collapsing the distinction between fine and decorative arts and putting artist and craftsman on equal footing. The craftsmen, however, got short shrift, as their names did not appear alongside the artists' in Germany's leading arts magazine.

In *Deutsche Kunst und Dekoration*'s Wiener Werkstätte issues, the text covered a wide range of topics, often completely unrelated to Viennese design. This produced an incongruous pairing of text and image; for example, one article about brightly colored wallpapers had illustrations showing the simple, whitewashed walls in the Wiener Werkstätte's showroom.[39] The lead articles, all ostensibly on the Wiener Werkstätte, varied widely in topic. Lux, who wrote essays for the first two issues, dated October 1904 and June 1905, barely addressed the aesthetic issues of the firm's designs, which differed radically from the dominant mode of decoration in bourgeois homes (Figure 6.1). He maintained that the extensive illustrations were to speak for themselves.[40] The third issue of *Deutsche Kunst und Dekoration*, published in December 1905, reiterated this theme, claming that the sheer mass of photographs already published rendered any further discussion of the images superfluous.[41] Indeed, *Deutsche Kunst und Dekoration* significantly contributed to the Wiener Werkstätte's rise as the epitome of Austrian design, a position it enjoyed until closing in 1932 in the wake of the Depression. Journal subscribers who read German gained a different sense of the firm and its mission than the international readership, who only looked at the pictures. Beyond Vienna, artists such as Dard Hunter, a designer for the Roycrofters, an arts and crafts workshop based in upstate New York, and Josep Pallau Oller, a textile designer in Barcelona, derived stylistic inspiration purely through the photographs, without reading the German texts.[42] In contrast, Austrian and German audiences read about the social and ethical ramifications of the decorative arts and learned about the Wiener Werkstätte's role in redefining design and taste. Thanks to this extensive publicity, the Viennese style of decorative arts quickly became instantly recognizable around the world.

Modern Ambitions: Culture, Power, and Identity

Established as a small-scale luxury goods producer, the Wiener Werkstätte quickly came to epitomize the modern Austrian style at home and abroad. Yet the firm exemplified more than just an Austrian style. The company evolved a distinctive approach to battling the ills of industrialization and modernization. In 1908, Hermann Muthesius's *The Economy of the Decorative Arts* pointed out that the Wiener Werkstätte, by focusing on unique, handmade luxury objects, was fundamentally different from German decorative arts workshops such as the Vereinigte Werkstätten für Kunst im Handwerk, which made standardized, low-cost objects accessible to the middle classes. Many of these German firms relied on "fashion intermediaries," to borrow Regina Lee Blaszczyk's concept, in response to consumer demands.[43]

Figure 6.1. Interior of the Wiener Werkstätte showroom in the Neustiftgasse 32, Vienna, Austria. Photograph published in the first Wiener Werkstätte issue in *Deutsche Kunst und Dekoration* 15 (1905): 4. Courtesy Fine Arts Library, Harvard University.

At the turn of the twentieth century, Austria lagged behind Germany and other European powers in its industrial, economic, and military strength. Because industrialization came late to Austria, the nation could not rival England or Germany, which prospered by making and exporting inexpensive consumer products. Austria-Hungary, a multiethnic empire headed by the aging Habsburg dynast Franz Josef and the state's extensive bureaucracy, exemplified in its political and economic development one of the "not-so-modern empires of not-so-European Europe."[44] By promoting handmade goods—both luxury wares, such as those produced by the Wiener Werkstätte, and peasant arts from the underdeveloped regions of the empire—Austria could assert dominance in one field: *culture*.

This emphasis on culture helped Austria forge an identity distinct from Germany. For too long, contemporaries complained, Austria had been mistaken for Australia, or worse, considered a German province.[45] In the early 1870s, Rudolf von Eitelberger posited the strategy of using cultural production, especially in the decorative arts, to bolster Austria's standing in the world.[46] As the first head of the new Austrian Museum of Art and Industry, Eitelberger had a stake in seeing the decorative arts recognized for their national importance. In an 1871 lecture, he asserted that Viennese goods were not only achieving a reputation abroad for their artistic quality, but they were also successfully penetrating world markets and helping improve the imperial economy.[47] Eitelberger also made another key observation central to the promotion of modern art by the Habsburg bureaucracy and the worldwide acceptance of these products after 1900. He claimed that Austria's "most dangerous" rival, and perhaps its "only enemy," was France, the European nation renowned for its luxury goods and fine fashions.[48] By 1914, however, modernist Germany and Austria had dethroned France in the kingdom of consumer goods. By then, German exports of home furnishings, fabrics, and the dyes and chemicals used in textile production dominated European markets, while Austria's innovative designs and excellent taste circulated throughout the world.[49]

The Imperial-Royal Austria Exhibition, held at Earl's Court in London from May to October 1906, put Austrian arts, crafts, and industry on show. The exhibition had been organized primarily by chambers of commerce from throughout Austria with explicit commercial goals.[50] Unlike international exhibitions, which rose to prominence in the nineteenth and early twentieth centuries by placing nations in competition with each other, this exhibition showcased Austria alone. It exhibited Austria's ambitions to escape economic and cultural marginalization, showcasing quality products made by the country's art workshops and manufactories. The official guidebook stressed that Austrian products were "not to be cheaper owing to the large number turned out, but are artistically and tastefully made and intended for art lovers."[51] Over a million visitors saw the Austrian exhibit in London.

The exhibition is best known today as the impetus for the book *Art-Revival in Austria*, which chronicled the nation's advances in painting, sculpture, architecture, and design. More than just a pattern book of new styles, this volume, published by the seminal English journal *The Studio*, put Viennese art before a wide English-speaking audience.[52] For the first time, middle-class consumers in Great Britain and the United States could read about the Wiener Werkstätte, rather than look only at the pictures. The exhibition had far greater significance for the development and reception of modern art and design in Austria, however. It demonstrated how the Austrian government, in association with various trade and cultural organizations, tried to shape international opinion about the empire's art, culture, and manufacturing goods. London was an apt venue because Austrians saw England as the ultimate measure of modernity.[53] For the exhibition's organizers, success in London meant success in the modern Western world. Most important, the exhibit testified to the Wiener Werkstätte's acceptability to elites in both Austria and England. The Wiener Werkstätte thereby became a central figure in the Habsburg government's attempts to promote Austria as a modern cultural power.

Moser remembered the London exhibition as a breakthrough moment for the Wiener Werkstätte.[54] From more than five hundred exhibitors, representing all aspects of the empire's artistic and industrial production, the *London Times* applauded the Wiener Werkstätte as the "typical" embodiment of the new Austrian style.[55] In Vienna, the *Neue Freie Presse*, widely regarded as Europe's best newspaper,[56] celebrated the Wiener Werkstätte's success by translating and reprinting the article from the *Times*. Both the *Times* and the *Neue Freie Presse* stressed the originality of the Wiener Werkstätte's goods on display, noting that for "persons who combine wealth with taste they offer an unusual opportunity, which has been appreciated by the King among other purchasers."[57]

The *Neue Freie Presse* excitedly reported that Edward VII, who ruled England from 1901 to 1910, had praised the Wiener Werkstätte's displays and promised to continue patronizing the firm.[58] An exceptionally fashionable man, Edward and Queen Alexandra, one of Europe's great aristocratic beauties, had a court known for its modishness, unlike that of his stodgy son George V.[59] According to the official Austrian report, the king purchased objects from the firm's metal workshops, including a silver box and candelabras.[60]

Edward was not the only European monarch to own objects made by the Wiener Werkstätte. The London exhibit showed a gold box from Emperor Franz Josef's private collection. This stupendous "Emperor's Box" had been a gift from the employees of the Skoda Steel Works in Pilsen (now Plzeň, Czech Republic) to commemorate the royal visit to the factory.[61] Despite their animosity toward Secessionist art and Jugendstil, the exhibition's organizers hailed the Emperor's Box as "a masterpiece of modern decorative arts."[62] The Wiener Werkstätte's reception in London showed that modernist Viennese design was fully compatible with imperial taste.

The Imperial-Royal Austria Exhibition positioned Austria as fulfilling the ambitions of power through culture. British and Austria commentators recognized that Austria's strength was not in cheap, mass-produced goods, but in the artistic quality of its products. In this way, Austrian design did not threaten British economic interests. As one critic noted, "This is because the exhibition did not set out to undersell the English in its own specific products, but instead invited them to look at the novel and the new that was being so richly offered in Austrian art workshops and factories."[63] Representatives from across the political spectrum, including liberals, Christian socialists, and German nationalists, accepted Austria's role as a cultural power, a *Kulturstaat*, rather than as a military or industrial leader.[64]

Though the exhibition fulfilled its political agenda, it had limited long-term commercial benefits. The *London Times* described the spectacle favorably, the show as a "place 'go shop or sight see.'"[65] But a report to the Austro-Hungarian Chamber of Commerce complained that Austrian businessmen were not prepared to fill orders from English customers, carping that they generally wasted the opportunities opened by the exhibition.[66] For the Wiener Werkstätte, this was certainly the case. The firm had no outlets or retailers in London, forfeiting any potential sales in the English market at the time.

Nearly a decade later, Xavier Marcel Boulestin planned to sell Wiener Werkstätte objects in London. A Frenchman better known to history for his culinary skills, Boulestin was an astute observer of popular taste with an eye toward profit. He noticed that English travelers to Paris, in search of something new, "thought nothing of spending six to eight pounds for one cushion—some bought several."[67] From his London flat, he began selling textiles and designs by Paul Poiret's Maison Martine, a workshop dedicated to decorative arts, along with other examples of modern design. Boulestin decorated the flat "in the modern manner" to prove to others "that rooms of this kind could be agreeable to look at and live in."[68] As he explained, "My stock was small, but modern and first-rate. I had made no concessions," carrying textiles, wallpapers, and various accessories from the Poiret's Maison Martine, the modernist French decorators André Groult, and Iribe, as well as examples of African art, which was all the rage in Europe and influenced a broad span of artists.[69] In collaboration with Poiret, Boulestin planned to open a new London shop, Modern Decoration, in October 1914, in which they planned to stock designs by the Wiener Werkstätte and from other German and French firms.[70] World War I put an end to those plans and to British interest in Viennese design.

While British consumers viewed Viennese design in a commercial setting, Austrian consumers found the Wiener Werkstätte's works displayed as high art. In Vienna, shows at the Galerie Miethke and the firm's own display room resembled modernist exhibition spaces like those Hoffmann created for the Secession. The popularity of the Wiener Werkstätte's metalwares at the 1906 London exhibition suggests that Viennese consumers may have been put off by the firm's approach to marketing at home. Designers had more success reaching middle-class consumers elsewhere by marketing their furnishings as trade goods rather than art, and by using sales venues such as department stores, mass marketers, and catalogs, which were more familiar than galleries.[71]

When the firm opened in 1903, its sole point of distribution in Vienna was at its showrooms, which shared the facilities with the workshops, in the city's seventh district. Because these showrooms were located outside the concentrated luxury shopping district in the city center and the egalitarian stores on the Mariahilferstrasse, the firm did not attract casual shoppers and was only visited by those who intentionally sought it out.[72] In 1907, the Wiener Werkstätte opened a salesroom on the Graben, Vienna's Fifth Avenue, followed in 1911 by a shop for fashion and textiles next door. It opened another fashion store on the Kärtnerstrasse, another major shopping street, in 1916.[73]

The Hohenzollern Kunstgewerbehaus, a department store in Berlin, had sold Wiener Werkstätte objects since 1904; other German outlets followed.[74] By 1916, the Wiener Werkstätte's products were widely distributed. In Germany they were sold by more than 150 shops in eighty cities. Retailers across the Habsburg empire and in Switzerland, the Netherlands, and Scandinavia carried these Viennese products.[75] In Berlin alone, seven shops carried Wiener Werkstätte objects. These retailers included the KaDeWe (Kaufhaus des Westens) and Hermann Gerson's department store, which had a strong relationship with French couturier Paul Poiret in the prewar period through its buyer, Hermann Freudenberg.[76] Increasingly, the firm also advertised as well, at first through advertisements placed by shops stocking their textiles.[77] Later it advertised in a broad range of newspapers, such as the *Neue Freie Presse*, the German society magazine *Elegante Welt*, and the Viennese fashion magazine *Wiener Mode*.[78]

From about 1913, Americans did not have to travel to Europe to buy Wiener Werkstätte products. In New York Joseph P. McHugh's Popular Shop, B. Russell Herts, and Rudolph Rosenthal all imported and sold the items.[79] The availability of Wiener Werkstätte textiles and housewares nearly ten years before the firm opened a shop on New York's Fifth Avenue in 1922 testifies to the firm's growing international prominence and appeal.

Fashion, Not Reform

French couturier Paul Poiret played a key role in spreading news about the Wiener Werkstätte abroad in the 1910s. Thanks to Poiret's interest, fashions and fabrics produced by the Wiener Werkstätte did not suffer the fate of reform dress, remaining a marginal style worn only by bohemians seeking alternatives to Parisian fashion. Instead, Viennese design became associated with the most fashionable advanced Parisian styles. As we have seen, the Wiener Werkstätte enjoyed substantial press coverage in the Viennese newspapers and German art and decorating magazines. In the 1910s, the Wiener Werkstätte began appearing in a broader range of international fashion and society magazines, even attracting the attention of leading American publications such as the *New York Times*, *Vogue*, and *Harper's Bazaar*.

In 1911, the firm established its couture workshop under the leadership of Wimmer-Wisgrill, dubbed the "Poiret of Vienna" by a German newspaper.[80] From the Wiener Werkstätte's first couture collection in 1911, Wimmer looked toward stylish French fashion rather than the German tradition of reform dress (Figure 6.2). Marie Gelber, who reviewed the fashion show for *Wiener Mode*, admitted that it was the French influence that made Wimmer's

Figure 6.2. Eduard Josef Wimmer-Wisgrill, Tea Gown, c. 1913, produced for the Wiener Werkstätte. Photograph from *Deutsche Kunst und Dekoration* 33 (1913–14): 300. Courtesy Fine Arts Library, Harvard University.

gowns appealing to Viennese women.[81] The Wiener Werkstätte's couture department did not create a radically new look or pioneer new cuts, handling of the fabric, or treatment of the body. Nevertheless Gelber explained, Hoffmann and Wimmer's designs were important for Viennese fashion. Together they "turned word into deed." "Without completely departing from the dominant trend of fashion," Gelber wrote, fashion designers at the Wiener Werkstätte had "created something completely original and new."[82] Vienna could be proud of the firm's venture into fashion.

In October 1912, a fashion exhibit in Berlin called the Galerie der Moden, or Gallery of Fashion, bolstered hopes that the Wiener Werkstätte could turn Vienna into a fashion center. The *Neue Freie Presse* reported that the Wiener Werkstätte was the "hit of the exhibition," despite its uncertain reception in the first few days. Success was sealed when German Crown Princess Cecilie ordered several of the firm's gowns, prompting Berlin's fashionable society to follow suit.[83] Like Edward VII, Cecilie was a trendsetter. A few months later, *Elegante Welt* named her the "best dressed princess in Germany."[84]

An international committee had organized the Gallery of Fashion, held at Hohenzollern Kunstgewerbehau, an important decorative arts store in Berlin that often held exhibitions of the latest designs. In October 1904, it had given the Wiener Werkstätte its first solo exhibition.[85] The Gallery of Fashion exhibition, at which all objects were for sale, showcased fashion magazines and the latest clothing designs by Poiret, the House of Redfern, Mariano Fortuny, the Wiener Werkstätte, and other fashion houses from throughout Europe.[86] The exhibit aimed to show that "artistic ideas can also be realized in the realm of fashion."[87] Although some of the organizers had supported the reform dress movement, they now embraced the commercial fashions produced by Parisian couturiers. Fashionable aesthetics replaced moral and ethical concerns among Austria and Germany's top critics, producers, and consumers of the decorative arts. Indeed, by 1910, the reform dress movement in Germany was dead. Magazines like *Deutsche Kunst und Dekoration*, which in the early 1900s had only shown reform clothes by local German producers and seamstresses, now reproduced apparel and accessories by Poiret, the House of Béschoff-David, and the Wiener Werkstätte.[88] When German writers talked about international fashion, they meant fashionable dress as defined by haute couture.

The Gallery of Fashion's organizers hoped to inspire German manufacturers to produce stylish mass-market apparel that would appeal to consumers. In turn, manufacturers faced an uphill battle, trying to convince consumers that German fashions were as good as French designs. Throughout Germany and Austria, the clothing industry—designers, manufacturers, and retailers—established trade organizations with the mission of convincing women to buy locally. In Vienna, comparable efforts dated to 1888, with the formation of the Wiener Mode Club (Viennese Fashion Club) and the magazine *Wiener Mode*. Sadly, little progress had been made as late as 1914. In Vienna as in Berlin, the *New York Times* reported that "women who cared to rank as well-dressed were still loyal to Paris fashions."[89]

Wiener Werkstätte and the Challenge to French Fashion

The outbreak of war on 1 August 1914 challenged Parisian hegemony in fashion. Within three weeks, Berta Zuckerkandl sounded the war cry, "freedom from Paris," in the Viennese paper *Wiener Allgemeine Zeitung*. On the front page of this leading liberal newspaper, Zuckerkandl announced: "With a victorious feeling of power and fulfillment, the Austrian nation, its audience and producers, frees itself from the bands of centuries of dependence on France's culture."[90] Other critics in Austria and Germany soon echoed Zuckerkandl's call.[91]

The importance of creating an independent fashion, in fact, pervaded the public discourse in the early days of the war.[92] Anton Jaumann, an early supporter of the Wiener Werkstätte, explained this position in *Deutsche Kunst und Dekoration*.[93] Creating a German fashion free of French influence was "a national, a socio-economic event of the greatest importance."[94] Critics transferred the same economic and political importance to fashion as they had ascribed to the decorative arts during the early twentieth century. Moreover, German and Austrian decorative arts had already beaten France, as Zuckerkandl stressed.[95] One anonymous critic asked why it should be any different with dresses.[96]

Max Eisler urged Viennese fashion producers to seize the moment. In the *Fremdenblatt*, the newspaper of the Habsburg foreign ministry, Eisler implored the fashion industry to redirect German taste and German gold away from Paris. Now, he wrote, "all of our charming weaknesses now are virtues. No one abroad will dispute our right as the path-setters when it comes to German fashion. Vienna must take the lead which has almost been deposited on our doorstep."[97] For Eisler, moreover, Hoffmann was the only person who could fulfill this task. German critics concurred. Rudolf Bosselt, a professor of fashion in Magdeburg, explained in a lecture: "Precisely the Wiener Werkstätten . . . , which—in contrast to French—we can regard as a home of German art, can be presented as the pillar of our greatest hopes."[98] In fact, Bosselt's students designed garments closely modeled on the Wiener Werkstätte, designs which in turn looked, even after the war broke out, toward Paris (Figure 6.3).

The Wiener Werkstätte's successes abroad—with Poiret in Paris, the exhibits in London and Berlin, and in American fashion magazines like *Vogue*—made it the best bet for the future of German fashion. Most established critics who had written extensively on fashion before the war recognized that the only way for German fashion to be truly successful was to be international.[99] Moreover, if German fashion was to play an economic role, it must also appeal to women in Allied and neutral countries. Ernst Friedmann, co-owner of the Hohenzollern Kunstgewerbehaus, explained that a true German fashion would only exist if it was desired and demanded by women of other countries.[100] Zuckerkandl, the first to use the phrase "freedom from Paris" in relation to fashion, agreed with Friedmann. She cautioned Austrians to resist the impulse to wear traditional costume or reform dress, even through these antifashions were a mark of patriotism in their rejection of Paris.[101] Rather than minimize the similarities between French fashion and the Wiener Werkstätte, which had been a dominant feature of its reception, Friedmann stressed the Wiener Werkstätte's continuing allegiance to French standards. He insisted that the Wiener Werkstätte "shows us the way which we also must travel for the time being. . . . It would be impossible to suddenly to want or make something completely from what the last season brought us."[102]

Stylistically, the Wiener Werkstätte's fashions produced shortly after the war began did not differ from reigning French styles. Its designs followed the silhouettes and styles emanating from Paris more than local trends. Wider skirts supplanted Poiret's narrow silhouette, which had dominated fashion magazines since 1908.[103] In late 1913 fashion editors from Paris to Berlin heralded the wider silhouette as a natural evolution from the minaret tunic and lampshade skirt.[104] Even Wiener Werkstätte dresses with overtly nationalist names, like Wimmer's Old Vienna and Maria Theresa, had a wide silhouette.[105] The Wiener Werkstätte remained true to the fashionable silhouette, as ever determined in Paris.

As critics from Vienna to New York agreed, the Wiener Werkstätte's distinctive contribution to fashion was in its brightly patterned fabrics.[106] In

Figure 6.3. Student design from class of Rudolf Bosselt, Kunstgewerbeschule Magdeburg, modeled on Wiener Werkstätte design. *Die Kunst* 38 (1918): 189. Courtesy Fine Arts Library, Harvard University.

fact, French couturier Poiret so liked these Wiener Werkstätte textiles that he purchased large quantities to use in his own designs.[107] Poiret even dressed his wife Denise in a Wimmer-designed silk during a visit to Vienna in November 1911.[108] Textiles marked the Wiener Werkstätte's greatest international success, and they were the most broadly distributed items in Europe and America. *Elegante Welt* suggested Wiener Werkstätte fabrics as the perfect, patriotic alternative to those of Liberty of London.[109]

Ironically, the features of the Wiener Werkstätte's fashions that attracted international praise dampened the firm's popularity at home among middle-class consumers. *Wiener Mode*, the local fashion magazine, had always been skeptical of the Wiener Werkstätte, which was too French and too advanced for its taste. In 1916, its critic Marie Gelber alluded to the firm's problems with pleasing local women, noting that Viennese women were finally warming up to the Wiener Werkstätte.[110] Although the firm took advantage of the war to consolidate its position, greater acceptance did not mean the company cast aside its founding ideals. The Wiener Werkstätte continued to produce international fashion, combining the silhouettes of Paris and distinctive Austrian textiles to define its own version of modern Viennese style.

Modern Style for Austria

As the driving force behind Austria's leading role in the decorative arts in the early twentieth century, the Wiener Werkstätte proved that in the area of culture, at least, Habsburg Austria could not only rival, but innovate and even dominate. The rivalry with Paris in luxury goods and fashion continued into the 1920s. In 1925 Hoffmann designed the Austrian pavilion at the Exposition des Arts Industriels et Décoratifs, which the French government mounted in Paris to regain France's role as the center of modern design.[111]

After World War I, Vienna's social, political, and economic situation dramatically changed, but the Wiener Werkstätte retained its position as the symbol of Austrian style. In celebration of the firm's twenty-fifth anniversary, Austrian commerce minister Hans Schürff explained that the Wiener Werkstätte was more than just a firm, it was an idea.[112] For the founders and for Austrian and German critics in general, the Wiener Werkstätte had always been about the ideas expressed by the decorative arts, rather than commercial success or popular appeal. The firm never made a profit and gained acceptance only after many years of struggle. The Wiener Werkstätte did not follow mass taste, but created its own vision of modern style for Austria.

CHAPTER SEVEN

American Fashions for American Women:
The Rise and Fall of Fashion Nationalism

Marlis Schweitzer

"IT LOOKS FOR the first time as if a distinct movement toward American-designed fashions for American woman were under way," the Philadelphia-based *Ladies' Home Journal* declared in 1913. Heralding a "new era of woman's dress," the *Journal* urged its readers to reject the whims of Paris design and embrace clothing made by those who understood what it meant to be American.[1] Although it was not the only advocate of "American Fashions for American Women" in the prewar years, the *Journal* was one of the loudest and most persuasive voices. Yet an optimistic outlook was not enough to transform consumer habits. It would be another three decades before fashion nationalists could convince Americans to choose domestic over foreign products. Despite this failure, the American Fashions campaign accomplished much more than previous accounts have suggested, sparking public debate about the possibility if not the reality of a full-fledged American fashion industry.

The resurgence of fashion nationalism in the prewar period was closely linked to the government's protectionist stance on trade. Analysis of the tensions surrounding women's fashion suggests that the leading proponents of economic nationalism were deeply troubled by American women's consumption habits, including their preference for Paris fashions. Indeed, as cultural historian Kristin Hoganson observes, while government officials, business leaders, and other cultural arbiters urged citizens to "buy American," many middle- and upper-class female consumers viewed themselves as members of an "imagined community of dress" that extended beyond national borders.[2] These women embraced a transnational aesthetic that was at odds with traditional American values favoring simplicity and moral rectitude. More than aesthetics was at stake, however. This cosmopolitan vision of modernity undermined the development of a national fashion industry and called into question the very definition of "American woman."

Fashion and business historians have paid little attention to the rise of American fashion nationalism in the early twentieth century. Most costume histories point to the 1914 closure of the Paris salons and *Vogue*'s subsequent "Fashion Fête"—a runway show organized by editor Edna Woolman Chase featuring clothes by Henri Bendel, Bergdorf-Goodman, and other native designers—as "the beginning of America's stylistic coming-of-age."[3] Others cite the promotion of Hollywood leisurewear in the 1920s or the "American Look" developed by Dorothy Shaver at Lord & Taylor in the 1930s as the real beginning of American fashion.[4] Studies that acknowledge the prewar American "revolt" against Paris tend to point to isolated incidents of fashion nationalism, weaving a narrative of inevitable failure that overlooks many of the exciting, if brief, collaborations among editors, dressmakers, pattern companies, and consumers.[5] A thorough examination of fashion nationalism prior to World War I suggests that efforts to promote American designs were hardly haphazard. Rather, early twentieth-century fashion nationalism was a carefully coordinated and persistent movement led by prominent men, notably *Ladies' Home Journal* editor Edward Bok. A gendered struggle over cultural and aesthetic power was a driving force behind the campaign. Whereas women seemed to have little difficulty reconciling their "Americanness" with foreign clothing styles, a growing number of American men feared that such consumption would erode the foundations of American society.

These competing and highly gendered visions of modernity help explain why early twentieth-century fashion nationalism failed. Although the movement managed to attract the public's attention and generate considerable discussion about fashion's role in American society, proponents of American fashion had trouble convincing female consumers to give up the "Paris idea." Compared to the shocking, modern creations of avant-garde Parisian couturiers, the conservative, practical designs promoted by American fashion nationalists seemed unimaginative and dull, hardly the clothes to define the modern American woman.

"It Was America That Made Paris"

American's sustained interest in Paris fashion dates back to the early nine-teenth century, when dressmakers and society women collected miniature porcelain dolls dressed in French gowns. Shipped from Paris twice a year in accordance with the changing fashion seasons, these "model" dolls gave dressmakers and their wealthy clients the necessary visual cues to design clothes in the newest French modes.[6] Beginning in 1830, *Godey's Lady's Book* facilitated the fashion education of middle-class American women by pub-lishing hand-colored fashion plates.[7] Similarly, international stage stars played an important role as disseminators of information about Paris fashion. In 1855, the French tragedienne Rachel arrived in the United States with forty-two trunks of Parisian gowns. At her first Saturday matinee in Boston, an audience "almost exclusively composed of women" filled the house, hop-ing to get a glimpse of her wardrobe.[8]

By the early 1890s, American socialites traveled annually to Paris to see the new collections and order custom-made wardrobes.[9] Reporters stationed in Paris avidly followed their exploits at home and abroad and filled society pages with vivid descriptions of their latest purchases.[10] Average women across the United States became increasingly fashion savvy thanks to these newspaper accounts. American department stores further fueled interest in French fashion, opening buying offices in Paris in the 1880s and showcasing original imported designs.[11] By 1900, the idea if not the reality of Paris fash-ion was present in the mind of most American female consumers and the words "from Paris" held considerable cachet.[12]

Yet when a group of avant-garde designers, led by Paul Poiret, began reinventing the female silhouette in dramatic, controversial ways, the hype surrounding Paris fashion reached an unprecedented level. Influenced by modern art and dance, these couturiers tested the limits of fashion, creating bizarre styles that reshaped the look and movement of the female body. The first major breakthrough occurred in 1908 when Poiret abandoned the S-curve corset and introduced a tubular, high-waisted silhouette that evoked the Napoleonic era's Empire style.[13] Gone were the puffed sleeves, bell-like skirt, and voluptuous curves of the 1900 ideal. In its place was a sleeker, form-fitting style—the sheath gown—that emphasized the legs and lower torso over the breasts and hips. This simplification and streamlining of the female silhouette marked the invention of the modern body.[14]

The new sheath gown had a high slit that shockingly offered a glimpse of the calf and upper thigh, usually accentuated by brightly colored stockings. In addition, the sheath was worn with sheer undergarments. A woman walking in the wind gave men passersby a peak of the body beneath.[15] With the sheath, we see the emergence of a thin ideal and the corresponding emphasis on maintaining a slender figure through diet and exercise.[16] Although women continued to wear corsets under their sheath dresses, the tight lacing necessitated by the S-curve line now gave way to a very different encasement of the female body, one that produced a "hipless, almost waistless figure."[17]

The sheath's focus on the lower half of the female body also reflected changing attitudes toward female sexuality. While the Victorian hourglass figure highlighted the maternal and reproductive aspects of a woman's body, the modern sheath emphasized the legs, transforming the wearer into a mobile and potentially dangerous sexual creature.[18] Whereas the original Empire style allowed for a certain looseness around the mid-section, the slim, streamlined look of the twentieth-century revival connoted youth, mobility, and a freer form of sexual expression.[19] In this respect, the sheath gown fortified the controversial theories of sexologist Havelock Ellis, who argued that women were not timid, passionless creatures (as asserted by nineteenth-century medicine), but passionate, desiring individuals, fully capable of experiencing sexual pleasure for its own sake.[20] As Victorian ideals of modesty began yielding to modern sensibilities, the sheath's explicit exposure of female limbs and its tight encasement of the torso aroused both fascination and horror.

The sheath gown was but one example of the radical styles promoted by Parisian couturiers like Paul Poiret, who took great pleasure in remodeling the female body each season.[21] Two extreme fashions took Orientalist inspiration: the Minaret skirt (a short skirt reminiscent of a lamp shade), and the *jupe culotte* (a variation on harem pants).[22] Poiret's most infamous design was arguably the hobble skirt of 1910, a tubular style that resembled the sheath gown with the exception of one crucial detail. In place of the side slit, Poiret placed a tight band around the knees, restricting rather than facilitating movement. "Yes, I freed the bust, but I shackled the legs," he later observed, presumably pleased with the irony of his design.[23] While Poiret was perhaps the most extreme avant-garde couturier, he was certainly not alone. Competitors Jacques Doucet, Jeanne Paquin, and others also drew inspiration from modern art in defining the look of the modern woman.[24]

Poiret and his competitors used new promotional techniques to publicize the female silhouette to an international audience. These self-styled "artists" commissioned visual and graphic artists to sketch designs and create labels, sent mannequins to highly publicized events like the Longchamps races, and collaborated with theater directors. Using such strategies, Poiret and his cohorts became household names in towns and cities around the world. They aimed, as art historian Nancy Troy explains, to sell dresses to wealthy clients while stimulating interest in their designs among mass-market garment manufacturers, retailers, and consumers.[25] These designers, especially Paquin and Poiret, recognized the vast potential of the American market and organized month-long lecture tours of the United States to attract consumers.[26]

Although Paris couturiers excelled at self-promotion, their success owed much to the support of American businesses: department stores, Broadway theaters, fashion magazines, and daily newspapers. With glowing copy, countless illustrations, window displays, and fashion shows, these commercial institutions sold the idea of Paris to American consumers. Their influence was so great that James B. Blaine, head designer for New York's Thurn, a retailer and importer of Paris fashion, declared that Paris was "American made."[27]

Elite American department stores made much of their relationships with designers like Poiret and Paquin. Gimbel Brothers and R. H. Macy & Company in New York and John Wanamaker in Philadelphia imported gowns from the leading couture houses each season, which they displayed in elaborate fashion spectacles that rivaled lavish Broadway productions like the Ziegfeld Follies. In 1913, the three stores staged exotic fashion shows complete with dramatic plots to showcase their recent acquisition of Poiret's Minaret designs.[28] American consumers stood in line for hours to gawk at the latest Poiret invention.

Women also visited Broadway theaters, attending matinees or evening performances to see French styles on display. To enhance their public profiles, female performers embraced Paris fashion in all of its extremity, modeling the most bizarre styles onstage and off. Actresses performed an important service for their female fans, providing them with a chance to see the new styles worn by fashionable woman abroad. In 1909 the fashion magazine *Harper's Bazaar* noted that at the theater "as nowhere else" women could "observe the effect and mark the shortcomings of a new style of gown."[29] Women of all ages attended the theater with notebooks in hand, ready to sketch styles that caught their eye.

The American press likewise contributed to the Paris mythos, offering readers constant updates on the latest style innovations. "With their accounts of Poiret and Dusset, Paquin and Cheruit, the newspapers have bewitched and hypnotized women," grumbled one complainant in the *New York Times*.[30] By the turn of the century, most major magazines and newspaper had fashion bureaus or correspondents in Paris, who reported on the new styles weeks before the shipments arrived in the United States. Innovations in communication and transportation, including the telephone, telegraph, and steam-powered ocean liners, further facilitated the transmission of design ideas between Paris and New York.[31] *Vogue* and *Harper's Bazaar* vied for the exclusive rights to publish haute couture designs, while the *New York World* and other newspapers enticed readers with pages of colored fashion sketches and *illustrations* of fabric swatches.[32] Newspaper sketches, however, rarely resembled actual Paris fashions. Instead, New York-based fashion syndicates paid illustrators without any training or experience in fashion $15 to $30 per week to create sketches, which they then circulated to newspapers nation-wide.[33] Readers who believed they were learning about Paris fashion in fact saw interpretations by an American sketch artist.

American dressmakers adopted French names and airs to attract local clients, while ready-to-wear clothing manufacturers and department stores across the country used imitation Paris labels to boost sales.[34] To further the French masquerade, some Northeastern dressmakers closed shop each sum-mer to give the impression that they were in Paris. In fact many simply visited New England's coastal resorts to watch high society at play. The fashions they later advertised as "direct from Paris" were actually adaptations of gowns seen at summer social events.[35] In 1909, a group of dressmakers, desperate to offer "Paris originals," participated in risky smuggling operations in an effort to avoid the 60 percent tariff on imported French gowns, coats, and gloves.[36]

Ironically, then, American cultural institutions, publications, and dress-makers—perhaps more than the Paris couturiers—shaped American percep-tions of Paris fashion. This celebration of Paris encouraged women from New York to San Francisco to view themselves as part of an international style community, as the American equivalents of European mavens. Although a Poiret sheath was beyond their means, these women imitated the styles they read about in the papers, sometimes managing to wear comparably flashy ensembles made by a clever dressmaker or purchased from a department store or pushcart vendor.[37] Jewelry and other factory-made accessories including hats, pins, scarves, and shoes provided another way to signal fashion knowl-edge. Emulation therefore allowed American women to possess and exude the cultural authority that, in many cases, lay beyond their grasp.[38]

Of course the question remains whether average American women actually. wore Parisian styles at their most extreme. While actresses and society women apparently took pleasure in shocking the crowds, most women seem to have *adapted* styles like the sheath or the hobble skirt to suit their lifestyles. In October 1908, one pattern magazine, *The Designer*, acknowledged that, while "No one really professes to admire the style in its extreme development, slashed at the side to show the silken tights or hose," less radical variations of the style were nevertheless "graceful and picturesque."[39] With careful modifications, Paris fashions could indeed suit American women.

American Fashions for American Women

Not all Americans greeted Paris fashion with enthusiasm, however. In fact some viewed the American fascination with a transnational aesthetic with growing suspicion and fear. In 1908 the Reverend W. A. Bartlett of Chicago's First Congregational Church condemned the new styles, drawing comparisons between the fashion-obsessed young woman and the alcoholic. "This passion for dress becomes as inexorable as the drink habit," he argued. "It takes the mind of the young from good books, it induces an artificial life, and the whole trend of it is away from stability of character and success in study or work."[40] For Bartlett, fashion threatened to transform American women into sinful hedonists, more concerned with appearance than spiritual well-being. More disturbing, fashion would divert women's attention from the domestic realm, undermining the stability of American society, initiating cultural decline and "race suicide."[41]

Economic nationalism and cultural concerns about Parisian hegemony were hardly new. Indeed, the early twentieth-century fashion critique reiterated ideas dating back to the American Revolution. Participants in the Boston Tea Party not only rejected British imports, but they also encouraged their fellow colonists to adopt an American style of dress. For these patriots, independence meant buying local goods and looking "American."[42] In the Victorian era, antifashion critics prioritized women's health and mobility over nationalism per se. During the 1850s, suffrage advocates shocked bourgeois crowds by wearing bloomers, a controversial bifurcated skirt introduced by English dress reformer Amelia Bloomer.[43] These early feminists emphasized bloomers' practicality, urging women to give up cumbersome, expensive garb that inhibited physical and psychic mobility. Three decades later, proponents of aesthetic reform in dress, architecture, and interior design called upon women to abandon the restrictive, and potentially damaging, corset for loose, flowing clothing like the tea gown.[44] These early critics of Paris fashion wanted American consumers to celebrate their inner beauty, rather than indulge in outward frivolity.

One feature separating modern fashion nationalism from Victorian critiques, then, was the gender and profession of the modern reformers. The founders of the "American Fashions for American Women" campaign were upstanding, progressive businessmen associated with the nation's most respected publications. Edward Bok, self-styled crusader and editor of the *Ladies' Home Journal*, led the charge, with assistance from the *New York Times*. Drawing on melodramatic tropes, these reformers positioned themselves as valiant heroes out to rescue American women from the evil clutches of the Paris couturiers. Yet the battle for American fashion was more than an exercise in male ego. It was a coordinated attempt to reshape consumer desires in accordance with national economic interests.

Following the Panic of 1893, some American manufacturers feared that a rising tide of foreign imports would erode their competitive position in the U.S. market. One solution involved the systematic manipulation of consumer desires. Manufacturers turned to advertising agencies to build brand recognition through national ad campaigns, while retailers engaged professional artists to create eye-catching window displays using color, light, and glass.[45] To assist American industrial development, in 1897 the U.S. Tariff Commission also raised duties on many European imports. Tariff rates on fashion imports varied considerably, however, according to the particular good and its country of origin. In 1908, a member of the American Chamber of Commerce complained that the varying scale on products such as French jewelry, glass, and fancy goods made it impossible to predict how much his New York firm would be charged from year to year.[46] The Payne-Aldrich Tariff of 1909 did little to simplify matters, introducing differing rates on cotton and wool clothing that in most cases doubled the original price of the item.[47] These measures primarily affected working- and middle-class consumers, however, and despite Payne-Aldrich, imports of Paris clothing actually increased.[48] Whereas imports of French goods declined by 50 percent in general in 1910, "the value of costumes America purchased from the Parisians nearly doubled over 1909, amounting last year to $2,406,674."[49] By 1912, however, the high tariffs seemed to be having the desired effect, prompting complaints about waning sales figures from the French minister of commerce.[50]

Domestic manufacturers of readymade clothing undoubtedly benefited from the higher tariffs. Between 1870 and 1900, the garment industry experienced rapid growth; capital investment increased threefold, from $54 to $169 million, while the size of the labor force nearly doubled, from 120,000 to 206,000 workers.[51] Expanded production of women's clothing, most notably cloaks, coats, and shirtwaists, began to encroach on the traditional territory of the professional dressmaker, as more women opted for cheaper ready-to-wear clothing. Although many female consumers continued to patronize dressmakers and tailors for complicated garments like dresses and suits, by 1914 few consumers did *not* own a factory-made garment.[52]

But while domestic production and consumption of readymade women's clothing increased in this period, the *idea* of Paris was hard to shake. The clean lines and simple practicality of a readymade shirtwaist or tailored skirt could hardly compete with the allure of a Paris label. In the 1890s, American middle-class women still ordered custom-made clothes from local dressmakers, often made along Paris lines.[53] The loose-fitting styles of the 1910s, however, were easier to sew at home or in the factory.[54] This new aesthetic permitted reformers like Bok to promote American fashion simplicity. The major challenge lay in convincing American women to accept the idea of American fashion. As editor of the *Ladies' Home Journal*, Edward Bok had the perfect mechanism for spreading the word about the new American look.

At the *Ladies' Home Journal*, Bok had long been an activist editor, waging a number of reform campaigns. Whereas most nineteenth-century editors had maintained a professional distance from readers, Bok became a visible presence in the *Journal*, addressing his readers in a folksy first-person voice in a monthly editorial column.[55] With a circulation of one million in 1901, *Ladies' Home Journal* was America's most widely read women's magazine, providing Bok with a platform for reform.[56] In 1903, he joined muckrakers from *Collier's* to battle the patent-medicine industry. For three years, Bok editorialized on the evils of "quackery" and refused to publish any advertisements for patent medicines. In 1906, Bok and other crusaders claimed victory with the passage of the Pure Food and Drug Act. After this success, he continued to use the *Journal* to advocate for social reform, turning to more "controversial causes" like sex education.[57]

In October 1909, Bok thrust the *Journal's* weight behind fashion nationalism, establishing "The First Department of American Fashions for American Women."[58] Bok's decision to turn fashion nationalism into his cause celebre is not surprising, given his rags-to-riches biography. Bok viewed himself as a successful example of the melting-pot phenomenon, a European immigrant who had made it big in the promised land. From humble beginnings in Holland, Bok rose to prominence in Philadelphia's Curtis Publishing Company, growing the *Journal* into America's best-selling women's magazine. Small wonder that he would so ardently promote the advancement of American design.[59]

The first "American fashions" appeared in the *Journal*'s October and November 1909 issues, along with descriptions of sewing patterns sold by the Home Pattern Company. The first run of patterns apparently sold well, and Bok considered the fashions a "success."[60] But finding American designs for the *Journal* proved difficult. In January 1910, Bok implored readers to submit their original fashion sketches to the *Journal*, shaming his audience with the banner headline, "Are the Only Clever Women in the World in Paris?" Bok appealed to his readers' ingenuity, patriotism, and pocketbooks. "We believe that the American woman is clever enough to create her own pretty things," he explained. "But we cannot make good that belief unless the American woman helps us" by sending in her original designs. In addition to publishing the designs, Bok promised to pay the winning applicants for their assistance. "Here is a new and truly feminine way, right at home, of making money," Bok noted, associating fashion design, femininity, and domestic economy.[61]

In February 1910, Bok published twenty pictures of "American-designed hats," sketched by illustrator H. Richard Boehm, in a two-page feature in the *Journal*. The article demonstrated that it was possible for America to "originate its own fashions."[62] As the copy explained, "All of these hats are of purely American design without regard to Parisian modes; they were designed as becoming to the face of the American woman."[63] Despite Bok's claims, the sketches depicted attractive hats in foreign modes. One was a version of the new "toque" style; another, the "Spanish turban"; the third, a "simple Panama." Throughout the American Fashions campaign, Bok continued to publish fashion sketches inspired by foreign art and national dress styles, as the Watteau hat in Figure 7.1 suggests. None of the hats were revolutionary or "American," except perhaps in their emphasis on simplicity and economy.

On his editorial page, Bok boasted that that *Journal* had "found ten clever women in America," whose published hat designs showed that "all the

Figure 7.1. Edward Bok's vision of "American Fashion" did not preclude borrowing from foreign sources, as this page of Watteau hats suggests. From "American Fashions for American Women: The Watteau Hat for the American Girl," *Ladies' Home Journal* (n.d.): 33. Author's Collection.

clever women are not in Paris." Yet, with the exception of "Charles Kursm," the winning designers were only identified by their initials. As a staunch cultural conservative, Bok may have sought to protect his readers' privacy by screening out the identities of the winning women. The Victorian cult of domesticity, which revered homemaking as the pinnacle of feminine achievement, dictated limited public participation for women. Some readers may not have deemed it appropriate to see their names in print. Nonetheless, Bok encouraged further submissions: "there certainly must be more than ten [talented women designers in America]," he urged. "We hope so, for we want the help in our American Fashion Department of every American girl and woman. We want this department to come direct from the American woman. So if you have a new thought in the way of a dress, a shirtwaist, a hat, a skirt, a sleeve, or a tie, pray send it to us."[64] Bok associated the success of the

Journal's fashion campaign with female involvement, believing the designs should come from American women.

To attract new readers and enhance the *Journal's* cultural cachet, Bok publicized his American fashions campaign in other magazines. In April 1910 an advertisement in *Harper's Bazaar* invited readers to look at the *Journal's* next issue, featuring women's shirtwaists, hats, and dresses as well as children's clothing. Bok avoided alienating *Bazaar's* readership with an open attack on Paris fashion. "No More Paris Alone in Women's Clothes; but Paris with America," reads the ad's tagline, suggesting a friendly collaboration between France and the United States.[65]

In the *Journal*, however, Bok more directly appealed to nationalist sentiments, stressing the differences between French and American women. Americans had "a New World cleverness" lacking among the French, he wrote in October 1910. "Above all, we have a knowledge of the needs of our own people" that other nations lacked.[66] Bok challenged the artistic supremacy of the Paris couturiers, arguing that their designers were historicist. Likewise, American designers could adapt historical clothing styles to meet the needs of contemporary consumers.[67]

Bok's detractors claimed that American Fashions for American Women was nothing more than an attempt to sell patterns. "Mr. Bok's business, next to selling magazines, is selling patterns," wrote *Dress* magazine editor T. L. McCready.[68] Indeed promoting patterns to home sewers seems to have been one of the driving forces behind the American Fashions campaign. In 1910, the Home Pattern Company published a four-page ad in the trade periodical *Dry Goods* touting the success of *Ladies' Home Journal* patterns. "We Make American Patterns for American Merchants to sell to American Women" the ad declared, exhorting merchants to recognize fashion nationalism's potential as a "selling idea." The ad claimed the stimulus came from home dressmakers, who demanded "common-sense American designs." With the growing demand, it remained "for a great all-around woman's publication to come to the aid of its readers; and incidentally open up a rich field that even the most experienced pattern manufacturers had been too shortsighted to cultivate."[69]

Curiously, in November 1910, Bok claimed that the *Journal* "had no interest in commercial fashions—it does not own a penny's interest in any dressmaking, millinery or even pattern establishment."[70] This evidence stands at odds with the Home Pattern Company's advertisement. Certainly, selling patterns was big business for the *Ladies' Home Journal* and rivals such as *McCall's*, *Pictorial Review*, and *Delineator*. Since 1904 the Home Pattern

Company had been selling *Journal* patterns to readers, channeling royalties to the Curtis Publishing Company. The *Journal* could publish apparel designs, but it lacked the capacity to manufacture its own patterns. The business agreement between the Home Pattern Company and the *Journal* allowed Bok's magazine to compete with *McCall's* and other magazines associated with pattern companies.[71] A successful American fashions campaign promised profits to the Home Pattern Company as well as the *Journal.*

Between 1909 and 1912, the *Journal's* circulation figures rose rapidly and pattern sales increased by "hundreds of thousands." More important, the *Journal* received thousands of letters from women praising the American fashions campaign with few complaints about the absence of Paris styles.[72] But higher circulation figures and growing pattern sales were not enough for Bok, who wanted American Fashions for American Women to become national news. Fittingly, the ambitious editor turned his attention to the *New York Times.*

The *New York Times* Rallies for American Fashions

In September 1912, Bok wrote to the *New York Times*, justifying the need for an American response to recent "freakish fashions" from Paris. According to Bok, Paris couturiers had deliberately sped up the fashion cycle to pay for their "gilded salons, with enormous salary lists." Consumed by greed, these French "tradesmen" had abandoned artisanry in favor of self-aggrandizement, offering an endless stream of new fashions to support their decadent lifestyles.[73] Bok urged readers to join his campaign for American fashions, citing the popularity of the *Journal's* fashions with women across the country. "The American woman has told me, in no uncertain terms, that she wants to get through with Paris," he concluded, "and that she wants American fashions. That is all I want."[74]

Bok's lengthy epistle to the *Times* seems to have been a calculated effort to enlist male support. By 1912 the *Times* had a reputation for journalistic excellence and integrity, eschewing the flashy, yellow journalism of Joseph Pulitzer's *New York World* and William Randolph Hearst's *New York Journal.*[75] Whereas the *World* and *Journal* appealed to working-class and immigrant readers, the *Times* directed its attention toward the middle class, including white-collar workers and business executives.[76] In writing to the

Times, Bok clearly hoped to enhance the credibility of his fashion crusade by attracting support from other conservative reformers, especially men.

Bok was not disappointed. *Times* readers praised his willingness to "enter the field" in a war "against foreign freakish modes" and leading women away from French domination.[77] "I have consistently maintained, as does Mr. Bok," wrote Louis M. Fisher of the New York textile manufacturing firm A. G. Hyde and Son, "that this country has no good reason to ape foreign creators of fashion." In Fisher's eyes, Bok had proven "by facts and figures that by introducing American fashions exclusively, he has succeeded in interesting his millions of readers."[78] While some businessmen tied to the garment industry defended Parisian authority, criticizing Bok for simply modifying older Parisian models for the general public, others spoke out against the frivolity of fashion-obsessed women, attacking Paris for its stranglehold on American ideas.[79] Bok responded to these letters in the pages of the *Times* and continued to encourage readers to share his vision for the future of American fashion.[80]

In bringing his campaign to the *Times*, Bok changed the tone and terms of the debate. Instead of appealing to the creativity of female readers, he now addressed men who shared his distaste for imports and concerns about American women's susceptibility to Paris fashion. To *Times* readers, Bok depicted himself as a rational, tireless crusader waging a war against the encroaching enemy. It was his burden to rescue American women, and by extension the country, from the decadence of the Old World.

Bok further implied that American women were unfortunate dupes, pawns in the couturiers' expanding commercial empires, and victims of fashion fraud.[81] The apparel sold by Paris couturiers to American dressmakers and department store buyers were *not* the same clothes worn by respectable Parisian women. Rather, they were the clothes worn by the demimondaine. Unaware, American women were making fools of themselves, walking about in gowns created for French whores.[82]

The suggestion that couturiers were secretly encoding the bodies of American women with sexual meanings was part of Bok's rhetorical strategy to represent female consumers as enslaved victims. In line with the twin themes of freedom and liberation, Bok and other fashion nationalists invoked the trope of slavery, characterizing American women as captives who must lift "the Paris Fashion Yoke" and "break free" from the "tyranny" of the Paris "masters."[83] Fashion nationalists played into contemporary fears about "white slavery," the entrapment of young white women by foreign men for the sex trade. They depicted Paris designers as corrupt Svengalis, manipulators of feminine desires, purveyors of "freakish fashions."[84]

These repeated references to "freakish fashions" highlighted associations among antimodernist sentiment, fashion nationalism, and gender anxieties.[85] The modernist tendencies of Paul Poiret, who drew inspiration from Ballet Russe's Orientalist designs, confirmed Bok's suspicions about the decline and depravity of the Old World.[86] In another *Times* letter, Bok assessed Poiret's latest designs, calling them impractical, unfeminine, and "slouchy."[87] An editorial went further, criticizing the couturier's "freakish, tasteless, and audacious models that have been set up for admiration and received only well-deserved ridicule."[88] American women's interests in "grotesque" designs like the sheath skirt, hobble skirt, and *jupe culotte* intensified masculine fears about the effect of French decadence on American society.

Underlying this anti-Paris rhetoric was the irrational fear that "freakish" Paris designs might infect the bodies of American women, rendering them infertile. Articles targeting Paris fashion repeatedly emphasized the "racial" differences between Latin and American bodies. Writers defined the average French woman as soft, "short and thick," and "monarchical in nature and taste." In contrast, the typical American woman was tall, thin, "broad shouldered," athletic, and "republican in every essence of her being."[89] American women who wore Paris fashions thus dressed for the "wrong" body and denied their republican natures. Only American designers could create clothes suited to the physical and temperamental needs American women, while reflecting republican virtue and sobriety.

Throughout fall 1912, the *Times* demonstrated its support for American fashions with a series of editorials that denigrated Paris fashion and praised native innovation.[90] In November the newspaper congratulated itself for facilitating Bok's campaign. The *Times* coverage stimulated national interest in the American fashions debate, with trade journals in "textiles and women's wear" now "devoting much space to the discussion."[91] With *Times* support, American Fashions for American Women was no longer limited to the pages of the *Journal*. It was national news and an important issue for national debate.

To further the debate, the *Times* initiated its own "American fashions" competition in December 1912. The editors wanted "to bring the question of American fashions to an issue for the purpose of discovering to what extent we have awakened." "The *Times* competition will afford an answer to this question which will show us just where we stand to date." To encourage participation, the *Times* promised "nine cash prizes" for the best "American-designed hats and dresses."[92] Ironically, however, judges told competitors to use a color forecast for the upcoming season, presumably created in Paris.[93] Although the contest aimed to free designers from Parisian dictates, the terms set by the committee demonstrated just how difficult this would be.

Bok chaired the *Times* committee that judged the fashion contest. The close ties between these judges, and their associations with the *Journal*, suggests that Bok was the driving force behind the competition. Grosvenor K. Glenn was editor of *The Illustrated Milliner* and a strong *Journal* supporter. Fashion illustrator Abby E. Underwood and style columnist Eleanor Hoyt Brainard had both recently joined the Curtis Publishing Company to promote *Journal* patterns. Actress Annie Russell, widely celebrated for her good taste in dress, later served as one of the *Journal*'s special guest fashion editors (Figure 7.2).[94] Most likely the competition was Bok's idea, as the *Journal* had much to gain.

In February 1913, the *Times* announced the winners and published illustrations of their designs. The newspaper had received more than a thousand submissions from designers, dressmakers, and milliners across the country. The committee awarded prizes for the best evening gown, afternoon dress, and hat. Like most of the American fashions profiled in the *Journal*, the winning designs reflected the prevailing Parisian silhouette but were "American" in their use of details. Irma Campbell, an in-house designer at New York's Lord & Taylor, created a "Quaker afternoon frock" with a Quaker-style hat and a long scarf reminiscent of a Quaker apron. Southerner E. Beatrice Chisholm, also living in New York, pleased the judges with a hat inspired by cotton balls.[95] These designers successfully incorporated aspects of American history, culture, and industry into their sketches. Yet numerous critics of the "American fashions" movement snickered that adaptation was not creation. Apparently Bok still had much to do.

The Success and Failure of American Fashions for American Women

By early 1913, hundreds of American newspapers, magazines, and trade journals had embraced fashion nationalism, publishing pages of designs "made in America."[96] Department stores stocked and advertised American fashions alongside those from Paris. Retailers reported that, "for the first time within

Figure 7.2. Actress Annie Russell endorses "American Fashions for American Women" as a special guest editor for *Ladies' Home Journal*. Russell also served as a judge in the *New York Times* fashion competition. From "Famous Actresses as Fashion Editors: A Girl's Three Dresses," *Ladies' Home Journal* (September 1913): 37. Courtesy Regina Lee Blaszczyk.

their knowledge," consumers were asking for American designs. In July 1912, the *Times* announced that fashion imports, including textiles, had declined by 50 percent in winter and spring, largely a result of the American Fashions campaign.[97] Bok proudly reported to *Journal* readers: "The whole manufacturer, the retailer, the department store, the newspaper, and the public, are lining up of on the side of what all declare to be 'the new era of women's dress in America.'"[98] To Bok, American Fashions for American Women had become a "great popular movement toward sensible designs!"[99] At the October 1913 meeting of the Curtis Publishing Company's advertising department, he suggested that victory was only a matter of time. History showed that all propaganda campaigns were initially met with public "antagonism and criticism," followed by "a time of questioning and quiet," and finally a "period of adoption." Bok saw the reform effort as entering the reflective second stage. "The criticism and the antagonism have largely died out." He had hopes for a bright future.[100]

Bok may have spoken too soon. By 1913, American Fashions had become national news thanks to major newspapers like the *Times.* Yet there was reluctance and resistance among businesses that depended on the goodwill of the Paris salons. Although some expressed interest in American fashions, the nation's leading department stores and fashion magazines continued to praise the ingenuity of Parisian couturiers, fearful of losing access to their designs.[101]

Others, including supporters of American innovation, pointed to the impractical aspects of fashion nationalism. In March 1913, *Dry Goods Economist* reminded retailers that the United States did not have the requisite infrastructure or resources to overturn the Paris fashion industry. Even if American designers introduced a radical new look, "it might very well happen that the design could not be made up, for lack of suitable materials." The American textile industry made mass-market fabrics, such as cotton broadcloth and worsteds. But only a handful of American firms made silk, the high-end fabric that constituted the backbone of high fashion. The *Dry Goods Economist* solemnly noted that the garment industry's "output must . . . accord with the kinds of materials turned out by the mills."[102] Without luxury materials, innovation would falter.[103]

Native design would also fail unless designers convinced ready-to-wear manufacturers that consumers would go for a distinctive American look. "Not only must the hundreds of garment concerns, employing thousands of operatives and having a capital investment of millions of dollars, make what they feel sure the women of the country will want," the *Dry Goods Economist* wrote.[104] The trade journal concluded that "for the basic idea of his garments the American manufacturer or dressmaker goes to Paris and will continue to do so."[105] Alphonus P. Haire, managing editor of *Dress Essentials*, made similar arguments in the *Times*, pointing out that American dressmakers did not copy Paris models, but used them as the basis for their own designs.[106] Like the *Dry Goods Economist*, Haire sympathized with Bok's fashion nationalism, but was reluctant to reject Paris.

But the greatest obstacle to American Fashions for American Women was consumer reluctance to abandon Paris. Bok acknowledged this in a 1913 address to Curtis's advertising department. American apparel designs got better every year, and interest in American fashion increased annually; by 1913 more artists and designers were pleased "to stand for the American idea than ever before." The real challenge, however, was "the Paris idea" so "deeply embedded in the American woman's mind."[107] Asked if the *Journal*'s "comparatively conservative idea" of dress frustrated readers, Bok assured his audience that the *Journal* had received "thousands and thousands" of letters from readers "telling us that we were right."[108]

Two years later, Bok baldly admitted that American Fashions for American Women had failed. He told Curtis admen, "We cannot change things that are fixed in a woman's mind. A magazine cannot reform. It can awaken interests, but it is up to the public to decide. Women must decide the style." Bok still believed that "economy in dress would be the greatest thing that could happen in this country." Yet he lamented the resistance: "But there is no use trying to jam it down their throats. For some reason or other they won't have American fashions."[109]

The reasons behind Bok's reversal are unclear. He may have been discouraged by *Vogue* magazine's decision to recant its support for homegrown fashion after a brief dalliance with fashion nationalism. *Vogue* went American when the Paris salons closed in 1914, but scuttled its support once the couture houses reopened in 1915. Ultimately the campaign for American fashions failed because Bok could only do so much to change consumer preferences. The *Journal*'s conservative, practical designs failed to capture his readers' imagination, and by September 1914 the *Journal* announced that "Paquin of Paris [was] the world's greatest fashion authority."[110]

Simply put, the American modernity offered by the *Journal* was at odds with the modernity envisioned by American women. The hegemony of the Paris "invisible empire" rested on the "the desire of woman to dress similarly to those of the world's smartest society," *Current Opinion* explained.[111] Those who felt that Paris styles opened the doors to an "imagined community of dress" had little incentive to wear the *Journal*'s American Fashions for American Women.

Nevertheless, American Fashions for American Women was far from a complete failure. While Bok conceded defeat in 1915, other economic nationalists continued to push American styles and products. During World War I textile and garment manufacturers promoted American designs, while trade journals debated whether to adopt the slogan "Made in America" or "Made in U.S.A."[112] In addition many participants in the *Times* fashion competition and *Vogue*'s fête went on to establish long careers in the fashion business.[113] Although short-lived, the "American Fashions for American Women" campaign enjoyed an impressive legacy.

CHAPTER EIGHT

Coiffing Vanity: Advertising Celluloid Toilet Sets in 1920s America

Ariel Beaujot

FROM 1917 TO 1929, E. I. du Pont de Nemours & Company, the nation's largest chemical company, aggressively advertised a new celluloid product: Pyralin Toilet Ware.[1] A type of personal grooming accessory kept on the bedroom dresser, vanity sets typically consisted of a comb, brush, and hand-held mirror, with dozens of add-ons such as cuticle pushes, glove stretchers, and perfume bottles. DuPont's Pyralin brand was made from celluloid, a plastic introduced at the International Exhibition of 1862 in London. Small plastics companies made celluloid vanity sets in the early 1900s, but these consumer goods were not widely advertised until 1917, when the DuPont Company launched a national campaign for its Pyralin brand.

Drawing on advertisements, trade literature, and corporate archives, this chapter examines how DuPont's Pyralin Department modified the cultural meanings of the vanity set in an effort to expand the line's appeal to consumers. Those efforts were not entirely successful. During the early to mid-1920s, DuPont advertisements for Pyralin Toilet Ware engaged a romantic vision of American womanhood, promoting vanity sets as a reflection of feminine character. When this campaign failed to stimulate sales, DuPont took a different approach. A new Pyralin ad campaign introduced in 1928 targeted the modern woman, appealing to her wider worldview and heightened interest in fashion. DuPont also changed the look of its Pyralin line, introducing modern styling, brighter colors, and themes that tied in with interior-decorating trends. Despite these efforts, sales of DuPont vanity sets slumped, forcing the firm to seek other markets for plastics during the 1930s.

The 1920s represents a distinctive phase in the history of American manufacturing, marketing, and advertising. Business historians have shown that this decade was a transitional period between the decline of the independent craftsman and self-promoter, and the rise of the professional industrial design and marketing consultant.[2] During this time of flux, national advertising grew by leaps and bounds, as American manufacturers sought to stimulate demand for new consumer products. In this golden age of national advertising, manufacturers and advertising agencies embraced dramatic new tactics for creating desire. Rejecting Victorian advertising methods emphasizing the product's inherent qualities, advertisers in the 1920s began to sell feelings, benefits, and experiences. They replaced "reason-why" copy with "atmospheric" themes that suggested how products might transform a consumer's life.[3] In other words, 1920s advertisers attributed new meanings to their goods, using psychological ploys to engage consumers' attentions. However, these intended meanings were not always accepted by the public. The case of Pyralin Toilet Ware is an example of such an advertising failure.

Even after consistent consultation with "fashion intermediaries"—style experts, merchants, retail buyers, and other interpreters of consumer desires—firms sometimes found themselves unaware of why their products were not selling. In DuPont's case, the firm tried several strategies to promote Pyralin Toilet Ware. Women rejected these, refusing to buy vanity sets, whether in the boom years of the Jazz Age or the hard times of the Great Depression. In the end, no matter how much DuPont spent on advertising, the company found that consumers simply would not purchase goods that did not meet their needs.

DuPont Meets Pyralin

DuPont became a celluloid manufacturer via a circuitous route. The company was extraordinarily successful with smokeless gun powder, establishing a monopoly by the early 1900s. In July 1907, the U.S. Justice Department charged DuPont with "conspiracy in restraint of trade" in accordance with the Sherman Antitrust Act.[4] To avoid prosecution, DuPont managers in 1909 began a broad-based program of industrial research and corporate acquisition designed to find new applications for the company's scientific and managerial expertise. Forced to diversify in 1911, the firm decided to concentrate on products using nitrocellulose, a basic component in smokeless powder. Du-Pont began acquiring companies that used nitrocellulose to make imitation silk, artificial leather, and celluloid plastics.[5]

As it diversified into plastics, DuPont bought the Arlington Company, one of the nation's largest celluloid manufacturers, for $8 million in 1915.[6] Originally known for its high-quality celluloid collars and cuffs, this New Jersey firm had expanded into the vanity-set business when the market for these detachable fashions began to decline. In 1910, Arlington had introduced a line of vanity sets sold under the brand name "Pyralin." At the time of the merger, DuPont managers knew that Pyralin toilet accessories had been profitable for Arlington; they hoped to use the line to move into consumer markets.[7] What DuPont's managers failed to anticipate was the remarkable changeability of women's wants and needs.

Shortly after the Arlington acquisition, World War I stimulated the demand for DuPont's smokeless powder by the Allied powers and, eventually, the American military. The war made consumer products a low priority for DuPont.[8] Between 1916 and 1920, the average return on investment at the Arlington Works was only 4.3 percent, far below the anticipated 15 percent.[9] Immediately after the war, DuPont returned to the vanity-set market, newly invigorated by several wartime lessons.

DuPont's adoption of a multidivisional, decentralized management structure in September 1921 had an important effect on Pyralin. The new structure included an autonomous Pyralin Department, whose managers had oversight for all aspects of celluloid: purchasing, manufacturing, engineering, and research.[10] This unit worked closely with the Sales Department, which was in charge of selling finished articles and raw Pyralin.[11] Managers at the Pyralin Department were based at DuPont's Arlington Works in New Jersey, while the Sales Department was located at DuPont headquarters in Wilmington. The Pyralin Department and the Sales Department also collaborated with Wilmington's Advertising Department to develop new looks for Du-Pont's vanity sets and create appropriate advertising campaigns. Together, the three departments experimented with new strategies and tactics designed expressly for plastics. Even before the reorganization, Arlington managers had launched new initiatives to improve Pyralin sales. Some of these took inspiration from wartime developments.

In 1919, *DuPont Magazine*, an in-house publication for investors and employees, explained how one wartime economy measure had changed the Pyralin business. "We believe that the idea of standardization originally developed by the government as a war measure should be adopted as a permanent improvement," noted an article about Pyralin. "Therefore we have decided to produce a minimum assortment of Ivory Pyralin design in any one line to properly provide for the needs and wants of the trade."[12] DuPont's move into a standardized line was based on its careful study of customer buying patterns. Sales managers noted that consumers who had chosen less-popular designs were often unable to complete their vanity sets because not all businesses stocked every line. Between 1918 and 1921, the company fazed out moderately popular shapes and colors, keeping the most basic pattern, Plain, and creating two new designs: Du Barry and La Belle.[13] Standardization increased efficiency for both the manufacturer and retailer, eliminating inventory buildups in factory warerooms and store stockrooms. In these years DuPont proved to be an innovative company, balancing explosives production and women's accessories with relative ease. Executives in charge of Pyralin had their fingers on the pulse of consumers and merchants, allowing them to redesign the line to suit the market.

A second wartime innovation—the federal government's excess profits tax—also had an impact on DuPont's Pyralin strategy. In effect, from 1917 to 1921 this federal policy enabled businesses to lower their taxable income by deducting advertising expenses. This tax policy may have motivated DuPont managers to launch the first national advertising campaign for Pyralin in 1920.[14] The Pyralin campaign coincided with a larger advertising boom in post-World War I America. Between 1916 and 1926, national magazine advertising increased by 600 percent. Full-page color advertisements appealed to customers' hopes and dreams in a ways that had rarely been seen in prewar America. Ushered in by the benefits of the excess profits tax, the golden age of advertising had arrived.[15]

William Coyne, vice president in charge of sales, believed that the sale of fancy goods depended on consistent and widespread advertising. Sales executives encouraged DuPont's Advertising Department to develop a national advertising campaign based on the belief that "the best advertised lines sell the best."[16] The advertising campaign thus targeted consumers at both the national and local levels. Full-page color advertisements appeared in national women's magazines, such as *Vogue*, *Harper's Bazaar*, and *Vanity Fair*, reaching a total readership of eight million.[17] On the local level, promotional materials, such as window display material, counter cards, circular letters, mailing enclosures, package inserts, moving picture slides, and newspaper electrotypes, were circulated to store managers in an attempt to heighten the visibility of Pyralin vanity sets and stimulate sales.[18] Local ads, designed to be shown in movie theaters and in local papers, featured dealers' names and suggested to consumers that Pyralin retailers would provide friendly personal service.[19] By 1924 C. F. Brown, director of DuPont's Advertising Department, estimated that managers of drug stores, jewelry stores, and department stores had placed 150,000 local newspaper advertisements in cities as large as New York and as small as Alexandra, Minnesota.[20]

The Advertising Department sent trade literature to merchants offering suggestions for local promotions. One idea was a beauty contest for the local high-school prom. Customers who bought Pyralin could vote for the prettiest girl at the prom. The gorgeous winner would receive a three-piece starter set of Ivory Pyralin, compliments of the store.[21] The Advertising Department also wrote puff pieces—advertisements in the form of genuine news articles— that merchants could use in the local papers. Furthermore, the advertising staff advised retailers on how to develop special Pyralin promotions and held contests for the best window displays.[22]

The Advertising Department also attempted to influence the way in which clerks sold vanity sets to consumers. A series of pamphlets addressed clerks specializing in toilet ware, outlining sales pitches designed specifically for Ivory Pyralin.[23] One such pamphlet encouraged clerks to sell DuPont vanity sets above all other brands: "Pyralin Toiletware is a line which we know you are proud to sell. . . . It does not always sell on sight, but fairly presented, many who come to look will stay to buy."[24] The brochure presents an imaginary conversation between a clerk and a customer, offering helpful display suggestions and persuasive sales pitches. The pamphlet is a step-by-step guide for turning an indecisive browser into the proud owner of a Pyralin vanity set. By targeting the sales clerk, the Advertising Department reinforced the messages of the national advertising campaign with friendly personal service at the point of sale.

The Advertising Department gathered promotional suggestions from local merchants and integrated these into trade literature so that other merchants could benefit from this experience.[25] The Sales Department took note of customer wants, collecting sales statistics on buying patterns, which helped to create the standardized line, and listened to the concerns of small merchants who would benefit from reduced stock and higher turnover. Through these efforts, the Pyralin campaign reached women at the national and local level. Mass-circulation women's magazines, local papers, window displays, direct-mail circulars, and retailers' promotions flooded the market with Pyralin news. In the direct-mail campaigns, retailers provided DuPont with mailing lists of consumers who had recently purchased Pyralin, and the Advertising Department wrote personalized letters encouraging those women to complete their vanity sets. DuPont in turn supplied these to retailers, who sent the letters and colorful promotional pamphlets in sealed envelopes to local customers.[26] By targeting women at home, the Advertising Department extended the vanity-set campaign into the private sphere, touching women's personal lives.

Imitation Ivory and Social Class

Despite the nod toward a reciprocal producer-audience relationship, the Pyralin advertising campaign misread the 1920s female consumer. Though it standardized shapes and patterns, the Pyralin Department continued to produce vanity sets in imitation ivory. By 1925 the mock ivory look, predicated on the assumption that middle-class consumers wanted to mimic the wealthy, was an outmoded style. "Imitation" appealed less to 1920s consumers than did authentic materials, even if they were "man-made."

Before DuPont's first national campaign for Pyralin, retailers advertised celluloid vanity sets in mail-order catalogs. In Toronto, the Perfumery and Toilet Articles section of the T. Eaton and Company catalog, for example, included choices in many different materials and prices. Between 1884 and 1918, celluloid appeared next to silver, ivory, ebony, and a few inferior woods.[27] Imitation ivory was among the lower-priced items on the list, giving the impression that celluloid was inferior to most other materials. Displaying vanity sets in this ranked fashion created the impression that toilet ware had predetermined qualities and classes, much like the people who bought it. In Chicago, Sears, Roebuck & Company's mail-order catalogs showed celluloid toilet sets in a similar way.[28] Such advertising may have eroded DuPont's hope to position Pyralin Toilet Ware as a quality product competitive with ivory and other precious materials.

Mail-order catalogs conveyed the notion that Pyralin was an inexpensive substitute for ivory, silver, and ebony, a lower-class imitation of the aristocratic "real thing." The Advertising Department challenged this bias by attempting to build a highbrow image for the celluloid vanity set. Borrowing the famous General Motors description of its ladder of automobiles, Du-Pont's national campaign for Pyralin offered vanity sets for "every taste and pocket book."[29] These claims about imitation ivory encouraged consumers of modest means to imagine themselves owning an article once enjoyed only by the wealthy.

Despite the references to elite consumers, the principal audience for Pyralin vanity sets, as demonstrated by DuPont's promotional literature, consisted of "men and women of limited means."[30] In 1924 the Advertising Department may have taken advantage of the Revenue Act of 1918, which stipulated that names and addresses of U.S. residents who filed tax returns be made pubic record.[31] This federal mandate enabled advertising agencies, which were pioneering the new field of market research, to gather information on consumers. The Sales Department made good use of statistics on possible Pyralin consumers in every American city by 1924.[32] In a trade catalog, *Selling Pyralin to Your Toilet Ware Market*, retailers were encouraged to "look in the following table and see the actual figures in *your own* city, and in the surrounding towns as well."[33] The family income bracket at which Pyralin vanity sets were aimed was the lowest taxable income bracket of $2,000 per year. This was a lower-middle-class level. Men and women of this class considered themselves to be upwardly mobile, and consumer economists of the time believed that the class as a whole sought to emulate their social betters, leaving them susceptible to the advertising of goods that remained just beyond their reach.[34]

Furthermore, evidence that the Advertising Department imagined their consumers to be from households of modest incomes is found in advertising pamphlets encouraging women to see vanity sets as affordable fancy goods. A 1923 leaflet, *Directing the Demand to You*, assured consumers that "exquisite" Shell Pyralin was "quite within your means." The brochure encouraged women to "build up a complete set of perfectly matched articles by starting with just a few pieces."[35] Pyralin retailers thus capitalized on the 1920s craze for installment buying, but with a twist. The 1920s experienced what the economic historian Martha Olney called a Consumer Durables Revolution, evidenced by increased purchasing of major durable goods (cars, appliances, radios) and steady purchasing of minor durable goods (china and tableware, jewelry and watches). This revolution coincided with a burgeoning credit economy and a fundamental change in middle-class attitudes toward acquiring credit and accumulating debt.[36] While there were some installment buying plans for Pyralin vanity sets, a more popular tactic was to suggest that women could buy their sets piece by piece as household money became available. Vanity sets were different from most consumer durables because they had many components, while a car or watch was purchased in its entirety. In other words, a vanity set could be purchased on an installment plan of the consumer's own making.

Another strand of Pyralin advertising promoted celluloid as a desirable replacement for other household materials for vanity sets. One such advertisement claimed that "Ivory Pyralin does not tarnish like metal, . . . shrink and swell like wood, nor chip and break like fragile compositions."[37] Occasionally these appeals stressed celluloid's superiority to real ivory, claiming "the man-made product proved definitely superior to ivory—it did not crack or discolor with age."[38] Celluloid was described as an improvement because it retained its original color and was not likely to crack along the grain. This appeal was directed toward practical consumers who wanted durable, long-lasting products rather than fragile fancy goods.

A third series of advertisements claimed that Pyralin was the "real thing," an authentic form of ivory from elephant tusks. Advice to sales clerks clouded the distinction between tusk ivory and Ivory Pyralin.[39] Once a customer entered the store, the sales clerk might suggest that Pyralin was in fact genuine. If this strategy proved successful, the customer might believe that Pyralin was real ivory—the same material aristocrats proudly displayed on their vanity tables. The 1920 booklet *Autobiography of an Ivory Pyralin Brush* pits "authentic" Pyralin against other brands of celluloid toilet ware. The hairbrush protagonist proclaims that only Ivory Pyralin is genuine, while all other celluloid products are false. "I was mighty pleased to discover that I was solid Ivory Pyralin through and through," the hairbrush declared. "They might have used a wooden core for me and, after building it up with wax, have wrapped around it a thin veneer of Ivory Pyralin. I mention no names, but I know some toilet brushes which put on great airs which are made in this fashion. But there is no sham about me, and although I say nothing, I know that these impostors will soon disappear from the face of the earth, while I am handed down from generation to generation."[40] The Pyralin brush accuses his counterfeit rival of "putting on airs," much like consumers who dressed above their station. The *Autobiography* implied that vanity sets, like people, came from different classes. In a world that could not distinguish tusk ivory from celluloid, Pyralin was upheld as genuine, allowing the owners of these vanity sets to imagine themselves as aristocrats enjoying the "real thing."

Pyralin, the Perfect Gift

In the nineteenth and early twentieth centuries, women's hairstyles had specific meanings, with certain styles marking the transition from girlhood to womanhood, from innocence to sexuality. The bound "up-do" symbolized maturity, the mark of a woman who was grown-up, married, and sexually unavailable. This hairstyle coexisted with two other iconic feminine styles: the long, loose hair of the innocent young girl, and the unkempt tresses of the hyper-sexed prostitute, stage actress, or vaudeville singer.[41]

Faced with an increasingly impersonal world, nineteenth-century Americans came to believe that the outer appearance of a woman was a sign of her inner character. In Victorian culture, a well-kept appearance indicated respectability. The brush, mirror, and comb—the three basic items in the vanity set—were the essential tools for creating the upswept coiffure that signified middle-class dignity and taste. The Victorian vanity set, then, was a gendered artifact that helped women to maintain the appearance so famously tied up with the middle class.

In the Victorian period, brides received vanity sets from male and female relatives at their weddings.[42] The vanity set marked the bride's journey from girlhood to womanhood, symbolizing maturity, much like the up-do. The gift vanity set was proudly displayed on the wife's dresser in the couple's bedroom, the only place where respectable women could "let their hair down," both literally and metaphorically. There it was a material representation of the woman's sexual and marital status. Hair brushing, done in the bedroom, was associated with sensuality. Finally, women used the vanity set as a beautification tool when they prepared themselves to be seen in public. As a cultural artifact, the vanity set had three functions: it was a object for giving, marking a transition in a woman's life; an erotic item associated with hair brushing and flirtatious foreplay; and a tool that helped to create a respectable middle-class public image.

DuPont's first national campaign for Pyralin drew on these associations, depicting toilet ware as a sexually enticing and respectably restraining artifact. Some ads in national magazines such as *Town and Country*, *Metropolitan*, and *Good Housekeeping* illustrate a woman sitting in her boudoir wearing a nightgown as she brushes her long, loose hair, which falls around her shoulders and onto her back. Other ads show a woman dressed up for a night on the town; she is bejeweled from head to toe, wears a beautiful flowing ball gown, and gazes into her hand-held mirror, admiring her up-do (Figure 8.1). Pyralin iconography had two sides: the images featuring brushes referred to the woman's sensuality, while pictures showing hand mirrors addressed her respectable public persona. The Pyralin vanity set, then, simultaneously symbolized the sexual siren and the monogamous wife.

Pyralin advertising drew on these associations to promote vanity sets as the ideal choice for male-to-female gift-giving. Building on the bridal gift tradition, DuPont's Advertising Department began marketing vanity sets as appropriate gifts for all occasions: graduations, birthdays, anniversaries, Christmas, and Easter. DuPont deliberately imagined the primary gift giver as masculine, increasingly fixing its gaze on the male consumer. This contrasted with nineteenth-century ads for vanity sets, which did not specify the gender of either the purchaser or the ultimate consumer. In 1921, *DuPont Magazine* explained that "men as well as women" were "potential buyers of the toilet articles."[43] The Advertising Department told store owners: "Wise dealers know that men do much of the actual buying. So display Ivory Pyralin where both men and women can see it."[44] In this context, DuPont managers envisioned men as *customers* needing instruction and advice, rather than *consumers* who understood the product's symbolism, function, and luxury value. The feminization of consumption, a process underway in the United States for decades, meant that men were less familiar with shopping customs than women. In fact, by the 1920s most businesses acknowledged that women were responsible for 80 percent of the nation's purchases.[45] DuPont's Pyralin advertisements sought to educate men by describing the composition of the vanity set, color choices, and other features (Figure 8.1).[46] Such instruction empowered men, who might have felt uncomfortable in stores, to select gifts that complemented their loved one's vanity set.

The Advertising Department fully understood the gendered dimensions of the vanity set, suggesting that these "intimate articles" were appropriate gifts to women by their sweethearts.[47] Sociologist Helmuth Berkin indicates that presents can function as "relationship signals," while David Cheal suggests that gift giving can be a way of "objectifying feelings."[48] According to Cheal, each gift is believed to contain the spirit of the giver, serving as a memory anchor. DuPont's ads suggested that the female recipient would remember her suitor every time she brushed her hair. DuPont assured him:

Figure 8.1. Respectable woman and her suitor, in the Pyralin gift-giving campaign. Advertisement from *Woman's Home Companion* (December 1924): 37. Courtesy Hagley Museum and Library.

"It will echo your Merry Christmas, whisper fair flattery, every morning of the year."[49] In the betrothed woman's bedroom, the vanity set stood in for the male gift-giver. As the brush stroked her locks, his fiancée could dream of the sweet nothings he would soon whisper every morning and evening. By Cheal's theories, the vanity set was the perfect communicative gift, both glamorous and utilitarian. The female recipient had a constant reminder of the thoughtful male giver.[50]

Selling Modern Womanhood

DuPont company records show that the Sales Department lost money on its vanity sets during the early 1920s. In part, the deficit stemmed from the costs associated with Pyralin as a start-up business. DuPont poured money into retail trade literature, national advertising, and implementing new production strategies such as standardization. Until 1924, the department kept prices artificially low, based on consumer expectations rather than actual costs.[51] The postwar recession of 1920–21 stunted sales of Pyralin and other luxury goods.[52] To put the Pyralin Department on a profitable basis, Pyralin executives recognized they must make changes. In 1924, the Pyralin division was split into separate units for toilet articles and plastic sheeting.[53] In early 1925, new products, such as fountain pens and radio dials, were introduced. Later that year, DuPont executives merged the Pyralin Department with the newly purchased Viscoloid Company into a single subsidiary called the DuPont Viscoloid Company.[54]

The economic boom of the mid-1920s may have provided F. B. Davis, Jr., general manager of the Pyralin Department and later president of the Viscoloid Company, with the impetus to introduce new vanity-set colors and styles. In a memo dated January 1925, Davis noted "the recent trend has been away from the conservative heavy ivory articles and toward the lighter vari-colored and more flashy lines." In another letter, Davis encouraged Fin Sparre, general manager of the Development Department, to seek an expert in the "psychology of colors" to advise DuPont on style matters. Like other big-business managers of the 1920s, Davis had begun to acknowledge fickle female tastes. The toilet-ware market, he wrote, was "dominated by the whims and fancies of the buyers, principally women. . . . If we had a tint which would produce subconsciously a favorable attitude of mind, the problem of making sales and popularizing the articles would be very much simplified."[55]

Davis implemented his plan for enticing female consumers with new styles and colors between 1925 and 1927. The Viscoloid Company began to experiment with exceptionally bright, unnatural colors, such as pink, green, and yellow pearl, as it designed a new product for a new consumer. The throwback Victorian ideals used in earlier advertisements were outdated. National advertising now had to target women who wore their hair bobbed and wanted personal-care tools in modern shapes and colors.

Back in 1911, Arlington managers had realized that the new bobbed hairstyle, popularized by dancer Irene Castle starting in 1909, affected Pyralin sales.[56] After World War I, the bob grew in popularity, affecting DuPont's Pyralin Toilet Ware business. In 1925 Davis expressed concern, noting that "the recent fad of bobbed hair" had "entirely upset" the hair ornament and accessories trade, reducing DuPont's sales of Pyralin vanity sets (along with Pyralin sheeting, bought by other toilet ware manufacturers).[57] By the late 1920s, DuPont managers realized that they had to take action to secure the interests of bob-haired women.

To reach this new market, the Viscoloid Company and the Development Department took stock of the ivory appearance of the vanity set and saw that it was outdated. The Consumer Durables Revolution, with its emphasis on products such as radios and automobiles, promised radical changes in the everyday lives of Americans. Historian Lois W. Banner argues that a new type of woman—the flapper—represented the hope and vitality of these new developments.[58] As the dominant physical ideal of the 1920s, the flapper, with her bobbed hair, heavy makeup, and slim, androgynous, flat-chested shape, was a new model of femininity. Advertisements and movies depicted flappers as free-spirited women functioning as secretaries, saleswomen, or college students, who danced the night away doing the Charleston. These young flappers did not have time to make themselves up in the privacy of their boudoirs, so they adopted the portable compact as a fashion accessory. Unlike Victorian women who hid their beauty rituals, the modern flapper coiffed herself in public—in the workplace, at restaurants, in dance halls—bringing attention to herself and the performance of her womanhood.[59] Vanity sets, with their Victorian associations, did not have much appeal to these women. The Advertising Department had to change its sales pitch, marketing strategies, and advertising iconography to fit this new model of womanhood.

In 1928, the newly formed Viscoloid Company announced the invention of a "new material" called Lucite.[60] Advertised as an entirely new substance, Lucite in fact was a celluloid product, just like Pyralin. Vanity sets made from Lucite, however, came in translucent bright colors and modern designs.[61] DuPont explained the rationale for Lucite toilet sets to retailers. "A new vogue in toiletware was needed—expressly keyed to the modern mode, purposely designed to harmonize with the present-day trends in interior decoration—something so radically different, so smart, so modern—that people who owned toilet sets of the old conventional type would recognize that they were out of date, and buy these new up-to-date creations."[62] The Viscoloid Company launched Lucite with a brand-new ad campaign.

This time, DuPont looked to fashion intermediaries "to find out what the public wanted and needed" from their toilet ware.[63] By the mid-1920s fashion experts, such as DuPont's premier colorist, H. Ledyard Towle, had successfully interpreted color fads, making Duco paints the trend setter in automobile finishes.[64] Seeking to repeat this success, DuPont hired six consultants with a mandate to create "a new vogue in toiletware."[65] These specialists included color experts, architects, and market researchers. The two women in the group contributed design expertise and knowledge of the "woman's viewpoint," while the men were managers and engineers who supervised the overall project.[66] The inclusion of women was due to the general recognition that women were the primary consumers, and that as market researchers, they were admitted more readily into homes, where they could solicit frank discussions about products.[67] Once the designers had proposed new styles, Rose Estelle Brown, one of the six consultants hired for her expertise as a stylist and field researcher, led a team of investigators to test the potential success of the product. During the research, Brown and her team showed Lucite to women of different incomes and social classes, from students at Columbia College to YMCA members. They discovered that seven out of ten women preferred the new Lucite sets over older designs.[68] With the help of fashion intermediaries, who had their fingers on the pulse of consumer wants, DuPont had tracked public demand and made plans to adjust its toilet ware line. With Lucite, DuPont created "a new vogue in toiletware," marketed toward the modern woman.

Based on this market research, DuPont Viscoloid introduced five new vanity-set designs: Ming, Watteau, Empire, Orchis, and Wedgwood. Advertisements for Lucite Toilet Ware featured a woman's slim white hand holding a mirror, so that the viewer could see the pattern on the back of the mirror but not the woman's face (Figure 8.2). The images on the backs of the mirrors

Figure 8.2. Lucite advertising campaign for women of the Jazz Age. From E. I. du Pont de Nemours & Company, *Modern Ways to Beauty* (Wilmington, Del.: E. I. du Pont de Nemours & Company, late 1920s). Courtesy Hagley Museum and Library.

varied, but all the patterns emphasized the exoticism of far-off places and times. This advertising imagery represented a break from the gift-giving campaign, which rested on the Victorian idea that a woman's possessions reflected her inner character and beauty. The Lucite campaign, on the other hand, turned the mirror around, shifting emphasis from the woman to the wider world.

Lucite marketers also capitalized on what historian Roland Marchand has called "the mystique of the ensemble," a 1920s design strategy that emphasized coordinated colors and styles in interior design.[69] Advertisements for Lucite vanity sets emphasized how the new hues and designs would "harmonize with the present-day trends in interior decoration," especially with the "colorful *ensemble* of the modern boudoir."[70] In this formula, women's responsibilities, which had long revolved around interior decoration and self-beautification, were updated for the Jazz Age. The modern, cultured woman had to understand the vocabulary of modernism, as expressed in the new Lucite designs.

Lucite colors marked a complete departure from the Ivory Pyralin tradition. DuPont invented new hues for the Lucite color palette and gave them exotic names: Napoleonic blue, imperial green, colonial buff, and mandarin red.[71] Should these exotic references be lost on consumers, the Lucite hand mirrors were decorated with foreign motifs. The advertisement for the Ming design featured an Asian woman and a mirror with an Oriental bird and flower motif (Figure 8.2). The female consumer, who had loomed large in earlier iconography, rarely appeared in the new advertisements. The Lucite campaign focused on the broader world, rather than inner-looking feminine vanity, appealing to women who saw themselves as worldly and modern. Unfortunately, DuPont soon found the vanity-set market in permanent decline.

The Demise of the Vanity Set

The romantic ideal of womanhood was partially embodied and maintained through the vanity set. At the moment when plastic vanity sets became accessible to middle-class consumers, the values embodied in them were being replaced by a modern viewpoint. With bobbed hairstyles, women stopped using vanity sets, needing only a single comb to style their hair. As it happened, Lucite vanity sets were introduced on the eve of the 1929 stock-market crash. By 1930, DuPont managers reported an overall reduction of vanity-set consumption in the United States.[72] By 1931, many American department stores no longer stocked vanity sets, so few consumers were buying them. Sales slumped even in December, traditionally the month with the highest turnover due to the gift-giving holiday season.[73] Though DuPont continued to advertise vanity sets until 1940, by the late 1920s the firm extended its plastics portfolio beyond women's boudoir accessories to include a wide variety of items, from toilet seats to airplane windshields. By 1937, the vanity set was no longer a profit-making consumer line. That year DuPont managers noted that more than 40 percent of the firm's products had not been on the market ten years earlier.[74] The vanity-set market had vanished. In 1936 a new Plastics Department took charge of Pyralin and Lucite, gradually phasing out vanity sets and focusing on other products.[75]

During the 1920s DuPont tried to establish a market for Pyralin plastics by attributing new meanings to the vanity set. In a national ad campaign in 1920–27, DuPont created a new meaning for the vanity set as an "intimate gift," by encouraging suitors to buy toilet ware for their sweethearts. The advertising campaign and related trade promotions reinforced Victorian ideology suggesting that a woman's character was reflected in her appearance and the objects that she used. DuPont abandoned this approach in 1928, as advertising managers acknowledged shifting cultural ideals, changing tastes, and women's expanded worldview. In the Lucite advertising campaign, DuPont encouraged women to see their toilet accessories as extensions of themselves as cultured individuals. However, DuPont found it could not entice women to buy the new product. The downfall of the vanity set was due to a number of factors: new trends in modern life, an unstable world market prone to booms and busts, and new chemical innovations that took precedence over celluloid toilet sets at DuPont. By the late 1920s, the heyday of the vanity set had passed.

PART III

Shaping Bodies, Building Brands

CHAPTER NINE

California Casual: Lifestyle Marketing and Men's Leisurewear, 1930–1960

William R. Scott

IN 1945, *FORTUNE,* the nation's leading business magazine, documented the rapid growth of Los Angeles from a fashion industry outpost in the early 1930s to the nation's third largest clothing center. *Fortune* highlighted the national reach of California's leisurewear industry: 85 percent of production was shipped over the Rockies, while shoppers in all 48 states looked for the "Made in California" label. California menswear manufacturers, in particular, were poised to play a crucial role in the postwar explosion of American consumption. Indeed Los Angeles would become the world's second largest fashion capital by the late 1950s, trailing only New York and surpassing older manufacturing centers such as Paris, London, and Chicago.[1]

The dramatic rise of the California clothing industry reflected important transformations in American men's fashion between the 1930s and 1960s. The three-piece suit, once the icon of the self-made man and a symbol of modern masculinity, remained a uniform only among conservative business professionals.[2] By the 1930s, men had stopped wearing hats in urban business districts on hot summer days. By the 1970s, the businessman's fedora was rare; top hats, once a requirement for evenings out, had become a veritable endangered species. In the 1920s, a few middle-class men daringly donned lightweight suits at summer resorts; by the 1960s, a man wearing any kind of suit at the beach looked ridiculous. Casual sportswear had become de rigueur. This new way of dressing was not limited to the Sun Belt. Men in Midwestern suburbs and New England towns enthusiastically adopted styles developed in Los Angeles and Palm Springs.

The rise of leisurewear was a national trend, but the Los Angeles clothing industry was fundamental to its development. "Los Angeles' Little Cutters," as *Fortune* termed them, designed casual clothing for "Hollywood's professionally perfect figures," and for people who aspired to the movie stars' casual lifestyle on weekends. Los Angeles manufacturers capitalized on the cultural shift toward informality, reworking masculine style in the process. This new masculine look integrated the high style of Hollywood and Palm Springs resort wear, the toughness of the Western frontier, and the informality of the suburb. California leisurewear fused seemingly incongruous references: the same garment might blend stylistic elements from the American ranch and the French Riviera. California leisurewear also lent itself to adaptation. By the late postwar period, West Coast clothing had become so widely copied that California casual became synonymous with American vernacular style.

A trade organization played a key role in the sartorial transformation of male America, notably through its innovative marketing practices. In 1934, local clothing producers anxious to lure retail buyers away from the traditional garment centers—Chicago, St. Louis, and New York—formed the Men's Wear Manufacturers of Los Angeles. When the Manufacturers mounted the first men's fashion show in history—the Sportswear Round Up at Palm Springs in 1942—the Los Angeles menswear industry made serious inroads into the national market. That year, the Manufacturers also helped launch the trade journal *California Men's Stylist*. By 1951, the New York-based trade publication *Men's Wear* started its "California Dateline" feature, acknowledging the importance of Los Angeles to the national industry. Today the Men's Apparel Guild in California (MAGIC), the successor to the Manufacturers, runs the largest exposition of men's clothing and accessories in the world.

MAGIC and its members forged a range of practices that by the 1960s came to be known as "lifestyle marketing." Their Sportswear Round Up attracted retailers from around the country who wanted to experience the "casual, easy" California "way-of-life," while they selected casual clothes for their stores. Sportswear manufacturers collectively and individually advertised in national magazines. Their ads associated California casual apparel with youth, celebrity, leisure, and heterosexuality. Los Angeles menswear manufacturers repeatedly emphasized that their designs emanated from the California lifestyle and catered to consumers' desires, rather than the other way around. Lifestyle marketing penetrated all aspects of the Los Angeles sportswear industry: responding to consumer demand and promoting the new casual lifestyle was as much the business as manufacturing apparel. Much earlier than other clothing companies—and thirty years before journalist-historian Thomas Frank documented the phenomenon—Los Angeles sportswear manufacturers oriented their business around lifestyle marketing.[3]

This rise of lifestyle marketing in California menswear signaled the ascension of consumerist masculinity during the mid-twentieth century. On the surface, this claim would seem to conflict with recent work on masculinity in this period. James Gilbert's analysis of the era's rhetoric considers how mass culture and suburbia were consistently portrayed as "feminizing" and "debasing." Clark Davis's study of Los Angeles describes rapidly developing corporate bureaucracies and the concomitant culture of "white-collar manhood."[4] Yet it was precisely these white-collar men who supported the California sportswear industry. "Organization men" who spent their workdays in business hierarchies inhabited less formal social worlds on weekends. Furthermore, marketing tactics that linked products to explicitly masculine values had tremendous appeal to men who shunned consumption's feminine associations. Just as most *Playboy* subscribers in the 1950s were married, California "frontier" clothes appealed to urban and suburban family men whose fantasies extended to rough-and-tumble living.[5] Men's penchant for fashionable clothing, long "hidden," was made visible though the simple act of dressing down.[6]

"On the Map as a Garment Town"

If Los Angeles appeared "On the Map of the Garment Town" by 1931, as *Southern California Business* argued, it was still only a lonely outpost.[7] Compared to New York and Chicago, it was at best a regional manufacturing center in the early 1930s, selling most of its clothes in California and the Southwest.[8] This changed gradually throughout the 1930s and dramatically in the 1940s. Department stores across the country established California departments. A high-end California Shop opened in New York City in 1938, with editors from major fashion magazines dropping in to see the exciting West Coast designs.[9] By 1945, an estimated 85 percent of clothing manufac-

tured in California was shipped over the Rockies, with a third of stores nationwide sending their buyers west to order stock.[10]

Other developments speak to California's emergence as a fashion center.
According to the U.S. Chamber of Commerce, the men's sportswear industry
was the fastest growing industry in Los Angeles between 1939 and 1942, out-
pacing defense spending in the region.[11] This growth accelerated after World
War II. In 1934, the men's sportswear industry in Los Angeles had $8 million
in sales; by 1957, it manufactured $160 million worth of garments.[12] Annual
sales among all Los Angeles clothing manufacturers grew from $50 million
in 1940 to $400 million in 1948. By comparison, the New York market,
which concentrated on men's suits, women's wear, and children's clothing,
dominated the industry, with a $1.5 billion market in 1945.[13] Small next to
this giant, the Los Angeles industry nevertheless exerted a powerful influence
over American men's fashion.

The rise of Los Angeles as a national sportswear center was facilitated by
historical phenomena not exclusively related to the clothing industry. Federal
laws creating the forty-hour work week in 1938 expanded leisure time for
middle-class Americans. The dramatic demographic expansion of Los
Angeles also certainly played a role. The city more than quadrupled in size
from 1920 to 1960, to more than 2.5 million. The swelling population, coupled with the rise of Hollywood, created an image of Los Angeles as the land
of limitless opportunity, the hub of commercialized leisure, and a major tour-
ist attraction. Such images, promoted by the mass media, stimulated a nationwide interest in all things Californian. Improved transportation between
the West and East allowed manufacturers and retailers to meet the demand
for California goods more easily.[14]

World War II played a crucial role in the development of the Los Angeles
sportswear industry and the California casual aesthetic. As the largest metrop-
olis on the West Coast and a major staging ground for the U.S. armed forces,
the city experienced rapid demographic growth and industrial infrastructure
development from American military operations in the Pacific. Los Angeles
clothing firms, like the Catalina Knitting Mills, reaped most of their profits
from wartime sportswear production. While other regional clothing centers
filled military orders for uniforms, parachutes, and other gear, California
sportswear firms expanded their output of civilian clothes.[15] World War II
also initiated a lifestyle shift by exposing thousands of soldiers and war workers to the Golden State's informal environment. As *Fortune* noted, workers
in Southern California's war plants starting buying and wearing sportswear.[16]

Ultimately, this trend spread beyond the factories and proved crucial to the dissemination of California leisurewear. Work clothing and sportswear came to be virtually indistinguishable by the late 1950s, with manual laborers wearing short-sleeved shirts on the job and white-collar workers wearing denim jeans in their free time.[17]

The economic growth of Los Angeles created opportunities for Southern California's industries, including factories that produced women's sportswear. Yet by the 1950s style leadership in women's clothing remained firmly centered in New York and Paris, with only minor inroads by sportswear manufacturers in California and Italy.[18] The women's wear market had always been larger and more diversified than the menswear industry, and successes of California women's sportswear firms never had a dramatic effect on the transnational industry, except in the niche business of swimwear. In contrast, menswear manufacturers capitalized on these developments to transform men's style and outdistance the local women's fashion industry. In 1971, the region's women's clothing magazine, *California Stylist*, folded, but the trade journal *California Men's Stylist*, created in 1942, was still going strong.

Between 1930 and 1960, California menswear companies moved from making coarse work clothes for the regional market to holding the reins of stylistic leadership for the American sportswear industry. The center of men's fashion had moved to the West Coast. From Manhattan, *Men's Wear* acquiesced in 1948, admitting, "The conquest of New York goes on steadily but not without some resistance from manufacturers in the east." Begrudgingly, the trade journal admitted that the "Pacific coast" was "largely responsible for the expansion of the leisure apparel market."[19] *Men's and Boys' Stylist* was even more direct: "Today California, no doubt, is the men's wear fashion center of the world."[20] In the short span of twenty years, Los Angeles had been transformed from a regional outpost to the nation's style center for men, by encouraging stores across the country to stock and promote casual sportswear.

Innovative marketing practices contributed to this success. The Men's Wear Manufacturers of Los Angeles, established in 1934, was in full swing by the following year. Representatives from well-established California firms helped create this important organization.[21] The oldest of these firms, Cohn Goldwater and Brownstein Lewis, dated from the 1890s, but most of founding companies had been established after 1920, during the startup years of the California leisurewear industry. The trade association grew steadily throughout the 1930s and 1940s. The Manufacturers claimed 62 members in

1935; by the time the association was renamed the Men's Apparel Guild in California (MAGIC) in 1948, an additional 179 firms had joined.[22] The association developed an institutional infrastructure, with officers, dues, and regular meetings. In 1941, the organization and its paid staff played a major role in launching the trade journal *California Men's Stylist*, later called the *California Men's and Boys' Stylist*. The next year witnessed the debut of the Manufacturers' premier promotional event, the Round Up, along with its Fall Market Week. Besides promotional activities, the Manufacturers addressed production concerns. In 1944, the organization contributed several hundred thousand dollars to construct independent textile mills in Los Angeles County, and in 1947 it sponsored an apparel training section at a local trade school in response to labor shortages created by the market's growth.[23]

The Manufacturers helped create the conditions for the region's success in apparel. The organization facilitated regional promotions and tie-ins as it marketed sportswear and the "Made in California" label. It cosponsored a West Coast promotion with women's clothing manufacturers in 1945 and invested thousands in group advertising in 1947.[24] More important, the trade association encouraged individual manufacturers and retailers to coordinate their marketing activities with its regional promotional efforts. Los Angeles retailers devoted major window space to tie-ins with the 1947 Palm Springs Round Up.[25] When *Men's Wear* started its "California Dateline" column in 1951, MAGIC members poured money into this national trade journal, surrounding the new feature with advertisements for West Coast leisurewear.[26] In sportswear ads, A-1 Manufacturing Company, Maurice Holman, and Catalina Knitting Mills proudly proclaimed their MAGIC memberships as they marketed the "California look."[27]

These cross-promotions and tie-ins had a synergistic effect. The two trade associations—the Manufacturers and later MAGIC—focused members' attentions on the entire region. Relatively small firms began to see themselves as competitors to brand-name manufacturers in New York, Chicago, and St. Louis.[28] Furthermore, the association's emphasis on publicity and marketing distinguished it from other manufacturers' organizations in the American clothing industry. For example, at its annual convention in October 1950, the New York-based Clothing Manufacturers Association focused on government clothing controls and disputes with the Wool Association, discussing advertising and marketing only as an aside. Labor relations, government "code problems," and industrial research preoccupied its members.[29] Traditional organizations like the Clothing Manufacturers Association did little to encourage marketing or boost sales. Its "Buy New York Products" campaign is a case in point. This 1939 effort emerged in response to the buoyant Los Angeles apparel trade, but failed in part because the plea for regional solidarity fell on deaf ears among New York retailers.[30]

A scrapbook found in the MAGIC corporate headquarters in Woodland Hills, California, reveals a very different trade organization—one that took marketing as its primary purpose. Compiled between 1947 and 1950, the scrapbook contains articles covering the group's activities and promotions, culled from an amazing range of local and national publications. While it documents only a fraction of the organization's activities, the scrapbook reveals MAGIC to be an activist association that did everything in its power to expand the California leisurewear industry.

Marketing a California Lifestyle

The MAGIC clippings show how the association used a wide variety of promotional strategies to generate a relatively cohesive message: buy California casual fashions! A marketing study by the New York-based Men's Apparel Research Guild outlined the basics of "California Fashion," themes reiterated in MAGIC's advertising, promotions, and articles:

"California Fashion" is best exemplified by:
A—Styled and made in California.
B—Casual, easy fitting apparel.
C—Broader shoulder expression.
D—Tradition slightly sacrificed for comfort.
E—Use of the unusual in colors or color combinations.
F—Often using motifs and details which stem from the Old West.[31]

California itself proved to be a major selling point for Los Angeles leisurewear, a decade before the mid- to late 1950s when Disney and *Gidget* surf movies marketed the Golden State.[32] Leisurewear represented the "California lifestyle" among marketers and journalists alike. Nearly every description of Los Angeles sportswear linked it to the "sunny" and "carefree" way of life in California.[33] This lifestyle was given expression in the "casual, easy fitting apparel" and bright colors made by the Los Angeles factories and promoted by MAGIC.

Just as fruit growers branded Sunkist orange juice and its sunny origins in the Golden State, Los Angeles sportswear manufacturers marketed the idea of casual living through the "Made in California" label.[34] The "distinctive styling" of California clothes reflected the close ties of producers and consumers.[35] The chief spokesman for the Western apparel manufacturers, P. G. Winnett, noted the principal differences between fashion design in the East and West. "In New York," he wrote, "the design may be something picked out of the air, or picked up in Paris. . . . California styles recognize and are an interpretation of the needs of the people."[36]

The smaller size of Western manufacturers enabled the responsive styling for which California producers became known. Rather than focusing on quantity and trying to cut costs when competition got tough, many Western operators tried to be nimble all the time. Their small, flexible production plants stood in stark contrast to New York's industry in the mid-twentieth century, which tended toward larger manufacturing operations and efficiencies of scale. The size of some New York-based factories allowed them to undercut the rest of the market in price. Californians parried with nimbleness, "chang[ing] designs overnight" to satiate consumer desires.[37]

This emphasis on the consumer reflected the distinctive marketing orientation of the California sportswear industry. Los Angeles manufacturers cultivated an image as "lifestyle" companies that understood the needs of men at play better than did Eastern competitors: "You can't design clothes like that"—casual, fun clothes for weekends in the sun—"huddled over a radiator."[38] Lifestyle marketing even reshaped the sites of production. When Catalina built a new manufacturing facility, a major feature of the site was an enclosed pool and patio area, presumably so employees could enjoy the California sunshine during their lunch breaks.[39] Perhaps employees also market-tested new product designs as they relaxed around the pool.

The heightened marketing orientation of California sportswear companies placed them at the forefront of American business practice. By mid-century, marketing had achieved status as an academic discipline and was becoming an important factor for companies concerned with satisfying the consumer. Practitioners who launched the "marketing revolution" in the 1940s and 1950s viewed their discipline as mediating the relationship between businesses and consumers.[40] Since the early 1900s, advertising agencies, mass-circulation magazines, and home economists, among others, had tried to understand, quantify, and respond to consumers' psychology, habits, and desires. Manufacturers also took up the charge of "imagining consumers," through informal observations of consumers or quantitative analysis of sales data.[41] The postwar marketing revolution codified these ideas and disseminated them to a wider range of companies and industries. New marketing practice aimed to reorganize *all* manufacturing firms to make them more focused on their customers. Like Catalina Knitting Mills, the ideal company would no longer simply be "production oriented" or even "marketing oriented," but "marketing controlled." In theory, the entire company was to be geared toward creating and meeting consumer demand. The California menswear industry put these theories into action: sportswear firms used innovative promotional techniques to help create demand and responded quickly to consumer taste with batch production and rapid-fire design.

California manufacturers developed advertising campaigns that linked their products to sensual longing, the pleasures of mass consumption, and status enhancement. Female-oriented advertising had used these tropes since 1911, when Andrew Jergens Company introduced sex appeal to resuscitate Woodbury's Facial Soap, a flagging brand. From 1907 to 1932, Peabody, Cluett and Company commissioned illustrator Joseph Christian Leyendecker to create the confident and masculine Arrow Man, which graced the firm's advertisements for celluloid collars from 1907 to 1931.[42] Nevertheless, most male-oriented advertisers emphasized durability, practicality, and social correctness to sell their products in the mid-twentieth century. California sportswear manufacturers were among the first men's businesses to foreground sensuality.[43]

MAGIC members emphasized masculine freedom to update the pleasure trope. As early as 1935, California manufacturers paired sportswear with freedom. "It has at last become good taste to be comfortable," noted the *Los Angeles Times*, "correct to be free."[44] Increasingly, California itself came to symbolize the freedom that came from informality and carefree living. Companies like Maurice Holman used California imagery, along with their MAGIC connections, to promote products. Holman's California MultiColored Short Jacket, advertised in *Men's Wear* in 1953, featured the long, pointed collar and the "broader shoulder expression" that epitomized West Coast styling. The sun picture at the top of Holman's ad and the "rainbow" colors of the clothes evoked California's bright, outdoor image. Maurice Holman typified MAGIC members who simultaneously marketed California *and* California style in trade publications like *Men's Wear*.[45]

This link between leisurewear, sunshine, and California styling became increasingly naturalized throughout the 1940s and 1950s, whether the marketer was on the West Coast or in the Midwest. Harry B. Pock, sportswear merchandising manager for the William H. Block Company of Indianapolis, launched a promotion titled, "Perfectly at Home in Indiana: California Shirts and Sport Shirts." His advertising text connected California styling and sunshine: "When the mercury soars, the Indiana male naturally turns to shirts from California (where hot weather styling is a year 'round specialty). . . . [T]hese sheer cool shirts have a light touch that makes them just right for a Hoosier summer."[46] The logic ran as follows: when Indiana's weather approached that of Southern California, Indianapolis men would "naturally" choose Los Angeles shirts. Stores throughout the country advertised similar promotions during the 1940s. In Michigan, Wurzburg's sold "Leisure Coats" from the "sunny playgrounds of California," while Hess Brothers in Allentown, Pennsylvania, "show[ed] men how to be smart, casual and comfortable under California influence."[47]

Promotions also portrayed the bright colors of California leisurewear as extensions of natural surroundings, including "native" Mexicans. Writing about women's leisure clothes, *California Stylist* articulated the link between sportswear, the landscape, and the state's colonial settlers. "The originality of color in California Sportswear is native to the environment," the *Stylist* reported. Chartreuse came "from the ever new leaves of the citrus groves." Fuchsia and Dusty Rose owed their hues to the glowing sunset, which gave "the mountain peaks" and "the valleys in between" their sensuous colors. "From the Pueblos come the sombre tones of Tile and Adobe Red, while the gay costume of Mexican inhabitants brings forth an array of brightest red and green and gold."[48] By reducing Mexicans to the category of the natural, alongside mountain peaks and citrus groves, the leisurewear industry adopted an imagined "Mexican peasant look" at the moment when racial tensions mounted between Anglos, blacks, and Hispanics in Los Angeles.[49] Naturalization of the Mexican "peasant" allowed the industry to appropriate Latino culture from a safe distance.[50]

Dusty Rose was perhaps too feminine a hue for menswear manufacturers, who preferred to promote California as "climate colored."[51] Pock framed this vibrant theme in ways that might appeal to men: "Bold color: The Decisive Masculine Trend in California Sport Shirts."[52] Color made the shirt, and hence the wearer, bold, decisive—and manly. *California Stylist* also framed colorful sportswear in masculine terms, relying on "nature" to legitimize the dye choices: "The natural expression of California interpreted in cloth would be the rugged rough types that lend themselves to the active out-of-door life."[53] Others found the color choices more shocking than daring. A *Fresno Bee* reporter wrote: "Hold tight, men. Colors for fall clothes will be gold and bronze, chartreuse and vermillion. The Men's Wear Manufacturers of Los Angeles are throwing the paint pot with wild abandon."[54] While some retailers may have relished California colors, others hesitated. The *Detroit Times* called the California styles "gaudy"; the *Rochester Democrat and Chronicle* labeled them "extreme."[55] Overall, however, sales continued to climb.

California sportswear manufacturers advertised their brightly colored garments by marketing the "natural" connection between California's warm climate, vibrant landscape, and California-made leisurewear. The advertisements and commentary repeatedly celebrated the "outdoor" lifestyle of Los Angeles and environs to explain the "style leadership" of Los Angeles: sportswear that men in the rest of the country could only wear in summer or at resorts could be tried out earlier and more often in sunny Southern California. Increasingly, it was this lifestyle itself that came to be advertised and marketed along with the clothes. This lifestyle marketing, or as one historian of consumer culture has put it, "aspirational merchandising," associated men's sportswear so closely with Southern California leisure practices that each came to stand in for the other.[56]

The more men nationally led laid-back, relaxed lives, the more they chose sportswear from Los Angeles (or at least in the Southern California style), a place continually associated with leisure through the rise of tourism to the region and the virtual tourism offered by motion pictures. The connection worked the other way, too: sportswear advertisements sold a leisure-filled lifestyle, or at least the fantasy of such a lifestyle, along with the clothes.

In 1953, one of Southern California's largest manufacturers, Catalina Knitting Mills, published an advertisement in *Men's Wear* illustrating the key elements of lifestyle marketing. Once called Pacific Knitting Mills, Catalina was a founding member of the Men's Wear Manufacturers of Los Angeles. Established as an underwear manufacturer in 1907, the firm shifted to swimwear in the 1920s. By the 1930s, it began making a popular line of sweaters and sportswear.[57] In the 1945 feature on Los Angeles, *Fortune* deemed Catalina's chief executive Edgar Stewart a "giant" of the Western clothing industry. Under his direction, Catalina sold $5 million worth of apparel each year.[58]

Catalina's advertisement for "Sun and Swim Fashions" used iconography that reiterated the key themes in lifestyle marketing: leisure, youthfulness, and consumer-inspired plenty (Figure 9.1). To twenty-first-century consumers, the advertisement's images of "beach boys" and "California girls"

[Left] Combining sun and sun in luxurious surroundings is the specialty of the exclusive Palm Springs Tennis Club. Against the post-background of flowered bougainvillea, left to right, Catalina's "Hayride" set, "Square" set, "Sol-Air" trunks.

[Below] Palm Springs community life revolves around the colorful Plaza with its quaint shops. Here Catalina Play-Abouts for women and Round-Abouts for men are a typical part of the scene. Photographed from left to right, "Engineers Stripes" dungaree, "Santa Rosa" shirt with Bermuda walking shorts, "Candy Dottins," "Hayride" and "Racquet Club" terry tennis shirt with gab tennis trunks.

SUN AND SWIM FASHIONS

...Previewed at Palm Springs

Fabulous Palm Springs, mecca of Hollywood film stars and socialites in the national picture, is the birthplace of fashion trends for summer months to come. Catalina, Official Swim Suit of the Miss Universe Beauty Pageant held annually at Long Beach, California, plays an important role in the Palm Springs resort season picture with styles that are colorful, comfortable, pretty and practical in the California tradition of casual, easy living.

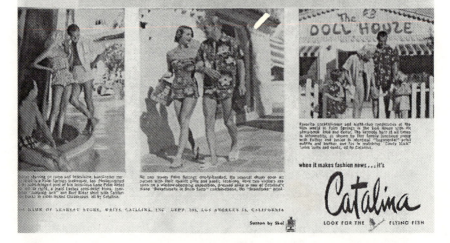

No one leaves Palm Springs empty-handed. Its newest shops stock all purses with their newest gifts and exotic fashions. Here two visitors are seen on a window-shopping expedition, dressed alike in one of Catalina's many "Beachwear" in Swim Suits" combinations, the "Snowflake" print.

Favorite cocktail-hour and night-club rendezvous of the film world in Palm Springs is the Doll House with its storybook look and decor. This keynote here at all times is informality, as shown by this lovely luncheon group with Fashion and Junior in identical "Regimental" pencil culotte and bodice and his in matching "Candy Stick" swim trunks and coats, all by Catalina.

Starring on radio and television, bandleader ... is at a Palm Springs makeup, top, photographed in sun-fringed pool of his luxurious Long Palm Hotel suit to right, a plaid Lastex semi-brief trunk, over "Jumping Jack" and Surf Rider shirt with California, trunk in color-locked Chessboard, all by Catalina.

FOR NAME OF NEAREST STORE, WRITE CATALINA, INC, DEPT. 303, LOS ANGELES 54, CALIFORNIA

when it makes fashion news...it's

Catalina

LOOK FOR THE FLYING FISH

Sutton by Skol

Figure 9.1. Catalina Knitting Mills advertised "Sun and Swim Fashion" in *Men's Wear* 126 (9 Jan. 1953). Courtesy Warnaco Inc.

look mightily familiar, part and parcel of a culture that values outdoor leisure and bodily display. For viewers in the 1950s, these images would have been new, exciting, and perhaps titillating. For one thing, the advertisement would have been visually arresting because of the five color photographs taken in "fabulous Palm Springs," a "mecca of Hollywood film stars and socialites" and the "birthplace of fashion trends for summer months."[59] In 1953, color images dominated the advertising pages of mass-circulation magazines like *Saturday Evening Post*, but they were rarer in trade journals like *Men's Wear*, probably due to costs. Second, the images depict scantily clad men and women, enjoying activities such as swimming, sunbathing, and shopping in Palm Springs, which had more pools per capita than any city in the world.[60] For context, it was only twenty years earlier when men first swam without shirts on a public beach in Florida.[61] Regardless of their age, everyone in the pictures looks youthful and tanned, photographs glow with naked legs, shoulders, and chests. "Catalina," the advertisement stated, "plays an important role in the Palm Springs resort season picture with styles that are colorful, comfortable, pretty and practical in the California tradition of casual, easy living." The name Catalina appears at the bottom, along with the firm's signature flying fish logo.

The imagery in this advertisement linked the "California tradition of casual, easy living" to bodily display and a barely-under-the-surface sexuality. Other lifestyle advertisers cultivated a meritocracy of the body, but California's clothing and film industries especially pushed these themes. Leisurewear promotions put the body on show along with the clothes. None of the Catalina men resembled celebrity bodybuilder Charles Atlas, who made muscularity popular in 1920s advertisements.[62] Atlas had to work out to look good. In contrast, the skinny, tan good looks of the Catalina models seemed effortless: the product of youthfulness, the right Anglo-Saxon gene pool, and a healthy outdoor lifestyle.[63]

The Catalina models differ from Atlas in another significant way. The Catalina ad steers the viewer's gaze in ways that reinforce heterosexuality and deflect implications of homoeroticism. The presence of women allowed readers to look safely at the men. This tension between advertising men's bodies and clothing while avoiding the threat of homoerotic reading of the images undergirded much of the lifestyle marketing in the pages of *Men's Wear*, *California Men's Stylist*, and other publications after the mid-1940s. The emergence of this tension reflected a declining acceptability of same-sex sociability, the rising perception that homosexuality was threatening, and, in some cases, a growing discomfort with men being objectified. California menswear marketers borrowed an obvious solution from *Esquire* and *Playboy*: encode the images with ebullient and obvious heterosexuality.[64] Images of young men in family situations and with women deflected suggestions of homoeroticism. Men in advertisements, when pictured together, often appeared looking off into the distance as if to avert homoerotic gazes.

The Catalina advertisement further supported a meritocracy of the body with celebrity tie-ins. For one, Catalina boasted that it provided swimsuits to the Miss Universe Beauty Pageant, held in Long Beach. Palm Springs as a location for the photo shoot implied links to Hollywood movie stars and other beautiful people. California manufacturers were well aware of the boost the entertainment industry gave to their growing businesses.[65] In the ad, bandleader-turned-hotelier Horace Heidt flirts with a young woman, suggesting celebrities were ubiquitous in Palm Springs. Decades earlier, California manufacturers had pioneered movie celebrity endorsements as a marketing strategy. Celebrity magazines such as *Photoplay* depicted stars lounging poolside in Palm Springs or relaxing in Hollywood; these images served as informal advertisements for California leisurewear and "easy" living.[66]

Los Angeles manufacturers were so successful at naturalizing the link between California and an informal, "breezy" lifestyle that Eastern manufacturers, eager to capitalize on the move to casual wear, began selling their products as "California-styled." West Coast manufacturers filed suit to protect the "Made in California" label, but in 1947 the court ruled against them. The court found that "California" referred to a type of garment rather than a place of origin.[67] California, casual living, and garment design had been conjoined so closely that outside manufacturers were legally allowed to name their leisurewear after the state. The conflict heralded the dramatic arrival of sportswear on the national picture. By the 1950s, West Coast sportswear and the marketing techniques used to sell it were copied by manufacturers throughout the country, transforming the industry in the image of California.[68]

Rounding Up Customers at Palm Springs

Perhaps the most novel and important innovation of West Coast manufacturers was the Palm Springs Round Up, an annual promotion created by the Men's Wear Manufacturers of Los Angeles in 1942. This Palm Springs event epitomized the sartorial and marketing changes led by Los Angeles apparel producers. Its centerpiece was a fashion show—the first in history to focus on men's clothing—featuring sportswear designed and made in Southern California.[69] More than a style show, the Palm Springs Round Up was also a merchandising forum, a market week, and a real-life demonstration of California living. Visiting buyers selected and ordered their lines, learned methods for promoting California wear, and experienced firsthand the sunny lifestyle. At New York's loosely organized Market Week, individual manufacturers set their own agendas, promoting their own new lines. At the Palm Springs Round Up, the Manufacturers cooperated to plan and host a convention that aimed to boost sales for all its members.

A major success from its start in 1942, the Round Up drew buyers, reporters, and manufacturers from all over the country only a few years later. In 1948, the trade journal *Men's Wear* previewed the Round Up with anticipation: "Interest in the proceedings is running at high pitch, tempo furioso, inasmuch as the world of men's apparel looks to California for its sartorial stimulation."[70] A guest register from the 1948 Round Up listed more than 1,200 attendees from cities and towns in every major region of the country: New York, Corpus Christi, Vancouver, Minneapolis, Honolulu, Chicago, Bakersfield, Birmingham, Washington D.C., and New Orleans.[71] The Round Up grew with the leisurewear market. A special American Airlines flight was chartered for attendees in 1950.[72] By the mid-1950s, approximately 2,000 people from 32 states and five countries traveled to Palm Springs for the Round Up. The arbiter of taste in menswear, *Apparel Arts*, called the Round Up the "talk of the industry," a "yearly masterpiece," and a "must on the calendar" for menswear retailers.[73] Today this annual MAGIC convention has moved to Las Vegas and become the world's largest trade show for men's goods.

In 1942, *California Men's Stylist* published a four-page spread of photographs from the first Palm Springs Round Up (Figure 9.2).[74] The photo essay illustrated the themes and marketing strategies behind California leisurewear. One page showed eight images that conveyed the distinctiveness of California casual. *Esquire* fashion editor O. E. Schoeffler posed with the "local color," sandwiched between six women to convey a "playboy" image. The *Esquire* picture linked the Round Up with the nation's most popular men's publication, a "modern," lifestyle-oriented magazine whose editors appreciated the "California way" and helped to publicize it. A poolside picture showed two male runway models in slacks and sport shirts by Duke of Hollywood and Hollywood Sportswear, with Mount San Jacinto rising up behind them.

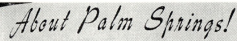

About Palm Springs!

re-orders, are still being received by the manufacturers who participated. The pictures on these pages show some of the outstanding styles as well as some of the atmosphere and fun.

notables taking in the sun and the fashion trends are Tom May (left), and Jack Dorsen (center), who seems amazed at something out of camera range. 9. Esquire fashion editor, O. E. Shaeffler, doesn't mind being surrounded by local color. 10. Duke of Hollywood showed this wool rayon and teca plaid sport shirt (left) with convertible collar, while Hollywood Sportswear countered with a "Buck Jones" frontier suit in gabardine. 11. Palm Springs resident Charles Farrell of former film fame displays and William Lundigan of present cinematic prominence admires the cup Charlie won for being the best-dressed sportsman in the country. 12. There is entertainment. 13. The ever-amiable Carrillo, emcee of the Round-up looks amiable again. 14. Guests line up for a western barbecue lunch under a sunny western sky. 15. The breakfast ride—sagebrush, stage-coaches, and exhilaration. 16. The Los Angeles Examiner put out a special front page for the event — but just for Palm Springs.

Figure 9.2. The first Palm Springs Round Up, *California Men's Stylist* 1 (April 1942). Courtesy Los Angeles County Museum of Art.

The style show was perhaps the most innovative event at the Round Up, signifying the incorporation of men into the fashion system. A third photograph of two Hollywood film stars, Charles Farrell and William Gargan, suggested that that men's fashionable presentation was not limited to magazines or staged events. At the event, the Manufacturers' honored Farrell as the country's "best-dressed sportsman." Finally, other photographs appropriated cultural icons from Hawaii, Texas, and Mexico to link California to the West and distinguish it from the East: grass skirts, cowboy hats, Western scarves, and a horse-drawn stagecoach. The event's title, the Round Up, conjured up images of the Old West as depicted by the movies and is indicative of the sportswear industry's debt to Hollywood.

Perhaps more striking than the beautiful setting, the male models were a major innovation and attraction. In the 1947 Round Up, the models began the fashion show by imitating mannequins in a "store" window before parading "out of the window onto the sidewalk, down the center lane of the audience." Their actions blended stage theatrics with catwalk practices. Clearly, men and their clothes were on display. The businessmen in the crowd watched the models keenly. The organizers of the event were careful in all their promotional material to call this event a "style show," but little appears to have separated it from a fashion show except that men were the audience and models.[75]

The Round Up's display of men and their clothes had precursors in *Apparel Arts* and in advertisements like Peabody and Cluett's Arrow Man. The all-male fashion show, however, was a markedly new development in the history of men's clothing. More than *Apparel Arts* or even *Esquire*, it symbolized men's entanglement in the fashion system. In this way, the Round Up fashion show prefigured the "peacock revolution" of the 1960s, the "glamorized male body" of the 1980s, and the "metrosexual" of contemporary parlance.[76] The Round Up show, in encouraging men to look at other men as models of style—which, as we have seen, was intimately connected to broader fantasies loosely captured by the term "lifestyle"—literalized the homosocial gaze of consumer aspiration. In addition to the clothes themselves, the act of exposure itself came to represent the comfortable, easy California way.

The Palm Springs Round Up had public relations tie-ins with retailers and publishers. Los Angeles department stores created special window displays linked to the event, while *California Apparel News* printed a special edition about it. Throughout Southern California, stores such as Silverwood's in Santa Barbara, Bullock's in Palm Springs, and Mullen and Bluett in Los

Angeles launched style events, including community parades and rodeos.[77] While helping to sell California sportswear, this systematic cross-promotion on the local and regional level attracted national media attention.

The Palm Springs Round Up was not only a style forum; it also put forward coherent messages about store merchandising and display.[78] California lifestyle marketing linked clothing style, mass marketing techniques, retail display, and point-of-sale promotions. Merchandisers who attended the Round Up were convinced by such promotions to return to their hometowns and open up California shops and departments selling sportswear in the ways they had witnessed at Palm Springs.[79] These departments around the country echoed the Round Up's emphasis on masculine leisure, bodily display, and an outdoors lifestyle, for these cultural tropes had become inseparably linked to California sportswear. Marketers' innovative use of scantily clad male models in the Round Up literalized this connection.

The Palm Springs Round Up style show, along with the inventive advertising of leisurewear, signaled a new relationship to marketing in the menswear industry. The California companies in MAGIC transformed the Round Up into much more than a market week. It was a tour-de-force performance that offered participants—store buyers from around the country—a taste of rodeos, swimming pools, and other symbols of the California lifestyle and the sportswear that was for sale. This reflected an orientation that was very different from East Coast manufacturers, at least until the mid-1950s. California sportswear companies may have produced clothes, but the Round Up illustrated that marketing, not manufacturing, drove their businesses. The associations with sexuality, leisure, and status aspiration sold the clothes.

In the 1930s, menswear manufacturers had promoted their clothing as appropriate and correct. The three-piece suit was, after all, appropriate for every occasion, a veritable male uniform. The success of California leisurewear not only changed men's wardrobes, but also changed the way men's clothes were viewed. After the marketing of California sportswear, men's clothing took on greater representational weight: it became symbolic of a lifestyle. The suit did not, of course, disappear. But it increasingly came to represent conventionality, business, and sobriety. Many men, on many more occasions, chose instead to align themselves with the informal ease and sexually laden imagery of leisurewear. California sportswear companies, in creating these cultural linkages, ensured their success and transformed the marketing of men's consumer goods.

CHAPTER TEN

Marlboro Men: Outsider Masculinities and Commercial Modeling in Postwar America

Elspeth H. Brown

ON 24 NOVEMBER 2004, the *Los Angeles Times* published a photograph that became one of the iconic images of the U.S.-Iraq war. Shot by *Times* photographer Luis Sinco, the picture depicted a battle-weary soldier, Marine Lance Corporal James Blake Miller, following a twelve-hour skirmish near Fallujah. Miller squinted beneath his helmet, his camouflage paint smudged and a cigarette dangling from the right side of his mouth. The photograph captured the nonchalant heroism of the ground troops, who were rugged, independent, hardworking, and, above all, masculine. It especially resonated among audiences back home because of an unintended reference to one of America's most successful advertising images: the Marlboro Man. Within a few days, more than a hundred newspapers had reprinted Miller's picture. The *New York Post* summarized its symbolic meaning: "Marlboro Men Kick Butt in Fallujah."[1]

As this portrait suggests, the iconic Marlboro Man epitomizes a particular version of heterosexual masculinity that gains power and coherence in symbolic spaces outside of the domestic, feminine, and urban realms. In the mid-1950s, the Chicago advertising agency Leo Burnett, collaborating with tobacco company Philip Morris, carefully fashioned this version of butch masculinity in response to postwar America's dominant vision of white-collar manliness. This essay explores Marlboro's re-branding, from a woman's luxury smoke to a man's cigarette, with reference to the Leo Burnett agency's use of the Marlboro tattoo to signify "outsider masculinities," and its discovery of Darrell Winfield, a real cowboy who became the quintessential Marlboro Man. The original Marlboro Man, depicted in print advertisements by professional models, was seen in a variety of occupations, from car tinkerer to bongo player. By 1962 the Marlboro Man appeared only as a cowboy, portrayed not by models but by real American cattlemen. The fact that the Marlboro Man was a working cowboy was central to the discourse of authenticity in the ad campaigns of the 1960s. Faced with the implicit feminization of the male model before the camera lens, brand executives sought to secure a dominant reading of the Marlboro Man as aggressively masculine and heterosexual, attributes that were coded through an emphasis on authenticity and "realness." Between 1954 and 1968, they produced an icon of heteronormative butch masculinity that allowed oppositional readings by some viewers who used the representation to craft new sexual subjectivities.

Sex, Gender, and Marlboro Marketing in the Interwar Years

Before cigarettes moved into mainstream American culture during World War I, Progressive reformers had labeled them as hazardous to Americans' moral health. Henry Ford even called cigarettes "little white slavers," believing they led consumers down an irrevocable path of moral decline. When the United States entered World War I in April 1917, cigarette sales were illegal in eight states and anti-cigarette bills were under consideration in another twenty-two. Mainstream white America associated cigarettes with foreigners and other lowlifes: working-class immigrants from southern and eastern Europe, actresses who flaunted their sexuality on stage, and effeminate men. Evangelist Billy Sunday urged men to eschew cigarette smoking, claiming that there "nothing manly" about it. "For God's sake, if you must smoke," Sunday exclaimed, "get a pipe."[2] Despite these condemnations, evermore Americans took up the habit, so that cigarettes accounted for 20 percent of the country's tobacco consumption by 1920. The war had legitimated cigarette consumption because the United States government sanctioned smoking by servicemen. Congress ordered the War Department to include cigarettes in army rations as a prophylactic that guarded against more objectionable vices, such as drinking or consorting with prostitutes. Widespread cigarette smoking by American soldiers associated the commodity with the culturally sanctioned norms, including heterosexual masculinity and jingoistic patriotism.[3]

In the 1920s, Philip Morris, a small South Carolina tobacco company, marketed Marlboro as a luxury cigarette for sophisticated urban men and young middle-class women. During the Jazz Age, women represented a significant percentage of the adult smoking population. In 1926, for example, *Advertising and Selling* reported that 15 percent of the cigarette market was female.[4] As they became more visible in films and novels, cigarettes emerged as an emblem of modernity for the "new woman" and her younger counterpart, the "flapper," who embraced public smoking as a symbol of newly defined personal autonomy.[5] This increased visibility of female smokers, especially in urban centers, sparked a new critique of the cigarette industry by middle-class reformers, who lobbied for legislation to curb women's public smoking. The cigarette industry worried about attracting "the lightning of the busybody element that brought about Prohibition—the long-haired men and the short-haired women whose lives are incomplete unless they are stage managing the lives and actions of the rest of us."[6] Fearing that reformist zeal might lead to a cigarette ban, tobacco companies and their advertising agencies approached female smokers only after much cautious deliberation.

The branding strategies and advertising campaigns used by Philip Morris, Liggett & Myers, and the American Tobacco Company in the 1920s reflected this careful approach.[7] In 1924, Philip Morris introduced Marlboro—today the world's best-selling brand—as a cigarette for ladies. Its 1926 advertising campaign featured the slogan "Mild as May," touting the new mild blend as fit for the female smoker's delicate tastes.[8] That year, Liggett & Myers introduced its "Blow Some My Way" advertising campaign, featuring a romantic couple enjoying Chesterfield cigarettes in the twilight. In one ad, a man lights his Chesterfield while the woman leans into the resulting halo of smoke. The tag line clearly signals to female readers, anxious that love and a delicious whiff of tobacco smoke blow their way. The campaign stirred controversy for its inclusion of women as subjects. Even though they did not show a woman smoking, the ads clearly suggested the feminine desire for romance and a smoke. The Chesterfield ads were the most direct appeal to women to date.[9]

In April 1927, Philip Morris became the first tobacco company to show a woman smoking in a national advertising campaign. The ads, published in *Bon Ton*, *Pictorial Review*, and other mass-market periodicals read by middle-class women, featured a "modern" young woman with bobbed hair, beads, and makeup reclining with a lit cigarette in her elegantly extended hand. The copy linked Marlboro to luxury: "Women—when they smoke at all—quickly develop discerning taste." Rather than raise the hackles of irate reformers, Philip Morris received favorable letters from female smokers who approved of the new campaign. According to the trade journal *Advertising and Selling*, the Marlboro campaign had "broken new ground," inaugurating what was "probably one of the most significant individual advertising efforts in several years."[10] As American cigarette manufacturers discovered the female consumer, Phillip Morris led the way with Marlboro, a "woman's cigarette."

The Marlboro campaign quickly inspired the competition to create ads that more closely linked women's smoking to fashions, both in the body and attire. By the late 1920s, advertisers and businessmen worried that parts of the consumer marketplace had grown saturated. In response, advertisers abandoned what historian Roland Marchand called the "great genteel hope" of the early 1920s—the belief that advertising might educate and uplift a mass audience—and embraced overblown testimonials, scare tactics, and competitive copy as a means of stimulating sales.[11] In cigarette advertising, the American Tobacco Company's Lucky Strike campaign, launched in 1928, directly engaged fear and fashion. American Tobacco's chief executive George Washington Hill violated one of the advertising industry's longstanding taboos when he developed a campaign that pitted the cigarette industry against the candy industry. More important for this discussion, the "Reach for a Lucky Instead of a Sweet" campaign linked smoking, fashion, and the body, creating a trope that would have a lasting impact on cigarette advertising. Hill hired publicist Edward L. Bernays to identify Lucky Strikes with fashionable slenderness and Jazz Age standards of beauty. Bernays asked commercial photographer Nicholas Muray to encourage other artists to hire svelte models, indirectly "praising slender women who lit cigarettes instead of eating sweets."[12] In his autobiography, Bernays later claimed that his collaboration with Muray led to the use of thin models for advertising work and the acceptance of Parisian "slim fashions" among fashion editors. To promote further Lucky Strikes, Bernays arranged for six Ziegfeld Follies chorus girls to pledge moderation, displaying their commitment to the "modern figure with its tantalizing, sinuous curves." When the Ziegfeld Follies went on tour, moderation became a part of the publicity theme.[13]

The Lucky Strike campaign is an explicit example of tobacco manufacturers' long-standing efforts to link smoking to fashions in dress and ideal body types. From Victorian times through the post-World War II era, advertising professionals, publicists, and others have linked commodities to ideal bodies to produce fashion, and vice versa. In the 1890s, tobacco companies illustrated their trade cards with voluptuous actresses. During the 1950s, the relationship between cigarettes, the body, and fashion was again reconfigured in terms of a new ideal: the nonconformist, outsider masculinity of the Marlboro Man.

Re-Branding and Re-Gendering Marlboro

Despite innovative marketing during the interwar years, Marlboro remained one of the weakest cigarette brands until the mid-1950s. In 1946, sales suffered dramatically, as military orders were cancelled, the domestic cigarette shortage ended, and smokers returned to other brands. In response, Philip Morris president Alfred E. Lyon restructured the company so that he could focus more energy on marketing and sales. By 1951, Philip Morris had recovered from the slump. Between 1946 and 1951, U.S. cigarette sales grew by 17 percent, Philip Morris sales by 77 percent. By 1954, however, Marlboro was still considered a "woman's cigarette." At this time, growing concerns about the health risks of smoking had boosted the popularity of filter cigarettes. Philip Morris lacked a strong brand in this expanding market segment. Filter-tip cigarettes represented only 3 percent of the industry in 1953, but *Fortune* predicted that nearly 15 percent of the market would be in filter tips by 1955.[14] Marlboro's lackluster performance combined with Lyon's desire to expand Philip Morris's presence in the popular-priced filter market led to a major re-branding effort.[15]

In the wake of the 1952 cancer scare, cigarette manufacturers turned to the filter as a means of assuaging public fears about health and taste.[16] In 1953, each tobacco company used a different type of filter, using their ad campaigns to tout the healthy attributes of the new cigarettes. P. Lorillard's Kent, the first major filter cigarette and the industry leader before Marlboro, used treated asbestos on crepe paper. Benson & Hedges's Parliament, a filter tip acquired by Philip Morris in 1953, used cotton. The tobacco companies competed for fickle "switch smokers," known to change brand loyalty with aplomb, by emphasizing their filter's unique features. Mid-1950s advertisements emphasized that a particular brand had less nicotine, that the filter removed harmful tars and irritants, and that the blend did not irritate the nose, lungs, throat, or mouth. By inference, the tobacco companies admitted that smoking was a harmful habit, but promised smokers that filters guarded against health risks. Each claimed that its filter best protected the body.[17]

At Philip Morris, public-relations director George Weissman, a career executive who joined the tobacco company in 1952, argued for a new moderately priced filter-tip cigarette. In early 1953, Philip Morris president O. Parker McComas authorized Weissman to launch a market-research program on the new cigarette. Weissman's team included Alfred's son, David Lyon, who worked as an executive in the Cecil & Presbrey advertising agency in Chicago.[18] Weissman and Lyon interviewed leading market-research firms, including those headed by Alfred Pulitzer and Ernest Dichter, before hiring Elmo Roper for the project.[19] As part of Marlboro's re-branding, Roper conducted the most extensive marketing research on cigarettes in the nation's history to that date. Roper undertook 10,000 home interviews to determine consumers' attitudes toward filtered cigarettes.

The results of the 1953 Roper survey revealed important information about consumers' perceptions of filtered cigarettes. Although 61 percent of interviewees had tried filters, most did not stick with these cigarettes for two reasons: taste and image.[20] Market research had shown that most smokers thought filters had an adverse effect on taste, and at a time when twice as many men smoked as women, Marlboro was thought to convey an effeminate, or "sissyish," image.[21] With Marlboro, the ivory-tipped filter and the luxury focus harked back to Progressive era associations between smoking, the immigrant classes, and non-normative masculine gender formations. In the 1950s, twice as many men smoked as women, and most did not feel comfortable with an effeminate masculinity. In this context, Marlboro's "sissy" connotations emerged as a key marketing focal point.

The Roper study served as a focusing device, leading Weissman's team to redesign Marlboro's packaging and the cigarette's taste to suit normative masculine gender expectations. At David Lyon's suggestion, the company hired a new package designer, Frank Gianninoto, to respond to the Philip Morris call for "a bold, masculine-type package." Production chief Clark Ames had recently returned from Germany with a flip-top box, hoping that it might serve as a prototype for the new Marlboro package. Initially the design team opposed the hard box, seeing it as a throwback to the 1850s, but they ultimately adopted it, eventually making rugged durability part of the brand's masculine image. Other elements, including the logo and color scheme, came under scrutiny.

To get a handle on these features, Philip Morris hired industrial designer Egmont Arens and Louis Cheskin's Color Research Institute of America in Chicago to research more than a hundred prototypical package designs. Working with Arens and Cheskin, the Container Corporation of America, a packaging giant that made cigarette boxes, tested eight trial packages among Chicago supermarket shoppers. From these eight trial packages, they focused on two designs, one picturing a filter-tip cigarette, another with a crest. Cheskin conducted eye-movement tests and surreptitiously photographed shoppers' movements and package choices to gauge the packaging's appeal. In a later oral history, Weissman remembered that the results had been "superb."[22] Next, Cheskin ran an association test among 805 smokers to gauge motifs and colors; 80 percent favored a crest design and a package with bold red accents. Cheskin reported that the crest unconsciously signified quality and prestige; red gave the package strong visibility.[23] These tests dictated the look of the final package. John Scott Fones, senior account supervisor for Publicity Consultants Inc., a company that had been working with Philip Morris during these years, told an audience in 1958 that these tests dictated which colors should be used in the final package design.

Cheskin, Roper, Burnett, Weissman, and others involved in Marlboro's re-branding represent what Regina Lee Blaszczyk has called "fashion intermediaries." As Blaszczyk has argued, these design professionals worked at the intersection of product development and demand, responding to consumers' perceptions and desires and redesigning commodities in an effort to increase market shares.[24] Marlboro's creative team members recognized the centrality of fashion and design as signifiers of both selfhood and social positioning. Looking back on the Marlboro re-branding project in 1958, adman Leo Burnett commented: "Outside the clothes and jewelry you wear, a cigarette package is your most frequently exposed possession."[25] The public display of material goods is central to the process of constructing and redefining social categories, including those organized around gender. As sociologist Pierre Bourdieu has argued, social classes are made intelligible to others through the everyday life of things, which constitute a symbolic system organized around the logic of difference. In Marlboro's re-branding, the primary organizing logic was gender: a system of power and social relations based on perceived differences between the sexes.[26] Fashion intermediaries involved with the brand's transformation used design to associate the cigarette with gendered meanings, new to Marlboro, but deeply entrenched within postwar American culture.

Sissies Versus Macho Men: Marketing a "Cigarette with Balls"

In 1954, market research told Philip Morris that consumers perceived Marlboro as a fancy smoke for dudes and women. Leo Burnett, the adman who relaunched the brand's identity in 1954, recalled that "people regarded the old ivory-tipped Marlboro as sissy." In contrast, the new Marlboro of 1954–55 had "a flavor you could get hold of and roll around in your mouth. There was nothing sissy about it."[27]

Postwar perceptions and definitions of masculinity figured into this transformation. The historian John Higham has observed that "sissy" became a gender-based term of derision in the 1890s, when middle-class men started defining their masculinity on the basis of their difference from women. Similarly, George Chauncey has noted that in the 1920s heterosexual observers used the vernacular terms "sissy," "fairy," and "pansy" synonymously to described men of effeminate character.[28] The mid-1950s cultural association of Marlboro with the sissy posed a double threat to Philip Morris. On the macro level, Marlboro's sissy-ness implied a failure of masculinity at a time when the boundaries of heteronormative gender roles were carefully policed.[29] On a micro level, the sissy's implicit lack of courage became problematic in the context of the cancer scare. If the public believed that cigarette smoking could kill, a masculine brand image might help to alleviate some of those fears. If audiences identified with an invincible strongman, they might see their own bodies as resistant to disease and decay.

To counter the effeminacy connotations, managers at Philip Morris and two advertising agencies—Cecil & Presbrey, and Leo Burnett—developed a campaign that introduced the public to a new Marlboro, the "cigarette with balls," a phrase coined by David Lyon in 1954, when he worked on the Marlboro account as vice president of the Cecil & Presbrey agency.[30] Lyon showed Philip Morris executives his ideas for a new image that included an advertisement of Red Sox outfielder Ted Williams announcing "I smoke Marlboro" as "an example of macho testimonials." According to Weissman, the "mission really was to create strong flavor, a masculine-looking pack and a macho campaign."[31] Adman Jim Cecil died in 1954, and his firm dissolved. Philip Morris executives turned to another Chicago agency, Leo Burnett, whose work on the Marlboro account developed the macho theme introduced by Lyon.[32]

As the founder of the "Chicago School of Advertising," Burnett had developed a world-class agency by capitalizing on Midwestern values that celebrated family, home, and soil. Established in August 1935, the Leo Burnett agency had $1.7 billion in annual billings by 1984. In the post-World War II era, Burnett built his agency's reputation by creating brand identities based on animation and live-action characters, including Tony the Tiger, the Jolly Green Giant, Charlie the Tuna, the Pillsbury Doughboy, the lonely Maytag repairman, and the Marlboro Man.[33] Advertising insiders have criticized Burnett's creative work as "corny, unsophisticated, almost childish," particularly in comparison to contemporary agencies such as those of David Ogilvy and Doyle Dane Bernbach.[34] Yet Burnett had the uncanny ability to measure Middle America's pulse. Personally, he enjoyed collecting vernacular, down-home phrases. On his desk, Burnett kept a folder labeled "Corny Language," filled with phrases that conveyed "a feeling of sod-buster honesty."[35] Burnett's intuition and his gut feelings for the myths that structured Americans' sense of place and cultural identity guided his decisions about Marlboro's new brand identity.

Marketing Outsider Masculinities: The Tattoo Campaign, 1954–59

For Marlboro, Leo Burnett crafted a masculine icon whose independence, vigor, and virility offered an alternative to the feminizing effects of postwar conformity, mass culture, and suburbanization. In large part, the campaign focused on "outsider" masculinities, that is, masculine gender positions that did not depend on family life, domesticity, or the breadwinning role as a means of anchoring heteronormativity. As a precursor of the famous cowboys, Marlboro Men of 1955–59 achieved this not with Western imagery, but with a tattoo embossed on the outside of the model's left hand. In print advertisements and television commercials, the tattoo symbolized a virile, outsider masculinity that provided a stark contrast to the cozy postwar domesticity.[36] The campaign featured older men with tattoos that signified a romantic past filled with travel adventures. Two audiences were targeted: the male smoker, who perhaps longed for an adventurous life unencumbered by mortgage payments and a nine-to-five job, and the female smoker, who might fantasize about the raw sexuality of such virile masculinity.

Unlike the familiar sailors' tattoos that testified to a World War II stint in the South Pacific, the Marlboro Man's ephemeral body art was produced in the studio. At the start of each photo shoot, Lee Stanley, the Leo Burnett executive who managed the Philip Morris account, inked a mock tattoo onto

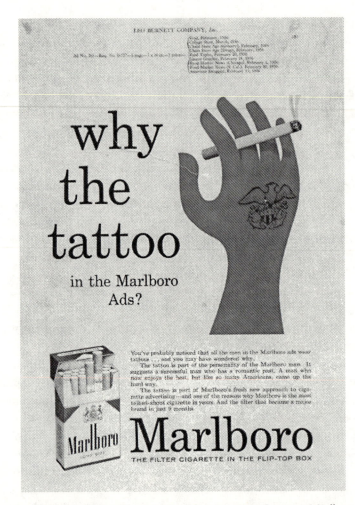

Figure 10.1. "Why the Tattoo?" 1956 print advertisement. Courtesy Marlboro Collection, National Museum of American History Archives Center, Series 4: Advertisements, 1926–86, box 16: Print Ads, 1927–1962.

the model's hand with a ballpoint pen, copying military designs published in a 1944 issue of *National Geographic*.[37] He drew the fake tattoos upside down, so when the model lifted the Marlboro to his mouth, the audience would see the image right-side up. The 1955 Marlboro tattoos included several designs based on naval motifs: lightning flashes crossed by an arrow, an anchor and the letters "USN," and two crossed anchors. One design portrayed a bald eagle gripping a striped shield flanked by two anchors, referencing the official seal of the United States and the U.S. navy (Figure 10.1). The tattoo connoted

American patriotism and the sailor's adventurous life. Although World War II stimulated interest in tattoos among enlisted men and civilians, by 1955 they had lost their significance as military status symbols. A 1946 a poll of servicemen found most new recruits uninterested in tattooing, and body art was in decline by the early 1950s.[38] Tattoo artist Samuel Steward, who researched the relationship between sexuality and tattooing for Alfred Kinsey, recalled the impact of the Marlboro campaign. Suddenly "young men wanted a tattoo on the back of the hand," preferably upside down as shown in the ads.[39] John Landry, brand manager at Philip Morris, described another unusual aspect of the 1954–59 Marlboro Man. For models, the ad campaign used "older men, much more mature men than was usual product advertising at the time—rugged men." Putting a tattoo on the hand of a mature man added to his "mystery and intrigue."[40]

The campaign separated Marlboro from other filter brands and helped the general acceptance of filter cigarettes. The tattoo campaign ran through 1959, when medical concerns over the spread of hepatitis ended the emphasis on tattooing as a sign of masculinity. The dominant ideal for white, heterosexual, middle-class men in the 1950s—the major audience for Marlboro's tattoo campaign—hinged on marriage, family, a white-collar job, a car, and a suburban home.[41] Between 1950 and 1956, the pressures of conformity attracted countless social commentaries, including David Riesman's *The Lonely Crowd*, William H. Whyte's *The Organization Man*, and Robert Lindner's *Must You Conform.*[42] During the 1955 campaign, Leo Burnett engaged contemporary versions of "outsider masculinity" in an effort to associate Marlboro with undomesticated "cool." As we have seen, tattoos signified the sailor's mobility and connoted initiation into his homosocial world. Other images, such as the bass player and bongo drummer used in a 1955 television commercial, defined outside masculinity in terms of beat culture.[43] The photographer in another commercial signified a third type of outsider masculinity: the virile creative artist. As Patricia Vettel-Becker persuasively argues, fashion photography and combat photojournalism had re-gendered professional photography as a "man's world."[44] In all these early Marlboro Man images, we can see an early example of what historian Thomas Frank called "hip consumerism."[45]

Gender, Modeling, and Representation

The use of male models in the early Marlboro campaign represented, however, a possible crisis in gendered representation. Throughout the history of

Western visual culture, and most especially in twentieth-century advertising, women have been represented as the object of a masculine gaze, while men have been understood to be the makers of those representations. John Berger famously summarized, "Men and women appear. Men look at women. Women watch themselves being looked at."[46] These early Marlboro Men, as macho as they strive to be, invite the desiring gaze—a subject position that has historically been seen as feminine. In a 1955 Marlboro commercial featuring an older man who enjoys tinkering with his car, for example, the camera lingers in a sustained close-up on the model's mature face, while a voiceover signifies an introspective interiority that positions its subject as mysterious, elusive, and implicitly an object of desire or identification (and the line between them is slippery). In the first of the cowboy commercials, also from 1955 and featuring what executives later dismissed as a "Hollywood Cowboy," the model's youthful face, crisp clothes, and stillness before the lens position him, implicitly, as the object of the gaze—and hence as "feminine." Leo Burnett faced a challenge with these early television ads. How to develop a male icon, an object of identification and desire, while safeguarding against the implicit feminization of appearing before the lens? In 1950s America, effeminate masculinity connoted the fairy; thus Burnett's challenge concerned both gender (masculinity) and sexuality (heteronormativity). To echo Berger's formulation, how could men "appear" before the lens and not be "women"?

Leo Burnett pursued several options for safeguarding the Marlboro Man's heteronormative masculinity. One approach was to use older models, which Burnett began to do with the tattoo campaign. A second was to begin including women in some of the ads, which he did with the 1958 Better Makin's campaign. The presence of a female figure, however marginal, worked to secure the narrative's heterosexual framework. A third approach considered that, if men's job was to act, rather than appear, then the Marlboro Men would have to start physically moving—their appearances before the lens would need to connote the "action" associated with masculinity. Rather than simply "appearing" before the lens, as women generally did in advertising of this period, Marlboro Men would need to be on the move.

Two 1955 cowboy commercials—one shot in a movie studio, another on location at a ranch—show how Leo Burnett executives constructed the Marlboro Man's image as a heterosexual, masculine icon. The first Marlboro commercial with a cowboy, "A Man and His Cigarette," features a model in Western dress—cowboy hat, ranch shirt, and bandana—securing a rope to a

Figure 10.2. Frame grab from Marlboro television commercial. Courtesy Marlboro Collection, National Museum of American History Archives Center, Television Commercials, reel 1: TV ads 1955–1956.

fence post against a painted cloud backdrop. When the commercial begins, the cowboy is already securing the rope in a minimalist gesture; the fact that nothing is attached to the rope, such as a horse, confirms that little exertion is necessary to accomplish this symbolic activity. As the narrator intones "guess I'll have a cigarette" and reaches for the Marlboros in the chest pocket of his crisp shirt, the viewer's eyes are drawn to the cowboy's body and attire. The camera view does not capture the model's lower body, so the viewer is asked to read macho virility in the head and torso alone. The viewer sees a dark cowboy shirt with light snaps, topped off by a knotted banana so new that the perky ends defy gravity. Neither the Western shirt nor the crisp new hat shows signs of weather, dust, or use outside the studio (Figure 10.2).

Looking back on the campaign thirty years later, Leo Burnett executive John Benson dismissed this image as "a Hollywood cowboy, a model cowboy, who was not very good." Although Benson doesn't spell out why he wasn't any good, I would argue that his youthful good looks, store-bought clothes, and lack of action onscreen presented a problem of gender, which later became coded as a problem of "authenticity." His performance of masculinity, already tainted by his status as a paid model rather than the "real" cowboys who later emerged in the campaign, was insufficient to counter the implicit feminization of appearing before the lens in clothing that "real" cowboys had been denigrating as signifying a "Montgomery Ward cowboy" since the late nineteenth century.[47]

In a second cowboy commercial, the Leo Burnett agency addressed concerns of gender, sexuality, and authenticity by featuring two cowboys in action, on location, on horseback. This 1955 commercial opens with a distant shot of two men on horseback riding down a hill, driving horses into a corral. The cowboys approach the audience, stop, and relax on their mounts while enjoying a smoke of Marlboro cigarettes. Their companionable dialogue disrupts the intimacy established with individual viewers, dissolving any implicit sexual tension between the implied male viewer and the on-screen male models. Furthermore, the models' purposeful movement on horseback deflects the implicit feminization of the lens; heteronormative masculinity is shored up through the manly work of corralling horses.

The cowboy soon emerged as Marlboro's iconic representation of outsider masculinity. John Benson, a Leo Burnett account executive who had worked on Marlboro since 1954, recalled that the creative team had brainstormed about the most macho representation of contemporary American masculinity. Benson recalled the crucial meeting where someone asked, " 'What's the best masculine image in the U.S. today?' Some people said, 'cab driver.' Then finally someone said, 'a cowboy.' And everybody said 'that's it.' " Leo Burnett produced a photograph of a cowboy on the cover of an old *Life* magazine, and, in Benson's memory, "The first Marlboro ad is almost identical to that *Life* magazine cover. . . . We reproduced as close as we could that cover."[48]

In these early years, each Marlboro cowboy wore a mock tattoo on his left hand. Eventually, however, campaign managers realized that the cowboy, rather the tattoo, registered with viewers as a mark of renegade masculinity. Benson remembered, "Every time we ran a cowboy, there was a bump in the Starch report," the ad research report compiled by Starch INRA Hooper.[49] Led by consumer research, the Leo Burnett agency focused the Marlboro campaign on the cowboy.

The cowboy was an inspired branding choice. Every time the cowboy appeared in a Marlboro commercial, audiences interpreted the icon through a cultural lens framed by nearly a hundred years of popular culture. For generations, the cowboy had inspired popular images: Buffalo Bill's Wild West shows of the late 1800s, Owen Wister's popular novel *The Virginian* (1902), and Edward S. Porter's *Great Train Robbery* (1904). The Marlboro Man was a brilliant, intertextual invention, where every spaghetti western worked to co-brand Marlboro and every Marlboro ad promoted the symbolic landscape that fueled the brand's campaign.[50]

Despite the emphasis on "authenticity," unmediated access to the mythic American West was impossible. Kenneth Krom, who joined Burnett's Marlboro team in 1966, had difficulty understanding the West as anything outside representation. Krom admitted that his limited knowledge came from repeated boyhood readings of Andy Adam's *Log of a Cowboy*, first published in 1903.[51] Adam's representation of cowboy life provided Krom with the knowhow to "document" authentic Western life on Marlboro shoots. By the 1960s, the international popularity of Hollywood Westerns helped usher the Marlboro brand into its place as world's most popular cigarette. John Landry, who joined Philip Morris in 1956 as a brand manager, urged Philip Morris to use the Marlboro cowboy in foreign promotions precisely because American Westerns had created a consistent perception of cowboys around the world.[52]

Despite enormous popular interest in the cowboy, Leo Burnett and Philip Morris did not immediately situate their Marlboro Man in the idealized Western landscape that came to be known as "Marlboro Country." The mid-1950s tattoo campaign was followed in the late 1950s by a campaign showing Marlboro men as "regular guys" who invited consumers to "settle back" and enjoy a smoke. By 1958, Marlboro had attained a 4.5 percent market share, but sales were not growing. The "settle back" campaign had failed to reinvigorate Marlboro.[53] In 1962, brand managers developed the "Marlboro Country" campaign, which forever linked the cowboy to the Marlboro Man. Confident in their decision, the Burnett team turned their attention to the selection of an appropriate symbolic landscape. Because most of Marlboro's sales were in major metropolitan areas, 1962 Marlboro Country ads featured model Bob Beck as a Marlboro Man in urban settings, such as an empty Yankee Stadium or Fifth Avenue at dawn. These images committed the Leo Burnett agency to the cowboy as icon.[54]

In 1962, the cowboy's landscape shifted from distinctive urban spaces to the open sky of the Old West. A member of Burnett's creative team came to the office with a record of Elmer Bernstein's soundtrack for *The Magnificent Seven* (1960). The team played the soundtrack while rolling the footage of a recently shot commercial. The linkage between the cowboy, the Western landscape, and the Marlboro cigarette was complete. After the Leo Burnett agency negotiated with United Artists and Yul Brynner for the rights to the soundtrack, the new Marlboro Country campaign went on the air in mid-1963. The thematic elements of Marlboro ads have remained relatively unchanged since that time, despite the ban on cigarette advertising on television after 1971.[55]

Modeling Masculinity: Professionals Versus the "Real Thing"

The Leo Burnett agency's most successful formula for anchoring the Marlboro Man's heterosexual, macho masculinity was to distance him from the term "model." As the brand's advertising managers developed the Marlboro Country campaign, which situated a working cowboy in a nonindustrialized, nonurbanized Western landscape, they also developed a discourse of authenticity and "realness" to describe the Marlboro Men. In contrast to the artifice of femininity, the "realness" of the Marlboro Men as working cowboys, rather than paid professional models, worked to secure a dominant reading of their representation as both heterosexual and masculine. As in other aspects of the Marlboro advertising campaign, this gender work took several years, between 1954 and the mid-1960s, to finalize. By the late 1960s the Marlboro Man was marketed consistently as a working cowboy, a "real" man whose implicit other was the feminized professional model, also known as the "Hollywood cowboy." In this equation, "realness" and "authenticity" become synonyms for heteronormative masculinity, while paid commercial modeling emerges as a synonym for femininity and, implicitly, queer masculinity.

Whether in 1954 or 1968, Philip Morris and Leo Burnett sought to depict the Marlboro Men not as professional models but as real working men.[56] In 1954, Leo Burnett vice president Owen Smith reported that Marlboro men were "businessmen, army and navy officers," and even antique dealers who had a hypermasculine appearance. By the 1960s, however, account executives, who had grown dissatisfied with surrogates, started recruiting actual ranch hands. The brand's macho image became anchored to the models' status as "working cowboys," rather than men who simply looked the part.

In the 1954–59 period, the campaign's photographer, Constantin Joffe, a leading photographer for *Vogue*, procured most of the tattoo models. Studio employees brought in friends from the local National Guard unit; commuter trains were searched for likely types. According to a trade article about the campaign in 1958, "to get the outdoor type for the cowboy, the suburbs were combed for healthy, manly looking faces."[57] The campaign was also distinctive for the dominant role of the photographic image in the print campaign, whether in magazines, newspapers, or outdoor advertising. Joffe departed from the fully lit set of contemporary ad campaigns and went back to the dramatically lit studio style of Edward Steichen's 1930s portrait work for *Vanity Fair*, where celebrity sitters such as Greta Garbo were portrayed with a modernist sparseness and intensity. Joffe sought, through lighting, to eradicate any softness and to create the sharp angles that connoted "as strong and masculine an image as possible."[58]

Throughout the 1950s and 1960s, Marlboro account executives distanced themselves from the term "model," stressing the men in their advertisements were not professionally trained mannequins. Disparaging models as fake and inauthentic, executives referred to the men in their television and print ads as "wranglers" (Tom Jarrard, a cowboy type who was hired as a model for a 1985 campaign, recalled, "I've never been called a wrangler until I worked . . . for Marlboro").[59] In John Landry's view, the authenticity of the cowboy as "real," rather than a paid model, was legible on his body. Landry believed that audiences could see the difference: "You can see it in their faces—these are people who have lived outdoors. In a subconscious way, people can identify with it because it is real."[60] Kenneth Krom, who began working on the Marlboro account for Leo Burnett in 1966, reiterated these themes when discussing television commercials. In his view, paid professional models did not know how to "hold the rope" or "cut up that steer." Even models who were good actors could not convince audiences they were real cowboys. "It's not believable. . . . It doesn't work!"[61]

Krom's marks suggest a "realness"—to the Western landscape, to cowboy life—that can somehow be effectively communicated, without mediation, to Marlboro viewers. In fact, Krom used the rhetoric of journalism, or documentary film, to describe his on-location work as creative director—how they "covered," or "documented," a cattle round up, for example. The campaigns paradoxically participated in the construction of an idealized landscape and way of life that bears a distorted relationship to history—Marlboro ads had no black or Hispanic cowboys, no all-terrain vehicles—but at the same time insisted on a rhetoric of documentary truth in their photographic realism. The account executives' insistence on the authenticity of the cowboy "wranglers" has been a constitutive element of this rhetoric. Executives' disparaging of the "professional model" and the "Hollywood cowboy" was a tactic designed to distance the campaign from the artifice of performance, which is the model's (and actor's) stock in trade. Furthermore the Marlboro Man's status as a "real cowboy" served to shore up his heterosexual masculinity, as the profession of male model, then as now, often connoted a more fluid sexual identity than the straight norm.

In 1968, Marlboro account executives found Darrell Winfield, the person who became the ur-Marlboro Man. Between the late 1960s and the 1980s, Winfield dominated Marlboro Country advertisements. Winfield was raised in a farming area of California's San Joaquin Valley by dustbowl migrant parents from Oklahoma. While working in a California feed yard, Winfield accepted a job on a Wyoming ranch, moving there in 1968 around age thirty-eight. Three months later, in March, Winfield met photographer Jim Braddy and Leo Burnett's creative director Ken Krom at a ranch, the Quarter Circle Five. In Wyoming to scout locations, the admen heard about Winfield's look and tried to track him down as a possible model. When they met, Winfield was digging ice out of an irrigation ditch. For Krom the moment was sublime: "I had seen cowboys, but I had never seen one that just really, like, sort of scared the hell out of me." Winfield embodied Krom's vision of the ideal Marlboro Man. Rugged and honest, he looked like a "born leader," a cowboy without "any enemies."

Over the next twenty years, the "constant camaraderie" between adman, photographer, and model fueled the men's creative energies.[62] The advertising campaigns that emerged gave material expression to the Marlboro Man of Krom's imagination. After Winfield's retirement in the late 1980s, the Leo Burnett agency looked high and low for a replacement. After spending more than $300 million in a talent search involving more than 10,000 candidates, the agency mourned the loss of the ur-Marlboro Man. "We probably have to face the fact that we will never find another Winfield."[63]

Krom's account of his "discovery" of Winfield, repeated in many Burnett stories about Marlboro's history, engaged the rhetoric of outdoor adventure and exploration. Like a natural resource borne of the Western landscape, Winfield was a "diamond in the rough" whose weathered face and outdoor squint anchored his authenticity, while distancing him from the artifice of paid professional modeling. By the postwar years, most commercial photographers found their subjects through professional modeling agencies, such as Eileen Ford's New York firm, Ford Models. By the 1950s the international fame of celebrated models such as Dovima (Dorothy Horan), Suzy Parker, and Lisa Fonssagrives, and the work of fashion photographers such as Richard Avedon and Irving Penn, had transformed American fashion modeling and turned fashion photography into a respected commercial art form. For the first time, as their models appeared on the covers of *Vogue* or *Harper's Bazaar*, photographers began to eclipse the role of designers in developing the season's "look," or feminine ideal. Patricia Vettel-Becker has argued that "nothing signified artifice more than the fashion photograph."[64] In contrast to this artifice and its associated femininity, Leo Burnett created the authentic masculinity of the "real" working cowboy and offered it to American audiences as the Marlboro brand's icon.

Winfield began posing as the Marlboro Man in fall 1968. For the first six or seven years, he worked part-time, retaining his summer job as a ranch foreman supervising four cowboys and managing a herd of 6,000 cattle. By the mid-1970s, Winfield began working full-time as the Marlboro Man. He had ten or so shoots a year, each five to ten days long. For each he received $350 per day for on-camera work and $200 for travel days.[65] Although Winfield helped the creative team locate additional wranglers, he mostly performed as the lead Marlboro Man. His relationships with Krom and Braddy grew increasingly close; he even vacationed with Krom and his family, as well as other Leo Burnett personnel, in Costa Rica.[66] While on the Marlboro payroll, Winfield distanced himself from the category of professional "model." Reflecting on his experience after his retirement, Winfield still maintained that the work was less like modeling and more like a real man's job. "To me, it's more like a ranch job, but with higher pay."[67] Having long been on the Philip Morris payroll, Winfield associated himself with the brand's image of authenticity and heteronormative masculinity.

With the shift to "real" cowboys as models, authenticity emerged as a key discourse in anchoring the heteronormativity of the Marlboro Man. To be a model—someone who is paid to perform with commodities before the lens—is to be implicitly feminized. Along with a variety of other strategies designed to counter the implicit feminization of the advertising model, including an emphasis on outsider masculinities and on action, the "realness" of the Marlboro Man as a working cowboy emerged in the 1960s as the brand's final approach in securing him as an icon of heteronormative masculinity.

But an image's meanings are produced through complex social relationships between viewer and image, shaped by the historical contexts in which the image is seen and interpreted. Though account executives might work to produce a dominant reading of the Marlboro Man's butch masculinity as heterosexual, specific historical viewers might make different readings of this iconic figure. In fact, Leo Burnett's crafting of a macho version of postwar masculinity appealed not only to straight viewers, but to gay ones as well.

Some postwar gay men, seeking to define new forms of gay sexuality, defined a new gender identity that joined both homosexuality and normative masculinity. This butch masculinity, increasingly articulated in the leather and motorcycle spaces of 1950s and 1960s gay male culture, and elaborated in the gay rodeo roundups of the 1970s, was increasingly defined against the feminized gender formations of the sissy or fairy.[68] For this group of men, for whom homosexuality and butch masculinity were coterminous, the Marlboro Man emerged as an important icon of both desire and identification.

CHAPTER ELEVEN

The Body and the Brand:
How Lycra Shaped America

Kaori O'Connor

ON THE MORNING of October 28, 1959, the world's fashion and trade press, along with leading manufacturers of foundation garments, textiles, and clothing, gathered at the Empire State Building on Fifth Avenue in New York City. Dominating the street synonymous with American style, the skyscraper symbolized American commercial supremacy, housing the offices of many top corporations, including E. I. du Pont de Nemours & Company. The world's largest chemical company and nylon's inventor, DuPont had summoned press and producers to announce its newest textile fiber.[1]

Developed in DuPont's laboratories and wear-tested under conditions of blanket secrecy, the new fiber had been the subject of intense speculation in the textile and garment industries. Anticipation was keen as the key members of DuPont's Textile Fibers Department spoke about the fiber, which DuPont had named "Lycra" so recently that many company employees still called it "Fiber K," its code name during development.[2] Lycra, the managers revealed, was an elastomeric fiber that stretched and snapped back into place like rubber but, unlike rubber, was resistant to the deterioration caused by perspiration and cosmetic oils and lotions. In addition, it could be dyed, machine washed, and machine dried with complete safety. Much lighter than conventional elastic thread but with two to three times as much restraining power,

Lycra could be used to make girdles that were light, soft, and sheer while providing the figure control of bulkier foundations. In an age when women of all ages wore girdles as a matter of course, the commercial potential of more comfortable and practical foundation garments was clear.

The guests were then invited to examine press kits that had been placed under their chairs. Each folder contained a sample of an innocuous white fiber that gave little hint of the more than twenty years of research and $10 million worth of investment that had gone into creating it. Alone, the new fiber did not look impressive, but it was not meant to. Lycra was what is now called an "ingredient brand," a fiber that was never used on its own. Instead, it was combined with other fibers like nylon to give them the invisible quality of stretch, thereby enhancing their performance and value. DuPont hoped that Lycra would bring about as great a change in the women's foundation garment industry as nylon had in the hosiery industry. And it did, although it is doubtful if anyone in that room on the day Lycra was launched could have foreseen quite how that would come about.

This chapter is an anthropological study of how Lycra came to occupy the position it holds today, as one of the world's top ten textile brands recognized by Interbrand, and one of the top fashion innovations of the twentieth century as designated by the Council of Fashion Designers of America.[3] It shows how fashion is produced, but it is not a straightforward account of how a particular fashion was created *by* a particular producer. This is an account of how Lycra was first accepted and then rejected by women consumers, only becoming successful after it returned to the market in an entirely different form from that originally envisioned by DuPont, as a result of sweeping social, economic, and demographic change.

The cultural turn in business history, which entails looking at commerce in broad social and cultural contexts rather than in narrow, purely economic ones, has brought anthropology and the anthropological method to the fore. By treating Western society like any of the exotic groups they are used to studying, anthropologists aim to shed the preconceptions that all people have about their own society, thereby gaining insights that may not be apparent to other disciplines. While conventional economics cast business as a wholly rational system of production driven by profit and manipulative of consumers, anthropology sees capitalism as a cultural system, sustained by the dynamic relationship between production and consumption, producer and consumer, culture and commerce, in which none is permanently dominant.[4] Anthropology differs from business history written in the tradition of Joseph

Schumpeter in that it does not focus on individual entrepreneurs whose personal qualities are often advanced as sole explanations for a company's success.[5] Unlike sociology, it is not concerned primarily with organizational studies and labor relations. Unlike design history, it does not focus on style, high fashion, and designers; unlike cultural and media studies, it is not interested mainly in image and personal identity.[6] For anthropologists, products are not just goods, but social values in material form. Fashion is not about elite or highly individualistic costumes but about broad sociocultural changes over time that are significant to the population as a whole, as manifested through what large numbers of people wear in everyday life.[7] The aim of the anthropological approach presented here is to investigate how business, technology, and society interact over time in the mass market to produce fashion. While most studies of fashion focus on clothes or individual designers, this one begins with the fiber that made the fabric that made the clothes, because for almost a century new manmade fibers have had more influence on mass-market fashion, and vice versa, than anything else.

A study of this kind requires three elements: a large-scale producer; an easily identifiable and statistically significant group of consumers; and a product that is ubiquitous and therefore widely relevant, one of sufficiently recent invention that it can be tracked against the background of contemporary social change. Here these are provided by the DuPont Company, Lycra, and the baby-boomer birth cohort born between 1946 and 1964, for whom DuPont's spandex fiber was invented. Normally a single company, however large, would not be considered sufficiently representative or influential, but DuPont is exceptional. As David A. Hounshell and John Kenly Smith, Jr., authors of a magisterial study of the company's research-and-development activities between 1902 and 1980, put it, "Understanding something about this institution is a key to comprehending the modern world."[8]

The larger study from which this paper is drawn involved both ethnography and archival research, notably in the DuPont corporate archives at the Hagley Museum and Library in Wilmington, Delaware. The DuPont archive is a meticulous record of the many products invented and developed by the firm since its founding in 1802. Altogether a remarkable collection, it constitutes a "private psychology and sociology of the consumer society," which gives unique insights into the way products came into being and reached their markets.[9] Although business historians are beginning to examine producers' records, they remain a largely neglected resource. Some historians are concerned that records created by producers may only give a positive view of products and their performance, but this is not the case with the DuPont archive. Professional researchers know how to critique self-produced accounts and will always consult other sources for comparative purposes. Nonetheless, it is still predominantly the case, as Regina Lee Blaszczyk has noted, that scholars continue to examine consumer society from every vantage point except that of the companies that made the goods.[10] For an anthropologist, to investigate how fashion is produced while ignoring the producers is like doing ethnography without asking the natives what they think. To help redress the balance, this paper has used the producer's archive as the primary source for the following account.

"To Serve a Market, Fill a Need"

Founded in 1802 by Eleuthère Irénée du Pont, a French émigré who had been trained at the government powder works by Antoine Lavoisier, the father of French chemistry, the DuPont approach to commerce from the outset was "to serve a market, fill a need."[11] In a nation expanding across an undeveloped continent, blasting and gunpowder products were indispensable commodities, and DuPont developed a distinctive market strategy based on inventing its own high-quality powders, and then tightly controlling every aspect of their manufacture and distribution. DuPont's powder salesmen were under explicit instructions to solve the customers' problems for them, building up loyalty through providing technical support and free advice, thus adding value to the firm's products. Salesmen were also ordered to question customers closely about their needs, and this information was fed back to the DuPont powder mills and laboratories where further refinements to the product were made in response to customer's requirement in a continuous process of research and development. By 1850, DuPont dominated the nation's explosives market.

In anthropological terms, the roots of the corporate culture that developed at DuPont were: (1) a shared family tradition that evolved into an exceptionally strong company identity and a veneration for particular ways of working associated with the founder amounting to something of an ancestor cult; (2) the belief that the company had a special relationship with chemistry, which produced an almost religious dedication to scientific research and development; (3) an identification between the growth and good of the company and the growth and good of the nation, which always led it to think in mass-market terms; and (4) a tradition of identifying closely with company products and developing them over time. It was this culture that helped the company make the transition from private family partnership to public corporation in 1902, and a diversification from general explosives into other areas of applied chemistry as a result of losing an antitrust suit in 1911.

In the early twentieth century, DuPont began to work on its new diversified products in the same way it had with explosives, with one significant difference. With very few exceptions, the company would never again expose itself to antitrust action by selling finished products on the open consumer market, as it had with powder. Instead, it would invent and develop raw products such as plastics, fibers, and finishes, and sell them to manufacturers to make up or incorporate in final consumer goods like radios, ornaments, polishes, tableware, cloth, and clothes. By 1935, when the advertising agency Batten, Barton, Durstin, & Osborn (BBDO) drafted DuPont's famous slogan "Better Things for Better Living . . . Through Chemistry," goods made from the company's chemical products were a fundamental and ubiquitous part of American material life.[12]

In the post-World War II era, DuPont's Textile Fibers Department, which was formed in 1952 out of the Rayon Department, became its most successful division, dominating the synthetic-fiber market worldwide. Ultimately, there were seven members of what DuPont called its "family of fibers," invented or developed in its laboratories: rayon, acetate, nylon, Dacron polyester, Orlon acrylic, Teflon flourocarbon, and Lycra spandex. DuPont entered the textile fibers business in the 1910s with cellulose or "artificial silk," later called rayon. Women had begun to emerge as a significant group of consumers, and most artificial silk was used for women's underwear and hosiery. As Ariel Beaujot has shown earlier in this volume, the company already had unrivalled experience with cellulose as a chemical raw material, and the new program of cellulose research and advanced engineering technology were legacies of the explosives business. To this expertise DuPont added the new field of market research, using it to investigate the nascent women's market with the aim of finding out what women wanted from textiles, then developing fibers to order. In time, DuPont built up a Textile Fibers Department unparalleled in the trade, embracing consumer research, advertising, promotion, publicity, and retail merchandising. Some studies, for internal use only and regarded as highly confidential, were used to guide the development of new processes and fibers by the research and technical divisions. Edited versions of the findings were used as aids in selling fiber to DuPont's customers, helping to take the guesswork out of buying decisions. There were also surveys on fashion trends and colors, and general information on consumer preferences. DuPont's immediate customers were able to share this information with their own customers, generating sales all the way down the chain. This was a service that few competitors could offer, and no manufacturer or retailer had the financial wherewithal to spend on comparable research. It provided a compelling incentive to work with DuPont, and it considerably enhanced the "value" of DuPont fibers. Preserved in the DuPont corporate archives, the records of these activities provide unique insights into something that is central to daily life, but little studied or understood, that is, the process through which a fashion or product comes into use, from start to finish.

The Lycra Innovation

Lycra, like rayon, had its origins in attempts by scientists to duplicate a natural material that resulted in the invention of a synthetic substance that far exceeded the natural one in capabilities. In the case of Lycra, that natural material was rubber, an essential element in products used for ventilation, insulation, electrical conduction, and hygiene. Because DuPont was a leading producer of the chemicals used in rubber processing, the firm was aware that natural rubber latex was not resistant to solvents, oxidation, sunlight, or heat. Through its growing experience with textile fibers and ladies' apparel, DuPont also knew the women's foundation-garment industry relied on rubberized yarn to give elasticity and support, despite widespread dissatisfaction with rubber's lack of durability and comfort. Putting the two together, DuPont managers identified a market opportunity for a synthetic material that did not have rubber's faults, and could do things that the natural product could not.[13]

American women's magazines of the immediate post-World War II era depicted the well-ordered world of what has been called the "togetherness age,"[14] characterized by a uniformity of look and lifestyle that both created and was created by a strictly gendered mass market.[15] In all areas of production and consumption, this was a "his and hers" world in which goods reinforced the gender distinction and women's place was seen as firmly in the home.[16] The ideal woman was always beautifully groomed, perfumed, and powdered, with every hair in place. However warm the weather, she never perspired, but simply "glowed." She was expected to be gentle in speech and manner, and from childhood she was taught to walk gracefully, not to run. Women wore skirts on a daily basis, and trousers were considered acceptable only for gardening or active leisure. In the spreading suburbs and in cities large and small, women's clothes, embellished with feminine trimmings, prints, and colors, emphasized their social identity as dependent, ornamental, and essentially passive supports to the dominant male. Women wore neat dresses, smart suits, fitted jackets, cocktail frocks, sweaters with slim pencil skirts, gathered skirts with well-defined waists, but the most significant element was what *couldn't* be seen—the girdle that every woman wore underneath her clothes.

Recently social historians have suggested that the degree of homogeneity depicted in the popular media of the period was misleading. But no matter what may have happened in private, this was indisputably a period of exceptionally strong conformity and social control in public, control which for woman was exemplified by the foundation garment known as the girdle. The role of the girdle was to control the physical and social female body. As the anthropologist Mary Douglas put it, "the social body constrains the way the physical body is perceived."[17]

Like the Victorian corset from which it evolved, the girdle was a garment that, in every sense, kept women in their place.[18] The socially acceptable body had to be firm, with no wiggle or movement. The phrase "a loose woman," with all its connotations, has its origins in the social horror of the uncontrolled female and her body. Throughout the 1940s and 1950s, it was taken for granted that all women would wear girdles—always in public, and very often in private. Not to do so was considered as shocking as appearing naked. For young women, donning a girdle for the first time was a kind of rite of passage, a sign of transition from childhood to young womanhood. Girdle advertisements were a mainstay of women's magazines, and department stores had extensive foundation sections that were often the most profitable in the store. Specialized ladies' foundation shops were a ubiquitous feature of the retail landscape, and mail-order catalogs like those of Sears, Roebuck and Company, which featured page after page of foundation garments, carried girdles into the hinterlands. Mothers and daughters of the 1950s found themselves in the embrace of an industry whose presence in their lives was unquestioned, and whose advertisements spoke to them in a special language in which words and phrases like "considerate," "controlling," "quicker than a diet," "very necessary," and "the foundation of good form" were repeated like mantras. Girdles were so taken for granted that even Mattel Inc.'s Barbie, launched in 1959 as the first "grown-up" doll with a contemporary fashion wardrobe, wore a girdle.

So completely has the once-ubiquitous girdle disappeared from general wear today that few people born after 1980 have any experience or recollection of it. There is no parallel in modern textiles to the stiffness of early girdle fabric, which compressed the body in a way that would now be considered intolerable, and which did not correspond in any way to the strong yet supple hold, so reminiscent of natural skin or muscle, that we think of today as "stretch." Getting into a girdle was a complex operation invariably described as a "struggle" or "murder" by women now in their seventies and eighties. This was the case even if the wearer was of normal weight because, to be effective, the girdle had to fit very tightly. One former girdle wearer recalled that easing into it was "like rolling dough with a rolling pin." Since they were so stiff, girdles couldn't simply be pulled on, but had to be fastened with hooks and eyes, or zippers, which often pinched the skin painfully. Once a woman was encased in the girdle, normal body movements like bending and sitting became awkward, perspiration was a problem, eating was often uncomfortable, and even attending to basic bodily functions could be difficult. As one woman put it, "We used to joke a lot about 'holding on' until we got home," while another said, "You went to the bathroom before you put on the girdle, you put on the girdle just before you left home, and you tried not to eat and drink while you were out."

Girdles were worn by women of all classes, across all income groups. The only thing that varied was the quality and quantity. Because rubber girdles were difficult to clean and took a long time to dry, a minimum of three was considered necessary. Also, since it was widely believed that it was impossible to look good in clothes without wearing a foundation garment beneath them, women sought to have a selection of girdles to suit different types of outerwear. There were many different kinds of girdles, the most common being panty girdles, high-rise girdles that covered the midriff, and long-line girdles that encased the body from underarms to hips, and sometimes to the knees. All girdles were fitted with tabs to hold up stockings.

The girdle was a significant item of mass production and mass consumption, a commodity with a firm grip on its market. But how and why did a garment that was uncomfortable and restrictive to a point that is unimaginable today come to occupy such a central position in both commerce and culture? In anthropological terms, whatever functional properties it possessed, the girdle above all was a symbol: a materialization, in commodity form, of beliefs and values relating to what it meant to be a "respectable" or "good" woman. And in the climate of the times, it set a standard from which few women felt willing or able to deviate.

In fashion terms, the girdle was as close to a "need" as it was possible to get, and it is no surprise that DuPont fixed its eyes on the market for a new elastomeric fiber. DuPont had become interested in developing a synthetic elastic fiber in the 1930s, but early results had been disappointing. As soon as World War II ended, the company resumed its efforts. Following established procedure, DuPont undertook consumer research, which confirmed the existence of a large potential market, but the performance requirements for an elastic fiber suitable for girdles proved to be more demanding than anticipated. Meanwhile, as the population grew steadily, so did the market for girdles. DuPont's exasperation was clear in a 1954 internal memo that began: "We have been knocking on this door for more than ten years. . . . We should not put off moving in this direction until we have a 'perfect' product. . . . There is no 'perfect' product because no one yarn will satisfy all elastic end-use requirements."[19]

DuPont's top secret stretch fiber project now moved into high gear. A promising new fiber called "Fiber K" was selected as the best candidate for development. There was no "eureka moment" for Lycra, no sudden and dramatic discovery in the laboratory, as there had been with nylon. Lycra was the result of DuPont's slow and painstaking work on polymer technology, which had gone on for many years and would continue for many more.

An existing DuPont plant at Waynesboro, Virginia, was adapted to produce the new fiber. Once prototypes of the new stretch yarn and fabric had been produced, DuPont teamed up with potential customers, such as the Warner Brothers Corset Company, to produce sample garments for wear-testing among consumers. DuPont also asked female employees at the Waynesboro factory to wear-test early girdle prototypes. This not only provided a control against which to compare results provided by professional testing agencies, but it also helped employees identify with the product on a personal level. To stimulate thinking about the future commercial applications of Fiber K while trials continued, the company held brainstorming sessions among marketing and management personnel at the head office. "Creativity" was a business buzz word of the 1950s, and the "brainstorming" technique developed by Alex Osborn at the BBDO advertising agency was used by major American companies, including the Campbell Soup Company and the Eastman Kodak Company. Brainstorming aimed to generate creative approaches to sales, merchandising, promotion, packaging, cost reduction, and product use and adaptation. For Fiber K, the problem posed was "What possible applications can you see for stretch yarn?" The brainstorming session produced many suggestions, including use in foundation garments, covers for sports cars, one-size clothing, and chinstraps to wear at night to correct double chins. Significantly, because the postwar baby boom was well under-way, many of the suggestions referred to children, including expanding toy bags to keep kids' rooms neat and Halloween costumes that would stretch over the years, making their purchase more economical.[20]

For more than thirty years, the mainstream foundation market had re-mained remarkably stable and manufacturers anticipated no change. It was in this positive atmosphere of commercial certainty that, after a large-scale trade evaluation of sample girdles, Fiber K was given the name Lycra and announced to the world at the Empire State Building in 1959. From the day it went public, every aspect of Lycra was tightly controlled by the company, beginning with the name itself. To emphasize the uniqueness of the trade-mark, DuPont insisted that the name should always be used in quotation marks, "Lycra." Reaching beyond DuPont's direct customers, marketing and promotion were aimed at the makers, sellers, and users of girdles. This pulled Lycra through the fiber chain from the front, augmenting the "push" sup-plied by production and sales, as shown in DuPont's diagram (Figure 11.1).

The marketing services for Lycra followed the pattern that had been developed for DuPont's earlier fibers, and covered four areas. Marketing re-search conducted and commissioned information that was used to inform product development. Advertising and promotion dealt with magazine ads, television commercials, store displays, and garment tags. Retail marketing educated store buyers and sales personnel on how to sell Lycra garments. Publicity generated news items and articles to take the story of Lycra to the garment trade and the public. Because Lycra was unlike any existing fiber, DuPont had to mount an intensive campaign to teach retail staff how to sell foundation garments made of it, and to show consumers how to wear them. DuPont provided retail sales staff with booklets entitled *How to Promote "Lycra" Spandex Fiber—and Have Better Sales Figures Too* and *How to Make "Lycra" Spandex Fiber E-x-p-a-n-d Your Sales*. One booklet gave a list of com-mon customer questions and figure problems, to which the salesperson was encouraged to respond by always suggesting a Lycra girdle.[21]

Since the late 1940s, DuPont had invested heavily in direct consumer

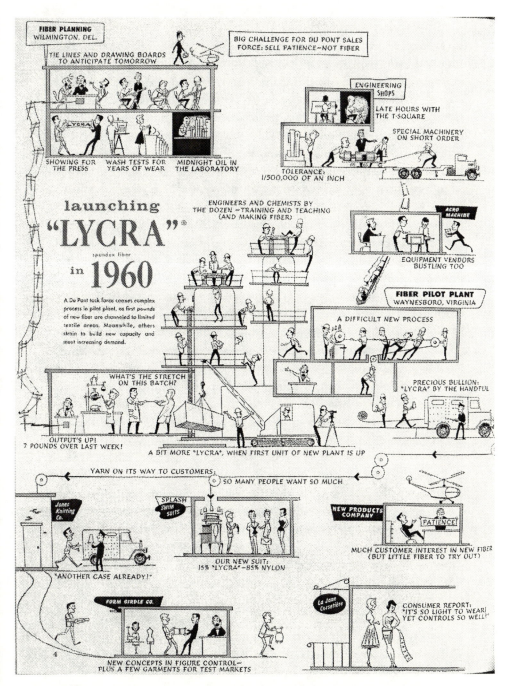

Figure 11.1. Launching Lycra in 1960. From "Stretch Plus Strength," *DuPont Magazine* 54 (Feb. 1960): 4. Courtesy Hagley Museum and Library.

advertising to promote its new synthetic fibers. In this vein, the company launched Lycra with an extensive publicity campaign, taking advertisements in newspapers and full-page ads in leading women's magazines such as *Vogue, Harper's Bazaar, Glamour, Mademoiselle, McCall's, Ladies' Home Journal,* and *Good Housekeeping.* Conventional girdle advertisements of the period showed perfectly groomed and girdled models modestly posed in tasteful settings, under anodyne captions like "The Intimate Story" and "The Line of Beauty." Because Lycra was an innovative fiber, the advertisements faced the challenge of conveying an invisible but significant difference. One advertisement did not show a Lycra girdle at all. Instead, an elegant hand with beautifully manicured 1950s nails held a girdle of rubberized thread disdainfully over an open garbage can, with the caption, "Your Girdle Is Out of Date . . . Thanks to Lycra." One ad in *Vanity Fair* promised, "Here is supple comfort that slithers in and out of modern compact cars." The "At Last" campaign was especially memorable. Instead of the rigid seated or standing poses of conventional girdle advertisements, this Lycra campaign showed girdles on bodies in dynamic motion. Bending, jumping, and high-kicking, the girdles danced across magazine pages partnered with exuberant captions that gave insight into the physical and social experience of girdle wearing before the invention of Lycra. The captions said things like "At last—a girdle that lets you breathe—even after shrimp, steak, French fries, salad, parfait and coffee."

Girdles with Lycra were an immediate success when they first came on the market, even though they were more expensive than other foundations. A girdle with Lycra cost $7.95 in 1961, compared to a Lastex rubber girdle at $5. Ironically, at the outset, DuPont was a victim of its own success. Girdles of Lycra were so comfortable that many women doubted they could do the job of figure control effectively, obliging the company to undertake more advertising to reassure customers of Lycra's efficacy. As with the first nylon stockings, demand for Lycra girdles far outran supply, and there was a justifiable air of satisfaction within the company. As *DuPont Magazine* summarized:

> A few years ago, DuPont textile men began asking a question that one wag noted went to the foundation of female fashions: "What are the characteristics of a good girdle?" . . . And in a series of surveys and test panels, American women replied in no uncertain terms. They wanted comfort, coolness, firm support, softness, ease of washing, contoured tailoring, fast drying and shape retention.

From such pronouncements stemmed sizeable events, notably continued development of a new product. . . . Justification: belief that
Lycra can be tailored to meet these demands and give the consumer
what she clearly wanted.[22]

But did she *really* want it, and who was "she"? Even before Lycra was
launched, hints were coming from the hosiery market that a new kind of
consumer would alter the consumption patterns that had remained stable for
so long. Like girdles and other foundations, the wearing of stockings by
women had long been considered obligatory, and during World War II, when
DuPont's entire nylon fiber output was allocated to military uses, women
had gone to extreme lengths to repair torn stockings, and to disguise bare
legs when mending failed. While sales of nylons boomed again after the war,
within a few years hosiery manufacturers and retailers began to notice signs
of change. In 1956, the year Fiber K went into development, DuPont commissioned a study on behalf of the hosiery industry that found younger
women were not buying stockings in the expected numbers, thinking them
"uncomfortable," "inconvenient," "requiring a girdle," and, particularly telling, "inappropriate with slacks." "It is a truism, applicable to many products,
that starting the young person as a consumer of a given product is perhaps
the most effective way of perpetuating product use in later years," the report
concluded. "*This is a danger signal.*"[23]

In hindsight, the hosiery survey's warning that younger women might
be a fundamentally different breed of consumer—to which DuPont responded by promoting stockings in fashion colors, which they hoped would
appeal to the young—was much more significant than was realized at the
time. Few other synthetic-fiber manufacturers matched DuPont's ability to
invent and develop fibers or its marketing and promotion capabilities. Yet
despite DuPont's efforts, and although the numbers of women in the population arriving at the age of girdle-wearing continued to rise dramatically year
by year due to the maturing of the boomers, the sales of girdles of all kinds
began to fall for the first time.

While DuPont had continued to focus on the technical side of fabric
innovation, a substantial demographic, economic, and cultural shift was taking place. World War II had been followed by a baby boom that produced
the largest birth cohort in history. In America, the baby boom coincided with
unprecedented postwar economic growth. Producing for the fledgling cohort
of "boomers," as they came to be called, became a boom industry in itself,

for, culturally as well as numerically, these children were at the heart of postwar life. At the center of the private world of their parents and the public world of mass marketers, this cohort grew up with the self-confidence and sense of entitlement that later earned them the nickname "the Me Generation." DuPont had been a leading producer of the synthetic materials that made up the boomers' hygienic nursing bottles, unbreakable plates, easy-care clothes, washable toys, and much more. DuPont and other producers had long anticipated that the aging of the boomer cohort would produce a larger adult consumer market. What had not been foreseen was how different from their parents these new consumers would be.

The Backlash Against the Girdle

By the time Lycra was finally launched, America was a society on the brink of transformation. Among consumers, the group who would be instrumental in cultural change during the 1960s and 1970s were the vanguard boomers, who became teenagers just as Lycra girdles came on the market. The introduction of the birth control pill in the 1960s gave women sexual freedom and the means to control reproduction. A rise in female employment outside the home increased female independence in spheres other than the sexual. The Vietnam War, the Civil Rights Movement, hippie anti-materialism, the emergence of youth culture, and Women's Liberation introduced boomers to liberal and radical politics in the widest sense. All these struck deep at postwar conformist culture and the assumptions about female dependency and identity underpinning it. These cultural changes produced a climate in which the girdle—a ubiquitous garment that seemed to embody conformist assumptions and values—became an anachronism.

   Where the girdle had been controlling of women, many women now wanted to be in control of themselves. Where it had been considered "natural" to wear girdles, girdles were now seen as unnatural, a barrier between a woman and her "real" self. Once seen to be healthy, girdles were now seen as the reverse. "Health" itself had come to have a wider meaning than simply being disease free. The new meaning implied independence and "wholeness," representing a movement away from a life now considered to have been only partial and unfulfilled. Above all, girdles came to be considered emblematic of an era that was now fast passing away. As boomers saw it, they symbolized older generations that were culturally and chronologically separated from their own by an unbridgeable gap.

Although the burning of bras is always cited as the great symbolic fashion event of the period, few women actually burned them.[24] Instead, brassiere sales rose in proportion to population growth, because so many "long-line" girdles had built-in bras. But if bra-burning was something of a myth, abandoning girdles was not. As they arrived at the girdle age, young boomers refused to wear them. Those who already owned some began throwing them away. Rejecting the girdle emerged as the defining sartorial event of female boomers' youth. Consumption patterns changed even more dramatically when mothers emulated their daughters by abandoning girdles, an act that many described as emblematic of their belated "emancipation" or "liberation."

By the mid-1970s, girdle sales in the United States and Great Britain were half what they had been in 1965.[25] This figure is startling because of the increase in the female population during the boomer era. The fiber and foundations industries now had to contemplate the possibility that the drop in girdle sales was not a temporary aberration or fad. Having wrestled for more than twenty years with the problems of stress decay, tensile strength, colorfastness, and resistance to degradation by gasses, solvents, and lights; having undertaken extensive market research to establish the existence of a consumer market for lighter girdles; having created Lycra for this market and having spent $10 million on research and development, DuPont now found that the market for girdles was fast disappearing for reasons that had nothing to do with the technological capabilities of the product, and everything to do with a change in culture that it did not understand.

DuPont was not entirely dependent on foundation garments or on a single fiber, but Lycra sales had been significantly affected by the girdle downturn. The decline of the girdle also affected the profits of DuPont's long-term customers, the girdle manufacturers and *their* customers, the foundation retailers. In 1975, DuPont initiated consumer research into the problem. The studies were done for the benefit of the foundation industry generally, but also in DuPont's own interest as the major manufacturer of stretch fiber. Reassuring in tone, the first studies suggested that "figure control garments can once again be the profit center they were in the past," blaming unimaginative retail displays and the ignorance of retail staff for the decline in sales.[26] A change in the language of girdle advertising was recommended, suggesting that words like "correct" and "hold" be replaced with new terms like "smoothing." As girdle sales continued to fall, DuPont commissioned further studies that focused on women aged thirty-five and younger, the boomer cohort. All but the youngest, the researchers found, had once been regular girdle wearers. Introduced to the garments by their mothers, who told them "'nice girls' always wear girdles," they had continued to wear them "as if there was a law stating that they must."[27] By the mid-1970s, however, most young women had given up girdles in favor of bras and pantyhose. As the researchers reported, the new generation "felt that new fashions or not, they would be damned if they would give up the 'new undergarment lifestyle' into which they had only recently and happily entered." With tongue in cheek, the study noted that "women used to believe that there was a 'law' that they had to wear girdles and most believe the law has been repealed."[28]

Further market research produced similar findings, but DuPont was not prepared to abandon a market in which so much had been invested. The company promoted a completely new kind of fashionable, light foundation garment aimed at young boomers. Called "form persuaders," "body garments," or "clothes smoothers," they were whole-body all-in-one foundations in the thinnest-ever stretch fabric, dyed in brilliant fashion colors like apple green, sapphire, and tangerine. The boomers ignored these new lines, despite catchy names like Free Spirit and Better Bottoms. The company continued its technological refinements of Lycra fiber and supported its customers as best it could. DuPont marketers brainstormed about converting the counterculture to girdle-wearing. Their fantasies about advertisements featuring rock stars like Grace Slick of the Jefferson Starship modeling all-in-one body garments in *Rolling Stone* magazine never materialized.[29] Despite DuPont's efforts, the "obligatory" wearing of foundations never revived. Even Barbie dolls no longer wore them. The girdle was dead, but elsewhere a new life for Lycra and the boomers was beginning.

A New Life for Lycra: Aerobics and the Me Generation

The aerobic fitness movement, which emerged in the 1970s and swept the country like a craze, is a prime example of the anthropological paradigm of sport as symbolic bodily practice. Symbolic practice involves the physical dimension of testing body and character to the limits; the creation of shared community with other participants; and the achievement of a ritual or heightened state through which the participant achieves insight into a cosmological worldview or meaningful connectedness to the social context. Aerobics as symbolic body practice had a particular resonance for boomer women of the Me Generation.

"Body consciousness" was very much a catchphrase and key concept of the period. Against the background of the cultural shifts outlined above, the body had taken on a new significance, both as metaphor and medium of social change, for young women who had been expected to buy and wear girdles. The birth-control pill had given women control over reproduction; now women wanted to be wholly responsible for themselves. As *Our Bodies, Our Selves*, the seminal book on women's health, asked, how could a woman work and enter into equal relationships with other people if "she drains her energy trying to change her face, her figure, her hair, her smells to match some ideal norm set by magazines and TV."[30] For women of the Me Generation, the aerobic-exercise ethos resonated with other emergent notions of control that had been instrumental in women's abandoning of the girdle. What was particularly striking was the totalizing nature of the phenomenon, of which the aerobics classes themselves were just one aspect. It spread into dietary practices, beliefs about health, and new codes of dress and behavior; it pervaded everyday life. No new practice can gain hold in such a way unless it reflects fundamental values or is expressive of fundamental change. Aerobics did both, and rarely has the concordance between social body and the physical body been so clearly manifested.

Aerobic exercise was perceived by its adherents as the wresting back of control of their bodies, their appearance, and their lives. If weight loss and change in body shape transpired as a result of exercise, these were by-products of a more meaningful activity, not an end in themselves. For women the very practice of strenuous exercise—smelly, sweaty, uncontrolled—was subversive. Far more important than an improved appearance was the empowerment—the improved bodily function and confidence—that could be achieved through aerobics. As both symbolic and physical practice, aerobics struck at the heart of 1950s female stereotypes and conventional behavior. And just as the position of women and the pertinent social values of the period had found their objectifying garment in the constricting girdle, for the new women of the Me Generation the objectifying garments became leotards and leggings or footless tights.

Aerobic exercise grew out of classical dance, finding a figurehead in the American actress Jane Fonda. In her best-selling *Jane Fonda's Workout Book*, she wrote about "Breaking the 'Weaker Sex' Mold" and finding empowerment through exercise.[31] Like many early adherents, Fonda had come to aerobics after classical ballet training, in which leotards and tights were the preferred gear because they fit better than one-piece cat suits. There was no variation in style or color: ballet leotards were always black, and leggings or tights always pink. Ballet wear was a small, specialist market, sold in specialty dance shops or, less frequently, in the hosiery sections of department stores. Although dancers were a small consumer group, they were a highly dedicated one. Ease of movement, shape retention, durability, moisture management, warmth, and *stretch* were the prime requirements for dancewear. For dancers, proper dancewear was considered as essential as spacesuits for astronauts: it was impossible to do what was necessary without it.

Although there was a well-established hierarchy of manufacturers of traditional ballet wear, there had always been a cottage industry of seamstresses, often retired or resting dancers, who made ballet wear to order as a sideline. In the 1970s, a new DuPont invention originally intended for use in lingerie and body-shaping foundations—a blend of shiny Antron nylon and Lycra spandex—proved vastly superior to existing dancewear fabrics. The blend made possible new cut-and-sew techniques that produced garments that hugged the body and moved with it in a way that had never been possible before. Dancewear manufacturers began to use it for traditional leotards and leggings in the classic black and pink color scheme, but the real changes emerged from another sector. As a result of the slump in the foundation market, there was a surplus of Antron-Lycra fabric in a range of fashion colors. A small craft business grew up, first around dance seamstresses who used the shiny stretch fabric to make colorful dancewear for private aerobics clients, then around early aerobics-wear entrepreneurs like Gilda Marx.

As aerobics swept the nation, enthusiasts were women who were coming to dance and to exercising to music for the first time. They found the physical experience of wearing leotards and leggings exhilarating, liberating, and revolutionary. This went beyond sartorial novelty, for Lycra was much more than just something new to wear. In the past, women had worn girdles beneath their garments to make the clothes look good; this can be thought of as women being worn by clothes. In contrast, Lycra leggings and leotards allowed women to wear their own bodies. Fitting like a second skin, Lycra enabled women to display a self-created, aerobicized, and empowered body—a "good" body that owed nothing to patriarchal notions of the erotic. This explains why women were now able to appear in public in a manner that would have been considered naked just a few years before.

Unlike ballet dancers, aerobicizers had no preconceptions about the "right" colors and styles. The introduction of fabrics that blended Lycra, cotton, and polyester turned leotards and leggings from functional garments into fashion items. Big manufacturers noticed the colorful dancewear that small specialists were producing as fast as they could, and followed suit. Leggings and leotards became standard items in department stores and general sporting-goods outlets. Aerobic workout videos and books flooded the market, all showing women in Lycra. There was even a Workout Barbie doll, dressed in Lycra leotard and leggings. Very quickly leotards and leggings danced out of the aerobics studios and onto the streets, worn with a skirt, a little wrap top, a pair of shorts, or sometimes nothing else at all. Using Lycra exercise clothes for street wear was not "just" a fashion statement. It was a social statement objectified in a new material form, one that, paradoxically, was not as new as it seemed. While girdles of Lycra were emblematic of dependency and control from without, leotards and leggings of Lycra symbolized control from within. What escaped comment at the time and still does today is how closely the aerobic leotards, leggings, and all-in-one cat suits favored by the boomers resembled the light, whole-body "form persuader" girdles they had rejected. This is a paradigmatic example of the way perceptions of the physical body and clothes are constrained by the social body, and an example of the ironies that arise from what anthropologists have called the "complex interplay of corporeality and culture."[32]

Ballet-wear manufacturers were small-scale consumers of fiber compared to the major foundation garment producers such as Maidenform. Because DuPont did not profit from the individuals and small companies who made the first aerobics leotards and leggings from surplus foundation fabric, the chemical giant initially took little commercial interest in these new developments. In addition, DuPont marketers still hoped that aerobics was just a passing fad, and that girdle-wearing would resume. Preoccupied with the downturn in traditional foundations, DuPont did not take aerobics seriously until the early 1980s. Then it conducted extensive market research into women's leotards. Foremost, the study confirmed that boomer women were the major buyers of leotards. In 1984, Americans purchased an estimated 21 million leotards worth $231 million at an average price of $10.90 for women aged fourteen and over, with 51 percent going to women between the ages of twenty-three and thirty-four.[33]

DuPont's 1984 leotard study also analyzed consumers and the retail trade. It established that the interest in exercise among American women, especially those of the boomer or Me Generation, was creating new and growing markets for the leotard, in addition to its use in aerobic, jazz dance, and figure-control exercise programs. First, leotards of the more revealing kind were replacing traditional boned and constructed swimsuits as the beachwear of choice of young women whose bodies had been made taut and lithe through exercise. The second new market for leotards had been created by their acceptance as street wear. Many new customers were not dancers, exercisers, or gymnasts, but they were attracted by the "fashion look" of the leotard worn with shorts, slacks, blouses, skirts, and leg warmers. This further popularized the wearing of separates as opposed to the dress, a garment linked with the traditional gender stereotype of women. Finally, researchers detected the beginnings of a move by manufacturers to take the leotard look into other kinds of active sportswear, including jogging, racquet sports, and gym activities, in which baggy clothes had long been customary. In contrast to the foundation retailers polled ten years earlier, American retailers of leotards, leggings, and related goods were positive and buoyant. In the end, DuPont researchers concluded "that the current market strength is a legitimate reflection of consumer interest in fitness which we consider now to have become a permanent and fundamental influence on American life styles."[34]

Despite these signals, DuPont marketers did not pursue the fitness market. Although the sales of stretch fiber to leotard and sportswear makers had reached substantial proportions, and although Lycra had become associated with style in the public mind, DuPont never developed the close relationship with the leotard and leggings that it had with the girdle and hosiery. Perhaps on a subconscious level it was difficult for the company to engage positively with a reconfigured market that had been responsible for the demise of products in which so much had been invested. For example, shortly after spandex girdles were launched, the company developed special Lycra fibers for use in the highly specialized field of women's support hosiery. With the death of the girdles that held them up, stockings experienced plunging sales. Seamless nylon pantyhose became popular in the 1960s along with the miniskirt, but early pantyhose had a tendency to sag or bag at the knees. Preoccupied with saving the girdle and stockings, DuPont did not promote Lycra for use in pantyhose until 1979, when the fiber's resistance to "sag" transformed the pantyhose market.

DuPont had become heavily involved in fashion campaigns when trying to save the girdle. After the girdle's death, the company retreated from the volatile style market, concentrating on developing Lycra for use in mass-market basics like recreational swimwear, children's clothes, sweaters, panties, and stretch jeans. It was only in the early 1990s that DuPont began to capitalize on Lycra's fashion potential, promoting the fiber's use in increasingly stylish outerwear and relaunching Lycra as a high-profile fashion brand with an iconic logo and extensive promotion. It was as though the producers were finally catching up with their product. Tellingly, when DuPont issued a fashion timeline showing milestones in Lycra's history, the aerobic leotard—the garment that most boomers associated with Lycra—was not included.[35]

Lycra's Legacy

In 2002, DuPont announced the sale of part of its textile fibers business, including Lycra, to Koch Industries. The divestiture provides a convenient vantage point from which to consider Lycra and DuPont's textile legacy. First, only DuPont with its unparalleled research and development program, fiber chain, and marketing resources could have invented, commercialized, and promoted a family of fibers that had an unparalleled influence on everyday life. Wash-and-wear fabrics, washable shrink-resistant sweaters, no-iron underclothes, and permanent-pleat skirts are just a few of DuPont's textile fiber innovations.[36] Lycra's significance and success, however, are due to more than its unprecedented capacity to stretch, or to DuPont's position in the industry. As Lycra's early years show, producers cannot always anticipate how social and economic change will affect consumer needs and wants. Products are not neutral—they are social values in material form, reflecting prevailing beliefs and standards. If there is no correspondence between them, neither technological excellence nor extensive advertising can compel consumers to buy. Conversely, if the "fit" is right, a product can virtually sell itself, and can go beyond simple commercial success to become embedded in the culture. When Lycra's technological capabilities and material qualities finally coincided with emergent social values and changing ideas about gender, beauty, and fitness, it became the essential ingredient in a new form of clothing that captured the zeitgeist, shaped the bodies and lives of the Me Generation, and ultimately transformed the market. Business, technology, and society were all involved in the process, and that, from an anthropological perspective, is how fashion is produced.

PART IV

Customer Reactions, Consumer Adaptations

CHAPTER TWELVE

French Hairstyles and the Elusive Consumer

Steve Zdatny

IN NOVEMBER 1910, Emile Long, the doyen of French coiffure, received a lesson in the serendipity of fashion when he paid a visit to several leading Parisian *modistes* (hatmakers). In his monthly column for *Hairdressers' Weekly Journal*, Long offered two reasons for this expedition. First, since hairstyles were inevitably subordinate to hat styles, Long wanted coiffeurs to be prepared for the next season's fashions. Second, Long suspected that these "purveyors of fashion" had learned to steer consumer taste in the most profitable directions, and he wanted to pass their secrets along to his hairdresser colleagues. Arriving at the workshops, Long was surprised to find nothing but toques—soft, brimless hats. "Why," he asked his hosts, "are you giving a preference to toques?" He surely expected an answer that combined sociological insight and marketing genius. What he got was something else: the capital's hat shapers had been on strike for four months, leaving *modistes* the choice between shapeless hats or no hats at all. So they bent to necessity and hoped for the best.[1]

It is impossible to say how often fashion was shaped by accident rather than calculation. Either way, the role of chance should already have been axiomatic to Long, for he began his career as the protégé of Marcel Grateau. In the early 1880s, the "master," as he came to be known, was a struggling coiffeur in the world capital of fashion, making wigs and coiffing "tarts" for half a franc. After years of trial and error, he finally perfected his technique.

Using a curling iron with two branches, one hollow and the other round, and twisting the iron in an unconventional manner around his skilled fingers, Marcel found he could create a soft, beautiful, and comparatively durable wave.[2]

No one could have predicted the impact of Marcel's invention on a profession dominated by chignons and doodads. But his wave caught the attention of Paris's most stylish women and quickly brought him fame and fortune. He charged 500 francs for his services and was soon earning 10,000 francs a month at a time when a coiffeur in a decent ladies' salon would be happy with 500 and a common barber with 200.

As marcelling became common practice in ladies' boudoirs and salons, it revolutionized both the business and the art of hairdressing. The leading coiffeurs of the day had made their reputations by weaving an assortment of jewels, combs, barrettes, feathers, and false hair into elaborate and expensive coiffures. When the marcel, offering radically simplified hairstyles, began to capture the public's fancy, the traditionalists reacted with scorn, if not downright panic.[3] But opponents of the marcel could not kill it any more than the "master" himself could have arranged its success. Indeed, they were soon glad of it, since the marcel brought ladies' hairdressers a considerable new source of income and propelled the profession toward prosperity. As Marcel's acolyte, Long more than anyone should have recognized the inscrutability of the process that produced new fashions and created new celebrities.

The truth is that Long could never make up his mind about whether fashion-makers could push consumers in a particular direction or were condemned to chasing after them. He wrote that hairdressers could "no more resist the on-coming of Fashion than we can stop the impetuous torrent of a mighty river."[4] At the same time, he helped found the fashion committee of the Institut des Coiffeurs des Dames, which brought together the capital's leading ladies' hairdressers to organize the profession and endorse the most lucrative coiffures. Naturally, the committee planned to make one season's hairstyles as different as possible from the next, "so that ladies may not be able to make use of the accessories of the previous season but be compelled to buy fresh ones."[5] In the end, the fashion committee lacked the means to enforce its decisions, even among its own members. But it is far from clear that more discipline and authority would have allowed the fashion committee to impose its will on the public. As the marcel had just proved and the bob would prove in the near future, the public's taste in hairstyles followed a logic of its own—if logic it was. Efforts to force it this way or that generally came to naught.

Discipline was further undermined by the division of the profession into two philosophical and aesthetic camps: "classicists" and "modernists." The "classicists" had quite fixed notions about what looked beautiful on a woman's head and disdained styles that offended their cultivated sense of proportion. The "modernists," by comparison, were flamboyant and unpredictable, producing coiffures that lacked the knickknacks and detail of the "classical" styles, but offering novelties like the "Bulgarian" colors—blue, green, and mauve—that helped make the reputation of the inimitable Antoine de Paris. Moreover, the "modernists" appealed especially to younger women seeking to break with their mothers' "look." In the end, the future of coiffure belonged to the modernists, with their youthful instincts and nose for business.

The outbreak of war in 1914 brought substantial changes to the system of hair fashion, although not exactly in the way one might think. To be sure, it meant hardship for the thousands of mobilized coiffeurs who had either to close their salons or leave them in the hands of their inexperienced assistants and wives. Meanwhile the economy geared up for a short, intense conflict. The government limited travel on the Paris metro, closed theaters, requisitioned horses from the racetracks of Auteil and Longchamps, and canceled the Tour de France.[6] Nonessential sectors of the economy like hairdressing suffered most, since the consuming classes "felt obliged to show respect by abandoning [their] normal frivolity."[7] Long's articles for the first few months of the war advised hairdressers to "lower their prices and resolutely attack the less pretentious tasks" simply in order to survive.[8]

All the fashion industries felt the first jolt of war. Couture was disrupted, as designers and tailors were called to military service, while fashionable excess disappeared in the initial impulse to patriotic austerity and sacrifice.[9] Yet the production and consumption of fashion reasserted themselves with remarkable speed. The government released the couturiers from military service. Restaurants and theaters reopened, even though officials restricted wearing formal "evening clothes." Old fashion magazines returned to publication, and new ones—Le Style Parisien and Les Elégances Parisiennes, for example— appeared to promote couture at home and abroad. They occasionally acknowledged the war, giving dresses patriotic names like Marseillaise or posing models with military props.[10] Mostly, though, fashion ignored the national emergency.

Those who reflect on the war's impact on fashion usually stress women's

new need for "practical clothes" and the "liberating" effects of war that freed
them from "from high-neck, ankle-length dresses."[11] But fashion styles had
already begun to change before 1914, and fashion historian Valerie Steele
argues convincingly that "developments in fashion were *not* primarily a response to changing patterns of work" and practical necessity.[12] Yet the war
did affect fashion in important ways. Even chic women now dressed with
"relative simplicity," while trousers "became acceptable female attire" for the
first time.[13] Essentially, the war accelerated the pace of change and passed
previous improvements in lightness and comfort down to the popular classes.
Corsets had been on their way out for years, shorter skirts and sweaters on
their way in. Only after 1914, though, did these trends reach working-class
women.[14]

Hairstyles followed the same trajectory. By the middle of 1915, the hairdressing business had returned to normal, with its parade of curls, waves,
chignons, and fancy combs. Everyday coiffures got shorter and simpler, as
the demand for fashionable hair worked its way across the lower classes. Long
was already complaining before the war about the cheap waves he saw "on
all the little typists of Paris." By the Armistice, he grumbled, virtually all
Parisian factory girls and shop hands had "acquired the habit of attending the
hairdresser's."[15] Long exaggerated, but he did have his eye on a fundamental
development: the inexorable democratization of the market for fashion.[16]

Young women from the *classes populaires* not only provided an expanding
customer base for hairdressers, they provided the hairdressers as well. With
so many coiffeurs called to service or drawn to more lucrative trades, young
françaises flooded into the salons to work. After two months training in a
hairdressing academy, fifteen-year-old girls could earn eight francs a day waving a dozen clients; older wavers could make double that. Hairdressing did
not pay as well as war work, but it was less unpleasant than factory or domestic labor. Between 1911 and 1921, the overall number of hairdressers in Paris
declined, but the number of coiffeuses more than tripled. Women, who had
comprised 8.5 percent of hairdressers around 1900, now accounted for almost
a third of them. By 1936, they made up 36.5 percent of the workforce in
coiffure, and the proportion continued to rise.[17]

A profession largely composed of young, inexperienced coiffeuses stood
even less chance of imposing its will on an increasingly diverse clientele and
left hairdressers with even fewer means to resist the menacing new taste for
women's short hairstyles. Many people have claimed credit for introducing
the bob to French women. One legend holds that American nurses brought

it with them to France in 1917. Celebrities also staked their claims. Antoine wrote that "Something just clicked in my head, and I decided the time had come for *cheveux courts* [short hairstyles]."[18] Coco Chanel explained how *she* invented the bob. One evening in 1917, while getting ready to attend the opera, her gas heater exploded, leaving her with a head of singed, smoky hair. With characteristic audacity, Chanel took nail scissors and snipped off her braids. She cut such a fashionable figure that evening, with her short hair and hip-waisted skirt, that other grandes dames quickly copied her.[19]

In reality, the bob reiterates the lesson of the marcel. Producers of fashion searched ceaselessly for forms that would grab hold of the public's imagination and pocketbooks, but on the rare occasions they succeeded, it was the residue as much of luck as of design. In other words, Antoine could have created the most beautiful short coiffures, but this alone could not have guaranteed their phenomenal success among women of all social classes across the Western world. A new fashion had to strike a particularly sensitive public nerve, and no one—not Antoine or Long or Lanvin or Chanel—knew exactly where that nerve was or hit it consistently. Paul Poiret, for example, who had been the toast of haute couture before the war, never caught the spirit of the "Roaring Twenties" and had to close his business in 1929.

Short hairstyles caught on in a gradual and anonymous manner. When Poiret first chopped the hair of his models for his 1908 collection, he adopted a look that had long been the signature of actresses and bohemians.[20] During the war, the vogue for *cheveux courts* spread among the "smart set," and short hairstyles were common on the privileged heads at the Victory Galas that followed the Armistice. But why did the bob become the very emblem of the "new woman" of the 1920s?

Everyone pointed to the effects of the war. Work and independence, they seemed to agree, had stimulated women's desire for emancipation and shaken up the inherited sexual order. They read *cheveux courts* alternately as "the psychological expression of femininity in crisis" or a "symbole de combat."[21] Observers also underlined the convenience of the bob, which rescued its wearers from the *corvées* required by the massive coiffures of an earlier fashion regime and allowed the energetic young women of the postwar generation to lead "active" lifestyles.

Whatever the inspiration, young women in short haircuts stirred up visions of the apocalypse among France's social conservatives, who saw them as evidence of androgyny and a "civilization without sexes."[22] According to Valerie Steele, however, the *garçonne* "was not so much boyish as she was [in] the style of a sophisticated schoolgirl."[23] Above all, short hairstyles symbolized youth and vigor, a new generation distinguishing themselves from their mothers. "The women who preceded us," wrote feminist Maria Vérone, "gave us a poor example of false hair, phony sentiments, marriage without love, and homes without intimacy. Whereas we wear *cheveux courts* and clothes that don't restrict us, and we want to have careers in order to be independent."[24]

Youth also linked symbolism to economics, since young women flocking to salons to have their hair cropped created new business opportunities. Indeed, the vogue for short hairstyles marks the moment when young women became the chief subjects of fashion. It was not "women in general," wrote sociologist René Koenig, "but above all the young women," who made this revolution, writing finis to the consumer society of the nineteenth century and ushering in that of the twentieth.[25]

Ironically, hairdressers initially tried to hold back the rising demand for *cheveux courts*. The campaign against the bob was led by the new journal *Coiffure de Paris*, published by Eugène Schueller, founder of L'Oréal. In December 1920, the magazine offered 5,000 francs for any new idea that might "erase every trace of this nefarious fashion."[26] The coalition against short hairstyles included virtually all the great artists of coiffure.

The public's taste for short hairstyles, however, proved stronger than coiffeurs' opposition—fortunately, since the bob turned out to be the greatest thing that had ever happened to the profession. René Rambaud, at the head of a new generation of coiffeurs, wrote that *cheveux courts* had "brought our trade an unprecedented prosperity," with a crush of eager new clients pushing into the salons.[27] If women were piling fewer ornaments in their hair, they were spending a lot more money on other things. Shorter cuts required more frequent visits to the salon, where women also had their hair tinted, shampooed, and waved. Even the demand for *postiches* remained lively, as these little hair pieces proved useful for dressing up short hairstyles for the evening.

Combined with technological advances that brought electricity and hot water to all but the meanest salon, the vogue for short hairstyles provided lucrative new markets for manufacturers of accessory products and services. Schueller's discovery in 1909 of a safe new formula for hair coloring fueled the growing taste for *teinture* and laid the foundation of a powerful new commercial fortune.[28] The sale of cheap dyes expanded fivefold by the early 1920s. "*Teinture* is not the most agreeable work in the profession," wrote Raul Patois, "but it is without comparison the most lucrative."[29]

The most spectacular new technology and the new workhorse of coiffure's profits was the permanent wave. Marcel's revolutionary wave had one fatal flaw: a cold mist or a hot bath would cause the most beautiful marcel to flop like wet spaghetti.[30] The technique for flattening and twisting hair follicles to create a *permanent* wave was an old secret of the *posticheur*'s trade, but it involved boiling hair in glue, an impractical solution for hair still attached to a client's head. The first assault on this technological barrier came from a German hairdresser working in London, Charles Nestlé (born Karl Ludwig Nessler), who brought his new invention to Paris for a demonstration in 1909. He soaked his model's hair in an alkaline solution, rolled it into several dozen *mèches* (locks), and attached them to a machine that, with its metal dome and dangling wires, looked like something out of a Frankenstein movie. He then turned on the current for several hours.[31] Hair had to be heated to over 200 degrees Fahrenheit, and severe burns were a constant danger. So was electric shock or the possibility that the rods might overheat, leaving the client with a head full of melted rubber—which might explain why, in its first year, only seventy-four women subjected themselves to Nestlé's treatment.[32]

The principle behind Nestlé's contraption was sound, however, and as others tinkered with the technology, permanent-wave machines became more reliable and practical. The "Eugene," introduced by Eugene Sutter in 1918, worked much more quickly and replicated the prettiest marcel[33] (Figure 12.1). Gaston Boudou built the first French machine, the "Gallia," right after the war, and hired René Rambaud as his principal spokesman. His Gallia clinics offered free instruction to those who purchased his apparatus. Rambaud helped by inventing the *mise en plis*, the "pin-curls" that enabled hairdressers to control the shape of the permanent wave. By 1929, Gallia had training facilities and salesmen on four continents.[34]

By then, the permanent wave, which added a stylish element to cropped hair, had become the decisive weapon in the coiffeurs' arsenal of art and profit. A first-class perm could cost a client well over 300 francs. In the much derided "hairdressing factories" of Jean Ricaud, women of the *classes populaires* could have their hair permed for a lot less.[35] Either way, it needed to be refreshed every week or so. As hair grew out it lost its curl, so customers needed a new session under the permanent-wave machine about every six months. Furthermore, the increased time women spent on their premises gave *salonniers* a perfect opportunity to launch the *soins connexes* of manicures and facials, introduced by high-end establishments in the 1930s.[36]

Figure 12.1. Advertisement for the "Eugène" permanent at the swanky Maison Défossé, Paris, 1923. Courtesy Collection Roger-Viollet.

In sum, the bob gave the hairdressing profession its modern form by speeding up the feminization of the profession and democratizing the demand for fashionable hair. Coincidentally, the revenue it brought to the salons immensely improved the working lives of hairdressers, the majority of whom could now enjoy livable wages and reasonable work schedules.

Even the most revolutionary style, however, obeyed the first law of fashion: evanescence. By the end of the Roaring Twenties, the bob was well on its way out. Once again, leading elements in the profession tried to hold back the tide of changing taste. They now argued, paradoxically, that *cheveux longs* would prove inimical to feminine beauty. But hairdressers were as powerless to save short hairstyles as they had been to resist them in the first place.[37]

Those who would like to read deep meaning into the forms of fashion have often seen counter-revolution in the more "feminine" styles of the 1930s, softer and more "sculptural" than the rebellious *garçonne*. René Rambaud, always among the most historically aware of coiffeurs, wondered if long hairstyles, along with floor-length dresses and prominent bosoms, fit the pessimism and conservatism of the Depression years, just as *cheveux courts* had expressed the optimism and proto-feminism of the twenties. Cultural historian Marylène Delbourg-Delphis is even more explicit. Compared to the *garçonne*, she writes, the 1930s woman "spoke less of her freedom than of her responsibility."[38]

These are the sorts of insights commonly offered by casual observers and cultural studies. There is no evidence, however, to support such contentions about the 1930s, which draw parallels between form and historical context and claim an organic relationship between, for example, tighter clothes and tighter morals. Even if the mood of the 1930s was less expansive, which it probably was, given the economic crisis, there is no reason on the face of it why hip-waisted dresses and bobs could not convey pessimism as well as longer skirts and longer hairstyles, or vice-versa.[39] Moreover the 1930s shift away from *garçonnesque* shapes was less complete than critics have implied. Fashion magazines continued to feature relatively short styles well into the decade, and hairstyles, while they got longer, never approached the length and volume of prewar coiffures. In a word, there is no reason to read the 1930s styles as a reactionary coup.

Without question, the Depression brought hard times to a lot of salons, as most women had less money to spend on their hair and there was less business to go around.[40] The structure of hairdressing businesses, small and lightly capitalized, deflected some of the effects of the economic crisis and helped limit unemployment among French coiffeurs.[41] At the same time, prices plummeted, especially for permanent waves. Salon revenues and personal income crashed with them.

Fashion continued to operate, even in a contracting economy. Women on tighter budgets spent less at the salons, but they did not abandon their hair altogether. At the top of the pyramid, celebrity coiffeurs continued to practice their art, ceaselessly creating new styles to satisfy their well-kempt clientele. They soon learned that longer styles themselves meant no loss of income. The new medium-length coiffures were still tinted in the latest colors, like the rose and mauve to which Antoine was partial, while they remained full of curls, jewels, flowers, feathers, and the other weapons of added value.[42] Antoine liked to sculpt his creations with lacquer. Rambaud preferred the softer look of pin curls. Fernand built his coiffures entirely without waves. The *Coiffure de Paris* in the early 1930s noted the "rage" for blonde tints, especially the "platinum" blonde featured in the 1934 film of the same name and starring Jean Harlow, who was bound to make the new look a "prodigious triumph." As the decade unfolded, other movie stars introduced new styles. In 1935, it was the Katherine Hepburn look. Two years later, according to the *Coiffure de Paris*, Joan Crawford's was the most asked-for hairstyle among *françaises*.[43]

The 1930s saw the arrival of a new generation of *hauts coiffeurs*. First among them was Guillaume, whose "Angel" hairstyle, based on a Botticelli painting and adopted by American couturier Hattie Carnegie and the cosmetics firm Elizabeth Arden, brought him international exposure and a place in Hollywood. Working for Rambaud at the Maison Emile, Guillaume repeated his success two years later with the "Star" hairstyle, which led to a documentary film and commercial collaborations with L'Oréal and Zoto. In 1936, Guillaume celebrated the opening of his own salon on the avenue Matignon by creating the "Pageboy," and completed his grand slam the following year with the "Eagle," shorter and more intensively worked than his earlier creations.[44]

By this time, the toniest modern salons were full of gleaming machines, luxurious, leather-bound chairs, polished mirrors, and shelves filled with hair-care merchandise from L'Oréal, Antoine, and Rambaud. The most elegant establishments added *instituts de beauté*, featuring pedicures and facials, paraffin baths, epilation for the eyebrows, appointments under ultraviolet lamps to restore "damaged" hair, double-brush therapy and massage for the scalp to prevent dandruff, and huge body rollers to reduce fat. Elizabeth Arden's range of beauty aids offered customers Venetian orange skin food, muscle oil, and "illusion" powder. Helena Rubenstein sold a similar line.[45]

When the elegant 1930s ended with the outbreak of World War II in September 1939, producers of French fashion faced a new set of challenges. At first, a wave of seriousness and austerity swept over the country, much as in 1914. The government banned public dances, closed restaurants, and curtailed theater and cinema hours. It put sandbags around the capital's most important monuments and packed children off to the countryside, where they would presumably be safe from German attacks.[46]

The great couturiers were forced to cancel their autumn shows, but they carried on as best they could in their patriotic duty to preserve *la belle française*, while reminding French women that they had a reciprocal obligation to be beautiful.[47] "Luxury," wrote the journal *Candide*, is not a sin but a useful expense and even a form of patriotism."[48]

Some hairdressers sought to turn the war to account by reviving the fashion for *cheveux courts*. Long, ornate hairdos, they told women, would be harder to maintain under wartime conditions. For the moment, however, the public remained loyal to longer styles that emphasized the "suppleness" and "natural lightness" of what it called "la mode d'Hollywood."[49]

Just as in 1914, mobilization emptied the hairdressing salons of many of their best and most experienced practitioners, closing them altogether or leaving them in the hands of wives and daughters. But the new war did not resemble the last one in the most critical respect: there was no "Miracle of the Marne" in 1940, and the "home front" that had proved surprisingly resilient in fashion between 1914 and 1918 now fell under a savage and rapacious German occupation. Indeed, hairdressers' tribulations from 1940 to 1944 are an accurate gauge of the difference between the civilian experiences of the two world wars. The first produced a moment of exuberance and creativity in coiffure, especially for young working women. Paris "on German time" was a drabber, sadder, more dangerous place.

Producers of hair fashions, whose needs ranked low on the scale of national priorities, felt the occupation most immediately as shortage. In September 1942, Marcel Bagnaud, proprietor of the Maison Marcel at the Place Victor Hugo in Paris and head of the rationing apparatus for coiffure, laid out the situation for his constituents: Brilliantine was almost impossible to find, with cotton and linen "reserved for priority needs." Hairpins were disappearing even from the black market. And things were about to get worse. Hairdressers could expect to get only half the shaving powder they needed, a quarter of the soap, 15 percent of the shampoo. L'Oréal, that bellwether of the hairdressing business, was doing more business with the Germans than with the French.[50]

The lack of coal, gas, and electricity made hot water a rare commodity. In 1942, the government forbade hairdressing salons from lighting their interiors before 10 A.M. or after 5 P.M. This meant that a coiffeur or coiffeuse, even if the materials could be found, could not offer tinting or permanent waves after 2 P.M. because these tasks took three hours to finish. In 1944, the Production Ministry issued an order that forced all *salons de coiffure* to close for two consecutive days a week, and by that summer they were forbidden to use *any* electricity without special permission.[51]

The most enterprising coiffeurs found ways of adjusting. Louis Gervais hired two men to ride a tandem bike that turned a generator eight hours a day. Albert Pourrière put his pampered clients out in the sun to dry their hair, while he provided manicures and pedicures al fresco. René Garraud invited his elite clientele to "drying teas," where hair could set and dry at leisure in amiable company. Antoine adapted toothpicks and pine needles to replace impossible-to-find hairpins. Roger Para collected bone marrow, which he used to treat his customers' hair.[52] Most hairdressers, however, had clients without the money or the time for such elegant deprivation. They found no clever, profitable way around the dearth of crucial materials. For them the war was a hard slog.

A sliver of the profession actually prospered during the Occupation, serving German officers and members of Parisian high society who found their company congenial.[53] On the whole, however, high fashion clashed with the conservatism of Vichy, which despised the *garçonne* and other expressions of modern womanhood. Official fashion policy urged women to avoid anything too cosmopolitan or sexy; rather, it sought to put women back into their kitchens and their corsets.

The high priest of reactionary opinion on fashion and femininity was Lucien François, editor of the journal *Votre Beauté*, part of the L'Oréal publishing empire. His book *Cent ans d'élégance* (*A Hundred Years of Elegance*), published in 1942, lambasted the liberal, androgynous woman of the interwar years who had helped plunge the country into its current predicament. "Today," François wrote, "France understands that she owes her defeat in large part to her slackening values," and he expressed his belief that when women returned to their "natural" functions, their bodies would regain their "natural" shape: bigger breasts, wider hips, and so forth.[54]

Stylish *françaises* ignored this conservative advice, while most ordinary women were too busy trying to find something comfortable, clean, and not unattractive to wear to worry about fashion philosophies. The lack of leather and wool forced women to wear wood-soled shoes and fabrics made from fibranne (spun rayon). Without silk for stockings, they had recourse to leg cream that gave the illusion of hosiery. L'Oréal introduced a wartime version of its best-selling soap, "Monsavon 30 percent"—a single bar of which, it claimed, would last two months. As the war continued and rationing bit harder, even these substitutes became impossible to find.

Under the circumstances, the hairdressing profession limped along. Hairstyles became somewhat shorter and less ornate. Actress Madeleine Sologne popularized a simpler, more natural style of medium-length hair. Other chic women adopted the look made famous by American actress Veronica Lake, their faces half-hidden by their straight, shoulder-length hair. Rebellious young women from the leisured classes adopted the "Zazou" style— short, pleated skirts, square shoulders, flat, heavy shoes, faces excessively made up, hair curled and swelled in the front, long on the neck. This jazzy, openly transgressive look mocked the "natural" and "austere" modes imposed by circumstance and official discourse.[55] The popularity of bicycles for local transportation and the difficulties of keeping hair clean made turbans a practical solution to daily haircare needs. There could be no better evidence, writes historian Dominique Veillon, of "the degree of precariousness into which the French population had fallen in the space of a few years."[56]

Precariousness did not disappear with liberation in the summer of 1944, and the second postwar era proved less effervescent than the first. The *salons de coiffure* in 1945 did not display the bustling optimism of 1919, and war produced no analogue to the *mode à la garçonne*; indeed, if it gave the world any representative hairstyle, it was the shaved head of "horizontal collaborators" and concentration-camp survivors. Yet the story of postwar fashion is not all drabness and depression. The *trentes glorieuses*, as the French call the thirty years of postwar prosperity, witnessed a huge expansion of the hairdressing trades, as they did of the fashion business in general. Women visited their hairdressers in almost constantly increasing numbers in the twenty-five years following the war, and the number of salons rose to meet demand.[57]

This prosperity did not rest, as it had in the 1920s, on one particular style, but was based on a series of demographic, economic, and cultural changes that inflated the demand for coiffure, whatever the fashion of the moment. The expansion of the hairdressing business was only a small part of a consumer revolution that also involved cars, televisions, refrigerators, telephones, vacations, and indoor toilets.[58] French women were urged forward in this revolution by growing media, principally the women's magazines whose articles and images sought to define au courant femininity. French *Vogue*, which began to publish again in 1945, continued to tweak the fashion imagination of the upper crust. More crucial to the mass market was the growth of a *presse féminine* aimed at middle- and working-class young women. The first issue of *Elle* appeared in November 1945. A magazine for readers more interested in ready-to-wear than in couture, it offered romantic stories and glossy color photographs of the latest styles and celebrities, alongside advice on love and employment and how to make the most of a small studio apartment.[59] *Marie Claire*, first launched in 1937, reappeared in 1954 as an "inexpensive, prestigious monthly" and sold out its first issue within hours. *Marie France* was born in 1944 out of the wartime resistance, and the initial number of *Mademoiselle*, with its even more explicit appeal to trendy young *françaises*, hit the kiosks in 1962.[60]

The French also took more care of their hair because they were taking more care about personal appearance and hygiene in general. At the turn of the twentieth century, even the most fashionable grandes dames seldom if ever washed their hair.[61] Every generation of experts over the twentieth century then recommended cleaner hair than the last one, and *françaises* clearly paid attention to their advice, although French standards of capillary hygiene lagged consistently behind British, German, and American ones.

In October 1951, *Elle* magazine published a survey that revealed a shocking deficit of cleanliness among *françaises*: 11 percent of French women reported washing their hair once a week; a quarter less than once a month. Although 54 percent claimed to use deodorant, only 17 percent changed their underwear every day; the same percentage brushed their teeth twice daily; 52 percent performed a full toilette every day, most using a bidet. But 14 percent did so less than once a week.[62]

Elle did not even bother to ask its respondents how often they bathed or showered, presumably because most of them still lived in apartments without such amenities. In the big cities, only a minority—often a small minority—had hot water, flush toilets, and bathrooms: *le confort*. And even when things had improved, by the end of the 1950s, the French possessed more televisions than bathtubs—although this was apparently also true of England, Germany, and the United States.[63] The rising threshold of personal hygiene is nonetheless detectable in the advertisements for soap, shampoo, deodorants, and toothpaste in women's magazines, along with the frequent articles counseling women to wash themselves and their underwear and to take off their makeup before going to bed.[64] The investment in new housing, which peaked in the 1970s, made an even bigger difference. By the middle of that decade, according to Mary Lynn Stewart, 70 percent of French homes had showers, and a quarter of the population bathed or showered daily.[65]

Following closely behind finer hygienic sensibilities and growing incomes, advertisements in the expanding women's press pitched an expanding array of products and services to make hair beautiful. As always, L'Oréal led the field, bringing new products to market virtually every year: baby shampoo, hair conditioner, coloring, setting lotions, and hairspray. The other French producers—Gallia-Eugène, Perma, and the newly franchised brands like Jacques Dessange and Jean-Louis David—followed closely behind.[66]

Elite hairdressers achieved new heights of prosperity and renown, as the 1950s mixed old celebrities with new. Rambaud and Antoine were nearing the end of their careers. Guillaume reached his pinnacle when he collaborated with Christian Dior for his revolutionary "New Look" collection of 1947, but continued working with major couturiers for the next twenty years, specializing in fantastical, medium-short styles.[67]

Two young sisters from Toulouse, Rosy and Maria Carita, made their mark when director Jean-Luc Goddard introduced them to Jean Seberg, the star of his first film, *A bout de souffle* (*Breathless*). The severe *garçonne* they gave her reduced Seberg to tears but helped make her, for a tragically short time, a star. The Carita sisters soon became the favorite coiffeuses of French cinema, working with the most celebrated directors and providing such actresses as Catherine Deneuve, Simone Signoret, and Jeanne Moreau with their signature hairstyles. They remained throughout this period the only women to crack the tight elite of *hauts coiffeurs*.[68]

Other young hairdressing celebrities included Louis Gervais, Albert Pourrière, and Jacques Dessange, who designed the "Choucroute" style that defined the sexy young starlet Brigitte Bardot. This and other high styles were made possible by the introduction of aerosol hairspray that, as the 1950s progressed, made it feasible to raise natural hair to unprecedented heights in teased bouffants. The various versions of the "Beehive" in the early 1960s, often stuffed with pads and finished with falls, marked the apex of "Big Hair." The master of these baroque creations was Alexandre "de Paris," Antoine's young protégé from Cannes, brought to Paris after the war especially to coif the Duchess of Windsor.[69]

Through the 1950s, the old fashion system survived in the glamorous salons of these elite coiffeurs, who created exquisite new styles for their clients from the world of cinema, theater, and high society, in much the same way designers created clothing fashions. These styles were then disseminated through films, magazines, and other media, by way of neighborhood beauty parlors, on to the heads of millions of *françaises*. Particular coiffures might strike a spark among the masses, but the flow of creation was largely from the top down.

In the 1960s, however, the fortunes of *haute coiffure*, as of haute couture, began to teeter, as the postwar generation rejected not merely the forms but the entire ethic of high fashion. Elaborate coiffures, too "done" and too "old," fell victim to this consumer-driven turnabout in values and sensibilities. French women now wanted less teasing, less hairspray, and more *authenticité*.

French hairdressers must have been especially displeased to see that the wind of generational change blew across the English Channel from London, where Vidal Sassoon, above all, had "redefined the bob for a 1960s audience."[70] Sassoon's geometric cuts, forever associated with Mary Quant's miniskirts, depended on conceptual audacity and skill with scissors, not volume and ornamentation (Figure 12.2). They became the badge of the "new woman" of the 1960s, exactly as the bob had defined her 1920s counterpart. From Carnaby Street to the Sorbonne, and in that mysterious way that new fashions always seize the public fancy, casual youthfulness pushed the old formality aside, as it had forty years earlier.[71] By the end of that remarkable decade, *haute coiffure* survived only in certain corners of the fashion world, at couture shows and professional competitions, while convenience and practicality established themselves as the foundation of women's everyday hairstyles.

This youthful aesthetic was tied more than ever to the democratization of fashion that had started to change coiffure before World War I. From the age of Marcel to that of Alexandre and the Caritas, the leading hairstyles had been imagined in the workshops and salons of the great designers, presented to high society, and passed down the social scale. The sixties all but completed the inversion of the traditional flow of fashion. Modern styles were increasingly born in the "street," among the young and hip. The ambitious young coiffeur would now have to pay less attention to the debutantes of the *seizième arrondissement* than to the students of the Latin Quarter and the gamines of the Marais district.

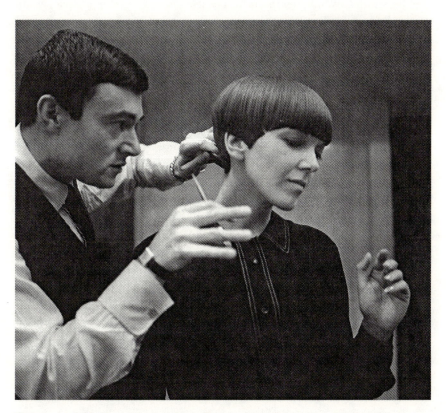

Figure 12.2. Vidal Sassoon gives Mary Quant a Five-Points Cut. Courtesy Getty Archives.

Even so, most hairdressers still produced fashion in a strictly mechanical manner. They kept an eye on the models in the professional publications, studied celebrity photos, and tried to satisfy customers who came in asking to be styled à la Juliette Greco or Catherine Deneuve. At the top of the profession, the great artists of coiffure, like artists of any stripe, looked for new forms and techniques to create beauty and set themselves apart from their colleagues. When it came to the business side of art, they engaged in exactly the same sort of quest that had led Long to the workshops of the *modistes* in 1910, constantly on the lookout for the new style that would capture the public's imagination, earning glory for themselves and profits for their colleagues.

Not surprisingly, famous hairdressers hit this target more easily than did the proprietors of ordinary salons. An Antoine coiffure was an event in itself; and when Guillaume created something for Dior, it appeared on runways and magazine covers and was widely copied. But even the most celebrated *haut coiffeur* could not set off a new secular trend on command. Antoine had not invented the bob; he had only helped propel it to prominence. Likewise Alexandre practiced his lavish art on queens and movie stars in the 1970s, but he did not create the fashion for big hair that became the idiom of his celebrity.

In other words, although historians and social critics have made much of the supposed "captains of consciousness"—manufacturers and advertisers, who are able to push cultural preferences this way and that—there is no evidence in the history of French coiffure that anyone actually had the power to predict or control what the public wanted.[72] The likes of Antoine, Rambaud, and Guillaume could count on long careers at the top, provided they were able to adapt their art to changing tastes. They could not, however, in the largest sense determine those tastes.

To say that fashion is ruled as much by providence as by logic does not deny that fashions themselves are a sharp reflection of their historical context. A careful dissection of the *garçonne*, or of any other version of *cheveux courts*, yields a treasury of insights into the historical moment. That short hair was regularly shampooed indicates changing standards of hygiene and urban reconstruction that brought hot water into homes and shops. Permanent waves entailed the progress of chemistry, electricity, industrial manufacture, and commercial distribution. The proliferation of beauty salons implies women with disposable income and the autonomy to spend it. The reach of the new hairstyles indicates the growing influence of magazines and films. The thousands of young customers from the *classes populaires* reflect the feminization, democratization, and "youthification" of consumption that swept France as it did other urban, industrial societies.

The evident symbolic richness of hairstyles has excited a lot of casual analysis of the "meaning" of it all. Recall the glib commentaries that attributed the popularity of the bob to women's desire for "emancipation," or that interpreted the slinkier dresses of the 1930s as a repudiation of that desire. Grant McCracken proposes similar thumbnail semiotics in his conventional remark that the "Big Hairstyles" of the 1950s were the embodiment of "subservient, domesticated femininity."[73] Other cultural critics have gone further in their efforts to "read" even deeper and more systematic meaning into the forms of fashion. Roland Barthes is only the best known of those who have deployed quite formal and complex techniques for historicizing fashion.[74]

The experience of French hairdressers suggests, however, that such speculation, while stimulating, does not make good history. For while hairstyles have much to say about the individuals who wear them and the society in which they are worn, the forms themselves are both empty and free-floating. They cannot be "read" in the manner of a literary text. In a world where suffragettes wore bulky chignons and society ladies sported *garçonnes*, there can be no reliable correspondence between a hairstyle and its *signification*, no equivalence between the coiffure and the politics. Perhaps that is why producers found it so difficult to anticipate the path of hair fashion. They could sail with the prevailing wind or try to tack against it, but the public soul remained enigmatic.

CHAPTER THIRTEEN

Ripping Up the Uniform Approach: Hungarian Women Piece Together a New Communist Fashion

Katalin Medvedev

Fashioning the Cold War

"IF I COULD place a single American book in the hand of every Russian, it would be the Sears, Roebuck catalogue," said Franklin D. Roosevelt.[1] Similar statements captured public attention during the political confrontations of the Cold War. The most famous exchange occurred during the "Kitchen Debate" between Richard Nixon and Nikita Khrushchev at Moscow's 1959 American National Exhibition. The American vice president and Soviet premier catapulted the capitalist-communist crisis from the military realm to the representational and gender front. As Khrushchev toured a model American kitchen, Nixon launched a scathing critique of the communist command economy. Arguing for the superiority of the capitalist system, Nixon evoked the image of the overworked, shabbily dressed communist woman, deprived of household help and suffering from a dearth of modern amenities. He contrasted her with the well-dressed American homemaker in a modern kitchen, as the epitome of Western freedom, prosperity, and fashion.[2]

Although widely circulated by the contemporary press and now often cited by historians, this politically motivated, homogenous portrayal of postwar women is skewed. It pits the frumpy, mannish "baba" from Eastern Europe against the feminine, stylish woman of the "free world." For one thing, the portrait does not acknowledge the enormous differences between the dress of urban and rural women. It also overlooks variations in the dress practices of different cultural, social, occupational, and generational groups, and between different geographical areas. Overall, the picture defies historical accuracy and needs correction.

There is no denying that the communist fashion Nixon dismissed was under considerable ideological influence and had coercive underpinnings. In Hungary from the late 1940s to the mid-1950s, the totalitarian communist regime had an antagonistic relationship with fashion. Newly released materials from the Radio Free Europe Archives testify to the importance of fashion to citizens behind the Iron Curtain. In a document titled "Fashion Problem," Radio Free Europe analysts, describing women's attitude toward fashion up until 1961, stated that many female defectors to the West claimed the lack of fashion as their primary reason for leaving communist Hungary.[3] Further, the analysts showed that Western authorities were aware of fashion's political potential and were ready to exploit it for their benefit.

Hungary shared many features with other communist bloc countries under totalitarian rule and Soviet influence after World War II. A close examination, however, shows that the development of Hungarian communist fashion was replete with internal contradictions. The gray image of people in the communist bloc constructed by Western officials and Soviet authorities was a far from accurate representation. The accounts of top communist designers and interviews with ordinary women in Hungary between 2003 and 2006 tell a different story. These sources show that the production and consumption of communist fashion was much more complex, dynamic, and context-specific than has been widely perceived.

Several salient features emerge from this new research. First, the evidence shows how private enterprise buttressed Hungarian fashion under the communist regime. Although private enterprise was not officially encouraged, it was not totally banned.[4] In fact, throughout the communist era, private dressmakers and small ateliers, with no more than five employees, continued to exist. Many people relied on their services. Second, the research shows that fashion never ceased to exist, at least in downtown Budapest. The wives of state officials, popular actresses, opera singers, and other political and cultural elites continued to dress stylishly under communism.[5] Third, interviews show that the general population also displayed some sartorial diversity. Before

World War II, Hungarian society was traditional; therefore, female gender socialization included learning sewing skills. With these skills, many women continued to create garments for themselves, their family members, and their friends after the communist takeover.

In sum, most Hungarians did not have to rely entirely on state supplied, mass-produced clothing and fashion articles. Nor did they subscribe to all-encompassing sartorial homogeneity. There were a few alternative outlets for producing unofficial fashion. Made from common fabric, the garments nonetheless showed some autonomy, individual variations in style, and women's individual aesthetic choices.[6]

Early Communist Aversion to Fashion

Karl Marx laid the foundation for the negative communist attitude toward stylish clothing when he described the "murderous, meaningless caprices of fashion" in his seminal work, *Das Capital*.[7] Because every communist in Hungary was expected to know this oeuvre inside out, Marx's critical evaluation may have automatically sealed the fate of fashion in a theoretical sense. Because fashion thrives best in democratic societies and advanced economies, the importance of fashion had to be dismissed by the communist regime.[8] The centralized, sluggish, planned economy could not keep up with the fickleness of fashion, nor would the authoritarian state tolerate its open, fluid meanings. On the one hand, the ambiguity of fashion left too much room for self-expression on the part of the wearer. On the other hand, fashion encouraged individual interpretation on the part of the viewer. Both scenarios presented a challenge to the totalitarian regime's modus operandi: repression and containment of the citizenry. So it was easier to declare fashion a public enemy.

Because dress is a public form of self-articulation, the totalitarian state strived for a monopoly over all its components: design, production, pricing, distribution, exportation, importation, meaning, and visual documentation. Fashion was ideologically suspect because of its links to uncontrolled consumption. The fact that fashion influences would have come mostly from the "reactionary and imperialist" West made it even more threatening.

After the 1948 communist takeover, the act of being fashion-forward carried radical connotations in Hungary. The authorities saw fashion as potentially disruptive because it represented a form of alternative, nonphysical power that was difficult to regulate and subsume under totalitarian control. But fashion was gradually coopted by the communist regime and became a measure of socialist success. At first glance this process might seem like a top-down initiative, imposed by the authorities. However, the imperative to integrate fashion into socialist society bubbled up from the bottom ranks of society, prompted by the actions of the female citizenry.

The "popular demands" of Hungarian women regarding their appearance and identity jump-started a crucial political process of renegotiation between the citizenry and the state. Women's demands for the right to enjoy fashion challenged the boundaries of state intervention in people's personal lives, questioning the official policy on entitlement, rights, and freedoms. Hungarian women asked: Does the regime have the right to regulate what people wear? Their psychological needs, desires, and affection for feminine and stylish dress not only shaped the Hungarian fashion scene, but also contributed significantly to the softening of totalitarianism and its eventual peaceful dismantling. In short, fashion played a key role in creating what was widely known in the communist bloc as "socialism with a human face."

From Hungarian Dress to Communist Uniform

To understand the emotions embedded in communist dress and learn how ideology shaped its parameters, we must first examine the historical antecedents. Dress has enjoyed cultural and political significance in Hungarian history for a long time. For example, in the nineteenth century, dress and fashion were anything but mundane concerns in the country. During the Habsburg rule, they were central to creating national, ethnic, and class consciousness. The Hungarian gentry wore the *diszmagyar*, the Hungarian gala dress, as a way of distinguishing themselves at the Habsburg court. Even after the 1867 Compromise, which established the formal equality of Austrians and Hungarians under the dual monarchy, the Hungarian gentry wore this attire as a symbol of national difference, ethnic pride, and aspirations for independence. The *diszmagyar* was a safe but extremely visible means of political opposition.[9]

The significance of fashion and elaborate dress for ordinary citizens grew over time. Hungary turned from a predominantly feudal society into modern one at the turn of the twentieth century. Before, the country was barely touched by industrialization, which had transformed England, France, Germany, Italy, and other European powers. During the 1920s and 1930s, however, Hungary began to catch up swiftly with the West. The capital, Budapest, became a fashion center, attracting wealthy shoppers from Eastern Europe and the Balkans who flocked to the city on buying sprees. The quality, styles, and standards of Hungarian fashions were comparable to Paris, but the prices were relatively moderate.[10]

As the Hungarian class system was undergoing a rapid change, people increasingly expressed their status and wealth in the sartorial realm. More and more Hungarians, especially in urban settings, relied on the services of skilled dressmakers to make their upward mobility visible to the world. But despite rapid commodification and social change, Hungary was still a "country of three million beggars" before World War II.[11]

Under communist rule, fashion continued to divide Hungarians. Those Hungarians who had suffered sartorial exigencies under the old class system for the first time had a basic wardrobe. They welcomed the homogenization of dress practices as historically justifiable. The new attire, which emphasized simplicity and functionality, served as a tangible marker of the change in social relations. In contrast, other citizens saw homogenization and the dissemination of low-quality attire as an arbitrary state policy that impeded self-actualization. In the early 1940s, a maid in her Sunday best could look as stylish as her mistress, taking satisfaction and a sense of autonomy from her "good" outfit. Under communism, the maid enjoyed an elevated social status, but the state's strict dress code mandated that she had to relinquish one of the most meaningful things in her life.

Even before the communist takeover, Hungarian women were already inclined to invest clothing with political meanings. At the first postwar political demonstration on 17 November 1946, thousands of angry women from all social classes gathered in front of the Hungarian Parliament in Budapest to protest the astronomical prices of clothing, calling for the death penalty for black marketers.[12] The women demanded sartorial stability: standardized and fixed prices of textiles and decent footwear. The protesters hoped that, in the new Hungary, the right to dressing well would not be the prerogative of a few. The authorities swiftly responded to their forceful demands. An upper limit was set on the cost of fabrics and the price of shoes was capped, the amount etched into the soles. Within a couple of years, communism's industrial sectors began producing some sartorial basics, which, although of mediocre quality and design, were available at affordable prices. This development undoubtedly pleased the general population.

In the beginning, then, the communist regime appeased women's key sartorial demands. Women seemed to relax as the government also promised social and economic benefits, such as better access to education and health care and decent-paying factory jobs. But when state totalitarianism took the form of censorship and intrusive regulations, citizens grew wary of speaking out against the regime. Soon women's exactions for access to fashionable styles were seen not only as insignificant, but also as an effrontery to the new ideals of communism. Essentially, women turned to dress as a safe, nonverbal means of communication to talk back to the regime. Because dress has open meanings and is nonverbal, women could use it effectively, if subconsciously, as a form of resistance.

How Communist Dress Made the Cut

The mission of communism was to overhaul the social order and economy, creating a new world order that challenged capitalism. Therefore, communist fashion also had to set itself apart from capitalist fashion. The social aspects of dress became more important than the aesthetic ones. The primary social role of "fashion" under socialism was to dress citizens in mass-produced readymade clothing, enabling them to concentrate all their energies on production.[13]

The new communist dress code was instrumental in the standardization of the population's lifestyles, too.[14] Communist dress was expected to prompt people to focus on commonality and solidarity, rather than to dwell on individuality and personal needs. It encouraged a puritanical mindset and discouraged sexual expression. Because of their class connotations, hats and jewelry, especially gold or precious gems, completely disappeared.[15] To mitigate clothing shortages, communist dress had to be spartan in the use of materials, ornamentation, and accessories.[16] For example, eyeglasses were mass-produced in only one style. Many people thought the glasses were ugly and refused to wear them. Medical necessities and uncommon dress sizes did not exist, largely because communist citizens were expected to have no physical weaknesses or irregularities.

Communism, in theory, aimed to erase all forms of social distinction, including the social inequalities between men and women. In the cultural realm, this translated into an official sartorial policy that tried to mask gender difference. Women's attire continued to be gender specific because Hungarian society was too conservative for a real, radical change. Nevertheless, it exhibited "mannish" characteristics. The shoulders of suits, popular at the time, were wide. Women also wore trousers, although strictly for factory and agricultural work. In the mid-1950s, nearly identical suits for men and women expressed not only the ideological blurring of genders but also the social elevation of the working masses.

With the exception of official state uniforms, women's work clothes were rarely made from good-quality fabric. Work clothes were pre-shaped, pre-fitted ready-to-wear. This made the wearer uniform and devoid of subjectivity. The primary objective of work attire was to protect the wearer during heavy physical labor and to allow ease in frequent washing. Women's work outfits usually had big, ungainly pockets for carrying tools and personal necessities. As a rule, women wore these simple, comfortable clothes with "sensible" shoes and a simple cotton scarf on the head.[17] The total effect made many look older than their age. Such outfits were intended to direct attention away from the working woman's body and sexuality. Besides work clothes, most women owned nearly identical house dresses made from cheap cotton. Called *otthonka* in Hungarian, these simply cut dresses were a staple of communist fashion.

Clothes worn outside the home and workplace were also understated. Communist citizens learned to police themselves, avoiding new styles and trying to remain inconspicuous. Both genders favored neutral colors, such as black, gray, and brown, because they did not show dirt and they helped people blend in. There was a material reason for the lack of vibrant colors, too. After the communist bloc was sealed off economically from the West, imported dyes were no longer available. Even the traditionally colorful attire of the peasantry was toned down considerably.

All mechanisms for expressing personal distinction fell out of favor under the totalitarian regime. Women were judged primarily by their ideological maturity and labor productivity. They were expected to achieve self-realization through beliefs and work, rather than through "shallow" things such as looks. Makeup fell by the wayside, as the regime valued the morality of the "natural." Most cosmetics would have been imported from the West because communist industries did not undertake such bourgeois ventures.[18] Women who wanted to enhance their looks used makeshift cosmetics made from everyday household items: burnt matchsticks as eyeliner, beetroot juice instead of rouge or lipstick. Hard work meant fingers with short nails. Nail polish was especially despised and ridiculed.[19]

Although scholars have studied the main features of early communist fashion, few have discussed the positive outcomes of these homogenizing practices.[20] Notably, the communist fashion system provided sartorial stability and affordable prices enjoyed by few Hungarians before World War II. The regime also published instructions on what people should wear and when. On the one hand, this suggests that the communist regime talked down to its citizens and unintentionally instilled them with petit bourgeois values. On the other hand, such initiatives provided crucial information to the proletariat, which had no awareness of social and sartorial etiquette.[21] Working-class citizens needed instruction about caring for a wardrobe because prior to the communist takeover they owned only the most basic items.[22] Ultimately, communist fashion relegated the power over sartorial presentation to the citizens, who were to become the true arbitrators of fashion. This meant that citizens told designers what they needed, rather than the other way around. Along the way, communist fashion developed its own distinguishing features, rather than imitating the West.

Because communist dress had to be inexpensive while effectively conveying egalitarian tenets, it was mass-produced and mass-marketed. Although the inflexibility of central planning clearly limited people's sartorial freedom, mass production was not the outcome of totalitarian thinking and economic strategy alone. In 1945, Hungary, an ally of fascist Germany, came out of World War II utterly devastated. Industry was in shambles, the infrastructure in a state of collapse. Factories had been looted by the retreating Germans and the Soviet occupation.[23] Industrial production came to a standstill. Vast quantities of clothing had disappeared during World War II, as city dwellers had given garments to peasants in exchange for food. While millions were inadequately dressed in the 1930s, the war exacerbated the miserable sartorial conditions. To equip citizens at least with basic items, the communist regime had to adopt mass production. Manufacturing had to be fast, the designs simple. In fact, one could argue that mass production was not only the logical but the most humane solution to postwar exigencies.

As the Cold War escalated, the Soviet and Hungarian governments pumped money into Hungary's heavy industry. Initially, the population endorsed the prioritization of heavy industry because of its defense potential. Heavy industrial progress was seen as a guarantee of military equilibrium with the West and a deterrent to confrontation. This type of industrialization led to shortages of necessities, including food and clothing, causing enormous hardship to the population. Hungarians sighed with relief when the state redirected some resources to light industry and garment manufacturing.

Dissemination of Communist Fashion

Fashion magazines were rare in Hungary under communism. Established in 1947, *Ez a divat* (*This Is Fashion*) had limited circulation because of chronic paper shortages. Initially the magazine had no photographs, only illustrations. Launched by fashion professionals from a prewar fashion school, *Ez a divat* looked like a throwback, but its content was strikingly new. To survive under the communist regime, the editors offered readers advice on how to recycle and refashion old attire for new conditions. For example, they popularized striped knitwear, cleverly showing how to make fashion from scratch. After all, striped garments could be made by unraveling old clothes and knitting new garments with, while creating eye-catching patterns.[24]

Another women's magazine, *Asszonyok* (*Women*), later renamed *Nők Lapja* (*Women's Magazine*), initially carried some beauty tips and fashion advice. As totalitarianism intensified in the early 1950s, it became a propaganda organ targeting women. Fashion disappeared completely from its pages. After the 1956 uprising, *Nők Lapja* reinstated fashion coverage, mostly by reproducing Western images. Many readers, however, probably saw the pictures of mostly film stars as "virtual fashion," because their Western attire remained inaccessible.

Certainly some Hungarian women had relatives or friends who could ship packages of clothes from the West. These parcels diversified the Hungarian fashion scene a great deal from the late 1950s onward.[25] A huge demand arose for stylish clothing, including nylon stockings. Because much of North America and Western Europe had become fashion-conscious throwaway societies, the turnover of dress items was high during the 1950s. In the United States, the expanding clothing industry put readymade fashions within reach of more people, including new Hungarian immigrants. Used clothing found in Salvation Army stores or donations to refugee relief groups found their way into Hungarian American households, eventually reaching East European relatives.

Communist Fashion Design

State-sponsored fashion design in communist Hungary had not only a functional but an explicit educational role.[26] Official fashion designers aimed to demonstrate through their creations the break with the old bourgeois world-view, to refine the tastes of the working population, and to inculcate them with an affinity for communist aesthetics. They hoped to eradicate the visual symbols of class standing; under socialism, being "well dressed" was no longer a measure of wealth. Instead, it reflected political and aesthetic maturity and, preferably, loyalty to the regime.

After the war, the Hungarian fashion system collapsed. Most fashion professionals either emigrated to the West or turned to other occupations.[27] The regime discouraged them from designing clothes, lest they brainwash young apprentices in profligate bourgeois ways. A new crop of designers, like other communist professionals, were recruited from reliable proletarian stock. After the late 1940s, citizens from other backgrounds had to be exceptionally talented to gain admission to the design schools. The education of the first communist fashion designers started at Budapest's College of Applied Arts in the Department of Textiles in 1949. Because faculty members were not fashion professionals, training initially focused on two distinct areas: classical drawing skills and Marxist-Leninist teachings. Consequently, the first graduates were more illustrators than designers and had few technical competencies. The curriculum did not include European costume history, and the art history courses stopped with French Impressionism.[28] Students' visual exposure to Western fashions was minimal. After graduation, they were placed in clothing factories. Their design sketches were juried by a committee of trade professionals and communist officials who knew very little about fashion. Remarkably, acceptable designs occasionally emerged and went into production.

The ideological demands on new designers were explicit: communist fashion was to develop its own characteristics. Accordingly, the 1953 rules of the College of Applied Arts cautioned students against following "decadent, formalist, cosmopolitan" trends. Instead, the College encouraged designers to shed European shackles by turning to their ethnic roots. For inspiration, students were supposed to look to Hungarian and Russian folk art instead of fads of the West.[29]

The first generation of communist designers were expected not only to reevaluate the goals of their profession but also to revolutionize the process of producing fashion. Officials hoped they would break away from "petit bourgeois taste." Such taste allegedly reflected a nonprogressive mindset and was inauthentic because it indiscriminately copied elements from all styles.[30] In contrast, communist design was to deliver clear and straightforward messages. It had compositional simplicity and was comfortable and functional.

Communist clothing design considered the body and focused on extending its physical capabilities. In the early 1950s, Comrade Zamushkin, director of the Tretyakov Gallery in Moscow, on his visit to Budapest lectured the staff and student body at the College of Applied Arts on the aims of communist fashion design. Differences between young and old, slender and rounded, urban and rural had to be eliminated from women's dress.[31] In addition, "good" designs also had to lend themselves to high-volume mass production, signaling the symbiosis of politics and economics under communism.

Communist designers were supposed to bring about a democratization of the design process that involved creators and the consumers. Thus the first communist fashion shows were held at factories to reach the target clientele: the proletariat. Workers often modeled the attire in these shows. Viewers sat at the same height as the models, stressing the idea of communist fashion as a key tool for social leveling. The arrangement also suggested the attainability of communist fashion, and that fashion was the right of every female worker. Viewers saw the designs on the "real" imperfect bodies of women like themselves, and they were allowed to touch the models and the clothes. Their feedback was also encouraged. Thus the working population helped produce fashion.

After the fashion shows, designers had informal conversations with the audience, who offered their opinions about the prototypes and suggested changes. Audience feedback was transcribed on paper and had to be directly transported to the drawing board. In winter 1952, *Ez a divat* reported that a fashion show organized in the National Theater of Pécs was a great success. Apparently, the designs incorporated the input of 10,000 women polled during the initial design process. Designers used their remarks and suggestions, creating final designs that reflected popular taste. In other words, working women were supposed to dictate fashion design and production principles. Most of the women polled in factories tended to be loyal communists, aware of mounting scarcities. They sought simple, functional, easy-to-mix-and-match designs, equating fashion with the pragmatic act of clothing the human body.

Communist designers were cautious about what they put on the runways, subjecting themselves to self-censorship. Those who received too many complaints were unlikely to keep their state employment for long. In fact, the state encouraged design partnerships so that creations could convey communal values and foster team spirit.[32] Cooperation was promoted in international fashion relations as well. Designers in the former communist countries showed their work in "fashion exhibitions," or "multi-lateral fashion shows," that emphasized collaboration instead of competition. Mrs. Rákosi, wife of the general secretary of the Hungarian Communist Party, explained the logic. Although friendly communist counties could not compete among themselves, they were strongly encouraged to compete against the West. [33] With time, some Soviet bloc countries were occasionally invited to participate in Western fashion contests. The Hungarian state rewarded designers who had been asked to show their collections in the West with extra funds for preparation.

Fashion, however, was not regarded as an equalizer of social conditions in every corner of Hungary under totalitarianism. Designers took into account the varying degrees of interest in fashion in different parts of the country and used this information to adjust their creations to different tastes. For example, one style went to Ózd, a working-class town, another to Sopron, a border town between Hungary and Austria, and still another to Budapest.[34]

Fashion shows were a popular form of light entertainment, a staple at communist holiday resorts. To judge by surviving photographs, the shows attracted men, perhaps because they provided a rare opportunity for the communist male gaze.[35] Communist public life was puritanical; women's bodies were not supposed to be sexualized or objectified.[36] Communist fashion shows were a "safe" site for gazing at a comrade's body rather than focusing on her intellect and political convictions.[37]

"Designer outfits" were unheard of in the totalitarian phase of communism, which lasted until 1956. A few prewar "boutiques," such as the Clara Rothschild Salon in downtown Budapest, catered to the diplomatic corps or wives of the political elite. Like Parisian couture houses, the salon kept life-size dummies of clients' shapes on hand, using these mannequins to make custom clothing for the wealthy. For example the wife of Yugoslav President Josif Broz Tito kept a fashion mannequin at the salon, which regularly sent her dress models. Unlike the Paris houses, the Clara Rothschild Salon did not create original collections. A former employee explained, it copied Western fashion and offered high-quality spin-offs for the Hungarian "elite."[38]

By the late 1950s rise of the János Kádár regime, Western fashion was seen as less threatening. The first independent design studio, Ruhatervező Studio, was launched in 1958, signaling the decentralization of Hungary's communist fashion scene. Ruhatervező Stúdió made clothing for the wives and daughters of doctors, lawyers, artists, and the like, reflecting the political changes that took place after the 1956 uprising.[39] Professionals, not just party cadres, also began to be socially valued. Around the same time, Hungary began exporting clothes to Western markets.[40] At first this apparel was designed in the West and manufactured in Hungary, taking advantage of low labor costs. Later communist designers took charge of design and production. Within Hungary, however, apparel designed for export was accessible only to the members of the power elite, creating social tensions.

Designers were pulled in many directions. They had to be experts in both the artistic and the industrial aspects of the design process. When working for the Hungarian elite, they had to study international fashion trends as they created high-quality models in limited quantity. When working for the masses, they received instructions from the state to produce versatile clothes that could be easily created by quantity production.

In a backlash against early 1950s suppression, some of Hungary's first communist fashion models and designers were elevated to star status. In 1962, designer Margit Szilvitzky received the highest government artistic distinction, the Munkácsy Prize. With official status, fashion designers like Szilvitzky had unique privileges. They were the only people in Hungary with access to Western fashion publications, such as the French *Vogue* or West German *Burda*. They could occasionally visit Western fashion houses and see the seasonal collections. But their expertise was harnessed, not for the masses, but primarily to create unusual apparel for state officials and boost Hungary's clothing export to the West. Although official superstar designers raised professional standards, their role in the ideological and political transformation of communist fashion was limited. The everyday sartorial practices of ordinary women proved far more decisive.

Communist Consumer Agency

Two case studies show how ordinary Hungarian women played a crucial role in changing perceptions about fashion under communism. Anni and Éva, interviewed in 2004, used dress to create and assert their selfhood under communism. While Anni benefited from the communist takeover, Éva suffered from it. Their stories show how Hungarian women developed a politically linked sartorial consciousness, while highlighting the production and consumption of Hungarian fashion from a new vantage point.

Although Anni and Éva came from different social backgrounds, they had remarkably similar sartorial experiences and feelings about clothing.

Their oral histories not only unfold deeply personal stories, but also epitomize two typical sartorial scenarios. Their accounts show how Hungarian
women of the 1950s and 1960s used dress to communicate views about the
gendered material provisions of the communist regime, providing powerful
examples of consumers' political agency. From their narratives, we learn how
Hungarian women under communism partook of the international fashion
scene as best they could, relying on whatever resources they could access.

In Communist Hungary, people judged each other's political leanings
through the nuances of appearance. Although most people looked somewhat
bland, they did not dress uniformly. Women set themselves apart by focusing
on details and the creative use of accessories, so these choices became deeply
meaningful. Communist citizens developed a keen ability to read between
the lines. They could discern and interpret sartorial signs of dissent or conformity with ease. The state was wary of verbal sanctioning or open politicali-
zation of dress practices, which would have shown that the regime could be
unnerved by a "lightweight" medium like fashion. While the regime was
lulled into a false sense of security, citizens like Anni and Éva steadily built
up their subversive strategies. Over time, similar tactics used by Hungarian
women became so pervasive that communist leaders had to reevaluate their
official stance on fashion.

Anni's Advantage

Anni is one of many Hungarian women who benefited from communism,
which made upward mobility available to the working class. With an extensive wardrobe, Anni felt as if she was able to transcend her humble background. Her clothes not only signaled, but constructed and produced, her
new middle-class identity.

Born in 1945, Anni was a war child. Her father was a policeman, her
mother a homemaker and skilled seamstress. They lived in a small town in
northeastern Hungary. Anni's fascination with dress is rooted in her childhood. In the war's aftermath, basic food was hard to come by and dress was
viewed as a luxury. Most Hungarians clothed themselves with what remained
from before the war. Children's apparel did not exist, so baby Anni's mother
made her newborn's clothes out of well-worn outfits whose fabrics would suit
the baby's delicate skin. For years, Anni was dressed in these homemade
creations or in hand-me-downs. Most dress items or textiles were available

only with ration cards. Shoes were the most difficult items to acquire. Anni was fortunate because her father, a state employee, was given extra leather soles for his boots. From these, the local shoemaker created Anni's footgear. Most communist citizens were forced to learn pragmatism as a way of life. Anni's mother made her daughters' dresses a size or two bigger, so that she could grow into them. Somewhat well clad, Anni stood out among the impoverished neighborhood children.

Items of apparel were the most valued gifts, linking dress to major celebrations in Anni's mind. Early on, she learned to be careful with an outfit, as it was meant to serve several generations. Anni's mother taught her girls never to sit on the floor in their outfits or engage in rough-and-tumble play. They were also socialized into being "feminine" and never dressed in pants. These expectations for ladylike behavior appeared to be especially important in Anni's family because her mother, who came from the working class, had endured a difficult childhood. Concerned to protect her children from similar hardship, she indulged them instead.

A "cultured appearance" was very important in Anni's household. Anni's mother explained that a girl in simple garb would be appreciated if she was clean and her dress displayed with care. As a girl, Anni usually had three outfits each season. The fanciest was taken out only for special occasions and the others were alternated weekly. The scarcity of clothes enhanced their "specialness," prompting extra care with maintenance. As soon as Anni got home, she would change into a pair of old track pants and top or into a tattered dress. Anni intensely disliked the ritual of changing after school because the well-worn house clothes were a constant reminder of deprivation and poverty. With bitterness, she recalled the humiliation of quickly having to change into a "presentable" dress when a friend dropped by unannounced. This shame carried into her adulthood, and she always made an effort to dress above her class status, displaying sartorial variety frequently. She also accumulated an extensive adult wardrobe.

In the 1950s, people began to run out of prewar apparel and the state mandated that children wear school uniforms. Anni believes that this move was intended not to eliminate class differences but rather to cover them up, which was indicative of double standards and the duplicitous nature of the regime. As was expected of a good communist citizen, Anni was well groomed and more presentable than many of her classmates. Judging others by their dress was so deeply ingrained in Anni that she would not make friends with unkempt children.

Anni's social relations were very much influenced by dress. The family lived in a small community where everybody knew everyone else, and people's outfits were often the talk of the town. Only the doctor and the pharmacist, who provided essential medical services to the community, could flaunt bourgeois tastes without criticism. Anni yearned to belong to this group and wear their more luxurious, better-fitting clothes, despite the fact that the political climate denigrated the petit bourgeois. In emulation, Anni developed a penchant for costume jewelry, adorning her dresses with pins and brooches. She also had a fondness for frilly dresses and flowery prints. Her accessories and flounces made an indirect political statement because they stood in opposition to the official state style—austere, functional, and mannish—worn by most women.

Communist Hungarians who created beautiful clothes enjoyed the admiration of their peers. Making a satisfying outfit entailed a lot of work and involved sacrifices. With so few materials available, a seamstress's transformative skills were equated with virtue. An early realization of this turned Anni not only into a clothes horse, but also into someone who used dress as a primary means to make public statements about her personal achievement and success.

After 1956, Anni's family's financial situation began to improve. By 1959, Anni's wardrobe already extended beyond functional apparel. For example, she owned a red rock-and-roll skirt, bought from a classmate with relatives in the West who regularly sent parcels filled with hand-me-downs. To get fashionable clothes, Anni's family also patronized the black market. Her aunt, who worked in a hospital and saw people from all walks of life, acquired some stylish smuggled goods. Eager to distinguish herself from others, Anni flaunted the black-market goods. Defining herself at a loyal Hungarian citizen, she saw nothing paradoxical in displaying Western goods made by the "enemy." What mattered to her was the visibility of these status symbols, which helped her gain entry and acceptance among the local "in" crowd.

In the 1960s, teenaged Anni used dress to emphasize her shapely figure (Figure 13.1). Her outfits show that she had begun to think of herself as a sexual being. Even her communist youth organization uniform fit tightly, unlike the modest dress of a regular cadre. She often accessorized it with high heels and left her long, dyed blonde hair loose.

Although Anni professed loyalty to the regime, she routinely violated its sartorial norms. She obsessed about her clothes and spent endless time, effort, and money to locate a matching pair of shoes, the right bag, or a color-

Figure 13.1. Anni (right) at age sixteen at her first ball, 1961. The girls wear white chiffon or tulle tea-length dresses and "adult" pumps. The girl in the middle wears a Western "parcel" dress that stirred Anni's envy. Anni completes her outfit with a black velvet belt that accentuates her narrow waist. All three girls accessorize with jewelry and gloves and had their hair professionally coiffed. Courtesy Anni Halmi.

coordinated scarf. She appeared in public overdressed and over-accessorized. In the postwar communal and egalitarian culture, no citizen was supposed to think that he or she was better than others. Dressing alike indicated identification with the political line and signified genuine communist consciousness. Dressing in an alternative fashion bespoke transgression. Furthermore, the desire for Western clothes was an indirect affirmation of capitalism's productivity, which implied the instability and ineffectiveness of the local economy. As such, dressing in Western apparel could be interpreted as covert political critique.

Subconsciously Anni contested the discrepancy between personal desires and public opportunities under communism. As a good citizen, she was expected to suppress her individuality and wear state-sanctioned dress without opposition. She was not supposed to nurture alternative sartorial desires. But her desires overrode any adherence to communist ideals. Many loyal Hungarian communist citizens behaved like Anni on the sartorial front.[41] Their transgressions signaled to others that material interests were not necessarily in opposition to communist consciousness and morals, and that suppression of their longings only weakened the regime's popular support. This resulted in women's increasing consumer demands, which fed into the New Economic Mechanism introduced in the 1960s. This policy gradually transformed communist Hungary's producer's market into a consumer's market. Soon, economic reforms were followed by limited political reforms. By 1968, Hungary had completely overthrown totalitarianism and embarked on a new socialist path. In this process, the sartorial revolts of many Annis, who otherwise supported communism, were crucial.

Éva's Angle

Éva was born in 1941 into a middle-class family of the type the state suspiciously labeled as a "class enemy." This made Éva's life under communism a constant struggle. Her mother, a homemaker, was a local beauty known for her stylish elegance (Figure 13.2). Neither she nor Éva's father, an agronomist who managed one of Hungary's biggest estates before World War II, allowed their children to dress sloppily. They instilled in the children a belief that dress is an integral part of one's self-concept.

Éva's first dresses were bought in stores in the nearby town, ordered from a children's salon in Budapest, or made by the local dressmaker. As expected of a middle-class child, her prewar wardrobe was extensive. It included a fur coat, laced-up leather boots, ruffled skirts, and jaunty hats. In contrast, peasant children living near the estate wore coarse linen dresses and went barefoot at the first sign of spring.

After the war, Éva's family's situation radically changed. Their income plummeted when her father went into hiding to avoid being taken to a labor camp. Éva and her mother found it increasingly difficult to keep up appearances, but they would not give up (Figure 13.3). The impoverished family received help from the West, as relatives sent parcels of clothes. Some of the material in these care packages—hats, cocktail dresses, fine gloves, and frilly children's attire—oozed prosperity and stirred a longing in Éva for another life, somewhere beyond the Iron Curtain.

An able seamstress, Éva's mother refashioned many of these items to suit the setting. Éva and her mother were especially glad to receive dress patterns. Their favorite pastime was poring over the patterns, trying to figure them out

Figure 13.2. Éva's mother before communism in her Sunday best or church dress, 1939. The simplicity and purity of the white color is broken up with contrasting dark, oversized buttons and a simple collar. Although she looks elegant and stylish, her overall appearance is rather conservative. Similar to other "better" class Hungarian women in the late 1930s, she wears silk hosiery and completes her outfit with dark dress shoes. Courtesy Éva Bartha.

or create new designs. Thanks to these patterns, which her peers didn't have, Éva was always a trendy dresser.

By the time she went to high school, Éva was a patient and devoted tailor who could sew, darn, crochet, and knit. She designed and executed all her dresses, mostly by hand. In the early era of communism, ordinary Hungarians did not have many outfits; this was true for Éva as well. What was different was her sense of style. She had limited resources, so she had to build her wardrobe consciously and systematically. She increased the number of

Figure 13.3. Éva's mother, her stylishness eroded, under the communist regime, 1948–1949. Here she wears a loose, mid-calf, dotted silk dress that is fraying. To make this simple garment festive, she added a white collar and eventually lengthened the dress by adding stripes, in an effort to emulate Christian Dior's "New Look." Courtesy Éva Bartha.

her outfits by combining different pieces and accessorizing them with unique details.

Paradoxically, communist scarcities made Hungarian women creative and resourceful. Putting together a look depended not only on a woman's individual taste and personal aesthetics, but also on her upbringing and cultural capital. Although their dresses were generally made of cheap textiles, they fit well due to the high level of home dressmaking skills. Real sartorial problems started only when women had to wear things they could not make themselves, such as shoes.

Negative sartorial and corporeal experiences—rough fabrics, low-quality shoes, lack of basic hygienic products—engendered many women with an antagonism toward the regime. The state had high expectations for women's political commitment and labor participation, but it failed to provide adequately for their basic needs. In hindsight, Éva believes that most women started to wonder about the regime's economic viability sooner than men. Women, after all, directly experienced the state's inefficiency while running their households and managing their families' daily lives.

Once the first real fashion publications appeared, Éva bought all the issues. Her favorite was the East German *Pramo* magazine, as it also contained dress patterns. From the late 1950s, women's magazines anxious to appease the population included occasional fashion briefs from Paris or London. These reports transported Éva to a world of abundance and fulfillment. As time went on, sewing became not only a survival skill but also Éva's favorite pastime. The sound of the foot pedal of her sewing machine, inherited from her mother, transported her to a world of fantasy and creativity. In a culture based on "truth and "realism," Éva embraced sewing as her form of escapism, which temporarily whisked away her gray reality. She felt that her creations transformed her physically and psychologically. Her aesthetics, innovations, and abilities gave Éva pleasure and satisfaction, helping her to construct a self-affirming identity that had dignity. Dress, as she put it, was a psychological shield that protected her inner self. Through her creations, Éva could articulate her difference and individuality, and this was a potentially alarming phenomenon to the political authorities.

Éva's appreciation for high-quality attire led her to illegal and black-market activities, which caused her great humiliation. She wondered why quality items came only from the black market, from under the counter, or through bribes and personal contacts in the West. Éva began to question the state, which could not provide for its citizens. She thought it "inhumane" that the simple act of buying fabrics or dress items almost always amounted to a crime.

. Dress was significant to Éva because it was one of the few aspects of life that she could control, providing her with a sense of freedom and personal choice. She accrued much personal and political confidence from her sartorial skills. Creating a nonconformist presence and, by extension, a "unique" sub-

Figure 13.4. Éva (in capri jeans) and her college friends, 1962. Young women under communism did their best to look fashionable and create an individual look. Éva's jeans and flat shoes were considered very fashion-forward. Courtesy Éva Bartha.

ject was a personal triumph under totalitarianism. With her outfits, Éva carried on her mother's stylish heritage and tested the limits of the regime (Figure 13.4). Officially, only the proletariat was allowed to be a trendsetter. In the state's eyes, all oppositional models of communist femininity, including the gentle female intellectual personified by Éva, had to be squashed. Through her alternative sartorial persona, Éva not only expressed her criticism of the regime, but she also demonstrated autonomy, resilience, and political finesse.

On one level, Éva's love of dressing with individuality and her Western flair could be interpreted as a mundane female desire for fashion. Through dress, however, Éva subconsciously defied the communist discourse of corporeal uniformity and contested her negative treatment by the regime. She knew that her sartorial sense affected her viewers, who instinctively understood that she was projecting an alternative standpoint. She refused to be crushed and be pressed into a confining mold on the sartorial front. Like Anni, she became one of the many Hungarian women who, through their sartorial presentations, were instrumental in stirring up an alternative consciousness and setting in motion winds of political change.

Toward a New Communist Fashion

Anni's and Éva's relationship to clothes defied the communist representation of women as uniform subjects, and tells the story of women who formed their political identities in the process of dressing their bodies. Anni and Éva used dress to define selfhood. For both, dress was a source of pleasure and a way of escaping the drudgery and stark reality of everyday life. In their efforts to avoid standardization, Anni and Éva circumnavigated around the sartorial provisions of the state. They used myriad resources—personal, familial, and at times illegal—to create their self-representation. Their sartorial strategies were neither passive nor unimaginative. Both manipulated social and ideological constraints on their appearance. Their narratives demonstrate how, through dress, many Hungarian women were able to state publicly without retribution their own and the population's dissatisfaction with the material and ideological aspects of the communist regime. By refusing to denounce material goods and the desire for them and by insisting on the right to enjoy fashion, ordinary women like Anni and Éva played a significant role in creating a shift in communism's momentum. By insisting on more humane standards of living and more personal choice, and by rejecting the state's power over their bodies, these women were pioneers of liberation who played an important role in the process that changed communist Hungary in fundamental ways. They reached their political consciousness through their daily struggles, rather than through indoctrination from institutions. By their relentless demand for the right to consume, they helped point the regime out of totalitarianism. Thus, they ended up not only refashioning themselves, but communism as well.

CHAPTER FOURTEEN

Why the Old-Fashioned Is in Fashion in American Houses

Susan J. Matt

In 1982, California realtors noted a "curious" trend in sales. Faux Victorian houses were selling at a rapid pace, but no one knew why. The *New York Times* reported the speedy sale of "houses featuring gables, turrets, gazebos, cupolas, leaded glass, parlors and yes, even front porches—houses built in 1981 with 1890 architectural touches." The backward-looking taste perplexed builders, who couldn't explain the popularity of "the anachronistic architectural gingerbread of a Victorian house." Some speculated that the Victorian revival reflected a renewed "interest in antiques and collectibles," while others believed that homeowners were "tired of lookalike bungalow-style homes." Hank Becker, the director of sales for a Victorian-style development near San Francisco, observed: "There seems to have been a turnaround in the country for things that are older; these homes have a touch of nostalgia; they conjure up a lot of pleasant things, peaceful things, from the past."

The most revealing analysis of the gingerbread revival came from Martha Levy, a consumer who wanted to purchase such a property. Levy, a computer programmer, was touring "Victoriana," a town-house development in Los Gatos, California. "'There's something cozy and substantial about the old styles," she said. "Inside they're just as modern" as other new houses, "but outside they look like the kind of home my mother grew up in Kansas." Levy longed for a house that looked old and that bore some connection to the way her ancestors lived. Similar yearnings undergirded the desires of countless Americans who wanted Victorian revival homes. For decades, American developers had been designing, building, and selling modern styles, such as the "California contemporary" and the ranch house. Consumers had been quietly longing for something else.[1]

For the last quarter century, middle-class consumers have gravitated toward old or old-fashioned houses and furnishings. Many have the same emotional responses as Martha Levy, finding them "cozy and substantial," and reminiscent of homes their families once occupied. Beginning in the 1980s, builders and developers responded to consumers' demand for old-fashioned homes. The Victorian housing fad, first observed in 1980s California, developed into a widespread national trend that has continued up to the present.

Market research surveys, consumer comments, and Web postings reveal the deep interest middle-class Americans have in old-fashioned houses and home goods. Their purchases also testify to this trend. The nostalgic goods sold by Restoration Hardware and Martha Stewart Omnimedia cater to the American hunger for what is imagined as traditional home life. Similarly, the spread of the "new urbanist" architecture, including planned communities like Celebration and Seaside, Florida, also reflects consumers' desires to live in structures reminiscent of another century. Even more common are the architectural features that grace many subdivision dwellings: Palladian windows, dormers, bric-a-brac, and wrap-around porches.

Such trends suggest that many twenty-first-century consumers want to create a domestic life tied to the past. Millions of Americans share a nostalgic iconography of home that seems to offer connections to ancestors and their lifeways, and they try to give this nostalgic ideal substance in their personal lives.

The nostalgic vision of home first appeared in the United States during the nineteenth century. It was jointly created by Victorian tastemakers who celebrated the idea of home in books, songs, and magazines, and middle-class Americans who adapted the ideal to fit their budgets and their emotional needs. Since then, the imagery of home has become so pervasive and familiar that modern consumers carry in their heads a vision of what home should look like. Consequently, while they may follow the advice of contemporary tastemakers, when making consumer choices they also rely on their own rich sense of what makes a house a home. This essay examines how the old-fashioned image of home was created in the nineteenth century and why it continues to hold meaning for modern consumers. The answer lies in the restlessness and instability that has characterized American social life for the last two centuries.

Creating Home in Nineteenth-Century America

Like many antebellum Americans, writer and editor Nathaniel Parker Willis (1806–67) was frequently on the move. During his sixty-one years, Willis lived in Maine, various parts of upstate New York, England, France, and Asia Minor. Yet, despite his peripatetic history, Willis encouraged his fellow Americans to settle down and celebrate the idea of home. In his 1855 collection of essays, he asserted the importance of joyful homesteads to American society. "Our plastic and rapidly maturing country would be bettered by a more careful culture of *home associations*," he argued. Anyone who had witnessed the mobility of American families and their tendency to "sell out and furnish new all over" undoubtedly yearned for the security of "'old homesteads'—to which the long absent can joyfully return."[2]

When building his own home, Willis tried to make it look old and long occupied (Figure 14.1). In 1857, architect Calvert Vaux wrote of Willis's newly constructed residence: "The new house was made to look *not* new, points of view were *not* sacrificed, and time was *not* lost in waiting for young trees to grow in place of old ones that would have had to be removed for the sake of a prospect, if less foresight had been exercised at starting. . . . Mr Willis's house looked like an old familiar settler almost before the roof was on."[3] To create "home associations" and the illusion of stability, Willis made his new house look old, sturdy, and rooted. Neither Willis's desire for an aged-looking house nor his record of relocation were uncommon. Antebellum Americans moved across state lines more than any other generation, before or since.[4] And, more than any other generation, they were responsible for the creation of home.

Despite high mobility rates, early nineteenth-century Americans celebrated the idea of a permanent home that might stay in a family for generations, and they created idealized images of what such a place looked like. Architect and critic Witold Rybczynski has argued that these images of home represent an "invented tradition," reflecting the human desire for custom and routine in a rapidly changing world. In early modern Europe, the middle classes established the idea of home as a site for family intimacy, privacy, and

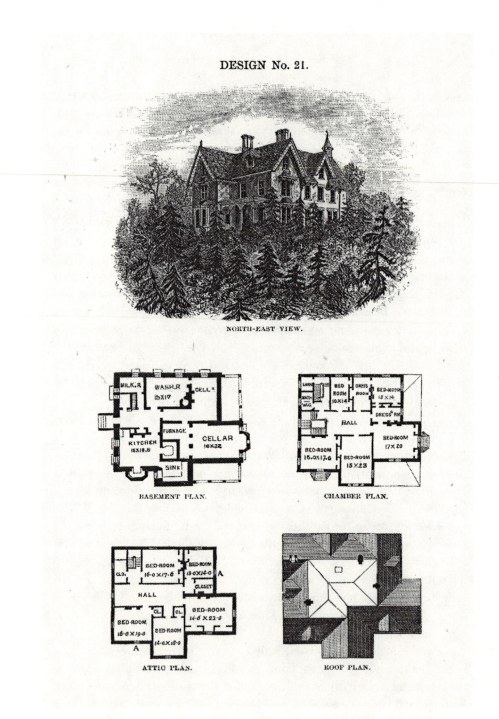

DESIGN No. 21.

NORTH-EAST VIEW.

BASEMENT PLAN.

CHAMBER PLAN.

ATTIC PLAN.

ROOF PLAN.

Figure 14.1. Design for Nathaniel Parker Willis House. From Calvert Vaux, *Villas and Cottages: A Series of Designs Prepared for Execution in the United States* (New York: Harper Brothers, 1857), 246. Courtesy Hagley Museum and Library.

comfort. The house had been a site of production; in the 1600s and 1700s, it became a location for family affection and sentiment.[5] Cultural historian Richard Bushman has shown how this ideal spread to America during the early 1800s.[6] Sociologist Peter Berger has argued that the creation of home represented an effort to offset the rootlessness that accompanied modernity.[7] Berger's observation is astute; home as envisioned by nineteenth-century Americans seemed to deny modern social patterns and presented the illusion that time and families stood still.

This vision of home did not grow organically but was created self-consciously in the antebellum era. Authors of songs, novels, poems, domestic advice manuals, and architectural guides spelled out what a home should be, offering rich images, detailed homemaking rules, and explicit house-building directions. Those celebrating the idea of home hoped that, with the proper design and care, this private family space might provide an antidote to American restlessness. In his 1852 book *Rural Architecture*, writer Lewis Allen explained that good architecture might help a family settle down. In the United States, the absence of primogeniture encouraged families to seek fortune and opportunity in new territories. The centrifugal force of social life, which sent people hurrying and scurrying away from home, was a "blemish in our domestic and social constitution." With everyone on the go, domestic architecture suffered. As a result, Americans had little "home feeling" or emotional "attachment to locality." Better architecture, however, might lead Americans to "cultivate a home feeling" and to enjoy the "virtue" of "home attachment."[8]

The American quest for this "home feeling" led to the proliferation of architecture guides in the mid-1800s.[9] According to these volumes, it was not a single style of architecture but a collection of features that made a house into a home. Lewis Allen suggested that Italian and English styles were particularly suited to America, but offered a range of designs for houses in an array of styles. English émigré and architect Calvert Vaux argued for eclecticism and historicism, urging Americans to take advantage of "all previous experience in architecture."[10] Similarly, architect and landscape designer Andrew Jackson Downing, recognized as the father of the American Gothic Revival style, encouraged a mix-and-match approach. In 1850, Downing's widely read book, *The Architecture of Country Houses*, endorsed "the Italian, Venetian, Swiss, Rural Gothic, and our Bracketed style, all modified and subdued forms of the Gothic and Greek styles," as the "most suitable for Domestic Architecture."[11]

By mixing styles, antebellum architects hoped to develop a new American domestic tradition, one well-suited to the nation's social life. They published house designs to fit a range of income levels. Their architectural guidebooks included elevations and floor plans for mansions, country houses, villas, and cottages. Guidebook writers promised that, despite differences in form, materials, and cost, all of these houses could be made into virtuous homes filled with love. For instance, Vaux praised the palatial house of Matthew Vassar, a self-made man who epitomized the mobile American of his time. An English immigrant who never learned to spell properly, Vassar created a New York brewing empire, became a millionaire, and later founded the eponymous women's college. Vaux estimated that Vassar's mansion cost $16,000, a large sum when an artisan's annual income was $375, and a clerk's, $610. Although spacious and grand, Vassar's house was nevertheless "very rural and homelike."[12] At the other end of the economic spectrum, the quaint working-man's cottage epitomized a more humble homeyness. In *The Architecture of Country Houses*, Downing wrote that "the love of home, rural beauty, and seclusion, cannot possibly be better expressed than in the English cottage, with its many upward pointing gables, its intricate tracery, its spacious bay windows, and its walls covered with vines and flowering shrubs."[13]

Although exterior style and ornament mattered, many architects believed that what made houses truly beautiful, appealing, and home-like were the associations conjured up in the minds of residents and observers. Downing claimed that his favorite styles, besides giving aesthetic pleasure, offered "another source of pleasure to most minds, which springs not from the beauty of form or expression in these styles of architecture, but from personal or historical *associations* connected with them."[14] This decidedly romantic notion held that a person's emotional responses to objects and places offered a true measure of their worth. The house's real value lay not in its structure or decorations, but in the sentiments it inspired. Much nineteenth-century advice literature played upon this romantic ideal.[15] Antebellum writers believed that all types of architecture—villas and mansions, farmhouses and cottages—could make fine homes if they possessed certain evocative qualities. Ideally, a house should be old, long-occupied, rural, unpretentious, and free of commercial associations.

The most important external feature that made a house into home was the appearance of age. In *Rural Architecture*, Allen wrote admiringly of "some of our ancient-looking country houses of the last century, which, in America, we call old." He celebrated "their ample dimensions; their heavy, massive walls; their low, comfortable ceilings; their high gables; sharp roofs; deep porches, and spreading eaves." These inspiring dwellings contrasted with "the ambitious, tall, proportionless, and card-sided things of a modern date." Allen concluded that "the old mansion, with outward features in good preservation," surpassed "in all the expression of home-bred comforts, the flashy, gimcrack neighbor."[16] Although antebellum Americans celebrated old houses, the newness of the United States and the constant shifting of its population meant that it was not always possible to live in ancestral farmhouses. As a remedy, many architects advised Americans to build new structures that simply looked ancient, much as Willis had done.

In the architects' minds, three key elements—the building materials, the setting, and the gardens—played an important role in turning new buildings into comforting homes. To achieve a sense of rooted perpetuity, builders needed to choose their materials carefully. Downing recommended "solid materials" like stone, which conveyed "the idea of eternal duration" and added much to the structure's emotional power.[17] Architects also urged builders to respect the landscape, preserving the pastoral setting that could lend a new structure the appearance of antiquity. Gervase Wheeler, who wrote *Homes for the People in Suburb and Country* (1856), lambasted the man who "grades, and blasts, and levels, and makes smooth . . . and succeeds in planting his house on a base of new-made ground, which looks slovenly for years, and has no trees of importance for a life-time." In contrast, he noted that "a well-cultivated farm, that has been tended for years, with fine old trees about the homestead, and thrifty orchards at hand, possesses so many charms" as the site for a future home.[18] Popular songs such as "The Old Oaken Bucket" also celebrated this vision, with lyrics extolling "the orchard, the meadow, the deep tangled wildwood" that surrounded the ideal home.[19] A house built on such a site would look natural—and almost as long established—as the surrounding trees, ponds, and rocks. Many architectural advisors also encouraged residents to beautify their houses with gardens and vines; Downing referred to the latter as the "drapery of cottages."[20] Well-tended gardens and walls covered with mature vines implied that a dwelling's owners had occupied a place long enough to plant seeds and suggested that they would stay to watch them come into flower.

Just as home exteriors should look old, so should their furnishings. Writing about furniture, Allen contrasted "old, familiar things" with bright shiny baubles fresh from the shopkeeper's shelves. "The furniture of a house ought to look as though the family within it once had a grandfather," he advised.

"Old things" testified to a family's roots and substance, exerting "an air of quietude, of comfort, and of hospitality."[21] Newly purchased furniture implied that a family had recently settled and perhaps recently arrived in their social class. The parvenu, or upstart, had no place in the tastemakers' recipes for home, sweet home. They recommended old furnishings that suggested that their owners had occupied the same spot, geographically and socially, for generations.

Besides being a repository of family history, the ideal home also functioned as a feminized bastion of domesticity and gentility. As industrialization created separate spheres for men and women, the home became the female domain, separate from the workaday world of business. In Harriet Beecher Stowe's words, the home was a place where "nothing ever seems to be doing or going to be done."[22] Likewise, historian Richard Bushman has written that the genteel house was "oblivious to business and work," its parlor and porch "regions of repose where ease ruled in defiance of the exertions of the economy."[23] Homes were to be feminized locations that stood outside of the male-dominated market economy, which so often disrupted family life and scattered individuals far and wide. Other scholars have demonstrated that in the nineteenth century home was imagined as the moral counterweight to the capitalist economy, as a place untouched by the fluctuating marketplace and shifting society.[24] In this context, architects often suggested that all signs of remunerative labor be tucked out of sight. Lewis Allen, in describing plans for a gentleman's country retreat, suggested that "the various offices and buildings of the farm itself, should be at a respectable distance . . . , so as not to interfere with its proper keeping as a genteel country residence."[25] To be a site of true domesticity, the house had to display its owner's freedom from want and the necessity of labor. A hint of market activity might suggest that families needed money and faced financial instability. Under such conditions they might not appear to be so very firmly planted after all.

Finally and most crucially, the house-as-home was supposed to be suffused with family affection. The happiness of family life sanctified a dwelling. In Catharine Sedgwick's 1835 novel *Home*, the fictional William Barclay explained this fundamental tenet to his children: "It is family love and happy domestic intercourse that attaches us to the inanimate objects of our home."[26]

The authors of architectural tracts and domestic novels hoped Americans would create permanent family residences and replace mobility with stability. To do this, they had to become emotionally attached to their residences.

Supposedly, the accouterments of home—furniture, vines, dovecotes, porches, trellises, and pleasant views—would conjure up the feelings that could bind people to one place. Under the influence of home, Americans would lose their restless habits and cultivate domestic virtues. Home, as so conceived, stood as a counterpoint to the tumult of antebellum life. It offered a safe haven, solidity in the face of change. It represented a fantastical wish for permanence in a world where much was in transit. Like other cultural manifestations of Romanticism, home called for a return to an imagined time, when life was simpler, society less changeable.

Created by tastemakers to ground and root a restless people, home was a brand-new tradition designed to seem old. The writers, composers, and architects who constructed this vision claimed their ideas drew on life in the past. Yet their imagined version of home bore little resemblance to the reality of earlier centuries. The homes they portrayed were supposed to have been handed down from generation to generation. In reality, few dwellings that matched their descriptions or carried their meanings had ever before existed.[27]

Despite the fact that home was a new and very self-conscious invention, it quickly took root in American culture. To greater or lesser degrees, American home owners adopted the housing styles recommended by Wheeler, Vaux, and Downing. As architectural historian Clifford Clark noted, "the vast majority of middle-class homes built at mid-century did reflect to some extent the house promoters and reformers' desire to create a new American domestic housing ideal. Yet once the ideal was accepted, the promoters and reformers lost control over it."[28] Clark points out that many adapted the designs from housing books in their own fashion and not always in strict conformity to pattern book drawings. More recently, scholars of vernacular architecture have shown how builders accommodated cultural expectations by fusing local carpentry traditions with the tastemakers' ideal.

As many American discovered, it was difficult to live up to the pictures and images presented in architectural books, novels, and poems. Elizabeth Margaret Chandler's experience is a case in point. In 1830, Chandler, along with her brother and her aunt, moved from Philadelphia to the Michigan Territory. There the Quaker frontierswoman struggled to create a home that matched the domestic ideal. In letters, Chandler showed her familiarity with sentimental domesticity, making repeated references to Nathaniel Willis's writings. Unfortunately, her small log cabin did not match the mythic vision of home. She told her aunt back in Philadelphia: "I can just fancy the mingled expression of curiosity and mirth, with which thee would eye our 'home manufacture' furniture and apartments. But I can assure thee that our house is by no means despisable." She described the rough furnishings: "On entering that apartment which may be best described by the comprehensive appellation of 'the room'—as it is conjointly 'parlour, kitchen, and hall'—the most conspicuous object is a large flour bin (situated by way of sideboard at the parlour end) over which from a wooden pin depends the looking glass. On either end of it stands Aunt Ruth's *walnut* box, and my cabinet."

Despite the simple layout and limited furnishings, Elizabeth labored to make her house match the romantic vision of home. Instead of calling her dwelling a log house or cabin, she referred to it as a cottage, giving it the quaint name Hazelbank. In an 1832 letter she referred to her dwelling in sentimental terms, confiding that her brother went to the woods for "ornamental trees of several sorts of a suitable size for planting round our *cottage*." He found several that Elizabeth thought would "be a great improvement to the looks of the house, and if I could get any body to send me a slip or two of honey suckle . . . to clamber about the door and windows, I think in process of time it would look pretty." By late summer 1832, Chandler expressed more satisfaction, writing that "the front part of our house looks quite pretty with the [morning glory] vines that creep round the door and over the windows." She still, however, longed for honeysuckle, the quintessential homey vine. She was "very impatient to see some growing about our house. They will give it such a home look."

Despite her efforts, Chandler was not convinced Hazelbank lived up to the homey ideal. In 1834, she expressed misgivings. Her house was too new, it was located in area too recently settled, and it did not match the popular images of home.

> I do not think my descriptions have done it more than justice,
> though they may have failed to give a correct idea of it. But you
> must not look for neatly railed fences, grass plots and flourishing
> shrubbery studding them at a graceful distances. No—we are new
> yet. Make up your minds for worm fences, girdled trees, and stumps.
> Do not expect to set [sic] at the window and inhale the scent of
> clover fields and newly mown hay, nor to see a picture cottage, with
> all its softened tints and its low mossy roof peeping up among the
> umbrage of beautiful trees.[29]

Chandler's language shows that she had read the sentimental literature, which shaped her expectations of domestic life. She clearly wanted her house to resemble the homes in such literature. Circumstances beyond her control limited Chandler's ability to create the ideal home. In reality, Elizabeth and her family *were* recently settled, their house *was* newly built. Her dwelling lacked the signs of age and permanence that were integral to the romantic vision of home. Nevertheless the domestic ideal guided her homemaking efforts.

In contrast, Elizabeth's aunt, Jane Howell, who remained in Philadelphia, came closer to achieving the domestic ideal. In 1834, she wrote that

> we have moved into a very neat new three story brick house[,] two handsome parlours[,] folding doors and marble mantels[;] a very commodious kitchen and four handsome chambers[,] close shutters in the 2nd story and green venitian [sic] to the 3rd. We have a beautiful yard about 66 feet clear of the buildings[,] a white painted fence with a border of flowers and shrubbery around it[,] a paved walk[,] and in the middle a long grass plot with an english walnut tree.

Aware that her Western kin lacked some of these homey touches, she added: "I have a coral honeysuckle in the yard in reserve for a dear niece when a suitable opportunity afford[s] to forward it on to her."[30]

Both Elizabeth Chandler and Jane Howell had visions of how their houses should look and an awareness of how those houses compared to the mythic American home. Their letters indicate that, by the 1830s, the tastemakers' image of home was no longer limited to novels and architectural guidebooks. It permeated middle-class American culture and the minds of ordinary women like Chandler and Howell. It could also be found, often in a vernacular form, in the wild of Michigan and on the streets of Philadelphia.

Nostalgic Styles in Contemporary Society

The vision of home that emerged in antebellum America has remained central to domestic imagery for more than a hundred years. When contemporary Americans celebrate home and "traditional" domestic life, they draw on images and ideals created in the 1800s. Evidence of the longevity of this invented tradition abounds.

In 1989, after interviewing home-owners, anthropologist Grant Mc-

Cracken enumerated the qualities of a "homey" house in North America. Many features mirrored those established in the nineteenth century. Mc-Cracken's subjects identified homey houses as diminutive: "ceilings are low, doors and windows are small," qualities that "give the domestic environment manageable proportions." Homey houses have variable elements as opposed to uniform or symmetrical surfaces. McCracken's respondents preferred "houses made of 'rubblestone' rather than cut stone." Homey dwellings also possess an "embracing property" that might enclose a resident or residence (fences around a yard, ivy on a house, low roofs, and full bookshelves, for example). This quality reflects family history and stability, for "ivy takes time to grow, the books take time to collect . . . the furniture time to buy and arrange, the family time to construct."

According to McCracken's informants, homey houses are "engaging" or welcoming; they have a "mnemonic property" that helps to "recall the presence of family and friendship relationships." They possess qualities of authenticity that make domestic space and objects "more 'real' and somehow more 'natural' than certain alternative styles of furnishings." The authentic home seems "untouched by the calculations of the marketplace." Homey houses are informal: "interior and exterior details of the house design are deliberately rustic, rural, cottagelike, and unprepossessing." Homey houses also successfully strip "possessions of their commercially assigned meanings."[31] Collectively, these features make up the modern definition of a homey house, a definition that has not strayed far from the nineteenth-century ideal.

In contemporary society, restless Americans rely on this notion of homeyness as they search for continuity, stability, and a sense of rootedness. To be sure, not every generation has needed the reassurance of old-fashioned furnishings. Indeed, some, like the high modernists of the 1920s through the 1960s, have celebrated technological progress and preferred more up-to-date styles. But since the 1980s, spending on home and housewares has reflected a hunger for tradition.[32]

Those most drawn to nostalgic domesticity, its goods and its architecture, include middle-class baby boomers, who grew up during an age of restless mobility and who themselves spurred rapid social changes. As children many boomers lived in new suburbs and moved repeatedly.[33] In 1956, sociologist William H. Whyte wrote about the widespread dislocation of their parents: "If by roots we mean the complex of geographical and family ties that has historically knitted Americans to local society, these young transients are almost entirely rootless."[34] Children born into such families became mobile adults. On average, between 1950 and 2003, 18 percent of Americans relocated each year. Between 1995 and 2000, more than 120 million people— roughly 45 percent of the U.S. population older than age five—changed residences.[35] While U.S. geographic mobility rates have fallen slightly in recent years, Americans still move around more than their counterparts in other industrialized nations.

Baby boomers, then, came of age in a highly mobile society. When they became adults, they became the driving forces behind other social changes. For instance, women of this generation who became mothers continued to work outside the home. In 1960, 70 percent of American families had a lone male breadwinner and a stay-at-home mother. By the late 1990s, only 10 percent fit this pattern. In 2001, 69 percent of all married women with children under eighteen worked outside the home.[36] Divorce also became more common during these years. In the mid-1970s the divorce rate doubled; overall since 1970 it has increased 30 percent. Currently, 51 percent of all marriages founder.[37]

Geographical mobility and dramatic transformations in family life left many baby boomers with an aching hunger for a home life rooted in tradition. Researchers have noted that baby boomers long for tradition precisely because they lacked it as children and young adults. In 1998, in an interview with *American Demographics*, J. Walker Smith of the market research firm Yankelovitch Partners noted: "Boomers are a bit scared of the way things have turned out. . . . There's been a negative fallout to their legacy that they don't feel comfortable with, so we're seeing a return to an interest in stability."[38] During the 1980s, studies by the American Council of Life Insurance drew a similar conclusion. Its researchers found that 93 percent of baby boomers believed that American society should accord greater importance to traditional family ties.[39]

In the late 1980s, the baby boomers' preoccupation with traditional domestic life found expression in a home-furnishings shopping spree. Between 1988 and 1998, consumer spending increased by 29 percent, but personal expenditures on home furnishings and accessories grew by 50 percent.[40] Among shoppers who bought housewares, a significant number gravitated toward nostalgic objects and furnishings. In a trade book for marketers, Yankelovitch Partners summarized its research on baby boomers, noting: "Boomers want home like it used to be. Not the house itself so much as that sense of security and well-being they remember fondly. They want homes and home products that appeal to this nostalgia."[41] Since the 1980s, then, baby boomers have reacted enthusiastically to businesses that supply them with the dwellings and furnishings that match their nostalgic notions of home.

For instance, old houses, or new houses built in traditional styles, have sold very well over the last quarter-century, with demand far outstripping supply. The editor of *Country Home* noted that "There is a finite number of old houses out there. . . . Everybody wants one, but most people can't have them." Marjorie Garber, author of *Sex and Real Estate: Why We Love Houses*, and chair of Harvard University's Department of Visual and Environmental Studies, points out that "In response to this desire there has developed a trend for the 'new old' house."[42]

. To get "new old" houses, prosperous home buyers have turned to the carefully planned "new-urbanist communities" that have proliferated since the early 1980s. At the dawn of the new millennium, developers were creating more than 300 towns according to "new urbanist" principles, and more than 100 smaller projects were underway nationwide.[43] Inspired by Jane Jacobs's and Lewis Mumford's critiques of modernist architecture, the "new-urbanist" movement coalesced in 1983, growing steadily since then. New urbanism is an approach to planning rather than an architectural school or style. Its practitioners combine traditional aesthetics and modern technologies to create pedestrian-friendly neighborhoods, largely in reaction to environmental degradation caused by the automobile. New-urbanist developments feature traditionally styled houses with front porches, alleyways, sidewalks, and old-fashioned town centers. As Sarah Boxer, a *New York Times* reporter and culture critic, noted in 1998, "new urbanism is, by definition, nostalgic."[44] People moving to these communities can buy brand-new houses that look old. In Disney's new-urbanist town, Celebration, Florida, housing styles range from Craftsman cottages to Italian villas. In a newly built neighborhood in Boulder, Colorado, a range of Victorian houses, complete with gingerbread trim, is available (Figure 14.2). Near Portland, Oregon, the town of Orenco offers English cottages and Arts and Crafts bungalows.[45] The demand for such houses is so great that they command extraordinarily high prices and appreciate at a faster pace than conventional houses.[46] As a result, only the affluent can currently afford to live in these communities.

Consumers explain why they are willing to pay high prices for old-fashioned houses. In 2001, builders in Onondaga County, New York, broke ground for a new-urbanist development called Annesgrove. Retiree Jerry Flanagan, the first person to buy a house, noted: "It's like coming back to your roots . . . when you lived in a neighborhood where you walked every-

Figure 14.2. New urbanist development in Boulder, Colorado, 2005. Photo courtesy Luke Fernandez.

where, knew your neighbors and had sidewalks, parks and stores. It was kind of neat." Similarly journalists Douglas Frantz and Catherine Collins, residents of Celebration, Florida, explained their reason for moving to Disney's planned community, writing, "Like many in our generation, we were always on the lookout for the next great place to live. . . . We were restless and, for the most part, rootless. . . . The locations that beckoned were places where we could walk, where a sense of history infused the community . . . and [there were] neighbors on whom you could count."[47]

Research by urban planners, the real estate industry, and other partisan groups suggest that the market for traditional housing in established neighborhoods is widespread but underserved. Some research suggests that one-third of all "home seekers" would prefer traditional neighborhoods like those offered by new-urbanist developments. Yet as of 2001, such developments represented a mere 1 percent of new housing construction.[48] A larger number of home buyers would like to live in old houses, or in traditionally styled houses, in communities without the rules and regulations imposed by new-urbanist towns. In 1980, Scott Kinzy, an architect and professor of design, surveyed homeowners about their housing preferences. He noted that 25 percent of respondents identified the farm house as their favorite house style, while 23 percent preferred the Tudor style. Modern and contemporary styles were far less popular, selected by a mere 4.7 percent and 7.8 percent of respondents respectively.[49] Such preferences have held steady over the past two decades. In a 1998 study of more than 400 home buyers in five states, researchers found that more than three-quarters of respondents favored "traditional" house and yard styles, "with garages hidden behind houses, front porches to encourage neighboring, and shade trees along the street." Nearly 60 percent objected to the "sterile uniformity" of suburban developments.[50] Further evidence of nostalgic tastes comes from Builder House Plans, a firm supplying architectural plans and blueprints to professional builders and individual home buyers. In 2006, its Web site described the top-selling house plans as "country," Colonial, farm house, and "European."[51]

Yet while the desire for an old house is widespread, most American consumers have little control over the type of house in which they live. Many people may long for older homes, but the constraints of supply and price may lead them to live in more modern buildings. This does not mean they wholly abandon their taste for nostalgic styles, however. While consumers cannot always choose the architecture of their houses, they can select their homes' interiors and furnishings. Here, too, they show a strong preference for the old-fashioned.

In the early 1980s, observers noted that in California, "older furniture including such items as antique roll-top desks and claw-foot oak dining tables have been so popular recently, and have become so scarce and expensive, that the production of replica antiques is now a major business here."[52] In 1994, business journalist Deborah Goldman, writing in *Brandweek*, described a related trend, the rise of the country style, which celebrated "roots and connections——the family farm handed down from generation to generation."[53] A year later, editorialist Stephanie Gutmann made similar observations in the *New Republic* about the rise of the "rustic look." Gutmann explained that rather than selling elegant and flawless furnishings, retailers from Pottery Barn to Spiegel had begun to offer furnishings made of distressed woods and rusted metal, as well as fabrics in faded colors. Gutmann herself appreciated the style: "I love the Rustic look. The 'washed' paint finishes are comforting. . . . A lot of people apparently have the same reaction." Rustic furnishings were designed to look "so permanent, so rooted," and, for Gutmann, this explained their appeal. Valerie Wilson, a Manhattan interior designer, explained that the style was "a reaction to newness, a way of giving things a history—in the same way that people started buying old photographs around five years ago and having someone else's whole family on their wall. It's another trend for baby-boomers that gives them a sense of place and history and time."[54] A 2002 market research study jointly conducted by Moen Inc. and Rooms of America, a consumer research organization, indicated that this longing for tradition and a sense of place remains strong in the twenty-first century and continues to drive consumer behavior. The study reported that 35 percent of consumers surveyed favored the "traditional style of decorating," while 27 percent chose a "country theme, which includes secondary themes such as Shaker, Country French and Mission." In sum, more than 60 percent of those surveyed wanted a backward-looking style of furniture in their houses.[55]

To capitalize on this longing, a host of retailers selling nostalgic home goods opened their doors in the 1980s and 1990s. Restoration Hardware, a national chain founded in California in 1980, offers mantle clocks, Mission style chests, garden arbors and stately dining room tables that, according to its advertising copy, are "traditional in detail and substantial in scale."[56] One reporter described the chain's clientele as "35–55, educated, and . . . earn[ing] more than $75,000 a year: a group that is increasingly fixated on the idea of traditional home life."[57] More famously, Martha Stewart, with her books, cable TV show, magazine, retail line, and housing developments, has gained popularity and earned a fortune over the last quarter century by capitalizing on middle-class nostalgia. In 1998, Steven Drucker, editor of *Martha Stewart Living*, explained that the magazine's major goal was "to build an archive of American traditions—a record of all the ways that families and regions and cultures set up home, celebrate the milestones of life, and pass along what they've learned to the next generation." The magazine filled a cultural void, he claimed, because so many traditions had disappeared during the twentieth century. Stewart's magazine promised to collect and revive them.[58]

While consumers learn decorating tips and style lessons from Martha Stewart and other retailers, ultimately, the success of the old-fashioned style is not the result of aggressive marketing. Instead, many shoppers already have a deep desire for traditional home life, a strong sense of what types of furniture and architecture make a house look homey and its residents rooted. They may not be familiar with the formal terms and labels of interior decor, but they know what gives a house an aura of stability. For example, in early 2006 a woman called "txbugaboo" described her decorating preferences on a *Better Homes and Gardens* online forum. About to relocate, txbugaboo hoped she would finally have the chance to buy her dream house, a pre-1980s dwelling with "more character than the newer ones." Although txbugaboo didn't have the professional vocabulary to clearly define her decorating style, she nevertheless narrowed her choices to a "few different 'decor types' and 'color schemes.'" She excitedly reported, for example: "I LOVE the country look— kind of a mish mash of different things found at flea markets, etc." She also loved "country" themes, colors, and motifs, such as "red/orange/yellow together—sunflowers, country signs, red checked curtains, etc." Her posting listed combinations of other "bright, summery colors" and country fabrics like toile. She concluded: "I'm so excited that I (might) get to start from scratch again in a house that is more 'country' than the brand new home I'm in now. . . . Where do I start, how do I decide what I like, etc.?"[59]

Txbugaboo had a clear idea of what made for homeyness. Frustrated by the style of her current, modern house, she hoped to gain the illusion of roots and a connection to the past by moving to a new town, buying a slightly older house, and decorating it with objects from a variety of styles, places, and periods. Txbugaboo's posting generated a flurry of advice from other readers. Suzieq775 suggested: "Look at decorating books leaning towards French/Country. That is what your taste sounds like to me. Good Luck!!!!" Mobarb2 wrote: "Sounds country to me too. . . . [L]ove your Love of colors. I have co[u]ntry and also have toile in one of my bedrooms. Doe[sn]'t mean its' not country or not necessarily french. I agree with the others. . . . take your time, start out by buying things you see that you really do love. In time, it will come together,' [sic] Congratulations too on being able to buy a new, older, home."[60]

In the *Better Homes and Gardens* online forum, participants exchanged advice on where to buy appropriate furniture, sometimes sharing pictures of their houses or ones they liked. For instance, one participant, SMLDesigns, noted that affordable country-style furnishings could be found at discount stores: "If you don't have accessories, I find a lot of stuff at TJ Maxx, Marshalls, Tuesday Morning—if you have one nearby or go to garage sales, flea markets and find something(s) that you really love or want to collect." Other participants discussed mantel pieces and moldings and offered pictures of their own or their favorite houses with shots of each room. For instance, DeAnn, writing under the alias dpowell, queried: "Is there still a website where everyone puts their home decorating photos for others to view? There used to be a couple, but I didn't know if they existed anymore."[61] People responded to DeAnn with links to helpful interior-decorating sites, some where they had posted pictures of their homes. In this way, participants in the *Better Homes and Gardens* forum have gradually become the authors of their own style books.

Consumers have adapted the nostalgic model of home life because they believe old-fashioned furniture, gardens, and architecture are more than just a style. In their own domestic spaces, they see values fulfilled and emotional needs met. Participants in a *Better Homes and Gardens* online discussion made this evident as they explained the deep appeal of old-fashioned furnishings. When asked their favorite styles, they used words like "romantic cottage," "country," "traditional with a English and French country twist," "rustic country clutter," "cottage/garden style," and "early American attic." Some liked the "country look" because it felt "so cozy and homey." Breezie explained that country styling gave a house a "relaxed comfy feel. It is also simple and I like that." Another participant volunteered: "I do love things and styles from the past. I love things that represent a simpler time . . . things that I remember my mother and grandmother having or using. I love a room now that feels like the quiet living room of my grandma's house that had certain smells and a feeling of safety and serenity. I'm also drawn to my roots which are in England. Country, cottage, Victorian, shabby chic . . . they're all based on the past, and that pleases me."[62]

These tastes for the antique combined the homemakers' memories of old family houses and their illusions about how houses looked in past centuries. Given the combination of memory and romantic imagination, it is perhaps not surprising that their taste for the old-fashioned often does not represent strict fidelity to one style or period. Instead, the domestic interiors American home owners create represent a diffuse yearning for a lost time and a strong belief that, in the past, life was simple and stable and people were connected to a place and to each other.

Andrew Jackson Downing, Calvert Vaux, Nathaniel Parker Willis, and other nineteenth-century tastemakers hoped Americans would borrow elements of European domestic architecture and develop a new, national style of home life. If they did, the country might become an orderly, stable, and moral republic.[63] To some extent, their efforts have borne fruit. Today, American consumers seem beset by the same romantic longing for a cozy, old-looking house harbored by many of their nineteenth-century counterparts. Such longings are the legacy of the sentimentalized view of home first presented in antebellum domestic style and advice books. Contemporary consumers are largely unaware of the origins of the homey ideal, and frequently imagine that the domestic life they are trying to create is based on a tradition that spans many centuries. The tradition they invoke, however, is a relatively new creation, a product of the restless, rootless, shifting society of antebellum America. The fact that the meaning and symbols of home are of rather recent vintage is a fact now obscured to contemporary consumers who find in them a comfortable sense of connection with the past. By now, the tradition, although consciously created and not as ancient or organic as some might imagine, has, in fact, become old. The style of home life that nineteenth-century advisors promoted thus has taken root.

Ironically, however, Americans themselves have not become rooted: the dream of stability and permanence undergirding the ideal of home is still unrealized. Nineteenth-century domestic advisors hoped that if Americans occupied attractive, old-looking, love-filled homes, they would stop moving. In contemporary America, such hopes have faded. Few believe in the possibility of grounding a restless nation. Instead, twenty-first-century Americans have reconciled themselves to the idea of moving, relying on the mythic image of home to give them a sense of place, wherever they go. This mythic image, with its retro architecture and furnishings, offers a sense of foundation and groundedness, even if the old-fashioned possessions are actually brand-new, and even if they are frequently loaded and unloaded from U-Haul trucks as their owners journey across the country, moving from one old-looking house to another.

NOTES

CHAPTER 1. RETHINKING FASHION

1. Estelle Ellis, "What Is Fashion?" speech for FIT Seminar Department, Fashion Institute of Technology, New York, 15 Nov. 1993, in folder 13: articles and speeches, box 40, acc. 423, Estelle Ellis Papers, National Museum of American History Archives Center, Washington, D.C. (hereafter cited as EE-NMAH).

2. Ellis, "What Is Fashion?"

3. On the creative economy, see Richard E. Caves, *Creative Industries: Contracts Between Art and Commerce* (Cambridge, Mass.: Harvard University Press, 2000); and Richard Florida, *The Rise of the Creative Class: And How It's Transforming Work, Leisure, Community, and Everyday Life* (New York: Basic Books, 2004).

4. For the recent history of New York's role in the transnational fashion business, see Teri Agins, *The End of Fashion: How Marketing Changed the Clothing Business Forever* (New York: Quill, 2000).

5. Roland Barthes, *The Fashion System* (Berkeley: University of California Press, 1990).

6. Ellis had this broad view of fashion for decades. See, for example, Estelle Ellis, "Fashion—Who Needs It?" address at Seventeenth Annual Convention of Schiffli Lace and Embroidery Manufacturers, Kaimesha Lake, New York, 9 May 1964, folder 13, EE-NMAH.

7. The most astute, self-confident, and articulate observers could venture educated guesses on the way certain styles or color palettes were going, based on where they had been. Such skilled anticipators of trends often worked as fashion forecasters or color forecasters. For more on forecasting, see my book, *The Color Revolution* (Cambridge, Mass.: MIT Press, forthcoming); and Ingrid Giertz-Mårtenson, *Att se in i framtiden—en studie av trendanalys inom modebranschen* (*Looking into the Future: A Study of Fashion Forecasting*) (Stockholm: Department of Ethnology, Stockholm University, 2006).

8. Early modern historians have been moving toward a similar perspective, as shown by Maxine Berg and Helen Clifford, eds., *Consumers and Luxury: Consumer Culture in Europe, 1650–1850* (Manchester: Manchester University Press, 1999).

9. For an overview of Chandler's influence, see Richard R. John, "Elaborations,

Revisions, Dissents: Alfred D. Chandler Jr.'s Visible Hand After Twenty Years," *Business History Review* 71 (Summer 1997): 151–201. For critiques, see Pamela Walker Laird, "Alfred D. Chandler Jr. and the Landscape of Marketing History," *Journal of Macromarketing* 20 (Dec. 2000): 167–73; Kenneth J. Lipartito and David B. Sicilia, eds., *Constructing Corporate America: History, Politics, Culture* (New York: Oxford University Press, 2004); and Regina Lee Blaszczyk and Philip B. Scranton, eds., *Major Problems in American Business History: Documents and Essays* (Boston: Houghton Mifflin, 2006).

10. For historians writing about the business and culture of innovation, see, for example, Kenneth J. Lipartito, "Picturephone and the Information Age: The Social Meaning of Failure," *Technology and Culture* 44 (Jan. 2003): 50–81; Steven W. Usselman, *Regulating Innovation: Business, Technology, and Politics in America, 1840–1920* (New York: Cambridge University Press, 2002); and Gerben Bakker, "Building Knowledge About the Consumer: The Emergence of Market Research in the Motion Picture Industry," in *The Emergence of Modern Marketing*, ed. Roy Church and Andrew Godley (London: F. Cass, 2003), 101–27.

11. Regina Lee Blaszczyk, *Imagining Consumers: Design and Innovation from Wedgwood to Corning* (Baltimore: Johns Hopkins University Press, 2000); Blaszczyk, "The Colors of Modernism," in *Looking High and Low: Representing Social Conflict in American Visual Culture*, ed. Patricia Johnston (Berkeley: University of California Press, 2006), 228–46; and Blaszczyk, "The Importance of Being True Blue: The DuPont Company and the Color Revolution," in *Cultures of Commerce: Representation and American Business Culture, 1977–1960*, ed. Elspeth Brown, Catherine Gudis, and Marina Moskowitz (New York: Palgrave Macmillan, 2006), 27–50. For comparable approaches, see Church and Godley, eds., *The Emergence of Modern Marketing*; and Sally H. Clarke, *Trust and Power: Consumers, the Modern Corporation, and the Making of the United States Automobile Market* (New York: Cambridge University Press, 2007).

12. Some historians have another take on one of my key points, the differences between tastemakers and fashion intermediaries. For example, see Per H. Hansen, "Networks, Narratives, and New Markets: The Rise and Decline of Danish Modern Furniture Design, 1930–1970," *Business History Review* 80 (Autumn 2006): 449–83. For sympathetic views by historians studying tastemakers, see Glenn Porter, *Raymond Loewy: Designs for a Consumer Culture* (Wilmington, Del.: Hagley Museum and Library, 2002); and Heather Hess's essay in this book.

13. Regina Lee Blaszczyk, "Styling Synthetics: DuPont's Marketing of Fabrics and Fashions in Postwar America," *Business History Review* 80 (Autumn 2006): 485–528; Orville C. Wetmore, interview by Regina Lee Blaszczyk, 8 Jan. 2007, Wilmington, Del. For a journalistic account, see Susannah Handley, *Nylon: The Story of a Fashion Revolution* (Baltimore: Johns Hopkins University Press, 1999).

14. See, for example, Valerie Steele, *Paris Fashion: A Cultural History*, 2nd ed., rev. (New York: Berg, 1998); Steele, *The Corset: A Cultural History* (New Haven, Conn.: Yale University Press, 2001); Kathy Lee Peiss, *Hope in a Jar: The Making of America's Beauty Culture* (New York: Metropolitan Books, 1998); Christopher Breward, *The Culture of*

Fashion: A New History of Fashionable Dress (New York: Manchester University Press, 1995); and Christopher Breward, David Gilbert, and Jenny Lister, eds., *Swinging Sixties: Fashion in London and Beyond, 1955–1970* (London: V & A Publications, 2006).

15. Dilys E. Blum, *Shocking! The Art and Fashion of Elsa Schiaparelli* (Philadelphia: Philadelphia Museum of Art, 2003); Dilys E. Blum and H. Kristina Haugland, *Best Dressed: Fashion from the Birth of Couture to Today* (Philadelphia: Philadelphia Museum of Art, 1977); Alexandra Palmer, *Couture and Commerce: The Transatlantic Fashion Trade in the 1950s* (Vancouver: University of British Columbia Press, 2001); and Lou Taylor, *The Study of Dress History* (New York: Palgrave, 2002).

16. Useful titles include Barbara Burman, ed., *The Culture of Sewing: Gender, Consumption and Home Dressmaking* (New York: Berg, 1999); Michaele Thurgood Haynes, *Dressing Up Debutantes: Pageantry and Glitz in Texas* (New York: Berg, 1998); Shaun Cole, *Don We Now Our Gay Apparel: Gay Men's Dress in the Twentieth Century* (New York: Berg, 2000); Dominique Veillon, *Fashion Under the Occupation*, trans. Miriam Kochan (New York: Berg, 2002); Eugenia Paulicelli, *Fashion Under Fascism: Beyond the Black Shirt* (New York: Berg, 2004); Irene Guenther, *Nazi "Chic"? Fashioning Women in the Third Reich* (New York: Berg, 2004); and Linda Welters and Patricia A. Cunningham, eds., *Twentieth-Century American Fashion* (New York: Berg, 2005). Also influential is Nancy J. Troy, *Couture Culture: A Study in Modern Art and Fashion* (Cambridge, Mass.: MIT Press, 2003).

17. Diana Crane, *Fashion and Its Social Agendas: Class, Gender, and Identity in Clothing* (Chicago: University of Chicago Press, 2000); Crane, "Globalization, Organizational Size, and Innovation in the French Fashion Industry: Production of Culture Theory Revisited," *Poetics* 24 (1997): 393–414; and Yuniya Kawamura, *Fashion-ology: An Introduction to Fashion Studies* (New York: Berg, 2005).

18. Claudia B. Kidwell and Margaret C. Christman, *Suiting Everyone: The Democratization of Clothing in America* (Washington, D.C.: Smithsonian Institution Press, 1974); *A Perfect Fit: The Garment Industry and American Jewry* (New York: Yeshiva University Museum, 2005).

19. Nicola White and Ian Griffiths, eds., *The Fashion Business: Theory, Practice, Image* (New York: Berg, 2000); Agins, *The End of Fashion*.

20. Ariel Beaujot, "Material Culture and the Vanity-Set Hairbrush: 1890–1940," Topics in Material Culture: A Graduate History Seminar at the University of Toronto, Canada, http://beaujot.com/vanity (accessed 7 Apr. 2007).

21. On the cultural history of New York fashion, see Caroline Rennolds Milbank, *New York Fashion: The Evolution of American Style* (New York: Abrams, 1996); and Valerie Steele, *Fifty Years of Fashion: New Look to Now* (New Haven, Conn.: Yale University Press, 1997). For its labor history, see Nancy L. Green, *Ready-to-Wear and Ready-to-Work: A Century of Industry and Immigrants in Paris and New York* (Durham, N.C.: Duke University Press, 1997); David von Drehle, *Triangle: The Fire that Changed America* (New York: Atlantic Monthly Press, 2004); Daniel E. Bender and Richard A. Greenwald, eds., *Sweatshop USA: The American Sweatshop in Global and Historical Perspective* (New York:

Routledge, 2003); and Richard A. Greenwald, *The Triangle Fire, the Protocols of Peace, and Industrial Democracy in Progressive Era New York* (Philadelphia: Temple University Press, 2005). Notable exceptions that look at the business side of the New York fashion industry are Agins, *The End of Fashion*; Andrew Godley, *Jewish Immigrant Entrepreneurship in New York and London, 1880–1914: Enterprise and Culture* (New York: Palgrave, 2001); and Goldstein, *A Perfect Fit.* Geographer Norma Rantisi is insightful on contemporary innovation networks in "The Local Innovation System as a Source of 'Variety'; Openness and Adaptability in New York City's Garment District," *Regional Studies* 36 (2002): 587–600, and "The Ascendance of New York Fashion," *International Journal of Urban and Regional Research* 28 (March 2004): 86–106.

22. For a sympathetic perspective, see Robert DuPlessis, Comments at the "Producing Fashion" conference, Hagley Museum and Library, Wilmington, Del., 28 Oct. 2005.

23. Sharon R. Ullman made similar arguments in her comments at the "Producing Fashion" conference, Hagley Museum and Library, Wilmington, Del., 29 Oct. 2005.

CHAPTER 2. SPREADING THE WORD: THE DEVELOPMENT OF THE RUSSIAN FASHION PRESS

1. Christopher Breward, "Femininity and Consumption: The Problem of the Late Nineteenth-Century Fashion Journal," *Journal of Design History* 7, 2 (1994): 71–89; Daniel L. Purdy, *The Tyranny of Elegance: Consumer Cosmopolitanism in the Era of Goethe* (Baltimore: Johns Hopkins University Press, 1998), 1–21. For a more general discussion of magazines on consumption, see Richard Ohmann, *Selling Culture: Magazines, Markets, and Class at the Turn of the Century* (London: Verso, 1996).

2. Gary Marker, *Publishing, Printing, and the Origins of Intellectual Life in Russia, 1700–1800* (Princeton, N.J.: Princeton University Press, 1985), 184–211.

3. Allan R. Raymond, "To Reach Men's Minds: Almanacs and the American Revolution, 1760–1777," *New England Quarterly* 51, 3 (September 1978): 370–71; and Lise Andries, "Almanacs: Revolutionizing a Traditional Genre," in *Revolution in Print: The Press in France, 1775–1800*, ed. Robert Darnton and Daniel Roche (Berkeley: University of California Press, 1989), 205.

4. Jennifer M. Jones, *Sexing la Mode: Gender, Fashion, and Commercial Culture in Old Regime France* (Oxford: Berg, 2004), 179–98.

5. Vyvyan Holland, *Hand Coloured Fashion Plates, 1770–1899* (London: Batsford, 1988), 48–60.

6. Catriona Kelly, *A History of Russian Women's Writing, 1820–1992* (Oxford: Clarendon Press, 1994), 19–78; and Gitta Hammarberg, "Flirting with Words: Domestic Albums, 1770–1840," in *Russia—Women—Culture*, ed. Helena Goscilo and Beth Holmgren (Bloomington: Indiana University Press, 1996), 297–315.

7. Mary Lee Townsend, *Forbidden Laughter: Popular Humor and the Limits of Repression in Nineteenth-Century Prussia* (Ann Arbor: University of Michigan Press, 1992), 171–91.

8. Charles A. Ruud, *Fighting Words: Imperial Censorship and the Russian Press, 1804–1906* (Toronto: University of Toronto Press, 1982).

9. Rossiiskii Gosudarstvennyi Istoricheskii Arkiv (Russian State Historical Archive, hereafter RGIA), f. 777, op. 1, d. 1629, ll. 1–6; and op. 2, d. 103, ll. 1–7.

10. "Modnyi svet," *Moda* 2 (15 Jan. 1851): 10–11.

11. "Kostium russkii i obshcheevropeiskii," *Moda* 14 (15 July 1856): 114–15.

12. RGIA, f. 777, op. 2, d. 1, ll. 2 ob. and 3.

13. An example can be found in *Moda* 2 (1858): 45.

14. An example can be found in "Zametka," *Moda* 16 (15 Aug. 1856): 136.

15. The magazine was originally titled *The Magazine of the Latest Sewing*, and was changed to *The Saint Petersburg Magazine of Various Kinds of Sewing and Embroidery*; in 1844, Safonova finally settled on *The Vase*. See RGIA, f. 777, op. 1, d. 1408 for a history of the magazine's name changes.

16. Ibid. *Fashion* also had many names. It began as *Pages for High Society: A Magazine of Paris Fashions*. Safonova shortened it to *Magazine of Paris Fashions* and finally *Fashion: A Magazine for High Society*. This frequent renaming of fashion magazines was common everywhere in Europe. The Elagin quote can be found on l. 69.

17. Ibid., ll. 59–62.

18. Cynthia L. White, *Women's Magazines, 1693–1968* (London: Michael Joseph, 1970), 58–77.

19. Louise McReynolds, *The News Under Russia's Old Regime* (Princeton, N.J.: Princeton University Press, 1991), 30–51.

20. Mark Steinberg, *Moral Communities: The Culture of Class Relations in the Russian Printing Industry, 1867–1907* (Berkeley: University of California Press, 1992), 11–12.

21. White, *Women's Magazines*, 75; and Helen Damon-Moore, *Magazines for the Millions: Gender and Commerce in the Ladies' Home Journal and the Saturday Evening Post, 1880–1910* (Albany: State University of New York Press, 1994), 1.

22. Jeffrey Brooks, *When Russia Learned to Read: Literacy and Popular Literature, 1861–1917* (Princeton, N.J.: Princeton University Press, 1985), 113.

23. RGIA, f. 776, op. 3, d. 450, ll. 1–5; d. 424, ll. 54–55; and f. 777, op. 2, d. 63, l. 2. For more on *Die Modenwelt* and its translations, see Holland, *Hand Coloured Fashion Plates*, 113. *Die Modenwelt* was actually published in thirteen languages.

24. "Ot izdatelia," *Vestnik mody* 1 (1 Jan. 1885): 1.

25. Carolyn R. Marks, "'Provid[ing] Amusement for the Ladies': The Rise of the Russian Women's Magazine in the 1880s," in *An Improper Profession: Women, Gender, and Journalism in Late Imperial Russia*, ed. Barbara T. Norton and Jehanne M. Geith (Durham, N.C.: Duke University Press, 2001), 1102–8; and "Sotrudniki *Vsemirnoi illiustratsii* vtechenii 10-ti let, 1869–1878," *Vsemirnaia illiustratsiia* 520 (16 Dec. 1878), supplement.

26. *Pamiati Germana Dmitrievicha Goppe, 1836–1885* (St. Petersburg: Tip. M. p. s., 1885), 2, emphasis in original.

27. These events in Russia mirror similar trends in Western Europe, where a few publishing houses controlled the fashion press, placing male publishers in charge of wom-

en's magazines. See Margaret Beetham, *A Magazine of Her Own? Domesticity and Desire in the Woman's Magazine, 1800–1914* (New York: Routledge, 1996), 115–30.

28. The censorship files do not contain the name of the author of this tale.

29. RGIA, f. 776, op. 3, d. 450, ll. 138–45.

30. RGIA, f. 776, op. 4, d. 98, ll. 53–54.

31. RGIA, f. 777, op. 2, d. 96, ll. 83, 105; and ibid., d. 63, ll. 37.

32. RGIA, f. 776, op. 4, d. 98, l. 68; and Marks, "Provid[ing] Amusement," 109–10.

33. Michelle Lamarche Marrese, *A Woman's Kingdom: Noblewomen and the Control of Property in Russia, 1700–1861* (Ithaca, N.Y.: Cornell University Press, 2002).

34. Christine Ruane, "The Development of a Fashion Press in Imperial Russia: *Moda: Zhurnal dlia svetskikh liudei*," in *An Improper Profession*, ed. Norton and. Gheith, 76–77.

CHAPTER 3. ACCESSORIZING, ITALIAN STYLE: CREATING A MARKET FOR MILAN'S FASHION MERCHANDISE

This chapter is the result of a joint effort; Elisabetta Merlo prepared the third and fourth sections and Francesa Polese the introduction and first two sections.

1. On La Rinascente, see Franco Amatori, *Proprietà e direzione: La Rinascente 1917–1969* (Milano: Franco Angeli, 1989).

2. Today the expression "fashion accessories" usually describes items that complement a clothing outfit: jewelry, shoes, handbags, scarves, hats, gloves, and umbrellas. Here we use the category "accessories" in a more restrictive way, based on definitions offered by Italian mail-order catalogs of the 1880s. Our analysis focuses on hats, umbrellas, and gloves. The detailed analysis of the assortment, styles, and prices has been limited to women's fashion, as the mail-order catalogs featured very few accessories for men.

3. Maria Teresa Olivari Binaghi, "La moda: le tendenze," in *Storia di Milano*, vol. 18, *Il Novecento* (Rome: Istituto della Enciclopedia Italiana, 1996), 516–17.

4. See Doxa, *Il consumo dei prodotti tessili nelle famiglie italiane (1953–54)* (Rome, 1956).

5. See the debate recalled in Vera Zamagni, *The Economic History of Italy, 1860–1990: Recovery After Decline* (Oxford: Clarendon Press, 1993); and Giovanni Federico and Jon Cohen, *The Growth of the Italian Eeconomy, 1820–1960* (Cambridge: Cambridge University Press, 2001).

6. The expression originated in a 1973 article by Luciano Cafagna, now commonly used to refer to Lombardy's mid-nineteenth-century economic development; see Luciano Cafagna, "Italy 1830–1914," in *The Fontana Economic History of Europe*, ed. Carlo Maria Cipolla (London: Fontana/Collins, 1973), 4: 279–328.

7. Giovanni Federico, *An Economic History of the Silk Industry, 1830–1930* (Cambridge: Cambridge University Press, 1997).

8. See Jonathan Morris, *The Political Economy of Shopkeeping in Milan: 1886–1922* (Cambridge: Cambridge University Press, 1993), 12.

9. Giuseppe Colombo (1836–1921) was one of the most important names in the Italian business and political community. He was a member of Parliament, professor of mechanical engineering at Milan's Politecnico, and founder of the Italian Edison Company. See Franco Della Peruta, *Milano: lavoro e fabbrica, 1814–1915* (Milano: Franco Angeli, 1987), 60–61; and Adrian Lyttleton, "Milan 1880–1922: The City of Industrial Capitalism," in *People and Communities in the Western World*, ed. Gene Brucker (Homewood, Ill.: Dorsey Press, 1979), 250–88.

10. Our analysis of commercial guides published in the late 1800s confirms the increasing importance of productive and commercial activities related to manufacture and distribution of accessories. As these firms grew number, they also became more homogeneous.

11. Renata Balestri, "Mestieri tradizionali e donne spregiudicate: le operaie del vestiario a Milano tra lavoro a domicilio e manifattura (1870–1923)," *Storia in Lombardia* I (1994): 73–105. Louise A. Tilly, *Politics and Class in Milan 1881–1901* (New York: Oxford University Press, 1992), does not consider the city's clothing industry as important to Milan's growth. Tilly claims, however, that the clothing industry was the only labor-intensive sector with a predominantly female workforce that showed evolutionary tendencies toward advanced capitalistic features. Our analysis of commercial guides confirms the large presence of women not only as workers but also as owners of production facilities and comercial establishments related to fashion.

12. Some historians suggest that the Bocconi brothers early on distinguished themselves from other itinerant sellers because they sold some readymade dresses produced on their behalf by home workers. Evidence on this point, however, is sketchy. See Ciro Poggiali, *Ferdinando Bocconi: Mercurio in finanziera* (Milano: Editoriale Domus, 1945).

13. At the beginning of the twentieth century, Ferdinando Bocconi (Luigi had retired in 1882) was considered one of the richest men in Italy. See ibid., 205ff.

14. Amatori, *Proprietà e direzione*, 28.

15. Department stores also introduced other innovations, including fixed prices clearly marked on a label and the possibility of touching or trying on goods without the obligation to buy them. See Geoffrey Crossick and Serge Jaumin, eds., *Cathedrals of Consumption: The European Department Store, 1850–1939* (Aldershot: Ashgate, 1999).

16. See debate on this issue in ibid.

17. Quoted by Amatori, *Proprietà e direzione*, 29.

18. See, for example, the description of the productive organization of Bon Marché, in Michael B. Miller, *The Bon Marché: Burgeois Culture and the Department Store, 1869–1920* (Princeton, N.J.: Princeton University Press, 1981), 55 ff.

19. Amatori, *Proprietà e direzione*, 29.

20. Although exact dating of surviving catalogs is still uncertain, it seems that the Parisian Petite Saint-Thomas had organized a mail-order service as early as 1844. In Italy in those same years, mail-order catalogs were also issued by other "traditional" shops, especially in the textile and clothing sectors. See Miller, *The Bon Marché*, 26, 31.

21. Ibid., 61. The catalog of the 1894 winter season was sent to more than 1.5 million

customers. Miller suggests that the mail-order service might have been started by Bon Marché as early as the 1860s.

22. Data for 1902–3 show that goods were sent more or less all over the world; see ibid.

23. Ibid.

24. Emile Zola, *Taccuini: un'etnografia inedita della Francia* (Milano: Bollati Boringhieri, 1986), 113.

25. Amatori, *Proprietà e direzione*, 31.

26. On the "great renunciation" see John Carl Flugel, *The Psychology of Clothes* (London: Hogarth Press, 1930).

27. Men's socks were limited to two types in wool (2.10 and 2.50 lire) and one in cotton (0.85). The ladies' assortment included pure wool stockings in different colored stripes (3.00 to 4.20); white cotton stockings at 1 lira a pair; and cotton stockings in red, blue, brown, and not dyed at 2 lire a pair. Children's socks cost from 1.15 to 2.90 lire, according to size. Shoes, generally made of soft kid leather, were included in only one catalog. This is not surprising, as mass manufacture of standardized footwear had yet to be introduced.

28. The prices are taken from the autumn-winter 1880–81 and spring-summer 1886 catalogs.

29. The catalogs feature both umbrellas and parasols; in the text we use the general term "umbrellas."

30. Raffaele Pareto and Giovanni Sacheri, eds., *Enciclopedia delle arti e industrie* (Torino: UTET, 1882), 3: 1240–1248. As described in this important technical encyclopedia, gloves had different names according to how the leather was treated. They were called glacés, or Swedish, when the outside of the glove was made from the side of the skin that rested on the animal's fat, treated by tanning with oil, egg yolk, water, and alcohol, and with the process of pumicing. The outside of suede gloves was made from the side of the skin that rested on the animal's fur. Gloves made of Scottish thread were woven, and their appearance was similar to leather gloves. They were preferred to knitted gloves.

31. Information about the organization and spread of glove production in Milan is taken from Luigi Carozzi, *L'industria dei guanti in Milano* (Milan: Ufficio del Lavoro della Società Umanitaria, 1908).

32. Pareto and Sacheri, eds., *Enciclopedia*, 6: 399.

33. These are the figures quoted by Franco Della Peruta, *Milano lavoro e fabbrica, 1815–1914* (Milano: Angeli, 1987), 14.

34. Giovanni Vecchi, "Il benessere dell'Italia liberale (1861–1913)," in *Storia economica d'Italia*, vol. 3, *Industrie, mercati, istituzioni*, t. I, *Le strutture dell'economia*, ed. Pierluigi Ciocca and Gianni Toniolo (Rome-Bari: Laterza, 2003), 71–98; and Vecchi, "I bilanci familiari in Italia (1860–1960)," *Rivista di Storia Economica* 2 (1994): 11–95, where the methodological aspects related to collecting and comparing data are described in detail according to the well-defined set of rules provided by the French statistician Frédéric Le Play from the mid-nineteenth century.

35. Vecchi, "I balanci familiari," 13.

CHAPTER 4. IN THE SHADOW OF PARIS? FRENCH HAUTE COUTURE AND
BELGIAN FASHION BETWEEN THE WARS

Many thanks to Madeleine Jacquemin for her help at the Archives Générales du
Royaume de Belgique, Brussels, and to Natacha Massar and Regina Lee Blaszczyk for
their help on the writing of this chapter.

1. Nancy J. Troy, *Couture Culture: A Study in Modern Art and Fashion* (Cambridge,
Mass.: MIT Press, 2003); Mary Louise Stewart, "Copying and Copyrighting Haute Couture: Democratizing Fashion, 1900–1930s," *French Historical Studies* 28 (2005): 103–30.

2. François Baudot, *Mode du siècle* (Paris: Assouline, 1999), 12.

3. Troy, *Couture Culture*.

4. Valerie Steele, *Paris Fashion: A Cultural History* (New York: Berg, 1988).

5. "L'influence parisienne," *International Textiles* 2 (28 Nov. 1934): 21, in Archives of
Art & Design, London, England (hereafter cited as AAD); "Le but de l'Officiel de la
couture et de la mode de Paris," *L'officiel de la couture et de la mode de Paris: organe de
propagande et d'expansion de l'art français* 4, 31(Mar. 1924): 1.

6. About the notion of intermediaries in the fashion-related industries, see Regina
Lee Blaszczyk, *Imagining Consumers: Design and Innovation from Wedgwood to Corning*
(Baltimore: John Hopkins University Press, 2000), 12–13.

7. Barbara Burman, "Home Sewing and 'Fashions for All,' 1908–1937," *Costume:
The Journal of the Costume Society* 28 (1994): 71–80; Kevin L. Seligman, "Dressmakers'
Patterns: The English Commercial Paper Pattern Industry, 1878–1950," *Costume: The
Journal of the Costume Society* 37 (2003): 95–113.

8. Joy Spanabel Emery, "Dreams on Paper: A Story of the Commercial Patron Industry," in *The Culture of Sewing: Gender, Consumption and Home Dressmaking*, ed. Barbara Burman (Oxford: Berg, 1999), 236–47.

9. Stewart, "Copying and Copyrighting," 103–30.

10. Guillaume Garnier, "Le milieu de la mode," in Guillaume Garnier, *Paris-
couture-années trente* (Paris: Musée de la Mode et du Costume, Palais Galliéra, 1987), 75.

11. Yuniya Kawamura, *The Japanese Revolution in Paris Fashion* (Oxford: Berg,
2004), 36–41; Didier Grumbach, *Histoires de la mode* (Paris: Seuil, 1993), 11.

12. Garnier, "Le milieu de la mode," 75.

13. Kawamura, *Japanese Revolution*, 66.

14. Grumbach, *Histoires*, 61–62; Germaine Deschamps, "La crise dans les industries
du vêtement et de la mode à Paris pendant la période de 1930 à 1937" (Ph.D. thesis,
Librairie technique et économique, Paris, 1937), 51.

15. *Im-ex. la grande revue belge pour le développement et l'expansion des industries du
vêtement* (Feb. 1926): 19.

16. Willy Devos, "L'utilité de l'intervention du commissionnaire pour l'acheteur
étranger," *Im-ex: la grande revue belge pour le développement et l'expansion des industries du
vêtement* (Feb. 1926): 28.

17. Grumbach, *Histoires*, 27.

18. Stewart, "Copying and Copyrighting," 112, 128.

19. Following the 1806 law, they had to be registered at the Prud'hommes. A third organization, Unis-France, also served as a registry for couture models. Its clients included Lanvin and Jenny.

20. Guillaume Garnier, "Quelques couturiers, quelques modes," in Garnier, *Paris-couture-années trente*, 9; Deschamps, "La crise," 54–55.

21. "Rochas, renouvellement dans la Haute Couture," *International Textiles* 2 (28 Dec. 1934): 12, in AAD.

22. Simona Segre Reinach, *La moda: un'introduzione* (Rome: Laterza, 2005).

23. R. Hirsch and L. Natan to M. Legrand, President of the Chambre de Commerce de Bruxelles, 11 Nov. 1929, folder 2264, in Archives Générales du Royaume de Belgique, I 288, Brussels (hereafter cited as AGR).

24. Gerdi Esch, Agnes Goyvaerts, and Simone Van Riet, *Mode in de lage landen: België* (Anvers: Cantecler, 1989), 15.

25. Content of the list from "Chambre syndicale de la Haute Couture de Belgique, à Bruxelles: statuts," *Annexes au Moniteur belge de 1936: recueil des actes des associations sans but lucratif et des établissements d'utilité publique jouissant de la personnalité civile: documents publiés en exécution de la loi du 27 juin 1921, année 1936* (Brussels: Imprimerie du Moniteur Belge, 1937), 1,638.

26. Copy of the Memorandum of the Second Meeting of the Committee of the Chambre Syndicale de Haute Couture, 13 Dec. 1929, 1, folder 2264, in AGR..

27. Steele, *Paris Fashion*.

28. Copy of the Memorandum of the Second Meeting, 13 Dec. 1929, 1–2.

29. Pierre Bourdieu and Yvette Delsaut, "Le couturier et sa griffe: contribution à une théorie de la magie," *Actes de la recherche en sciences sociales* 1 (Jan. 1975): 9.

30. Folder 2265, in AGR.

31. Copy of the Memorandum of the Second Meeting, 13 Dec. 1929.

32. Press Clippings ([s.d.]), 2, folder 2268, in AGR.

33. Chambre syndicale, Ecole de Couture, 1933, folder 2306, in AGR.

34. Copy of the Memorandum of the Second Meeting, 13 Dec. 1929.

35. Roland Barthes, *Système de la mode* (Paris: Seuil, 1967).

36. "Dans la haute couture," *Textilia: Organe professionnel des fabricants, négociants et détaillants* 1 (1 Dec. 1929): 3.

37. Copy of the Memorandum of the Second Meeting, 13 Dec. 1929.

38. Stewart, "Copying and Copyrighting," 110.

39. Deschamps, "La crise," 53–54.

40. Véronique Pouillard, *Hirsch & Cie, Brussels, 1869–1962* (Brussels: Editions de l'Université Libre de Bruxelles, 2000), 9–14, 29–37.

41. Pouillard, *Hirsch*, 41–42.

42. Minutes of the general meetings, 1930–31, Réunion du Comité, 15 Oct. 1930, in Chambre Syndicale de la Haute Couture, Paris. Many thanks to Gérald Chevalier for this reference.

43. J.-P. Hirsch à Mrs. Hirsch & Cie, Pragestrasse, 6/8, Dresden (21 Feb.1938), folder 2199, in AGR.

44. Ibid.

45. Robert Hirsch was manager of Hirsch & Cie with his brothers Lucien and Jean-Paul Hirsch.

46. Grumbach, *Histoires*, 35; Philippe Simon, *La haute couture, monographie d'une industrie de luxe* (Paris: Presses Universitaires de France, 1931).

47. Geoffrey Jones, *The Evolution of Multinational Business: An Introduction* (London: Routledge, 1996), 9, 27.

48. Deschamps, "La crise," 21–22, 45–46.

49. Grumbach, *Histoires*, 12. Nancy Troy, however, shows that the copying process goes back to the 1910s at least. Troy, *Couture Culture*.

50. Stewart, "Copying and Copyrighting," 109.

51. Garnier, "Le milieu de la mode," 99–100.

52. Chambre Syndicale de Haute Couture, short note, 9 Feb. 1931, folder 2264, in AGR.

53. Guillaume Garnier, "Callot sœurs," in Garnier, *Paris-couture-années trente*, 243.

54. Deschamps, "La crise," 9.

55. L. Natan and R. Hirsch, Circular of the Chambre Syndicale de Haute Couture Belge, 985, Brussels, 10 Feb. 1932, folder 2265, in AGR.

56. Véronique Pouillard, "Entretien avec Milly Clarenburg, directrice de la Haute Mode chez Hirsch & Cie," *Cahiers de la fonderie: revue d'histoire industrielle de Bruxelles* 30 (Sept. 2004): 52–54.

57. Pierre Hirsch, interview by Véronique Pouillard, Brussels, July 2004; Garnier, *Paris-couture-années trente*, 242.

58. Pouillard, *Hirsch*, 60–62.

59. Press Clippings, folder 2268, in AGR.

60. Press Clippings, *Le Soir*, 29 Mar. 1931, folder 2268, in AGR.

61. Christine Bard, *La garçonne: modes et fantasmes des années folles* (Paris: Flammarion, 1998).

62. Lou Taylor, "The Hilfiger Factor and Flexible Commercial World of Culture," in *The Fashion Business*, ed. Nicola White and Ian Griffiths (Oxford: Berg, 2000), 126–27.

63. Press Clippings, folder 2268, in AGR.

64. Press Clippings, *Spectacles*, Apr. 1931, folder 2268, in AGR.

65. Press Clippings, *L'indépendance Belge*,1931, folder 2268, in AGR.

66. Bourdieu and Delsaut, "Le couturier et sa griffe," 7–33.

67. Daniël Christiaens, "Variétés en l'art vivant: Kunstschriften en Belgische mode tijdens het Interbellum," *Vlaamse vereniging voor oud en hedendaagse textiel, Bulletin 1990* (1991): 61–68; Daniël Christiaens and B. Van Doorslaer, "De relatie beeldende kunst en mode: 1910–1930. Met bijzondere belangstelling voor Erté en Sonia Delaunay" (M.A. thesis, Art History, Leuven, 1982), 2, 111–37.

68. Daniël Christiaens, "De Belgische bijdrage tot de mode en de jaren twintig," *Interbellum Cahier* (Ghent: 1985), 2, 5–7.

69. Nele Bernheim, "Couture Norine: Avant-Garde Belgian Fashion, 1918–1952" (M.A. paper, Fashion and Textile Studies, History, Theory and Museum Practice, Fashion Institute of Technology, New York, 2006).

70. Jules Hankenne, *La mode féminine* (Liège: n.p., 1913).

71. Martin Margiela, for example, acknowledged this complex as a part of the Belgian identity in the early years of his career, adding that he aimed at a change. Press clippings, Martin Margiela; and Agnès Goyvaerts, "Margiela, de Limburger die openbloeide in Parijs," *De Antwerpse Morgen* (18 Sept. 1985), in Mode Museum Archives, Antwerp, Belgium.

72. Esch, Goyvaerts, and Van Riet, *Mode in de lage landen*, 49.

73. Pouillard, "Entretien avec Milly Clarenburg, 52–54.

74. "Histoire d'un chapeau de 49 francs acheté 1000 francs à Paris," *Reflets: le magazine de la vie belge* (Apr. 1939), 38–40.

75. Deschamps, "La crise," 6–7.

76. René Bizet, *La mode* (Paris: F. Rieder & Cie, 1925), 21.

77. R. Goetz, Hirsch & Cie, Amsterdam, to R. Hirsch, 14 Feb. 1939, folder 2200, in AGR.

78. J.-P. Hirsch to Mrs. Hirsch & Cie, Reesendamm, Hamburg, 13 Aug. 1930, folder 2198, in AGR; J.-P. Hirsch to Mrs Hirsch & Cie, Pragestrasse, 6/8, Dresden, 18 Feb. 1933, folder 2199, in AGR; J.-P. Hirsch to Mrs. Hirsch & Cie, Pragestrasse, 6/8, Dresden, 11 Feb. 1935, folder 2199, in AGR.

79. *Textilia: organe professionnel des fabricants, négociants et détaillants* 2 (1 Apr. 1930): 28.

80. Fédération de la Couture de Belgique, Memorandum of the General Meeting, 16 Nov. 1948, 1–7; and annexes, folder 2295, in AGR.

81. P.G. v. H.-N. [Paul-Gustave van Hecke, Norine], "La Mode en Belgique," *L'art vivant* 3 (1 Oct. 1927): 815.

82. "Copier veut dire voler: la mode contre l'espionnage," *International Textiles* 3 (26 Apr. 935): 26, in AAD.

83. Grumbach, *Histoires*, 37.

CHAPTER 5. LICENSING PRACTICES AT MAISON CHRISTIAN DIOR

1. In French, *maison* means "house." It can also describe a group of people, such as a family or a clan. In business use, it means "enterprise." In this essay, *maison* is used to mean "enterprise" or "store."

2. "Dictator by Demand," *Time* (4 Mar. 1957).

3. Didier Grumbach, *Histoires de la mode* (Paris: Éditions du Seuil, 1993), 73–78.

4. Press release, "Une prestigieuse aventure commerciale," 1975, Christian Dior S.A., in Bibliothèque du Musée des Arts Décoratifs, Paris, France.

5. Dorothy L. Wallis, "What the Customers Say Tells the Story in U.S.," *Women's Wear Daily* (hereafter cited as *WWD*), 14 July 1953.

6. On Poiret, see Paul Poiret, *En habillant l'époque* (Paris: B. Grasset, 1986). On Gabriel Chanel, see Jean Leymarie, *Chanel* (Genève: Art Albert Skira S.A., 1987); and Edmonde Charles-Roux, *Le temps Chanel* (Paris: Éditions de la Martinière/ B.Grasset, 2004).

7. Valerie Steele, *Fifty Years of Fashion: New Look to Now* (New Haven, Conn.: Yale University Press, 1997), 18.

8. Diana de Marly, *The History of Haute Couture, 1850–1950* (New York: Holmes & Meier, 1980), 108–18.

9. On the Dior family, see "Les Dior avant Dior—saga d'une famille granvillaise," exhibition catalog, 12 Feb.–30 Apr. 2005, Archives départementales de la Manche, Saint-Lô, France; Musée Christian Dior, *Christian Dior—Man of the Century* (Versailles: Éditions Artlys, 2005), 4–8; Dorothy L. Wallis, "Background of the Empire Ranges from Art to Fashion" *WWD*, 14 July 1953.

10. Christian Dior, *Christian Dior et moi* (Paris: Amiot-Dumont, 1956), 13–39, 199–209.

11. On the role of Boussac in launching the *maison de couture*, see Tomoko Okawa, "Investment and Launching of a Couture House: Groupe Boussac and Maison Christian Dior" (M.A. thesis, Tokyo Metropolitan University, 2005).

12. Henri Fayol was a son of Jules Henri Fayol (1841–1915), who founded the Centre d'Études Administratives and who in 1916 published *Administration industrielle et générale*, a book that influenced French industrialization during the early twentieth century. On Henri's career, see *Christian Dior, Marcel Boussac, 1947–1978: l'industriel et le créateur, la rencontre de deux génies* (Husseren-Wesserling: Musée du Textile et des Costumes de Haute Alsace, 1998), 18.

13. Musée Christian Dior, *Christian Dior—Man of the Century*; Valerie Steele, *Paris Fashion: A Cultural History* (New York: Oxford University Press, 1988), 273–75. On wartime fashion, see Dominique Veillon, *La mode sous l'occupation* (Paris: Éditions Payot, 1990). On Snow (1887–1961), see Penelope Rowlands, *A Dash of Daring: Carmel Snow and Her Life in Fashion, Art, and Letters* (New York: Atria Books, 2005).

14. Grumbach, *Histoires*, 74.

15. "Christian Dior Launches "'Corolla' and 'Figure 8,'" *WWD*, 13 Feb. 1947.

16. Document on the authorization of foreign remittance by CIC to Office des Changes, 14 Oct. 1946, Ref. No. 1987–003–0418, in Groupe Boussac (Comptoire de l'Industrie Cotonnière, Manufacture de Senones), Centre des archives du monde du travail, Roubaix, France (hereafter cited as GB-CAMT).

17. Frank Engle, "Dior American Line Success Story Strong After 4 Years," *WWD*, 24 May 1952; Dorothy L. Wallis, "Many Contribute Talents to Mosaic of a Great Business," *WWD*, 15 Jul. 1953.

18. Document on CIC's inter-correspondence, 25 Nov. 1947, Ref. No. 1987–003–0418, in GB-CAMT.

19. Document on the authorization of foreign remittance, 14 Oct. 1946. After New York, Groupe Boussac established Dior branches in Mexico and Argentina. The New

York office was the key branch in Groupe Boussac, and Marcel Boussac became its largest shareholder. Groupe Boussac's subsidiaries each had their own investors, the tradition since the firm's 1911 formation.

20. Guillaume Garnier, *Paris-couture-années trente* (Paris: Musée de la Mode et du Costume, Palais Galliera, 1987), 216.

21. Interview with Pierre Balmain, *Women's Wear Daily Japan* (hereafter cited as *WWDJ*) 11 May 1981.

22. "ELLE à Paris, on parle d'eux," *Elle* (28 Jan. 1947), 5.

23. Christian Dior, *Dior by Dior* (London: Penguin, 1958), 51–52; and Dior, *Christian Dior et moi*, 69–71.

24. Document of a handwritten draft of correspondence (n.d.) and a typed document (19 Sept. 1946) for the registration of the establishment Société Christian Dior, Ref. No. 1987–003–0251, in GB-CAMT. In this document, the role or activity of Rouët is mentioned as banking (deposit and withdrawal), regulation, and administrative service in general.

25. For celebrations of Dior's work, see Diana de Marly, *Christian Dior* (London: Batsford, 1990); Esmeralda de Réthy and Jean-Louis Perreau, *Monsieur Dior et nous 1947–1957* (Paris: Anthèse, 1999); Françoise Giroud, *Christian Dior* (Paris: Éditions du Regard, 1987).

26. Christian Dior S.A., *Plaquette* (Paris: Christian Dior S.A., 1953), in Christian Dior Couture S.A. Archives, Paris (hereafter cited as CDA). A *plaquette* is a small volume, or a booklet.

27. "First U.S. Dior Collection to Be Shown Nov. 1," *WWD*, 7 Sept.1948.

28. Harry Berlfein, "Dior Has 30% Reorders on His First U.S. Collection," *WWD*, 28 Jan. 1949; company profile, 1969, Christian Dior S.A., in Bibliothèque du Musée des Arts Décoratifs, Paris; Grumbach, *Histoires*, 74.

29. After the Maison Dior experience, Legrez became Maison Chanel's license director from 1963. See Grumbach, *Histoires*, 78, 80.

30. Musée Christian Dior, *Christian Dior et le monde* (Versailles: Éditions Artlys, 2006).

31. Dorothy L.Wallis, "Specialized Operations Extend Dior Scope from Head to Foot with Varied Accessories," *WWD*, 16 July 1953.

32. Document on CIC's correspondence, 13 Oct. 1955, Ref. No. 1987–003–0253, in GB-CAMT.

33. "Christian Dior Is Dead at 52; Designer Created 'New Look,'" *New York Times*, 24 Oct. 1957; Lucien François, *Comment un nom devient une griffe* (Paris: Éditions Gallimard, 1961), 221–22.

34. Wallis, "Background of the Empire."

35. Wallis, "Specialized Operations Extend Dior Scope."

36. Dorothy L.Wallis, "Where Is It All Going? Glimpsing the Dior Future," *WWD*, 20 July 1953.

37. Philippe Le Moult, Director for Institutional Relations of Christian Dior Cou-

ture Archives, Paris, interview by Tomoko Okawa, 7 June 2006, at CDA; Soizic Pfaff, manager, Christian Dior Couture Archives, Paris, communication with Tomoko Okawa, 28. Feb. 2007. Le Moult worked the licensing division in the late 1970s and 1980s.

38. Catalogs shown in the exhibition "Christian Dior et le Monde," Musée Christian Dior, Granville, France, 2006. The model San Francisco is found in Dior, *Christian Dior—Man of the Century*, 76–77.

39. Christian Dior S.A., *Plaquette*.

40. Press release, "Une prestigieuse aventure commerciale."

41. Grumbach, *Histoires*, 74.

42. Christian Dior S.A., *Plaquette*.

43. "The Brilliant Boussac," *Daily Express* (London), 11 Nov. 1958, in CDA.

44. Ibid.

45. Grumbach, *Histoires*, 46.

46. Dior, *Dior by Dior*, 141–42; Dior, *Christian Dior et moi*, 178.

47. "Une interview exclusive du grand couturier; Yves Saint Laurent: Je suis né avec une dépression nerveuse. . . ," *Le Figaro* (Paris), 11 July 1991.

48. "Christian Dior est mort," *Le Monde* (Paris), 25 Oct. 1957.

49. Guillaume Hanoteau, "Christian Dior s'en va," *Paris Match*, 2 Nov. 1957.

50. Pierre Borie, "La mort de Christian Dior sonne-t-elle le glas de la Haute Couture," *Noir & Blanc* (Paris), 2 Nov. 1957, in CDA.

51. "Dictator by Demand."

52. "7th Ave. Feels Death of Dior a 'Great Loss,'" *WWD*, 25 Oct. 1957.

53. "Dior Worldwide Sales Rated at $22 Million," *WWD*, 25 Oct. 1957.

54. Marie-France Pochna, *Christian Dior* (Paris: Flammarion, 1994), 387–88.

55. "Une interview exclusive du grand couturier."

56. Musée Christian Dior, *Christian Dior et le monde*, 24; Grumbach, *Histoires*, 45; "Bohan to Continue Casual Look," *WWD*, 27 April 1961.

57. Lucien François, *Comment un nom devient une griffe*, 221.

58. Bernadine Taub, "Guy Douvier—New Fashion Star," *WWD*, 22 Sep. 1961.

59. "Dior Modified in U.S.," *New York Times* (int. ed.), 18 Oct. 1961.

60. Grumbach, *Histoires*, 79.

61. Lucien François, *Comment un nom devient une griffe*, 221.

62. Marie-France Pochna, *Bonjour, Monsieur Boussac* (Paris: Éditions Robert Laffont, 1980), 296–300.

63. Document on CIC's correspondence, 8 Aug. 1946, 2 Oct. 1946, Ref. No. 1987-003-0251, in GB-CAMT.

64. "Behind the Doors at House of Dior," *WWD*, 19 Sept. 1977.

65. Grumbach, *Histoires*, 80.

66. "Marc-ing 25 years at Dior," *WWD*, 24 Jan. 1983.

67. Miss Dior was the name of Maison Christian Dior's first perfume, introduced in 1947, in homage to Dior's sister, Catherine. See "Dior France: historique du groupe, Christine Dior S.A.," http://www.dior-finance.com, accessed in 2004.

68. "Those Diorings," *WWD*, 26 Nov. 1968.

69. Press release, "Une prestigeuse aventure commerciale."

70. "The Sign Game," *WWD*, 31 Jan. 1969.

71. "Americans Buying More RTW in Paris," *WWD*, 23 Oct. 1975.

72. "Activity (in Japan) Mainly Composed of Prêt-à-Porter: Rouët, President of Christian Dior, Talks about the Cooperation with Kanebo" *Senken Shinbun* (Toyko), 12 May 1964.

73. Ibid.

74. Ibid.

75. Alexandra Palmer, *Couture and Commerce: The Transatlantic Fashion Trade in the 1950s* (Vancouver: University of British Columbia Press, 2001), 117–21. El Palacio de Hierro, a specialty shop in Mexico got both American and French patterns. El Encanto, a specialty and department store in Havana, Cuba, got Paris patterns for made-to-order coats, suits, and dresses, as well as patterns from the American line. The House of Youth in Sydney, Australia, contracted only for American patterns. See Engle, "Dior American Line Success Story Strong after 4 Years."

76. Marc Bohan, interview by Jean-Luc Dufresne, Joëlle-Anne Robert, and Philippe Le Moult, in Musée Christian Dior, *Christian Dior et le monde*, 31.

77. "Dubois Who Is an Executive Director, Talks About Japanese Market," *WWDJ*, 7 Jan. 1980.

78. Soizic Pfaff, communication with Tomoko Okawa.

79. "Activity (in Japan) Mainly Composed of Prêt-à-Porter." According to "Dior Hoping to Find a New Partner," *New York Times*, 2 Sept. 1981, copy in CDA, the United States accounted for 35 percent of sales, Europe 33 percent, and Japan 22 percent. The remainder was in Central and South America.

80. The reason for Sherman's departure was that he couldn't get equity; this was a major difference between French and American companies. See "Sherman Out, Rouët Heads: Dior-N.Y.," *WWD*, 11 June 1970.

81. "Toubeix Out at Dior N.Y.," *WWD*, 15 Sept. 1970.

82. Grumbach, *Histoires*, 70.

83. Press release, "Une prestigieuse aventure commerciale."

84. Ibid.

85. "Increasing Two and Half Times on Its Turnover Within Five Years—Christian Dior Announces a Long-Range Plan for the Restructuring," *WWDJ*, 3 Sept. 1979.

86. "Dior Hoping to Find a New Partner."

87. Ibid.

88. The archives of Maison Christian Dior S.A. are confidential and not open to the public. The CAMT documents are limited from the point of chronology and content. Given this situation, I carefully screened CAMT documents and selected the most useful.

89. When Groupe Boussac faced financial difficulty in 1978, it was purchased by the French textile company Agache-Willot, which went bankrupt in 1981. After three years

under the watch of the French government's Institut de Développement Industriel, the Groupe was put up for auction, purchased by Bernard Arnault, and eventually merged with his LVMH Group.

90. *Bilan* (Balance Sheet), Société Christian Dior, 31 Dec. 1947–31 Mar. 1977, Ref. No. 1987-003-251, GB-CAMT.

91. "État comparatif des chiffres d'affaires et résultat" (Comparative statement of sales and results), Christian Dior S.A., 31 Dec. 1977, Ref. No. 1994-020-112, in GB-CAMT. Most likely, this document was prepared for the consolidation of Groupe Boussac and Agache-Willot in 1978.

92. Musée Christian Dior, *Christian Dior et le monde*, 30.

93. Of Dior's private clients, were American 30 or 40 percent, while the United States fashion business purchased 40 percent of the total Dior models going to commercial firms. See "Dior to Celebrate 10th Birthday," *WWD*, 1 Feb. 1967.

94. Grumbach, *Histoires*, 76.

95. "Dubois, Who Is an Executive Director, Talks About Japanese Market."

96. Although Maison Dior was Groupe Boussac's most prestigious asset, most of its profits had to be diverted to the Groupe. As a result, the maison's managers were paralyzed. They didn't have the cash for improvements such as boutique remodeling.

97. "Christian Dior Couture reprend en main sa diffusion au Japon," *Les Echos*, 10 Feb. 1997, in CDA.

98. Dior, *Dior by Dior*, 9–10, 37–43; Dior, *Christian Dior et moi*, 9–10, 53–60.

99. "Christian Dior et le Monde" exhibited the perfume offered by Dior to Boussac's wife. On the day when Dior presented his first collection, he prepared to deliver a bouquet to Boussac's house. See Pochna, *Christian Dior*, 168.

100. "Hereafter for Designers' Licensing Business," *WWDJ*, 1 Mar. 1982.

101. "Pierre Balman Speaks on His Fashion History," *WWDJ*, 26 Nov. 1979.

102. Ibid.; "Fashion Is My Life," *WWDJ*, 11 May 1981.

103. Le Moult interview.

104. "Does the License Business Certainly Come Back to Life?" *WWDJ*, 19 April 2004. In 1981, Rouët noted, "In many countries we haven't sold licenses because there's not a high quality manufacture." See Susan Heller Anderson, "Dior Hoping to Find a New Partner," *WWD*, 2 Sept. 1981.

105. Bernard Arnault, interview by Yves Messarovitch in his book *La passion créative* (Paris: Polon, 2000), 2.

106. Xavier Lambert, "Christian Dior réorganise sa distribution au Japon," *La Tribune*, 10 Feb. 1997, in CDA.

107. "The End of Men's Line License, Christian Dior Kanebo," *Senken Shinbun*, 20 Jan. 2001; "The License Production Has Finished, Dior Men's Line," *Senken Shinbun*, 24 Jan. 2001.

108. "Interview with Toledano, CEO at Christian Dior; Giving the Full Picture of Dior Ginza Flagship Store," *WWDJ*, 24 May 2004.

109. Wallis, "What the Customers Say."

CHAPTER 6. THE WIENER WERKSTÄTTE AND THE REFORM IMPULSE

Unless otherwise noted, all translations are my own. I am grateful for the research support of the Metropolitan Museum of Art fellowship program and the Austrian-American Fulbright Commission.

1. For the concept of the "taste professionals," see Leora Auslander, *Taste and Power: Furnishing Modern France* (Berkeley: University of California Press, 1996), 195–96.

2. Here I use Peter Bürger's rigorous definition of the avant-garde as in *The Theory of the Avant-Garde*, trans. Jochen Schulte-Sasse (Minneapolis: University of Minnesota Press, 1984), 109 n. 4. Others disagree with my position; see, for example, Michael Huey, *Viennese Silver: Modern Design, 1780–1918* (Stuttgart: Hatje Cantz, 2003), 284–335; and Christian Witt-Dorring, introduction to *Viennese Silver*.

3. [Josef Hoffmann], "Arbeitsprogramm der Wiener Werkstätte," *Hohe Warte* 1 (1904): 268.

4. Hoffmann, "Arbeitsprogramm," 268.

5. On the key role age played in establishing status in fin-de-siècle Vienna, see Stefan Zweig, *The World of Yesterday* (1942; Lincoln: University of Nebraska Press, 1964), 25–26.

6. On the significance of the School of Applied Arts for modern Viennese art, see Gottfried Fliedl, *Kunst und Lehre am Beginn der Moderne: Die Wiener Kunstgewerbeschule 1867–1918* (Salzburg: Residenz Verlag, 1986).

7. Kirk Varnedoe, *Vienna 1900: Art, Architecture, and Design* (New York: Museum of Modern Art, 1986), 83.

8. Peter Vergo, *Art in Vienna, 1898–1918: Klimt Kokoschka, Schiele and Their Contemporaries* (London: Phaidon, 1975), 68–70; *Max Klinger Beethoven, XIV: Kunstausstellung der Vereinigung bildender Künstlers Österreichs. Secession* (Vienna: n.p., 1902), 12, 79.

9. The date of 1909 is based on the archival research of Herta Neiss, *100 Jahre Wiener Werkstätte: Mythos und ökonomische Realität* (Vienna: Böhlau, 2004), 79.

10. Paulus Rainer, "Eine Chronologie der Wiener Werkstätte," in *Der Preis der Schönheit: 100 Jahre Wiener Werkstätte*, ed. Peter Noever (Stuttgart: Hatje Cantz, 2004), 50.

11. Joseph August Lux, "Die Wiener Werkstätte," *Deutsche Kunst und Dekoration* 15 (Oct. 1905): 11: "Die soziale Frage hört in diesem Betrieb zu existieren auf."

12. Neiss, *100 Jahre Wiener Werkstätte*, 243.

13. On Waerndorfer, see Peter Vergo, "Fritz Waerndorfer and Josef Hoffmann," *Burlington Magazine* 125 (July 1983): 402–10.

14. *Versteigerung des gesamten Warenlagers der Wiener Werkstätte* (Vienna: Eigenverlag, 1932).

15. Lux, "Wiener Werkstätte," 13.

16. On the Sanatorium, see Leslie Topp, "An Architecture for Modern Nerves: Josef Hoffmann's Purkersdorf Sanatorium," *Journal of the Society of Architectural Historians* 56 (Dec. 1997): 414–37.

17. On the Stoclets, see Annette Freytag, "Close to Paradise: The Stoclet House: Masterpiece of the Wiener Werkstätte," in *Yearning for Beauty: The Wiener Werkstätte and the Stoclet House* (Stuttgart: Hatje Cantz, 2006), 360–64.

18. Oscar Bie, *Das Kunstgewerbe* (Frankfurt am Main: Literarische Anstalt Rütten & Loening, 1908), 7–9.

19. Ivan T. Berend, *History Derailed: Central and Eastern Europe in the Long Nineteenth Century* (Berkeley: University of California Press, 2003), 182.

20. See Mark Jarzombek, "The Kunstgewerbe, the Werkbund, and the Aesthetics of Culture in the Wilhelmine Period," *Journal for the Society of Architectural Historians* 53 (Mar. 1994): 7–19.

21. Hermann Muthesius, *Wirtschaftsformen im Kunstgewerbe* (Berlin: Verlag von Leonard Simion NF, 1908), 5–6: "die Kunstgewerbe ist zu einer Kulturbewegung im weitesten Sinne des Wortes geworden, die unsere Sitte des Wohnens, des Umganges, der Geselligkeit beeinflußt."

22. Hoffmann, "Arbeitsprogramm," 268: "Unser Bürgerstand hat seine künstlerische Aufgabe noch lange nicht erfüllt."

23. Henri van de Velde, "Das neue Prinzip in der modernen Frauenkleidung," *Deutsche Kunst und Dekoration* 10 (Apr.–Sep. 1902): 363–86.

24. "Mode und Handarbeit: Frauentracht vor Hundert Jahren," *Hohe Warte* 3 (Mar. 1906): 22.

25. Anna Muthesius, "Die Ausstellung künstlerischer Frauen-Kleider im Waren-Haus Wertheim Berlin," *Deutsche Kunst und Dekoration* 14 (Apr.–Sept. 1904): 441.

26. "Poiret Gastspiel," Feuilleton-Beilage, *Fremden-Blatt* 328, 28 November 1911. "Es war einfach, aber es war nicht schön."

27. [Adolf] Vetter, "Reform der Mode," *Wiener Mode* 28 (1 July 1915): 592; Stella Mary Newton, *Health, Art, and Reason: Dress Reformers of the Nineteenth Century* (London: John Murray, 1974), 166–67.

28. Berta Zuckerkandl, "Durch Kunst zu künstlerischer Mode," *Wiener Allgemeine Zeitung*, no. 10482, 15 Mar. 1913.

29. The photographs appeared in one of the special Wiener Werkstätte issues discussed below. See also *Deutsche Kunst und Dekoration* 18 (1906): 65–73.

30. *Deutsche Kunst und Dekoration* 16 (1905): 523–25. On Klimt's relationship with Flöge, see Wolfgang Fischer, *Gustav Klimt and Emilie Flöge: An Artist and His Muse* (New York: Overlook Press, 1987).

31. The other villas were for Carl Moll, Hugo Henneberg, and Friedrich Spitzer. Henneberg and Spitzer were amateur photographers and leaders of the Vienna Camera Club, the city's modernist art-photography movement. Moll was a Secessionist painter and head of the Galerie Miethke, where the Wiener Werkstätte and the Vienna Camera Club exhibited together in 1904. On the villas, see Eduard Sekler, *Josef Hoffmann: The Architectural Work* (Princeton: Princeton University Press, 1985), 45–56.

32. Alexander Koch, "Kunst-Zeitschriften," *Deutsche Kunst und Dekoration* 33 (Oct. 1913–Mar. 1914): 469.

33. Peter Gay, *Pleasure Wars*, vol. 5, *The Bourgeois Experience: Victoria to Freud* (New York: Norton, 1998), 105.

34. Auslander, *Taste and Power*, 195–96.

35. Regina Lee Blaszczyk, *Imagining Consumers: Design and Innovation from Wedgwood to Corning* (Baltimore: Johns Hopkins University Press, 2000), 12.

36. Ludwig Hevesi explained his role as a critic in a letter to Moser, quoted in Bernhard Kleinschmidt, *Die "gemeinsame Sendung": Kunstpublizistik der Wiener Jahrhundertswende* (Frankfurt am Main: Peter Lang, 1989), 208.

37. Hermann Bahr, "Zur Kritik der Kritik," in *Das Junge Wien: Österreichische Literatur- und Kunstkritik, 1887–1902*, ed. Gotthart Wunberg (Tübingen: M. Niemeyer, 1972), 23–29.

38. Nancy Troy, *Couture Culture: A Study in Modern Art and Fashion* (Cambridge, Mass.: MIT Press, 2002), 26.

39. "Buntpapiere und Tapeten-Fabrikation," *Deutsche Kunst und Dekoration* 20 (Apr.–Sept. 1907): 332.

40. J. A. Lux, "Die Moderne in Wien," *Deutsche Kunst und Dekoration* 16 (June 1905): 529.

41. [Der Redaktion], "Wiener Werkstätte," *Deutsche Kunst und Dekoration* 17 (Dec. 1905): 149.

42. Josep Casamartina I Parassols and Silvia Carbonell I Basté, "Josep Palau and the Textile Designers of the Early Twentieth Century," in *Josep Palau Oller, del Modernisme a l'Art Decó* (Barcelona: Centre de Documentació i Museu Tèxtil, 2003), 245; Dard Hunter, *My Life with Paper* (New York: Knopf, 1958), 45–49; Wendy Kaplan, *The Art That Is Life* (Boston: Museum of Fine Arts, 1987), 93.

43. Hermann Muthesius, *Wirtschaftsformen im Kunstgewerbe* (Berlin: Verlag von Leonard Simion NF, 1908), 26.

44. Scott Spector, "Introduction: Uneven Cultural Development? Modernism and Modernity in the 'Other' Central Europe," *Austrian History Yearbook* 33 (2002): 147. The Russian and Ottoman empires were the other laggards.

45. Hermann Heller, foreword to *Die Österreichische Ausstellung in London 1906 in Wort und Bild nebst einer Vorgeschichte und Chronik der Ausstellung*, ed. Hermann Heller (Vienna: Verlag Hermann Heller, 1906), 5.

46. The Österreichisches Museum für Kunst und Industrie, today known as the Museum für angewandte Kunst, was founded in 1863 and was the first decorative arts museum in continental Europe. It was modeled after London's Victoria and Albert Museum.

47. R. Eitelberger von Edelberg, *Die Österreichische Kunst-Industrie und die heutige Weltlage* (Vienna: Wilhelm Braunmüller, 1871), 19.

48. Eitelberger, *Die Österreichische Kunst-Industrie*, 20.

49. Berta Zuckerkandl, "Los von Paris!" *Wiener Allgemeine Zeitung*, 18 Aug. 1914; Kenneth E. Silver, *Esprit de Corps: The Art of the Parisian Avant-Garde and the First World War* (New Haven, Conn.: Yale University Press, 1989), 174.

50. Heller, foreword to *Die Österreichische Ausstellung*, 5.

51. "Position of Austria-Hungary in the Commercial World," *Imperial-Royal Austrian Exhibition: Official Catalogue and Guide* (London: n.p., 1906), 27.

52. Charles Holme, ed., *The Art-Revival in Austria* (London: The Studio, 1906). In the United States, *Studio* was published as *International Studio* until 1922.

53. This was one of the few things Hoffmann and Adolf Loos could agree on. See Eduard F. Sekler, "Hoffmann, Loos and Britain: Selective Perceptions," *9H* 6 (1983): 2–8.

54. Koloman Moser, "Mein Werdegang," *Velhagen & Klasings Monatshefte* 31 (1916–17): 259.

55. "The Austrian Exhibition at Earl's Court," *The Times*, 17 Aug. 1906; "Englische Blätter über die 'Wiener Werkstätte,'" *Neue Freie Presse*, 4 Oct. 1906.

56. Allan Janik and Stephen Toulmin, *Wittgenstein's Vienna* (New York: Simon and Schuster, 1973), 45.

57. "The Austrian Exhibition at Earl's Court"; Englische Blätter über die 'Wiener Werkstätte.'"

58. "Der König von England in der 'Wiener Werkstätte,'" *Neue Freie Presse*, Abendblatt, 23 May 1906.

59. Farid Chenoune, *A History of Men's Fashion*, trans. Deke Dusinberre (Paris: Flammarion, 1993), 113. I am grateful to Andrew Bolton, Associate Curator at the Costume Institute, Metropolitan Museum of Art, for sharing his knowledge of fashion and the British royal family.

60. "Der König von England in der 'Wiener Werkstätte,'" in Heller, ed., *Die Österreichische Ausstellung*, 2: 48. I thank Deidre Murphy, curator of collections of the State Apartments, Kensington Palace, for her assistance in trying to confirm the exact objects Edward acquired.

61. "Kassette für den Kaiser von Oesterreich," *Deutsche Kunst und Dekoration* 18 (Apr.–Sept. 1906): 417.

62. "Der König von England in der 'Wiener Werkstätte,'" 48.

63. "Ein Nachwort zur Londoner Ausstellung," *Neue Freie Presse*, 8 Oct. 1906. "Das kam daher, weil die Ausstellung nicht darauf berechnet dem Engländer ein Unterbieten seiner eigenen spezifischen Erzeugnisse anzudrohen, sondern ihn vielmehr einlud, sich das Neuartige und Neue anzusehen, das ihm so überreichlich durch die österreichischen Kunstwerkstätten und Fabriken angeboten wird."

64. It marked a rare instance when the antipodes of Vienna's press, the conservative *Reichspost* and the liberal *Neue Freie Presse*, agreed. See "Feuilleton: Oesterreich in London," *Reichspost*, 19 June 1906. For the concept of the *Kulturstaat*, I am indebted to Stephen Beller and Diana Reynolds. See Stephen Beller, "The Tragic Carnival: Austrian Culture in the First World War," in *European Culture in the Great War: The Arts, Entertainment, and Propaganda, 1914–1918*, ed. Aviel Roshwald and Richard Stites (New York: Cambridge University Press, 1999), 130–31; and Diana Reynolds, "Die österreichische Synthese," in *Kunst und Industrie*, ed. Peter Noever (Ostfildern: Hatje-Cantz, 2000), 203–18.

65. "The Austrian Exhibition at Earl's Court."

66. Oscar Guttmann and Emil Hecht, *Bericht über die Österreichische Ausstellung London 1906: Erstattet an die Österreichisch-Ungarische Handels- und Gewerbekammer in London* (Vienna: Moritz Perles, 1907), 45–46.

67. Xavier Marcel Boulestin, *Myself, My Two Countries* . . . (London: Cassell, 1936), 156.

68. Xavier Marcel Boulestin, *Ease and Endurance*, trans. Robin Adair (London: Home & Van Thal, 1948), 57.

69. Boulestin, *Ease*, 58.

70. Ibid., 59–60.

71. Leslie Greene Bowman, "Industry and Ideals: McHugh, Stickley, and the American Arts and Crafts Movement," *The Distinction of Being Different: Joseph P. McHugh and the American Arts and Crafts Movement*, ed. Anna Tobin D'Ambrosio (Utica, N.Y.: Munson-Williams Proctor Institute, 1994), 28.

72. Ludwig Hevesi, "Wiener Werkstätte," in *Acht Jahre Secession* (Vienna: Carl Konegen, 1905), 484.

73. See Neiss, *100 Jahre Wiener Werkstätte*, 53–54; Advertisement, *Neue Freie Presse*, 31 Mar. 1916.

74. Rainer, "Eine Chronologie," 250.

75. Wiener Werkstätte advertisements, *Elegante Welt* (7 June 1916): 23; (19 July 1916): 20; Advertisement, Silks of the Wiener Werkstätte, *Elegante Welt* (13 Sept. 1916): inside cover.

76. On his friendship with Freudenberg, see Paul Poiret, *King of Fashion: The Autobiography of Paul Poiret*, trans. Stephen Haden Guest (Philadelphia: J.B. Lippincott, 1931), 157–58.

77. Advertisement, Wiener Werkstätte fabrics and fashions at the Hohenzollern Kunstgewerbehaus, Berlin, *Elegante Welt* (7 May 1913): 26.

78. Examples include *Neue Freie Presse* 18537, 31 Mar. 1916 and no. 18543, 6 Apr. 1916. See also advertisements in *Elegante Welt* (24 May 1916). Some advertisements included silk swatches; see "Bedruckte Seidenstoffe der Wiener Werkstätte" (Printed silks of the Wiener Werkstätte), advertisement, *Wiener Mode* 30 (15 Oct.1916): back cover.

79. Advertisement for Joseph P McHugh, *Dress and Vanity Fair* (Nov. 1913): 90; "Fabrics Created, Signed, and Copyrighted," *Vogue* (15 Apr. 1914): 48, 110; "Modern German and Viennese Fabrics," *Arts and Decoration* 4 (July 1914): 331.

80. Werner Schweiger, *Wiener Werkstätte: Design in Vienna, 1903–32*, trans. Alexander Lieven (New York: Abbeville Press, 1984), 233.

81. Marie Gelber, "Die Wiener Werkstätte und ihre Modellschau," *Wiener Mode* 24 (15 May 1911): 930.

82. Gelber, "Die Wiener Werkstätte und ihre Modellschau," 930.

83. "Wiener Werkstätte—Mode in Berlin," *Neue Freie Presse*, Morgenblatt, 9 Oct. 1912.

84. *Elegante Welt* (22 Jan. 1913): 5.

85. *Galerie der Moden, Ausstellung im Hohenzollern Kunstgewerbehaus* (Berlin: n.p., 1912), 5.

86. Ibid., 6.

87. "Wiener Werkstätte—Mode in Berlin."

88. For examples, see photographs in *Deutsche Kunst und Dekoration* 27 (1910): 70–71; 31 (1912): 111, 436–37.

89. "Berlin Faithful to Paris Fashions," *NYT*, 29 Mar. 1914.

90. Zuckerkandl, "Los von Paris": "mit einem siegreichen Gefühl von Kraft und Erfüllbarkeit löst die österreichische Nation, Publikum und Produzent, die Bande einer Jahrhunderte währenden Abhängigkeit von Frankreichs Kultur."

91. Helene Tuchak, "Los von Paris!" *Wiener Mode* 28 (1 Oct. 1914): 1; a.b. [sic], "Los von London und Paris," *Elegante Welt* (Aug. 17, 1914): 4.

92. Bruno Paul, "Unzeitgemäße Notwendigkeiten," *Deutsche Kunst und Dekoration* 35 (Oct. 1914–Mar. 1915): 185.

93. Anton Jaumann, "Von Primitiven in der Angewandten Kunst," *Deutsche Kunst und Dekoration* 16 (1905): 547ff.

94. A[nton] Jaumann, "Deutsche Kleider und Deutsche Zutaten," *Deutsche Kunst und Dekoration* 35 (Oct. 1914–Mar. 1915): 104: "Ein nationales, ein volkswirtschaftliches Ereignis von höchster Wichtigkeit!"

95. Zuckerkandl, "Los von Paris," 1.

96. X, [Anonymous letter], *Deutsche Kunst und Dekoration* 35 (Nov. 1914): 183.

97. Max Eisler, "Wiener Kunstmode (Eine Zeitfrage)," *Fremden-Blatt*, Feuilleton-Beilage, Morgenblatt, 17 Oct. 1914. "alle unsere liebenswürdigen Schwächen werden hier zu Tugenden, die der Sache förderlich sind. Niemand draußen wird uns das Vorrecht des Wegweisers bestreiten, wenn es um die deutschen Mode geht. Wien muß die Führung nehmen, die man ihm geradezu ins Haus trägt."

98. Rudolf Bosselt, *Krieg und Deutsche Mode* (Magdeburg: Heinrichshofen, 1915), 34: "Gerade die Wiener Werkstätten . . . , und die wir doch, im Gegensatz zur franz-öischen, als eine Stätte deutscher Kunst ansehen dürfen, die können als Stützpunkt kühns-ter Hoffnung angeführt werden."

99. This position is outlined in Eisler, "Wiener Kunst-Mode," 19; Paul Westheim, "Deutsche Mode," *Dekorative Kunst* 23 (1915): 48; Berta Zuckerkandl, "Die Wiener Mode-Ausstellung," *Deutsche Kunst und Dekoration* 38 (1916): 81.

100. Ernst Friedmann, "Der Weg zur Deutschen Mode," *Deutsche Kunst und Dekoration* 35 (Oct. 1914–Mar. 1915): 103.

101. Zuckerkandl, "Die Wiener Mode-Ausstellung," 81.

102. Friedmann, "Der Weg zur Deutschen Mode," 103: "Daß sie . . . zeigt uns den Weg, den auch wir für die nächste Zeit gehen müssen. Es wäre unmöglich, plötzlich etwas ganz neues oder anderes machen zu wollen als die letzte Saison uns gebracht hat."

103. Editorial, *Vogue* (15 June 1914): 17; "Going, Going, Almost Gone Is the Tight Skirt," *Vogue* (1 Apr. 1914): 33; "Das Rokoko von 1914," *Elegante Welt* (13 May 1914): 15.

104. "Die Krinoline ist wieder da!" *Elegante Welt* (3 Dec. 1913): 17–18.

105. Edward Wimmer-Wisgrill, Dress design, Alt Wien (Old Vienna). Watercolor and ink on paper. Dated 19 June [19]14. Wiener Werkstätte Archiv, Museum für angewan-dte Kunst, Vienna, Austria (hereafter cited as WWA), Box 12, File 7, K.I. 13365/106; E. J. Wimmer, "Maria Theresa" dress, executed by the Wiener Werkstätte Fashion Depart-

ment, 1914, Photograph, WWA, K.I. 13365/108. For an interpretation of these dresses as examples of nationalist fashion, see Angela Völker, *Wiener Mode und Modefotografie: Die Modeabteilung der Wiener Werkstätte 1911–1932* (Munich: Schneider-Henn, 1984), 74–76. I disagree with this interpretation.

106. Gelber, "Die Wiener Werkstätte und ihre Modellschau," 930; "Originality and Exclusiveness," *Vogue* (October 1, 1913): 50; "Fabrics Created, Signed, and Copyrighted," 48, 110.

107. Wolfgang Georg Fischer, "Paul Poiret à Vienne, Emilie Flöge à Paris," in *Vienne 1880–1938: L'apocalypse joyeuse*, ed. Jean Claire (Paris: Editions du Centre Pompidou, 1986), 558.

108. "Eine Toilette der Madame Paul Poiret," *Neue Freie Presse*, 2 Dec.1911.

109. "Ratgeber der *Elegante Welt:* Ersatz für Liberty-Seiden," *Elegante Welt* (10 May 1916): 25.

110. Marie Gelber, "(Untitled)," *Wiener Mode* 29 (15 Sept. 1916): 770.

111. Henry Russell Hitchcock, *Architecture: Nineteenth and Twentieth Centuries* (Baltimore: Penguin, 1958), 351.

112. Hans Schürff, as quoted in "Jubiläumsfeier der Wiener Werkstätte," *Deutsche Kunst und Dekoration* 62 (Aug. 1928): 335.

CHAPTER 7. AMERICAN FASHIONS FOR AMERICAN WOMEN: THE RISE AND FALL OF FASHION NATIONALISM

1. "The Coming of American Fashions," *Ladies' Home Journal* (hereafter cited as *LHJ*) (Feb. 1913): 5.

2. Kristin Hoganson, "The Fashionable World: Imagined Communities of Dress," in *After the Imperial Turn: Thinking With and Through the Nation*, ed. Antoinette M. Burton (Durham, N.C.: Duke University Press, 2003), 260–78.

3. Caroline Seebohm, *The Man Who Was* Vogue (New York: Viking Press, 1982), 102; Jane Mulvagh, "Introduction," *Vogue History of Twentieth Century Fashion* (London: Viking-Penguin, 1988), 33.

4. Sarah Berry, *Screen Style: Fashion and Femininity in 1930s Hollywood* (Minneapolis: University of Minnesota Press, 2000); Tiffany Webber Hanchett, "Dorothy Shaver: Promoter of the 'American Look,'" in *The Fashion Reader*, ed. Linda Welters and Abby Lillethun (London: Berg, 2007).

5. Valerie Steele, *Paris Fashion: A Cultural History* (New York: Oxford University Press, 1988), 233–36; Caroline Rennolds Millbank, *New York Fashion: The Evolution of American Style* (New York: Abrams, 1989), 59–62.

6. Lois W. Banner, *American Beauty* (Chicago: University of Chicago Press, 1983), 67; Wendy Gamber, *The Female Economy: The Millinery and Dressmaking Trades, 1860–1930* (Urbana: University of Illinois Press, 1997), 111.

7. Sharon Marcus, "Reflections on Victorian Fashion Plates," *differences* 14 (2005): 4–33.

8. Banner, *American Beauty*, 69; quoted in Richard Butsch, "Bowery B'hoys and Matinee Ladies: Re-Gendering of Nineteenth Century American Theatre Audiences," *American Quarterly* 46 (Sept. 1994): 388–89.

9. William R. Leach, *Land of Desire: Merchants, Power, and the Rise of a New American Culture* (New York: Pantheon, 1993), 93.

10. Hoganson, "The Fashionable World," 264.

11. Joseph Herbert Appel and Leigh Mitchell Hodges, comps., *Golden Book of the Wanamaker Stores*, vol. 1 (Philadelphia: John Wanamaker, 1911), 68, 195.

12. Susan Hay, ed., *From Paris to Providence: Fashion, Art, and the Tirocchi Dressmakers' Shop, 1915–1947* (Providence: Museum of Art, Rhode Island School of Design, 2000), 21, 27, 32.

13. Valerie Mendes and Amy de la Haye, *20th Century Fashion* (London: Thames & Hudson, 1999), 32.

14. Mary Louise Roberts, "Samson and Delilah Revisited: The Politics of Women's Fashion in 1920s France," *American Historical Review* 98 (June 1993): 658.

15. French Modistes Differ on the Directorie [sic] Gowns," *New York Times* (hereafter cited as *NYT*), 24 May 1908; Margaret Alice Friend, "Hips Eliminated by the New Corset," *New York Daily Tribune*, 13 Sept. 1908, "Women's Realm," 1.

16. Valerie Steele, *Fashion and Eroticism: Ideals of Feminine Beauty from the Victorian Through the Jazz Era* (New York: Oxford University Press, 1985); Joan Jacobs Blumberg, *The Body Project: An Intimate History of American Girls* (New York: Vintage, 2002).

17. Friend, "Hips Eliminated by the New Corset."

18. Robert C. Allen, *Horrible Prettiness: Burlesque and American Culture* (Chapel Hill: University of North Carolina Press, 1991), 146.

19. Sarah Nixon Gasyna, "Women, Witnesses, and Words: Gynocentric Historiography and the *bals des victims*," conference paper, Association for Canadian Theatre Research, Toronto, 26 May 2006.

20. John D'Emilio and Estelle B. Freedman, *Intimate Matters: A History of Sexuality in America*, 2nd ed. (Chicago: University of Chicago Press, 1997), 224–25.

21. Roberts, "Samson and Delilah," 666.

22. Nancy J. Troy, *Couture Culture: A Study in Modern Art and Fashion* (Cambridge, Mass.: MIT Press, 2003), esp. chap. 2–3.

23. Paul Poiret, *King of Fashion: The Autobiography of Paul Poiret*, trans. Stephen Haden Guest (Philadelphia: J.B. Lippincott, 1931), 97.

24. Troy, *Couture Culture*.

25. Ibid., 6.

26. Steele, *Paris Fashion*, 234–35; Caroline Evans, "The Enchanted Spectacle," *Fashion Theory* 5 (2001): 285; Nancy L. Green, *Ready-to-Wear and Ready-to-Work: A Century of Industry and Immigrants in Paris and New York* (Durham, N.C.: Duke University Press, 1997), 118.

27. "It Was America That Made Paris," *NYT*, 22 Dec. 1912.

28. Troy, *Couture Culture*, 223.

29. Gustav Kobbé, "The Stage as a School of Costume," *Delineator* (Jan. 1905): 63; Sheila Stowell and Joel H. Kaplan, *Theatre and Fashion: From Oscar Wilde to the Suffragettes* (New York: Cambridge University Press, 1994); Troy, *Couture Culture*, chap. 2.

30. "It Was America That Made Paris."

31. Hoganson, "The Fashionable World," 264; Leach, *Land of Desire*, 93.

32. Edna Woolman Chase and Ilka Chase, *Always in Vogue* (New York: Doubleday, 1954), 125–26; Nicholson Baker and Margaret Brentano, *The World on Sunday: Graphic Art in Joseph Pulitzer's Newspaper* (New York: Doubleday, 2005), 9.

33. Ninth Annual Conference of the Advertising Dept., [Jan.] 1913, 165–66, box 16, Mss. Coll. 51, Curtis Publishing Company Records, Rare Books and Manuscripts Collection, University of Pennsylvania (hereafter cited as Curtis, RBM, Penn).

34. Banner, *American Beauty*, 32; Troy, *Couture Culture*, 233–34.

35. "Ladies' Tailors Bar Styles from Paris," *NYT*, 7 Sept. 1910.

36. "Smugglers' Bribe Raised to $260,000," *NYT*, 20 Apr. 1909; "Smugglers Formed Over-Sea Express," *NYT*, 22 April 1909.

37. Kathy Peiss, *Cheap Amusements: Working Women and Leisure in Turn-of-the-Century New York* (Philadelphia: Temple University Press, 1986), 62; Nan Enstad, *Ladies of Labor, Girls of Adventure: Working Women, Popular Culture, and Labor Politics at the Turn of the Twentieth Century* (New York: Columbia University Press, 1999), 78.

38. Hoganson, "The Fashionable World," 264, 267.

39. "A Careful Selection of the New Models," *The Designer* (Oct. 1908): 523.

40. "Calls Dress a Snare," *Chicago Record-Herald*, 24 May 1908.

41. Martha Banta, *Imaging American Women: Ideas and Ideals in Cultural History* (New York: Columbia University Press, 1987).

42. Dana Frank, *Buy American: The Untold Story of Economic Nationalism* (Boston: Beacon Press, 1999), 10–12; Lawrence B. Glickman, "'Make Lisle the Style: The Politics of Fashion in the Japanese Silk Boycott, 1937–1940," *Journal of Social History* 38 (Spring 2005): 573–608.

43. Elizabeth Reitz Mullenix, "Private Women/ Public Acts: Petticoat Government and the Performance of Resistance," *Drama Review* 46 (Spring 2002): 104–17.

44. Mary W. Blanchard, "Boundaries and the Victorian Body: Aesthetic Fashion in Gilded Age America," *American Historical Review* 100 (Feb. 1995): 29.

45. Leach, *Land of Desire*, 39–70.

46. "Calls Tariff Benighted," *NYT*, 14 June 1908.

47. "Jokers in Cotton Schedule," *NYT*, 5 Apr. 1909; "Payne-Alrdich Bill Revision Upward," *NYT*, 2 Aug. 1909.

48. "The Clothing of the Poor," *NYT*, 21 June 1909.

49. "The Woman in Variety, by the Skirt," *Variety* (4 Feb. 1911): 13.

50. "America Lifting Paris Fashion Yoke," *NYT*, 14 July 1912.

51. Green, *Ready-to-Wear and Ready-to-Work*, 46.

52. Ibid., 46–47.

53. Rob Schorman, *Selling Style: Clothing and Social Change at the Turn of the Century* (Philadelphia: University of Pennsylvania Press, 2003), esp. chap. 2, 45–75.

54. Gamber, *The Female Economy*, 216.

55. Mary Ellen Zuckerman, *A History of Popular Women's Magazines in the United States, 1792–1995* (Westport, Conn.: Greenwood Press, 1998), 49; Jennifer Scanlon, *Inarticulate Longings: The* Ladies' Home Journal, *Gender, and the Promises of Consumer Culture* (New York: Routledge, 1995).

56. Zuckerman, *A History of Popular Women's Magazines*, 26.

57. Hans Krabberdom, *The Model Man: A Life of Edward William Bok, 1863–1930* (Amsterdam: Rodopi, 2001), 104.

58. "Are the Only Clever Women in the World in Paris?" *LHJ* (Jan. 1910): 3.

59. Edward Bok, *The Autobiography of Edward Bok* (New York: Charles Scribner's Sons, 1921). See also Krabberdom, *The Model Man*.

60. "The Editor's Personal Page," *LHJ* (Jan. 1910): 3; "Can We Make Pretty Hats in America?" Advertisement, *Harper's Bazar* (Feb. 1910): 117.

61. "Are the Only Clever Women in the World in Paris?" 3.

62. "Can We Make Pretty Hats in America?" *LHJ* (Feb. 1910): 69.

63. Ibid.

64. "We Have Found Ten," *LHJ* (Feb. 1910): 3.

65. "No More Paris Alone," *Harper's Bazaar* (Apr. 1910): 278.

66. "What We Mean by 'American Fashions," *LHJ* (15 Oct. 1910): 3.

67. Ibid.

68. "The French Fashions," *NYT*, 16 Sept. 1912.

69. Home Pattern Company, advertisement, *Dry Goods* (Feb. 1910): 114.

70. "The Difference Between 'Paris Fashions' and 'American Fashions,'" *LHJ* (15 Nov. 1910): 3.

71. Ninth Annual Conference of the Advertising Dept., 135–36, 153; Krabberdom, *The Model Man*, 108.

72. "Paris Fashion and Our's [sic]," *NYT*, 6 Sept. 1912.

73. Ibid.

74. Ibid.

75. Frank Luther Mott, *American Journalism: A History of Newspapers in the United States Through 260 years: 1690 to 1950*, rev. ed. (New York: Macmillan, 1950), 550–51.

76. Mott, *American Journalism*; Ted Curtis Smythe, *The Gilded Age Press, 1865–1900* (Westport, Conn.: Praeger, 2003).

77. "Freakish French Fashions," *NYT*, 12 Sept. 1912.

78. Ibid.

79. "How Styles Are Got," *NYT*, 17 Sept. 1912; "The French Fashions," *NYT*, 16 Sept.1912; "Mr. Bok's Sincerity," *NYT*, 27 Sept. 1912.

80. "Gowns and Hats Fresh from Paris," *NYT*, 15 Sept. 1912; "If America Had Her Own Fashions," *NYT*, Sept. 25, 1912.

81. "Paris Fashion and Our's."

82. "Gowns and Hats Fresh from Paris"; "Mr. Bok's Sincerity."

83. "Paris Losing Its Vogue," *NYT*, 1 Dec. 1912; "Freakish French Fashion."

84. "Freakish French Fashion."

85. T. J. Jackson Lears, *No Place of Grace: Antimodernism and the Transformation of American Culture, 1880–1920* (New York: Pantheon, 1981).

86. Steele, *Paris Fashion*, 233.

87. "Gowns and Hats Fresh from Paris."

88. "Paris Losing Its Vogue."

89. "What We Mean by 'American Fashions,'" 3; "Nazimova for American Modes," *NYT*, 14 Dec. 1912; Justia, "Nationalism in Dress," *NYT*, 1 Jan.1909.

90. "Paris Losing Its Vogue"; "Our National Need," *NYT*, 25 Sept. 1912.

91. "American Fashions," *NYT*, 3 Nov. 1912.

92. "Fashion Contest for Times Readers," *NYT*, 5 Dec.1912; "Nine Cash Prizes for American Designed Hats and Dresses," *NYT*, 6 Dec. 1912; Millbank, *New York Fashion*, 59–62.

93. "Prefer French Fashions," *NYT*, 11 Dec. 1912.

94. "Fashion Contest for Times Readers"; "American Fashions for American Women: Famous Actresses as Fashion Editors," *LHJ* (Sept. 1913): 37–38.

95. "American Fashions for American Women Results," pt. 2, *NYT*, 23 Feb. 1913.

96. "American Fashions," *NYT*, 3 Nov. 1912; "Paris Fashions," *NYT* [reprinted from the *New York Post*], 9 Jan. 1913; "Our Views Endorsed," *Dry Goods Economist* (hereafter cited as *DGE*) (8 Mar. 1913), 32: Harriet Edwards Fayes, "American Fabrics Not American Fashions," *Ladies' World* (June 1914): n.p.

97. "America's Lifting Paris Fashion Yoke," *NYT*, 14 July 1912.

98. "The Coming of American Fashions," *LHJ* (Feb. 1913): 5.

99. Advertisement, "American Fashions for American Women," *Dry Goods* (Feb. 1910): 111–14.

100. Tenth Annual Conference of the Advertising Dept., [29–31 Oct.] 1913, 299, 1 vol. box 17, Curtis, RBM, Penn.

101. Ibid., 300.

102. "Our Views Endorsed," *DGE* (8 Mar. 1913): 31.

103. James Chittick, *Silk Manufacturing and Its Problems* (New York: James Chittick, 1913); Charles W. Hurd, "Mallinson Campaign to Popularize American-made Styles," *Printer's Ink* (2 Sept. 1915): 3–8, 74–84; "American Fabrics Not American Fashions," *Ladies' World* (June 1914): n.p.

104. "Our Views," *DGE* (8 Mar. 1913): 31.

105. Ibid.; "The Origin of Fashion," *DGE* (5 Apr. 1913): 103.

106. "A Type of Dress That Is American," *NYT*, 18 Sept. 1912.

107. Tenth Annual Conference of the Advertising Dept., 299.

108. Ibid.

109. "The Journal and Fashions," Condensed Report of Advertising Conference, 1915, 7, box 18, Curtis, RBM, Penn.

110. Quoted in Steele, *Paris Fashion*, 235.

111. "The Agitation for American Fashions," *Current Opinion* (Mar. 1913): 253.

112. "Shall We Label Our Goods 'Made in U.S. of A.'?" *Printers' Ink* (24 Sept. 1914): 17–21; "'Made in U.S.A.' Movement Gathers Strength," *Printers' Ink* (5 Nov. 1914): 42; "Paterson's Exposition of 'Made in America' Products a Big Success," *Dry Goods* (Nov. 1914): 26; "'Made in U.S.A.' Tells the Story," *DGE* (21 Nov.1914): 24.

113. Milbank, *New York Fashion*, 59–61.

CHAPTER 8. COIFFING VANITY: ADVERTISING CELLULOID TOILET SETS IN 1920S AMERICA

I am very grateful to several people for their assistance. Initial encouragement came from Professor Adrienne Hood, whose graduate course Topics in Material Culture encouraged an investigation into celluloid hairbrushes. I am indebted to the Hagley Museum and Library for giving me a grant-in-aid to offset the costs of research. The academics, archivists, and librarians at Hagley were all very helpful, especially Roger Horowitz, Regina Lee Blaszczyk, Marge McNinch, Linda Gross, and Debra Hughes. For their useful suggestions and constructive criticisms, I thank the Women, Gender, and Sexuality Group at the University of Toronto; Sarah Amato; Professor Tim Blackmore; Professor Mike Pettit; and Professor Patricia Skidmore.

1. An earlier exploration of this article can be found at: Ariel Beaujot, "Material Culture and the Vanity-Set Hairbrush: 1890–1940," Topics in Material Culture: a Graduate History Seminar at the University of Toronto, http://beaujot.com/vanity (accessed 7 Apr. 2007).

2. Regina Lee Blaszczyk, *Imagining Consumers: Design and Innovation from Wedgwood to Corning* (Baltimore: Johns Hopkins University Press, 2000), 12.

3. Roland Marchand, *Advertising the American Dream: Making Way for Modernity, 1920–1940* (Berkeley: University of California Press, 1985), 9–16.

4. Graham D. Taylor and Patricia E. Sudnik, *DuPont and the International Chemical Industry* (Boston: Twayne, 1984), 30–32.

5. David A. Hounshell and John Kenly Smith, Jr., *Science and Corporate Strategy: Dupont R&D, 1902–1980* (New York: Cambridge University Press, 1988), 65.

6. Ibid., 73.

7. Taylor and Sudnik, *DuPont and the International Chemical Industry*, 61.

8. "Ivory Py-ra-lin During the War and After," *DuPont Magazine* 10 (Feb. 1919): 14.

9. Hounshell and Smith, *Science and Corporate Strategy*, 73.

10. Ibid., 107.

11. F. B. Davis Jr., General Notice, 20 Sept. 1924, folder: Plastics Department (formerly Pyralin Department), acc. 1662: Papers of the President's Office, E.I. du Pont de Nemours & Company, Hagley Museum and Library, Wilmington, Del. (hereafter cited as PP-HML).

12. "Ivory Pyralin During the War and After," 14.

13. *Ivory Pyralin Toiletware, with Exclusive Features in Amber Pyralin, Shell Pyralin, Colortone Pyralin* (Wilmington, Del.: E. I. du Pont de Nemours & Company, Pyralin

Division, 1921), 3, Trade Catalog Collection, Hagley Museum and Library, Wilmington, Del. (hereafter cited as TC-HML).

14. Marchand, *Advertising the American Dream*, 6.

15. Ibid., 5–7; Frank Presbrey, *The History and Development of Advertising* (New York: Greenwood Press, 1968), 565–68; Martha L. Olney, *Buy Now Pay Later: Advertising, Credit, and Consumer Durables in the 1920s* (Chapel Hill: University of North Carolina Press, 1991), 4.

16. W. M. Coyne to C. W. Phellis, 13 Jan. 1923, folder: Plastics Department, box 62, PP-HML.

17. *Catalog of Dealer Advertisements and Electrotypes* (Wilmington, Del.: E. I. du Pont de Nemours & Company, Pyralin Division, 1921), TC-HML.

18. *Pyralin Toiletware: The Leader in Popular Demand, Now Complete and Standardized in Every Price Class* (Wilmington, Del.: E. I. du Pont de Nemours & Company, Pyralin Division, 1925), TC-HML.

19. *Catalog of Dealer Advertisements and Electrotypes.*

20. C. F. Brown to Irénée du Pont, 11 Jan. 1924, folder: DuPont Advertising Department, 24 Jan. 1924–Nov. 1927, box 3, PP-HML; *Directing the Demand to You* (Wilmington, Del.: E. I. du Pont de Nemours & Company, Pyralin Division, 1923), TC-HML; *Pyralin Toiletware; This Plan Has Helped Other Dealers Increase Their Profits on Pyralin: It Will Help You*, Oct. 1923, folder 2: Pyralin Products—Advertising Materials 1917–1924, box 35, acc. 1803: Advertising Department, E. I du Pont de Nemours & Company, Hagley Museum and Library, Wilmington, Del. (hereafter cited as AD-HML).

21. *Directing the Demand to You.*

22. *100% Hook Up* (Wilmington, Del.: E.I. du Pont de Nemours & Company, Pyralin Department, 1922), 12, TC-HML.

23. C. F Brown to Irénée du Pont, 6 June 1924, folder: DuPont Advertising Department, 24 Jan. 1924–Nov. 1927, box 3, PP-HML.

24. *Your Profession—Salesmanship* (Wilmington, Del.: E. I. du Pont de Nemours & Company, Pyralin Division, 1921), 2, TC-HML.

25. *Get a Big Share of the Christmas Gift Money by Pushing Pyralin Now*, Dec. 1923, folder 2: Pyralin Products—Advertising Materials, 1917–1924, box 35, AD-HML.

26. *This Plan Has Helped Other Dealers.*

27. See, for example, "Perfumery and Toilet Articles," *T. Eaton Co., Dry Goods Importers* 1 (1884): 24, and "French Ivory (or Grained Celluloid)," 124 (Fall and Winter 1917–18): 456–58. As of 1918, Pyralin was separated from other materials within the mail-order catalogs. By 1910, catalogs changed from using the generic name "celluloid" and began to use brand names such as "Parisian Ivory" and later "Pyralin Ivory."

28. "Celluloid Combs," *Sears, Roebuck & Company* 106 (1897): 641; "Combs," 113 (1904): 961; "Combs, Curling Irons and Hair Brushes," 121 (1910–11): 914; "Combs, Pocket Cases and Infant Hair Brushes of Quality," 125 (1912–13): 614; "Combs and Pocket Necessities," 137 (1918): 773. For a similar analysis of mail-order catalogs, see Miles Orvell, *The Real Thing: Imitation and Authenticity in American Culture, 1880–1940* (Chapel Hill: University of North Carolina Press, 1989), 43–45.

29. *Pyralin Toiletware.*

30. Ibid.

31. Gerald Carson, *The Golden Egg: The Personal Income Tax—Where It Came from, How It Grew* (Boston: Houghton Mifflin, 1977), 104–5.

32. In the late 1920s, DuPont's advertising agency was Frank Seaman, but it is unclear which agency the company used for the 1924 Pyralin campaign.

33. *Selling Pyralin to Your Toiletware Market* (Wilmington, Del.: E. I du Pont de Nemours & Company, Pyralin Division, 1924), 16, TC-HML.

34. Daniel Horowitz, *The Morality of Spending: Attitudes Toward the Consumer Society in America, 1875–1940* (Baltimore: Johns Hopkins University Press), 138–39; Robert A. Wilson and David E. Jordan, *Personal Exemptions and Individual Income Tax Rates, 1913–2002*, bulletin prepared for the Internal Revenue Service, Publication 1136 (Washington, D.C.: GPO, 2002), 219.

35. *Directing the Demand to You.*

36. Olney, *Buy Now Pay Later,* 1, 86–90, 130–31; Lendol Calder, *Financing the American Dream: A Cultural History of Consumer Credit* (Princeton, N.J.: Princeton University Press), 183–84, 199–201.

37. *Ivory Pyralin,* 1922, folder: Trade Catalogs, Pamphlets, 1917–1921, box 34, AD-HML.

38. "The Wonder World of Chemistry," 1936, folder: VC 49 Advertising Department, box 37, Series H, acc. 228: Irénée du Pont Papers, Hagley Museum and Library, Wilmington Del.

39. *Points on Ivory Py-Ra-Lin for the Retail Clerk* (Wilmington, Del.: E. I. du Pont de Nemours & Company, Arlington Division, 1917), 3, TC-HML.

40. *Autobiography of an Ivory Pyralin Brush* (Wilmington, Del.: E. I. du Pont de Nemours & Company, Pyralin Division, 1920), 10–12, TC-HML.

41. On the sexual symbolism of hair, see Elisabeth G. Gitter, "The Power of Women's Hair in the Victorian Imagination," *Publications of the Modern Language Association* 99 (Oct. 1984): 936–54; Wendy Cooper, *Hair: Sex Society Symbolism* (New York: Stein and Day, 1971); Raymond Firth, *Symbols: Public and Private* (London: Allen and Unwin, 1973); and Heidi Humphrey, *Hair* (Baskerville: Eastern Press, 1980).

42. See, for example, "Phillips's Minton China: Wedding Presents," *Illustrated London News* 98 (May 1891): 583.

43. "The Standardized Pyralin Line," *DuPont Magazine* 14 (Jan. 1921): 10.

44. *Seasonable Which Changed to a Staple—and Why?* (Wilmington, Del.: E.I. du Pont de Nemours & Company, Pyralin Division, 1920), n.p., TC-HML.

45. Blaszczyk, *Imagining Consumers,* 17; Regina Lee Blaszczyk, *American Consumer Society: From Hearth to HDTV, 1865–2005* (Wheeling, Ill.: Harlan-Davidson, forthcoming 2008).

46. *Catalog of Dealer Advertisements and Electrotypes, 1921: Ivory Pyralin* (Wilmington, Del.: E. I. du Pont de Nemours & Company, Pyralin Division, 1920), n.p., TC-HML.

47. *100% Hook Up.*

48. Helmuth Berkin, *Sociology of Giving,* trans. Patrick Camiller (London: Sage, 1999), 5; David Cheal, "'Showing Them You Love Them': Gift Giving and the Dialectic of Intimacy," *Sociological Review* 35 (Feb. 1987): 154.

49. "That Glamour Gift," *DuPont Magazine* 30 (Dec. 1936): inside front cover.

50. Cheal, "'Showing Them You Love Them'," 161–62.

51. Irénée du Pont to F. B. Davis Jr., 2 Jan. 1924, folder: Plastics Department, Oct. 1921–Aug 1927, box 62, PP-HML.

52. Taylor and Sudnik, *DuPont and the International Chemical Industry,* 79.

53. F. B. Davis, Jr., General Notice, 20 Sept. 1924, folder: Plastics Department, Oct. 1921–Aug.1927, box 62, PP-HML.

54. Irénée du Pont to department heads, 28 Apr. 1925, folder: Plastics Department, Oct. 1921–Aug. 1927, box 62, PP-HML.

55. Fin Sparre to Irénée du Pont, 8 Jan. 1925, folder: Plastics Department, Oct. 1921–Aug. 1927, box 62, PP-HML; Regina Lee Blaszczyk, "The Importance of Being True Blue: The Du Pont Company and the Color Revolution," in *Cultures of Commerce: Representation and American Business Culture, 1877–1960,* ed. Elspeth H. Brown, Catherine Gudis, and Marina Moskowitz (New York: Palgrave Macmillan, 2006), 34.

56. "History of DuPont's Plastics Department," folder: Plastics Department History, box 42 acc.1410: Public Affairs Department Records, E. I. du Pont de Nemours & Company, Hagley Museum and Library, Wilmington, Del.

57. Davis to Sparre, 8 Jan. 1925.

58. Lois W. Banner, *American Beauty* (New York: Knopf, 1983), 279.

59. Kathy Peiss, *Hope in a Jar: The Making of American's Beauty Culture* (New York: Metropolitan Books, 1998), 186.

60. *Behind the Scenes: How a New Vogue Has Been Created* (Wilmington, Del.: E. I. du Pont de Nemours & Company, Viscoloid Company, 1928), 14, TC-HML.

61. *DuPont Boudoir Accessories: Lucite-Pyralin 1929: Dealers' Price List for 1929* (Wilmington, Del.: E. I. du Pont de Nemours & Company, Viscoloid Company, 1929), 2, TC-HML.

62. Ibid.

63. *Behind the Scenes,* 10.

64. Blaszczyk, "The Importance of Being True Blue," 29.

65. *Behind the Scenes,* 12.

66. Ibid., 10.

67. Marchand, *Advertising the American Dream,* 34–35.

68. *Behind the Scenes,* 12.

69. Marchand, *Advertising the American Dream,* 132.

70. *Behind the Scenes,* 14.

71. *DuPont Toiletware: Lucite & Pyralin* (Wilmington, Del.: E. I. du Pont de Nemours & Co, DuPont Viscoloid Company, 1928), n.p., TC-HML.

72. Sales Report to Willis F. Harrington, Sept. 1930, folder 6: 1930 DuPont Visco-

loid Company, box 3, acc. 1813: Willis F. Harrington Papers, Hagley Museum and Library, Wilmington, Del. (hereafter cited as WFH-HML).

73. Monthly Report to Board of Directors, DuPont Viscoloid Co., Oct. 1931, folder: Willis F. Harrington 1931, DuPont Viscoloid Co., Minutes, Memoranda regarding Purchasing, box 7, WFH-HML.

74. Taylor and Sudnik, *DuPont and the International Chemical Industry*, 145.

75. "History of DuPont's Plastics Department," 4.

CHAPTER 9. CALIFORNIA CASUAL: LIFESTYLE MARKETING AND MEN'S LEISUREWEAR, 1930–1960

Thanks to Paula Fass, Kerwin Klein, Don Romesburg, Amanda Littauer, Chris Agee, Regina Lee Blaszczyk, and Sharon Ullman, who provided helpful suggestions and encouragement.

1. "Los Angeles' Little Cutters: Their Sportswear Always Had Honor in Its Own Country," *Fortune* 31 (May 1945): 134, 182; "L.A. Ranks 2nd in World as Apparel Industry Center," 1958, clipping, folder: "Garment Industry—Los Angeles," Vertical File, Los Angeles Public Library, Los Angeles.

2. For background on men's dress, especially the rise of the three-piece suit, see Christopher Breward, *The Hidden Consumer: Masculinities, Fashion and City Life, 1860–1914* (Manchester: Manchester University Press, 1999); David Kuchta, *The Three-Piece Suit and Modern Masculinity: England, 1550–1850* (Berkeley: University of California Press, 2002); Michael Zakim, *Ready-Made Democracy: A History of Men's Dress in the American Republic, 1760–1860* (Chicago: University of Chicago Press, 2003).

3. Thomas Frank, *The Conquest of Cool: Business Culture, Counterculture, and the Rise of Hip Consumerism* (Chicago: University of Chicago Press, 1997).

4. James Gilbert, *Men in the Middle: Searching for Masculinity in the 1950s* (Chicago: University of Chicago Press, 2005); Clark Davis, *Company Men: White-Collar Life and Corporate Cultures in Los Angeles, 1892–1941* (Baltimore: Johns Hopkins University Press, 2000).

5. "The Playboy Reader," *Playboy* 2 (Sep. 1955): 36–37.

6. Consumption was coded as feminine in the late nineteenth and early twentieth centuries, leaving masculine consumption hidden in plain sight. But historians should not confuse this gendered understanding of consumption with the reality, in which men arguably consumed more than women. Breward, *The Hidden Consumer*; Mark A. Swienicki, "Consuming Brotherhood: Men's Culture, Style and Recreation as Consumer Culture, 1880–1930," in *Consumer Society in American History: A Reader*, ed. Lawrence B. Glickman (Ithaca, N.Y.: Cornell University Press, 1999), 207–40.

7. James H. Collins, "On the Map as a Garment Town," *Southern California Business* 10 (Mar. 1931): 13.

8. On the regional nature of California's apparel industry, see Seward C. Simons, "The West's Greatest Garment Center," *Southern California Business* 4 (Oct. 1925): 17.

9. The California Shop's Guest Book from 1938 included visitors from *Vogue*, *Es-*

quire, Women's Wear Daily, Town and Country, Harper's Bazaar, Parents, Mademoiselle, and *Glamour.* See box 1, series 3, acc. no. 572, California Shop Records, Archives Center, Smithsonian National Museum of American History, Washington, D.C. (hereafter cited as CS-NMAH).

10. "Los Angeles' Little Cutters," 134; Charles S. Goodman, *The Location of Fashion Industries with Special Reference to California Apparel Markets* (Ann Arbor: University of Michigan Press, 1948), 36

11. Cited in Phil Lansdale, "An Unliterary Digest of Los Angeles Sportswear," *California Men's Stylist* 1 (Jan. 1942): 45.

12. Robert J. Sullivan, "Stitch in Time," *Wall Street Journal,* 20 Jan. 1948; Art Ryon, "Plunging Neckline in Male Styles," *Los Angeles Times,* 28 Oct. 1957.

13. "Los Angeles' Little Cutters: Their Sportswear Always Had Honor in Its Own Country," *Fortune* 31 (May 1945): 134.

14. For the image of California, see Kirse Granat May, *Golden State, Golden Youth: The California Image in Popular Culture, 1955–1966* (Chapel Hill: University of North Carolina Press, 2002).

15. Gwendolyn June Bymers, "A Study of Employment in Women's and Misses' Outerwear Manufacturing" (Ph.D. dissertation, University of California, Los Angeles, 1958).

16. "Los Angeles' Little Cutters," 134, 186.

17. U.S. Department of Commerce, Business and Defense Services Administration, *Leisure and Work Clothing* (Washington, D.C.: GPO, 1961), 3.

18. The women's clothing industry remained more diversified throughout this period. Although California took a lead in many casual styles and was the home to "star" designers like Edith Head and Adrian, both couture and quantity production remained firmly rooted in the East. For triumphal histories of California women's fashion, see Marian Hall with Marjorie Carne and Sylvia Sheppard, *California Fashion: From the Old West to New Hollywood* (New York: Abrams, 2002); Maureen Reilly, *California Casual: Fashions, 1930s-1970s* (Atglen, Pa.: Schiffer, 2001); and "Iconic to Ironic," Exhibition, Oakland Museum, Oakland, Calif., Mar.–Sept. 2003. The exhibit presented a celebratory narrative focusing on the influence of beach wear, California jeans, and Hollywood glamor.

19. E. M. Ruttenber, "Palm Springs Preview," *Men's Wear* 120 (24 Sept. 1948): 61–67, clipping, MAGIC Archives, Woodland Hills, Calif. (hereafter cited as MA).

20. Fred Grunwald, "California Futurization," *California Men's and Boys' Stylist* (Nov. 1947), clipping, MA.

21. "Fact Sheet: Men's and Boys' Apparel Guilds in California" (Los Angeles: Men's and Boys' Apparel Guilds in California, 1956), MA.

22. Jack Hyde, "Thorsen Heads Men's Wear Manufacturers of Los Angeles," *Daily News Record,* 9 Jan. 1948, clipping, MA.

23. "Fact Sheet: Men's and Boys' Apparel Guilds in California"; "Huge Growth Forecast for Apparel Industry," *Los Angeles Times,* 4 June 1944; "Manufacturers Plan Training Program," *California Apparel News* (28 Nov. 1947), clipping, MA.

24. "California Styles," *Wall Street Journal*, 27 Aug. 1945; Hyde, "Thorsen Heads Men's Wear Manufacturers of Los Angeles."

25. "Los Angeles Retailers Pledge Bank of Windows for Roundup," *Boys' Outfitter* (Sept. 1947), clipping, MA.

26. Jack Hyde, "California Dateline," *Men's Wear* 122 (12 Jan. 1951): 168.

27. A-1 Manufacturing Company, advertisement in *California Men's Stylist* 4 (July 1945): 12; California Sportswear Company, advertisement in *Men's Wear* 123 (27 Apr. 1951): 91.

28. One trade journalist urged menswear manufacturers to act ethically as they built the California industry: "Ask yourself if, by what you are getting away with, you are building a strong, ethical business for the future, if you are contributing to a greater Los Angeles market . . . or if you are simply making money." Will Chappel, "There'll Come a Day," *California Men's Stylist* 3 (Oct. 1944): 85.

29. "CMA Convention," *Men's Wear* 122 (Mar. 1950): 89–93.

30. "'Buy New York Products' Drive Is Begun to Offset Diversion of the Apparel Trade," *New York Times*, 6 Apr. 1939.

31. "The California Market and Its Importance to Men's Wear Retailers" (New York: Men's Apparel Research Guild, 1947), MA.

32. May, *Golden State, Golden Youth*.

33. See, for example, "Milady Had Nothing on the Gentlemen," *American-Statesmen* (2 Nov. 1947); Fred Grunwald, "California Futurization," *Men's and Boys' Stylist* (Nov. 1947), clippings, MA. The link between the California lifestyle and leisurewear marketing dates back at least to the 1920s. See Frank Anderson, "New Styles Are Set at Palm Springs," *California Men's Stylist* 1 (Jan. 1942): 19; Seward C. Simons, "Dressing Up Los Angeles," *Southern California Business* 7 (Feb. 1928): 18; Mary Braggiotti, "California Clothes Bring Sunshine," *New York Post*, 17 Oct. 1940, clipping, box 1, series 3, CS-NMAH.

34. "California Styles," *Wall Street Journal*, 27 Aug. 1945.

35. Sullivan, "Stitch in Time."

36. "Leadership of California Sportswear Stressed," *Los Angeles Times*, 28 Apr. 1948.

37. Bill Becker, "California's Sartorial Outlook Is Making Inroads on 'Ivy' East," *New York Times*, 9 Feb. 1964; Charles S. Goodman, *The Location of Fashion Industries*, 36.

38. Sullivan, "Stitch in Time."

39. "Sportswear Concern Opens $2 Million Unit," *Los Angeles Times*, 25 Sept. 1960.

40. Robert Bartels, *The History of Marketing Thought*, 3rd ed. (Columbus, Ohio: Publishing Horizons, 1988).

41. For seminal texts, see Stuart Ewen, *Captains of Consciousness: Advertising and the Social Roots of the Consumer Culture* (New York: McGraw-Hill, 1976); Roland Marchand, *Advertising the American Dream: Making Way for Modernity, 1920–1940* (Berkeley: University of California Press, 1985), 52–87. For a revisionist analysis, see Regina Lee Blaszczyk, *Imagining Consumers: Design and Innovation from Wedgwood to Corning* (Baltimore: Johns Hopkins University Press, 2000); and for the British context, Paul Jobling, *Man Appeal: Advertising, Modernism and Menswear* (New York: Berg, 2005).

42. Regina Lee Blaszczyk, *American Consumer Society: From Hearth to HDTV, 1865–2005* (Wheeling, Ill.: Harlan Davidson, 2008 forthcoming); Carole Turbin, "Collars and Consumers: Changing Images of American Manliness and Business," in *Beauty and Business: Commerce, Gender, and Culture in Modern America*, ed. Philip Scranton (New York: Routledge, 2001), 87–108.

43. Tom Pendergast, *Creating the Modern Man: American Magazines and Consumer Culture, 1900–1950* (Columbia: University of Missouri Press, 2000): 60. His observations are borne out by the slogans in William Borsodi, *Men's Wear Advertising* (New York: Advertisers' Cyclopedia, 1910).

44. Robert Fairchild, "For the Modern Man," *Los Angeles Times*, 20 July 1935.

45. "Of Course . . . When You Say CALIFORNIA You're Saying Maurice Holman," *Men's Wear* 127 (24 Apr. 1953): 133.

46. "Palm Springs . . . Countless Promotional Opportunities," *Men's and Boys' Stylist* (Sept. 1948), clipping, MA.

47. "Promoting California," *California Men's Stylist* 3 (Jan. 1944): 43; "California 'Sells' for You," 39.

48. "Sportswear: How California Captured the Sportswear Market," *California Stylist* 3 (Feb. 1939): 5. Leisurewear's bold colors and California origins parallel another popular consumer product of the period, Fiesta ware. See Blaszczyk, *Imagining Consumers*.

49. Douglas Monroy, *Rebirth: Mexican Los Angeles from the Great Migration to the Great Depression* (Berkeley: University of California Press, 1999); George Sánchez, *Becoming Mexican American: Ethnicity, Culture and Identity in Chicano Los Angeles, 1900–1945* (New York: Oxford University Press, 1993); and Eduardo Obregón Pagán, *Murder at the Sleepy Lagoon: Zoot Suits, Race, and Riot in Wartime L.A.* (Chapel Hill: University of North Carolina Press, 2003).

50. On the representational trope of Indians as part of the natural environment, see Philip Deloria's *Playing Indian* (New Haven, Conn.: Yale University Press, 1998); and Kerwin L. Klein's *Frontiers of Historical Imagination* (Berkeley: University of California, 1997).

51. "Sheriff of Los Angeles," *California Men's Stylist* 4 (Jan. 1945): 46.

52. "Palm Springs . . . Countless Promotional Opportunities."

53. "Sportswear: How California Captured the Sportswear Market."

54. "Gold and Bronze, Other Vivid Hues Will 'Color Men,'" *Fresno Bee*, 21 May 1948, clipping, MA.

55. "Gaudy Shirts, Slacks Shown for Men, Boys," *Detroit Times*, 10 Jan. 1950; "Extreme Styles Shown at Men's Wear Exhibit," *Rochester Democrat and Chronicle*, 9 Jan. 1950, clippings, MA. For the phrase "sun-ripe," see "California Fashion Scene, as Viewed by the Matilda Bergman Resident Buying Office of Los Angeles," 1942 Report, Special Collections Department, Gladys Marcus Library, Fashion Institute of Technology, New York.

56. The term "aspirational merchandising" is from Daniel Thomas Cook, *The Commodification of Childhood: The Children's Clothing Industry and the Rise of the Child Consumer* (Durham, N.C.: Duke University Press, 2004).

57. Frances Anderson, "The Tale of the Flying Fish," *California Men's Stylist* 2 (Jan. 1943): 48–51.

58. "Los Angeles' Little Cutters," 136.

59. "Sun and Swim Fashions," *Men's Wear* 126 (9 Jan.1953): 39.

60. Anderson, "New Styles Are Set at Palm Springs."

61. "What with Repeal and All, the Shirtless Swimmers Are Going in for a 'Nude Deal' All Their Own"; see *Apparel Arts* 4 (1934): 71.

62. *Athletic World* (Aug. 1924): 11, cited by Pendergast, *Creating the Modern Man*, 135.

63. In the pool behind bandleader Heidt is a man with his back to the camera and his hand on a beach ball. His muscular definition approaches that of Atlas. Anne Hollander has called this informal exposed look "unselfconscious readiness," with a studied "artlessness" undercutting the exposure's eroticism. See Hollander, *Sex and Suits: The Evolution of Modern Dress* (New York: Kondasha, 1994), 175. On the "double-bind" of female beauty as needing to be both constant and effortless, see Elizabeth Haiken, *Venus Envy: A History of Cosmetic Surgery* (Baltimore: Johns Hopkins University Press, 1999).

64. For a critique of using sex to sell to men in the 1950s, see Philip Wylie, "The Abdicating Male," *Playboy* 4 (Nov. 1956): 23–24. On the history of these two men's magazines, see Bill Osgerby, *Playboys in Paradise: Masculinity, Youth, and Leisure-Style in Modern America* (New York: Berg, 2001); Pendergast, *Creating the Modern Man*; Kenon Breazeale, "In Spite of Women: *Esquire* Magazine and the Construction of the Male Consumer," in *The Gender and Consumer Culture Reader*, ed. Jennifer Scanlon (New York: New York University Press, 2000), 226–44. On homosexuality and appearance, see "Fashion Is a Fairy," *Esquire* 10 (Apr. 1938): 35–36.

65. "Men's and Boys' Market Began Century Ago," *California Apparel News* (13 Jan. 1950), clipping, MA.

66. *Photoplay*, the original celebrity magazine, was first published in 1911 and followed by a host of imitators. On celebrity magazines, see Richard Dyer, *Stars* (London: BFI, 1979); and Richard Meyer, "Rock Hudson's Body," in *Inside/Out: Lesbian Theories, Gay Theories*, ed. Diana Fuss (New York: Routledge, 1991), 259–88.

67. Goodman, *The Location of Fashion Industries*, 29.

68. On East Coast manufacturers copying California specialties and turning them into "strange hybrids," sold as "California styles," see Ruttenber, "Palm Springs Preview."

69. Earlier California fashion shows focused on women's clothing, with one exception, the Manufacturers' 1926 "peacock parade"; see "Styles for the City of Los Angeles," *Southern California Business* 5 (Feb. 1926): 28.

70. Ruttenber, "Palm Springs Preview," 61–62.

71. "P.S.R.U. [Palm Springs Round Up] Guest Register," *California Apparel News* (29 Oct. 1948); "Over 1,200 to Attend Palm Springs Roundup Starting Tomorrow," *Los Angeles Daily News Record*, 23 Oct. 1947, clippings, MA.

72. "Dignitaries Welcome Visitors," *California Apparel News* (29 Oct. 1948); "MAGIC Arranges for Visitors to Fly to Palm Springs Roundup," *Los Angeles Daily News Record*, 23 Dec. 1949, clippings, MA.

73. "Fact Sheet: Men's and Boys' Apparel Guilds in California"; William Watts Rose Jr., "Palm Springs: Highs in the Roundup," *Apparel Arts* (December 1949); clipping, MA.

74. "They're Still Talking About Palm Springs!" *California Men's Stylist* 1 (Apr. 1942): 29.

75. "California Glamour Comes to Life at Roundup Show," *California Apparel News* (31 Oct. 1947).

76. For accounts of these moments, see Osgerby, *Playboys in Paradise*; Shaun Cole, *"Don We Now Our Gay Apparel": Gay Men's Dress in the Twentieth Century* (New York: Berg, 2000); Frank Mort, *Cultures of Consumption: Masculinities and Social Space in Late Twentieth-Century Britain* (New York: Routledge, 1996); Mark Simpson, *Male Impersonators: Men Performing Masculinity* (New York: Routledge, 1994); Colin McDowell, *The Man of Fashion: Peacock Males and Perfect Gentlemen* (New York: Thames and Hudson, 1997); Lynne Luciano, *Looking Good: Male Body Image in Modern America* (New York: Hill and Wang, 2002).

77. "Los Angeles Retailers Pledge Bank of Windows for Roundup," *Boys' Outfitter* (Sept. 1947), "P.S.R.U. Guest Register"; "Roundup Huge Success," *California Apparel News* (5 Nov. 1948), clippings, MA; "Sportswear Round Up at Palm Springs," *California Men's Stylist* 1 (Jan. 1942): 51; Jack Hyde, "California Dateline," *Men's Wear* 125 (20 Mar. 1953): 132–34.

78. Ruth Miller, "Palm Springs Round Up," *Display World* (Dec. 1948), clipping, MA.

79. One such merchant, A. H. Silverman from Minnesota, was profiled in Lois P. Hatton, "Palm Springs Show Inspires New Shop," *St. Paul Pioneer-Press*, 4 Dec. 1948, clipping, MA.

CHAPTER 10. MARLBORO MEN: OUTSIDER MASCULINITIES AND COMMERCIAL MODELING IN POSTWAR AMERICA

Thanks to Sharon Ullman, Regina Lee Blaszczyk, and Woody Register for their helpful suggestions.

1. Patrick J. MacDonnell, "Marlboro Man Would Trade Fame for Smokes," *Los Angeles Times*, 14 Nov. 2004.

2. Cassandra Tate, *Cigarette Wars: The Triumph of "The Little White Slaver"* (New York: Oxford University Press, 1999), 45, 66; Michael E. Starr, "The Marlboro Man: Cigarette Smoking and Masculinity in America," *Journal of Popular Culture* 17 (Spring 1984): 45–57.

3. Tate, *Cigarette Wars*, 65–92; Richard Klein, *Cigarettes Are Sublime* (Durham, N.C.: Duke University Press, 1993), 136–38.

4. Lin Bonner, "Why Cigarette Makers Don't Advertise to Women," *Advertising and Selling* 7 (20 Oct. 1926): 21, 46–47.

5. On women's smoking, modernity, and the overthrow of Victorian gender expec-

tations, see Nancy Bowman, "Questionable Beauty: The Dangers and Delights of the Cigarette in American Society, 1880–1930," in *Beauty and Business: Commerce, Gender and Culture in Modern America*, ed. Philip Scranton (New York: Routledge, 2001), 52–86; Sara M. Evans, *Born for Liberty: A History of Women in America* (New York: Free Press, 1989), 175; Tate, *Cigarette Wars*, 93–117; Peter G. Filene, *Him/Her/Self: Gender Identities in Modern America* (Baltimore: Johns Hopkins University Press, 1998), 139–40.

6. Bonner, "Why Cigarette Makers Don't Advertise to Women," 21, 46–47; Michael Schudson, "Women, Cigarettes and Advertising in the 1920s: A Study in the Sociology of Consumption," in *Mass Media Between the Wars: Perceptions of Cultural Tension, 1918–1941*, ed. Catherine L. Covert and John D. Stevens (Syracuse, N.Y.: Syracuse University Press, 1984), 71–83; and Tate, *Cigarette Wars*, 93–117.

7. Bowman, "Questionable Beauty," 78.

8. Bonner, "Why Cigarette Makers Don't Advertise to Women," 21, 46–47.

9. Roland Marchand, *Advertising the American Dream: Making Way for Modernity, 1920–1940* (Berkeley: University of California Press, 1985), 97.

10. "Marlboro Makes a Direct Appeal," *Advertising and Selling* 8 (23 Mar. 1927): 25.

11. Marchand, *Advertising the American Dream*, 88–116.

12. Edward Bernays, *Biography of an Idea* (New York: Simon and Schuster, 1965), 383. For more on Bernays's work, see Regina Lee Blaszczyk, "The Colors of Modernism: Georgia O'Keeffe, Cheney Brothers, and the Relationship Between Art and Industry in the 1920s," in *Seeing High and Low: Representation and Social Conflict in American Visual Culture*, ed. Patricia Johnston (Berkeley: University of California Press, 2006), 228–46; and her forthcoming book, *The Color Revolution*.

13. Bernays, *Biography of an Idea*, 385.

14. "The Uproar in Cigarettes," *Fortune* 48 (Dec. 1953): 130–33, 161–65. In 1952, *Reader's Digest* published "Cancer by the Carton," alerting the public to links between smoking and cancer. A longstanding critic of big tobacco, *Reader's Digest* drew on medical literature to accuse the cigarette industry of covering up the perils of smoking. See Richard Kluger, *Ashes to Ashes: America's Hundred-Year War, the Public Health, and the Unabashed Triumph of Philip Morris* (New York: Knopf, 1996), 152.

15. "Alfred E. Lyon and O. Parker McComas: More Production for More Sales," *Business Week* (17 May 1952): 72–74.

16. On filter cigarettes and health concerns, see "Marlboro Sticks to Tried and True Tattoo-Man Motif," *Advertising Age* 27 (Oct. 1958): 3, 100.

17. "The Uproar in Cigarettes"; "In a Rabbit's Eye," *Time* (18 Feb. 1952): 96; "Cigarette Trade Yawns at FTC Rules," *Business Week* (1 Oct. 1955): 56.

18. Other Marlboro account team members included Ross Millhiser of the advertising department; Clark Ames, head of production; and Bob DuPree, director of research. See George Weissman, interview by Scott Ellsworth at Philip Morris Inc., New York, 27 Apr. 1987, Marlboro Oral History and Documentation Project, Archives Center, Smithsonian National Museum of American History, Washington, D.C. (hereafter cited as MC-NMAH). Historian Scott Ellsworth interviewed thirty people involved with the Marlboro account as part of a 1980s collecting initiative by the Archives Center.

19. On Dichter and the origins of motivational research, see Daniel Horowitz, *The Anxieties of Affluence: Critiques of American Consumer Culture, 1939–1979* (Amherst: University of Massachusetts Press, 2004), 48–78.

20. Philip Morris created a new tobacco blend, or "recipe," that became the focus of the Better Makin's advertising copy in the mid-1950s. The new blend was also central to Marlboro's re-branding, much like the tattoo. See Weissman interview; "PR Man Fones, Adman Burnett Bare 'Secrets' of Modest Marlboro He-Man," *Advertising Age* 29 (17 Nov. 1958): 3, 99.

21. Weissman interview; "Bad News Can Mean Good Growth," *Forbes* 102 (15 Nov. 1968): 50–51. Weissman worked as a Hollywood public-relations specialist before joining Philip Morris. In 1945, he publicized the Academy Award-winning film *The Best Years of Our Lives*. See "Marketing Man at the Top," *Sales Management* 99 (15 Dec. 1967): 34–38.

22. Weissman interview; "PR Man Fones," 3, 99. Many thanks to Regina Lee Blaszczyk for the information on Egmont Arens's involvement in Marlboro packaging redesign.

23. Louis Cheskin, *How to Predict What People Will Buy* (New York: Liveright, 1957), 104; David G. Lyon, *Off Madison Avenue* (New York: Putnam's, 1966), 66; "The Marketing Merlins of Philip Morris," *Dun's Review* (Apr. 1968): 32–33, 77–79.

24. Regina Lee Blaszczyk, *Imagining Consumers: Design and Innovation from Wedgwood to Corning* (Baltimore: Johns Hopkins University Press, 2000), 13.

25. Leo Burnett, "The Marlboro Story," *New Yorker* 34 (15 Nov. 1958): 41–43 (quotation 43).

26. On "habitus" and material culture, see Pierre Bourdieu, *In Other Words: Essays Towards a Reflexive Sociology* (Stanford, Calif.: Stanford University Press, 1990), 131. On gender, see Joan Scott, *Gender and the Politics of History* (New York: Columbia University Press, 1988).

27. "The Marlboro Story"; Weissman interview.

28. George Chauncey, *Gay New York: Gender, Urban Culture, and the Making of a Gay Male World, 1890–1940* (New York: Basic Books, 1994), 15, 115.

29. Joanne Meyerowitz, "Beyond the Feminine Mystique: A Reassessment of Postwar Mass Culture, 1946–1958," in *Not June Cleaver: Women and Gender in Postwar America, 1945–1960*, ed. Joanne Meyerowitz (Philadelphia: Temple University Press, 1994), 229–62; David K. Johnson, *The Lavender Scare: The Cold War Persecution of Gays and Lesbians in the Federal Government* (Chicago: University of Chicago Press, 2004); Marc Stein, *City of Sisterly and Brotherly Loves: Lesbian and Gay Philadelphia, 1945–1972* (Philadelphia: Temple University Press, 2004), 200–225.

30. Karen Singer, "Ex-Adman Has Untargeted Audience—in the Bag," *Adweek* (14 Apr. 1986): 54.

31. Weissman interview. George Weissman did not remember if these ads actually ran.

32. Ibid.

33. Gary M. Levin, "Burnett—an Animated Celebration of Longevity," *Advertising Age* (1 Aug.1985): 15; Leo Burnett, *Communications of an Advertising Man* (Chicago: np, 1961), 331.

34. Hooper White, "Drive to Be the Best Attracts Many," *Advertising Age* (1 Aug. 1985): 21.

35. David Ogilvy, *Ogilvy on Advertising* (New York: Crown, 1983), 201; Simon Broadbent, ed., *The Leo Burnett Book of Advertising* (London: Business Books, 1984), 3–4.

36. My discussion of the tattoo campaign draws on television commercials and print advertisements, MC-NMAH, dating from the mid-1950s.

37. There are different accounts of the sources of the tattoo iconography. Photographer Constantin Joffe claims he presented the idea to Burnett, expanding on suggestions from his wife (and employee). In Joffe's account, Burnett studied tattoos from around the world, including India and Japan, but rejected this research and directed the creative team to use simple military insignia. See Robert Glatzer, *The New Advertising: The Great Campaigns from Avis to Volkswagen* (New York: Citadel Press, 1970), 129.

38. Alan Govenor, "The Changing Image of Tattooing in American Culture, 1846–1966," in *Written on the Body: The Tattoo in European and American History*, ed. Jane Caplan (Princeton, N.J.: Princeton University Press, 2000), 212–33; Maarten Hesselt van Dinter, *The World of Tattoo: An Illustrated History* (Amsterdam: KIT Publishers, 2005), 260.

39. Samuel M. Steward, *Bad Boys and Tough Tattoos: A Social History of the Tattoo with Gangs, Sailors, and Street-Corner Punks, 1950–1965* (New York: Haworth Press, 1990), 58.

40. John Landry, interview by Scott Ellsworth at Philip Morris Inc., New York, 12 Mar. 1986, MC-NMAH. For a nearly identical quotation, see William F. Gloede, "Agency Executives Feel at Home in Marlboro County," *Advertising Age* (1 Aug. 1985): 46.

41. The classic account of middle-class formation is Elaine Tyler May, *Homeward Bound: American Families in the Cold War Era* (New York: Basic Books, 1988). For a recent look at heterosexual masculinity in the postwar era, see James Gilbert, *Men in the Middle: Searching for Masculinity in the 1950s* (Chicago: University of Chicago Press, 2005).

42. David Riesman, *The Lonely Crowd: A Study of the Changing American Character* (New Haven: Yale University Press, 1950); William H. Whyte, Jr., *The Organization Man* (New York: Simon and Schuster, 1956); Robert Lindner, *Must You Conform* (New York: Rinehart, 1956).

43. Normal Mailer, "The White Negro: Superficial Reflections on the Hipster," *Advertisements for Myself* (New York: Putnam, 1959), 335, 339–40.

44. Patricia Vettel-Becker, *Shooting from the Hip: Photography, Masculinity, and Postwar America* (Minneapolis: University of Minnesota Press, 2005).

45. Thomas Frank, *The Conquest of Cool: Business Culture, Counterculture, and the Rise of Hip Consumerism* (Chicago: University of Chicago Press, 1997), 108, characterizes Burnett as "the Chicago-based celebrator of middle-American values" who supported his younger colleagues' revolt against hackneyed late 1960s advertising strategies.

46. John Berger, "Ways of Seeing," in *The Feminism and Visual Culture Reader*, ed. Amelia Jones (London: Routledge, 2003), 37–40.

47. Mail-order retailer Montgomery Ward began selling cowboy dress through its

catalogs by the 1890s. See Laurel Wilson, "American Cowboy Dress: Function to Fashion," *Dress* 28 (2001): 40–52.

48. John Benson, oral history interview by Scott Ellsworth, 14 Apr.1986, at Leo Burnett Co., Inc., Chicago, Ill., MC-NMAH. The *LIFE* image was probably the 22 Aug. 1949 cover portrait of cowboy Clarence Daily Long. Many thanks to Woody Register for this connection; see also Pat McGeehan, "Cowboy Image Connects," *Advertising Age* (1 Aug. 1985): 46, in folder 2, box 3, series 1, MC-NMAH.

49. Benson interview; see also McGeehan, "Cowboy Image Connects."

50. The voluminous historiography on representations of the American West includes Richard Slotkin, *Regeneration Through Violence* (Middletown, Conn.: Wesleyan University Press, 1973); Stanley Corkin, *Cowboys as Cold Warriors: The Western and U. S. History* (Philadelphia: Temple University Press, 2004); Bruce A. Lohof, "The Higher Meaning of Marlboro Cigarettes," *Journal of Popular Culture* 3 (Winter 1969): 443–50; Christopher L. Salter, "The Cowboy and the City: Urban Affection for Wilderness," *Landscape* 27 (1983): 43–47; John Fleckner, "Marlboro Country: Discovery, Domination, Disappearance" (paper, annual meeting of the National Council on Public History, Victoria, British Columbia, Canada, 1 Apr. 2004).

51. Ken Krom, interview by Scott Ellsworth, Leo Burnett Co. Inc., Chicago, 15 Apr. 1986, MC-NMAH.

52. Landry interview. For the fascination with American westerns and Marlboro's popularity in Europe, see John Blair, "Cowboys, Europe, and Smoke: Marlboro in the Saddle," *Revue Française d'Études Américianes* 10 (May 1985): 195–212.

53. Scott Ellsworth, "Introduction to the Marlboro Oral History and Documentation Project," 10, folder 2, box 1, MC-NMAH.

54. In response to declining cigarette sales, Philip Morris led the tobacco industry's product diversification and foreign expansion efforts in the early 1960s. See "Embattled Tobacco's New Strategy," *Fortune* 67 (Jan. 1963): 100–131.

55. Landry interview; Norman Muse, interview by Scott Ellsworth, Leo Burnett Co. Inc., Chicago, 16 June 1986, MC-NMAH. Muse critiqued the cowboy-in-the-city ads as "too stylized"; he thought they failed to make Marlboro Country into a "real" place. Landry expressed a similar opinion in William F. Gloede, "Agency Execs Feel at Home in Marlboro Country," 40.

56. Account executive John Benson remembered: "Then we had a Hollywood cowboy, a model cowboy, who was not very good. . . . do an introductory commercial talking about this new filter cigarette with the flip box." John Benson, interview by Scott Ellsworth, Leo Burnett Co. Inc., Chicago, 14 Apr. 1986, MC-NMAH.

57. "Marlboro Won Success by Big Newspaper Ads," *Editor and Publisher* (6 Dec. 1958): 26, 30.

58. Ibid., 26; for further claims about the masculine gender of the photographic element of this first campaign, see J. L. Watkins, *The 100 Greatest Advertisements* (New York: Dover, 1959), 216.

59. Tom Jarrard, interview by Scott Ellsworth, Lander, Wyoming, 28 Aug. 1986, MC-NMAH.

60. Landry interview.

61. Krom interview.

62. Ibid.

63. "Cowboy Talent Search," T. A. Dudreck to Nancy Lund, 31 May 1990, Bates no. 2048475407/5409; and "Marlboro: The Search for New Faces," 3 Feb.1994, Bates no. 2040848029/8051; both from Legacy Tobacco Documents Library, http://legacy. libray.ucsf.edu/ (hereafter cited at LTDL) (accessed 7 June 2006).

64. Vettel-Becker, *Shooting from the Hip*, 87.

65. Contract between Darrell Winfield and Filmfair Inc., 22 Sept. 1975, Bates no. 2024979980, from LTDL (accessed 7 June 2006).

66. Cap Adams, interview by Scott Ellsworth, Philip Morris Inc., New York, 24 Mar. 1986, MC-NMAH.

67. Darrell Winfield, interview by Scott Ellsworth, Riverton, Wyo., 27 Aug. 1986, MC-NMAH.

68. Angela M. Blake, "He Looked like the Devil," radio documentary, June 2004, aired on *To the Best of Our Knowledge*, Public Radio International.

CHAPTER 11. THE BODY AND THE BRAND: HOW LYCRA SHAPED AMERICA

The support of the Center for the History of Business, Technology, and Society at the Hagley Museum and Library, Wilmington, Delaware; the Pasold Fund for Textile Research (UK); and the Economic and Social Science Research Council of Great Britain (award PTA-026–27–0089), in the preparation of this work is hereby gratefully acknowledged, as is the assistance of Regina Lee Blaszczyk, the volume's editor.

1. Unless otherwise stated, the material in this chapter draws on Kaori O'Connor, "Lycra, Babyboomers and the Immaterial Culture of the New Midlife: A Study of Commerce and Culture" (Ph.D. dissertation, University College London, 2004). The ethnographic portion of the study involved interviews with 400 women between 1999 and 2003.

2. Robert B. Gardner, Jr., merchandising manager, Intimate Apparel, Textile Fibers Department, E. I. du Pont de Nemours & Company, transcript of launch presentation, 1959; Arthur M. Saunders, Jr., director of the Sales Division, Textile Fibers Department, transcript of launch presentation, 1959, both in box 3, acc. 84.259, Textile Fibers Product Information files, Pictorial Collections, Hagley Museum and Library, Wilmington, Del. (hereafter cited as PI-HML).

3. Press releases circulated in London, "The World's Top Ten Textile Brands" and "Top Fashion Innovations of the Twentieth Century," ca. 2000–2002, E. I. du Pont de Nemours & Co, Geneva, Switzerland, author's possession.

4. Marshall Sahlins, *Culture and Practical Reason* (Chicago: University of Chicago Press, 1976).

5. John Comaroff and Jean Comaroff, *Ethnography and the Historical Imagination* (Boulder, Colo.: Westview Press, 1992), 38. See Alfred D. Chandler, Jr., and Stephen

Salsbury, *Pierre S. du Pont and the Making of the Modern Corporation* (New York: Harper and Row, 1971), for a paradigm example of this genre relating to DuPont.

6. See Susannah Handley, *Nylon: The Man-Made Fashion Revolution* (London: Bloomsbury, 1999), for a study of nylon from a design-history perspective.

7. Mary Douglas, *Natural Symbols* (London: Routledge, 1970); Mary Douglas and Baron Isherwood, *The World of Goods* (London: Routledge, 1979).

8. David A. Hounshell and John Kenly Smith, Jr., *Science and Corporate Strategy: DuPont R&D 1902–1980* (New York: Cambridge University Press, 1988), 601.

9. William M. O'Barr, *Culture and the Ad: Exploring Otherness in the World of Advertising* (Boulder, Colo.: Westview Press, 1994), 201.

10. Regina Lee Blaszczyk, *Imagining Consumers: Design and Innovation from Wedgwood to Corning* (Baltimore: Johns Hopkins University Press, 2000), ix.

11. "The Long Road to Market," *DuPont Today* 2 (1980): 1–5.

12. Roland Marchand, *Creating the Corporate Soul: The Rise of Public Relations and Corporate Imagery in American Big Business* (Berkeley: University of California Press, 1998); and Roland Marchand, *Advertising the American Dream: Making Way for Modernity, 1920–1940* (Berkeley: University of California Press, 1985).

13. Paul Sampson, "Two Contributions to Chemistry's Progress," *DuPont Magazine* 27 (May–June 1933): 8–9.

14. Gary Cross, *An All-Consuming Century* (New York: Columbia University Press, 2000).

15. Roger Horowitz and Arwen Mohun, eds., *His and Hers: Gender, Consumption and Technology* (Charlottesville: University of Virginia Press, 1998); Regina Lee Blaszczyk, "Cinderella Stories: The Glass of Fashion and the Gendered Marketplace," in ibid., 139–64.

16. Nancy Walker, *Shaping Our Mothers' World: American Women's Magazines* (Jackson: University of Mississippi Press, 2000); T. J. Jackson Lears, *Fables of Abundance* (New York: Basic Books, 1994); Michael Kammen, *American Culture, American Tastes: Social Change and the 20th Century* (New York: Basic Books, 1999); Bernard Rosenberg and David Manning White, eds., *Mass Culture: The Popular Arts in America* (Glencoe, N.Y.: Free Press, 1956).

17. Douglas, *Natural Symbols*, 69.

18. Valerie Steele, *The Corset: A Cultural History* (New Haven, Conn.: Yale University Press, 2001); Jill Fields, "Fighting the Corsetless Evil: Shaping Corsets and Culture, 1900–1930," in *Beauty and Business: Commerce, Gender and Culture in Modern America*, ed. Philip Scranton (New York: Routledge, 2000), 109–40.

19. E. I. du Pont de Nemours & Company, "Elastic Yarn Program," 17 Dec. 1954, 1–8 and appendices, box 14, acc. 1771: Papers of the Textile Fibers Department, E. I. du Pont de Nemours & Company, Hagley Museum and Library, Wilmington, Del. (hereafter cited as TF-HML).

20. James H. McCormick, "To Advertising Department Brainstorm Panel Chairmen," 3 July 1956, and attached "Stretch Yarn" session results, 9 Aug.1955, file: Form Letters 1956–57, box 27, series I, acc. 1803: Advertising Department Papers, E. I du Pont

de Nemours & Company, Hagley Museum and Library, Wilmington, Del. (hereafter cited as AD-HML).

21. DuPont sales leaflets and advertisements for Lycra, Product Information, TF-HML; also vol. 613, box 43, acc. 500, DuPont Museum Files, Advertising Department, E. I. du Pont de Nemours & Company, Hagley Museum and Library, Wilmington, Del.

22. "Launching Lycra in 1960," *DuPont Magazine* 54 (July–Aug. 1960): 2–5.

23. National Analysts Inc., "Nylon Hosiery–A Study of the Consumer, made for Textile Fibers Department, E. I. du Pont de Nemours & Company, 1956," 8, box 29, PI-HML.

24. For more on the myth of bra-burning, see Susan Faludi, *Backlash: The Undeclared War Against American Women* (New York: Crown, 1991).

25. Brand Gruber and Company, "A Limited Study of Retail Foundation Department Buyers and Managers for E. I. du Pont de Nemours, Inc.," June 1975, box 25, PI-HML.

26. Ibid., 7.

27. Brand Gruber and Company, "Opportunities for the All-in-One Undergarments for E.I. du Pont de Nemours Inc." July 1975, 5, box 25, PI-HML.

28. Ibid., 14.

29. Charlie Willis, "Lycra Ideas Generation Meetings, 16–17 July 1965," box 25, PI-HML.

30. Boston Women's Health Collective, *Our Bodies, Our Selves* (Boston: Boston Women's Health Collective, 1973), iii.

31. Jane Fonda, *Jane Fonda's Workout Book* (New York: Simon and Schuster, 1986), 45.

32. Comaroff and Comaroff, *Ethnography and the Historical Imagination*, 77.

33. R. T. Brigham, "Retail Sales—Women's Leotards, 1984 Profile," Apr. 1985, 1, Textile Marketing Division, Textile Fibers Department, E. I. du Pont de Nemours & Company, Wilmington, Del., author's possession

34. Herbert E. Mencke Associates Inc., "Quantitative Assessment of the Market for Leotards and Related Garments," Mar. 1983, appendix A, submitted to the Textile Fibers Department, E. I. du Pont de Nemours & Company, Wilmington, Del., author's possession.

35. Press release circulated in London, "Lycra, the Past, Present and Future of Fashion," 2002, E. I. du Pont de Nemours & Company, Geneva, Switzerland, author's possession.

36. E. I. du Pont de Nemours & Company, "The 1970s General Summary," file: Technological Information, box 77, acc. 2215: External Affairs, E. I. du Pont de Nemours & Company, Hagley Museum and Library, Wilmington, Del.

CHAPTER 12. FRENCH HAIRSTYLES AND THE ELUSIVE CONSUMER

1. *Hairdressers' Weekly Journal, Supplement* (hereafter cited as *HWJS*) (Nov. 1910): 162. For all Long's reports from Paris, see Steve Zdatny, *Hairstyles and Fashion: A Hair-

dresser's History of Paris, 1910–1920 (Oxford: Berg, 1999). For a broader history of French hairdressing see, Zdatny, *Fashion, Work, and Politics in Modern France* (New York: Palgrave, 2006).

2. On the marcel, see André Bardet, *Technologie de la coiffure* (Paris: Dervy, 1950), 175; *Cheveux Courts* (Jul. 1931): 3; René Rambaud, *L'ondulation bouclée: trois méthodes d'ondulation en une seule* (Paris: Société d'Éditions Modernes Parisiennes, 1949), 46–47.

3. *Moniteur de la Coiffure* (Oct. 1892): 6.

4. *HWJS* (Nov. 1910): 162.

5. *HWJS* (Jan. 1914): 1.

6. On the disruption of amusement and consumption, see Jean-Jacques Becker, *The Great War and the French People* (New York: Berg, 1985), 9–102; Charles Rearick, *Pleasures of the Belle Epoque: Entertainment and Festivity in Turn-of-the-Century France* (New Haven, Conn.: Yale University Press, 1985), 214; and William Wiser, *The Crazy Years: Paris in the Twenties* (New York: G.K. Hall, 1983), 73.

7. Charles Rearick, *The French in Love and War: Popular Culture in the Era of the World Wars* (New Haven, Conn.: Yale University Press, 1997), 4.

8. *HWJS* (Nov. 1914): 161.

9. Valerie Steele, *Paris Fashion: A Cultural History* (New York: Oxford University Press, 1988), 236; and Gabriel Perreux, *La vie quotidienne des civils en France pendant la grande guerre* (Paris: Hachette, 1966), 261.

10. See Paul de Léon, "La semaine féminine," *La Femme de France* (23 May 1915)—or, indeed, virtually any issue of the magazine.

11. Modris Ecksteins, *Rites of Spring: The Great War and the Birth of the Modern Age* (New York: Anchor, 1989), 259. For similar sentiments, see Wendy Cooper, *Hair: Sex, Society, Symbolism* (New York: Stein and Day, 1971), 106; and Arthur Marwick, *The Deluge: British Society and the First World War* (New York: Norton, 1965), 92.

12. Steele, *Paris Fashion*, 241; Valerie Steele, *Fashion and Eroticism: Ideals of Feminine Beauty from the Victorian Era to the Jazz Age* (New York: Oxford University Press, 1985), 234; also Anne Hollander, *Seeing Through Clothes* (New York: Viking, 1975), 339.

13. Jane Mulvagh, *Vogue's History of Twentieth-Century Fashion* (London: Viking, 1988), 45; and Christobel Williams-Mitchell, *Dressed for the Job: The Story of Occupational Costume* (Poole: Blanford Books, 1982), 112–14.

14. On corsets, see Béatrice Fontanel, *Corsets et soutiens-gorge: l'épopée du sein de l'antiquité à nos jours* (Paris: Éditions de la Martilères, 1992), 91; and Valerie Steele, *The Corset: A Cultural History* (New Haven, Conn.: Yale University Press, 2001).

15. *HWJS* (Nov. 1918): 161.

16. See, for example, Catherine Lebas and Annie Jacques, *La coiffure en France du Moyen Age à nos jours* (Paris: Delmas, 1979), 310; Mary Louise Roberts, *Civilization Without Sexes: Reconstructing Gender in Postwar France, 1917–1927* (Chicago: University of Chicago Press, 1994), 79.

17. Ministère du Travail, Statistique générale de la France, *Résultats statistiques du recensement général de la population effectué le 5 mars 1911*, vol. 1 (Paris: Imprimerie Natio-

nale, 1913), 28; *Résultats statistiques du recensement de la population effectué le 6 mars 1921*, vol. 1 (1923), 51, 148–49; *Résultats statistiques du recensement effectué le 8 mars 1936* (1943), vol. 1 (1943), 58, vol. 2, 4, 8. Also see Annie Fourcault, *Femmes à l'usine en France dans l'entre-deux-guerres* (Paris: François Maspéro, 1982), 216. On the parallel trend in the United States, see Dewey Anderson and Percy E. Davidson, *Occupational Trends in the United States* (Stanford, Calif.: Stanford University Press, 1940), 2; and Julie A. Willett, *Permanent Waves: The Making of the American Beauty Shop* (New York: New York University Press, 2000), 29–30.

18. Quoted in Paul Gerbod, *Histoire de la coiffure et des coiffeurs* (Paris: Larousse, 1995), 212; also Antoine [Cierplikowski], *J'ai coiffé le monde entier* (Paris: La Table Ronde, 1963), 25; also *Vogue* (Mar. 1920): 60–61.

19. Pierre Galante, *Les années Chanel* (Paris: Éditions de Pierre Charon et Mercure de France, 1972), 70; and Marcel Haedrich, *Coco Chanel sécrète* (Paris: Robert Lafonte, 1971), 149.

20. Mary Trasko, *Daring Do's: A History of Extraordinary Hair* (Paris: Flammarion, 1994), 109–11.

21. René Rambaud, writing in *Gallia Journal* (May 1926); see also Caroline Cox, *Good Hair Days: A History of British Hairstyling* (London: Quartet Books, 1999), 50–51.

22. The phrase was coined by the fascist writer Pierre Drieu la Rochelle. For other condemnations, see the tract against bobbed hair in Richard Corson, *Fashions in Hair: The First Five Thousand Years* (London: Peter Owen, 1965), 615; René Rambaud, *Les fugitives: précis anécdotique et historique des coiffures féminines à travers les âges, des égyptiens à 1945* (Paris: René Rambaud, 1947), 241; and Gonzague Truc, "De l'église et des cheveux courts," *La Grande Revue* (Apr. 1926): 317–18.

23. Steele, *Paris Fashion*, 246.

24. Quoted in Rambaud, *Les fugitives*, 253; also see *La Mode Illustrée* (14 May 1922).

25. René Koenig, "La diffusion de la mode dans les sociétés contemporaines," *Cahiers Internationaux de Sociologie* 63 (July–Dec. 1967), 40; also Koenig, *Sociologie de la mode* (Paris: Petite Bibliothèque Payot, 1969).

26. *Coiffure de Paris* (Dec. 1920): frontispiece.

27. *Coiffure de Paris* (Jul. 1925): 17.

28. On the origins of L'Oréal, see *International Directory of Company Histories*, vol. 3, Adèle Hast, *Health and Personal Care Products-Materials* (London: St. James Press, 1991), 46; and Michèle Ruffat, *175 Years of the French Pharmaceutical Industry: History of Synthélabo* (Paris: La Découverte, 1996), 195–96.

29. *Coiffure de Paris* (Jan. 1920): 6; also see *Hebdo-Coiffure* (22 July 1939).

30. Mrs. Robert Henrey, *Madeleine Grown Up* (London: J. M. Dent, 1952), 39.

31. *Hairdressers' Weekly Journal* (Mar. 1909): 435.

32. Cox, *Good Hair Days*, 143.

33. *HWJS* (June 1917): 88; (Mar. 1919): 34–35.

34. For a biographical sketch of Boudou, see *Coiffeur de France* (May 1948). On the Gallia, see *Coiffure de Paris* (Mar. 1925): 17; *Gallia Journal* (Feb. 1926); Volo Litvinsky,

Toute la permanente: tous les procédés et tours de mains (Paris: Société d'Éditions Modernes Parisiennes, 1958), 13–14.

35. On Ricaud, see Archives Nationales, Paris (hereafter cited as AN), F²² 422, "Coiffure–8 heures": booklet from the Fédération nationale des syndicats des ouvriers coiffeurs (hereafter cited as FNSOC), "Le problème des heures de travail dans la coiffure," n.p.; and "Association des grandes maisons de coiffure de Paris." Also Archives de Paris, 1070, "Status des syndicats professionnels," carton 10, #1704: Institut des coiffeurs des dames de France; *Coiffure de Paris* (December 1933): 17; Archives de la Préfecture de Police, Paris, "Bureau des Affaires Réglementaires—Dossiers des Syndicats," dossier #5321: Association des grandes maisons de coiffure de Paris.

36. Paul Gerbod, "Les métiers de la coiffure en France dans la première moitié du XXe siècle," *Ethnologie Française* (1983/1): 40.

37. On the defense of the bob, see *Cheveux Courts* (10 Mar. 1930): 1–2; Union fédérale des maîtres-coiffeurs de France, d'Algérie, et des Colonies, *Xe congrès national, Nantes, 20–22 August 1928* (Paris: Imprimerie Parisiennes Réunies, 1929), 9–10; also the report on the fifteenth congress, in Saint-Etienne, in *Bulletin des Maîtres-Coiffeurs de l'Oise* (Sept. 1933).

38. Marylène Delbourg-Delphis, *Le chic et le look: histoire de la mode féminine et des moeurs de 1850 à nos jours* (Paris: Hachette, 1981), 148; René Rambaud, *Les fugitives*, 269; also *Votre Beauté* (Feb. 1938): 6.

39. Hollander, *Seeing Through Clothes*, 313. Jean Baudrillard, among the most frequently cited authorities in studies of culture, writes that "the signs of fashion are freefloating and not grounded in the referential": quoted in Shari Benstock and Suzanne Ferriss, eds., *On Fashion* (New Brunswick, N.J.: Rutgers University Press, 1994), 5; also see Elizabeth Wilson, *Adorned in Dreams: Fashion and Modernity* (Berkeley: University of California Press, 1985), 8–9.

40. *Hebdo-Coiffure* (Dec. 1935): 2; also *Coiffeur du Sud-Ouest* (Mar. 1938). Julian Jackson calculated that shopkeepers' income in general fell by 18 percent during the Depression; see Jackson, *The Popular Front in France: Defending Democracy, 1934–1938* (New York: Cambridge University Press, 1988), 20.

41. Gabrielle Letellier et al., *Le chomage en France de 1930 à 1936* (Paris: Librairie du Receuil Sirey, 1938), 81–83, 156–57; also *Journal des Maîtres-Coiffeurs* (June 1933): 19.

42. See, for example, the story on "Le charme des boucles," *Vogue* (Dec. 1933): 26–29.

43. *Coiffure de Paris* (Jan. 1934): 2; (Jan. 1935): 5; and (Apr. 1937): 2.

44. Guillaume, *Guillaume raconte . . . la coiffure et ses métamorphoses* (Argenton-sur-Creuse, France: Imprimerie de l'Indre, 1982), 53–61; and Vincent Chenille, *La mode dans la coiffure des françaises: "La norme et le mouvement," 1837–1937* (Paris: Harmattan, 1996), 11.

45. Gisèle d'Assailly, *Fonds et beauté: ou l'éternel féminin* (Paris: Hachette, 1958), 203; and *Gallia Journal* (Jan.–Feb. 1932): 7.

46. Dominique Veillon, *Vivre et survivre en France, 1939–1947* (Paris: Payot, 1995), 17–19.

47. *Vogue* (Dec. 1940): 10.

48. *Candide* (25 Oct. 1939).

49. *Vogue* (Apr.–May 1940): 26.

50. See *Coiffure de Paris* (Apr. 1941): 41; (Aug. 1942): 2–3; also AN F¹² 11993, "Procès-verbal du comité d'organisation de la coiffure et de professions annexes, 1er février 1943." On L'Oréal, see Archives de Paris, 901/64/1 1. 282, dossier "Scheuller: Affaire l'Oréal," part of the records of the Comité Interprofessionnel Régional d'Epuration for Paris; Raymond Abiello, *Ma dernière mémoire III: Sol Invictus, 1939–1947* (Paris: Editions Ramsey, 1980), 213–17; Pascal Ory, *Les collaborateurs, 1940–1945* (Paris: Seuil, 1976), 99; and Henry Rousso, *La collaboration: les noms/les thèmes/les lieux* (Paris: MA Editions, 1987), 130–31.

51. *Eclaireur des Coiffeurs* (5–20 June 1944): 1; and AN F²² 1955, note from Pierre Jardelle, Sept. 1942. Also see Alain Beltran and Patrice Carré, *La fée et la servante: la société française face à l'électricité, XIX–XXe siècles* (Paris: Belin, 1991), 280.

52. Jean Camus, "Les coiffeurs pendant la guerre," in *Coiffure 46* (Paris: Imprimerie Curial-Archereau, 1945), 55–56.

53. Dominque Veillon, *Fashion Under the Occupation* (Oxford: Berg, 2002), especially chap. 7, "Fashionable Paris Dresses Up," 107–24.

54. Lucien François, *Cent ans d'élégance* (Paris: Société d'Éditions Modernes Parisiennes, 1942), 21.

55. Veillon, *Fashion Under the Occupation*, 135.

56. Veillon, *Vivre et survivre*, 162.

57. Catherine Gavend, "Les coiffeurs de Lyon (1948–1975)," Centre Pierre Lyon d'Histoire Économique et Sociale, *Métiers et Statuts: Bulletin* (1999): 134.

58. Jean Fourastié, *Les trentes glorieuses, ou la Révolution invisible de 1946 à 1975* (Paris: Fayard, 1979), 23; and Dominique Veillon, *Nous les enfants (1950–1970)* (Paris: Hachette, 2003), 133–35.

59. Colombe Pringle, *Telles qu'Elle: cinquante ans d'histoire des femmes à travers le journal* Elle (Paris: Grasset, 1995), 14.

60. Samra-Martine Bonvoisin and Michèle Maignien, *La presse féminine* (Paris: Presses Universitaires de France, 1986), 20–22. For a more in-depth treatment of *Elle* and *Mademoiselle*, see Susan Weiner, *Enfants Terribles: Youth and Femininity in the Mass Media in France, 1945–1968* (Baltimore: Johns Hopkins University Press, 2001), especially chap. 1, "From *Elle* to *Mademoiselle*," 21–66.

61. See, for example, Pauline Laure Marie de Broglie, Comtesse de Pange, *Comment j'ai vu 1900* (Paris: Grasset, 1975), 86; also Marie-Christine Auzou and Sabine Melchior-Bonnet, *La vie des cheveux* (Paris: Gallimard, 2001), 56; Alain Corbin, *The Foul and the Fragrant: Odor and the Social Imagination* (London: Papermac, 1996), 179–80; Georges Vigarello, *Concepts of Cleanliness: Changing Attitudes in France Since the Middle Ages* (New York: Cambridge University Press, 1988), 83; and Eugen Weber, *France: Fin-de-Siècle* (Cambridge, Mass.: Harvard University Press, 1986), 60.

62. *Elle* (Oct. 1951): 14–16.

63. Lawrence Wright, *Clean and Decent: The Fascinating History of the Bathroom & the Water Closet* (New York: Viking, 1960), 263.

64. Kristin Ross, *Fast Cars, Clean Bodies: Decolonization and the Reordering of French Culture* (Cambridge, Mass.: MIT Press, 1995), 78–79.

65. Mary Lynn Stewart, *For Health and Beauty: Physical Culture for Frenchwomen, 1880s–1930s* (Baltimore: Johns Hopkins University Press, 2001), 68.

66. Gerbod, *Histoire*, 297–324.

67. See Joyce Asser, *Historic Hairdressing* (New York: Pitman, 1966), 122; and Jean Keyes, *A History of Women's Hairstyles, 1500–1965* (London: Methuen, 1967), 63.

68. Gerbod, *Histoire*, 257.

69. Alexandre, *Sous le casque d'Alexandre* (Paris: Presses de la Cité, 1972).

70. Trasko, *Daring Do's*, 128–29.

71. For a fascinating reflection on this process, see Malcolm Gladwell, *The Tipping Point: How Little Things Can Make a Big Difference* (New York: Little, Brown, 2000).

72. Stuart Ewen, *Captains of Consciousness: Advertising and the Social Roots of Consumer Culture* (New York: McGraw-Hill, 1976); similarly see Rosalind Williams, *Dream Worlds: Mass Consumption in Late Nineteenth-Century France* (Berkeley: University of California Press, 1982).

73. Grant McCracken, *Big Hair: A Journey into the Transformation of the Self* (Woodstock, N.Y.: Overlook Press, 1995), 36–37.

74. Roland Barthes, *The Fashion System* (New York: Hill and Wang, 1983).

CHAPTER 13. RIPPING UP THE UNIFORM APPROACH: HUNGARIAN WOMEN PIECE TOGETHER A NEW COMMUNIST FASHION

1. David M. Potter, *People of Plenty: Economic Abundance and the American Character* (Chicago: University of Chicago Press, 1954), 80.

2. Elaine Tyler May, *Homeward Bound: American Families in the Cold War Era* (New York: Basic Books, 1988), 16–20.

3. Radio Free Europe (RFE) was a radio station in Munich, West Germany, run by the Central Intelligence Agency (CIA). During the Cold War, it fought communism by broadcasting news and features assembled by Eastern European émigré political and economic analysts. Broadcasts to Hungary started in 1950; the Hungarian Desk was terminated in 1993. In the 1990s, RFE archives were transported to Hungary and deposited with the Open Society Archives (hereafter cited as OSA), founded by George Soros in Budapest in 1995. The OSA is now open to researchers. The documents used here are numbered and catalogued as "items." The document *Fashion Problem*, for example, is Item No. 540/61. It was compiled by anonymous analysts of the RFE's Research Department in 1961.

4. RFE, "An Independent Dressmaker's Work in Communist Hungary," Item No. 7341/55, OSA.

5. RFE, "The Most Elegant Beauty Salon in Budapest," Item No. 711/59, OSA.

6. Magda Vámos, Budapest, personal communication with Katalin Medvedev, 24 May 2004.

7. Karl Marx, *Capital* (London: Laurence and Wishart, 1974), 1: 450.

8. Giles Lipovetsky, *The Empire of Fashion: Dressing Modern Democracy* (Princeton, N.J.: Princeton University Press, 1994), 18–54, 134–55, 203–25.

9. Katalin F. Dózsa, *Letünt idők, eltünt divatok 1867–1945* (Budapest: Gondolat, 1989), 11–34.

10. Ibid., 138–41.

11. János Botos et al., *Magyar hétkoznapok* (Budapest: Minerva, 1988), 27.

12. See *Asszonyok* 16, 18 (1946). At this time, Hungarian women's magazines did not have page numbers.

13. Ernone Lukacs, ed., *Nok Enciklopediaja* (Budapest: Minerva, 1966), 471–72.

14. I write about the characteristic features of communist dress after examining approximately two thousand photographs in *Fotótár*, the Photo Collection of the National Museum, located in Budapest, and reading *Asszonyok*, later *Nők Lapia*.

15. "Akik jól dogloznak," *Asszonyok* 5 (1947).

16. See "Tótágas," *Asszonyok* 16 (1947).

17. See "Mit visel a dolgozó nő," *Asszonyok* 9 (1947).

18. RFE, "The Most Elegant Beauty Salon in Budapest," Item No. 711/59, OSA.

19. See "Belvárosi öntudat," *Assxonyok* 13 (1947).

20. Francine du Plessix Gray, *Soviet Women, Walking the Tightrope* (New York: Anchor Books, 1999); Nadezdha Azhgikina and Helena Goscilo, "Getting Under Their Skin: The Beauty Salon in Russian Women's Lives," in *Russia—Women—Culture*, ed. Helena Goscilo and Beth Holmgren (Bloomington: Indiana University Press, 1996), 94–121; David Crowley and Susan E. Reid, eds., *Style and Socialism: Modernity and Material Culture in Postwar Eastern Europe* (New York: Berg, 2000); Slavenka Drakulic, *How We Survived Communism and Even Laughed* (New York: HarperPerennial, 1993); Katalin Medvedev, "Socialism, Dress and Gender" (M.A. thesis, University of Northern Iowa, 1999); Olga Vainshtein, "Female Fashion, Soviet Style: Bodies of Ideology," in *Russia—Women—Culture*, 64–93.

21. In 1957, *Nők Lapja* published a series of lessons on how to dress properly, titled "Öltözködés Iskólaja."

22. Tibor Valuch, *A lódentől a miniszoknyáig* (Budapest: Corvina, 2004), 15.

23. László Kontler, *Millennium in Central Europe: A History of Hungary* (Budapest: Atlantisz, 1999), 95.

24. Also see "1 ruha = 7 ruha" (1 dress = 7 dresses) *Asszonyok* 16 (1946).

25. RFE, "Fashion Problem," Item No. 540/61, OSA.

26. See "Öltözködés Iskolája," regular feature in *Nők Lapja* (1957).

27. Many of these fashion professionals ended up working in New York and Hollywood.

28. Margit Szilvitzky, Budapest, personal communication with Katalin Medvedev, 21 July 2006.

29. Ilona Bundev-Todorov, "Magyar Iparmúvészeti Főiskola Története 1945–1973," *Ars Hungarica* 1 (1979): 103–16; Judit Fekete, "Divatot a dolgozó nőnek!" *Magyar Iparművészet* 2 (2006): 8–10.

30. Szilvitzky communication.

31. Fekete, "Divatot a dolgozó nőnek!"

32. Vámos communication.

33. Ibid.

34. Ibid.

35. In Fotótar, the Photo Collection of the National Museum, I came across many pictures of communist fashion shows. In these pictures, most audience members are men.

36. Eric Naiman, *Sex in Public* (Princeton, N.J.: Princeton University Press, 1997), 214.

37. The same explained the popularity of sports in communist Hungary, such as figure skating, gymnastics, or swimming.

38. Gréti Oravetz, Budapest, personal communication with Katalin Medvedev, 16 June 2004; RFE, "Independent Dressmaker's Work in Communist Hungary," Item No. 7341/55, OSA.

39. There was an uprising against the totalitarian regime in Hungary in 1956.

40. In fact, Hungary began exporting clothes to the West in 1948, amid the biggest sartorial shortages; see "Magyar ruhák mennek külföldre," *Asszonyok* (July 1948).

41. Between 2003 and 2006, I conducted twelve in-depth interviews with former communist women on their sartorial experiences. The women wish to remain anonymous.

CHAPTER 14. WHY THE OLD-FASHIONED IS IN FASHION IN AMERICAN HOUSES

1. Robert Lindsey, "A Renaissance of Victorian-Style Houses," *New York Times*, 7 Jan. 1982.

2. "Willis, Nathaniel Parker," *Appleton's Cyclopaedia of American Biography*, ed. James Grant Wilson and John Fiske (New York: D. Appleton, 1889), 4: 539–41; N. Parker Willis, *The Rag-Bag: A Collection of Ephemera* (New York: Scribner, 1855), 101, 136.

3. Calvert Vaux, *Villas and Cottages* (1857; New York: Da Capo, 1968), 248.

4. Patricia Kelly Hall and Steven Ruggles, "'Restless in the Midst of Their Prosperity': New Evidence on the Internal Migration of Americans, 1850–2000," *Journal of American History* 91 (Dec. 2004): 829

5. Witold Rybczynski, *Home: A Short History of an Idea* (New York: Viking, 1986), 9; Eric Hobsbawm and Terence Ranger, eds., *The Invention of Tradition* (New York: Cambridge University Press, 1983); Kenneth Jackson, *The Crabgrass Frontier: The Suburbanization of the United States* (New York: Oxford University Press, 1985), 50–51

6. Richard Bushman, *The Refinement of America: Persons, Houses, Cities* (New York: Knopf, 1992).

7. Peter L. Berger, Brigitte Berger, and Hansfried Kellner, *The Homeless Mind: Modernization and Consciousness* (New York: Random House, 1973), 184–85.

8. Lewis F. Allen, *Rural Architecture* (New York: C.M. Saxton, 1852), 21–22; Clifford

Edward Clark, Jr., *The American Family Home, 1800–1960* (Chapel Hill: University of North Carolina Press, 1986), 23–24.

9. Bushman, *Refinement of America*, 244; Clark, *The American Family Home*, chap. 1.

10. Allen, *Rural Architecture*, 50; Vaux, *Villas and Cottages*, 31.

11. Andrew Jackson Downing, *The Architecture of Country Houses* (1850; New York: Dover, 1969), 28.

12. Vaux, *Villas and Cottages*, 277: George Alter, Claudia Goldin, and Elyce Rotella, "The Savings of Ordinary Americans: The Philadelphia Saving Fund Society in the Mid-Nineteenth Century," *Journal of Economic History* 54 (Dec. 1994): 750, 763.

13. Downing, *The Architecture of Country Houses*, 26.

14. Ibid., 26–27; Katherine C. Grier, *Culture and Comfort: Parlor Making and Middle-Class Identity, 1850–1930* (Washington, D.C.: Smithsonian Institution Press, 1988), 9–17.

15. David P. Handlin, *The American Home: Architecture and Society, 1815–1915* (Boston: Little, Brown, 1979), 42.

16. Allen, *Rural Architecture*, 20.

17. Downing, *The Architecture of Country Houses*, 49.

18. Gervase Wheeler, *Homes for the People in Suburb and Country: The Villa, The Mansion, And The Cottage* (1855; New York: Arno Press, 1972), 263, 367.

19. "The Old Oaken Bucket," in *Popular Songs of Nineteenth-Century America* (New York: Dover, 1976), 168–70.

20. Henry W. Cleaveland, William Backus, and Samuel D. Backus, *Village and Farm Cottages* (New York: D. Appleton & Co., 1856), 173; Downing, *The Architecture of Country Houses*, 207.

21. Allen, *Rural Architecture*, 236–38.

22. Harriet Beecher Stowe, *Uncle Tom's Cabin, or Life Among the Lowly* (New York: Signet Classics, 1966), 172.

23. Bushman, *The Refinement of America*, 249, 263.

24. Kathryn Kish Sklar, *Catharine Beecher: A Study in American Domesticity* (New Haven, Conn.: Yale University Press, 1973); Nancy Cott, *The Bonds of Womanhood: "Woman's Sphere" in New England, 1780–1835* (New Haven, Conn.: Yale University Press, 1977).

25. Allen, *Rural Architecture*, 133, 149.

26. Catharine M. Sedgwick, *Home* (Boston: James Munroe, 1835), 94.

27. Bushman, *Refinement of America*, 108, 110, 137, 229; Rybczynski, *Home*, 15–77; John Lukacs, "The Bourgeois Interior," *American Scholar* 39 (Autumn 1970): 616–30; Phillipe Ariès, *Centuries of Childhood: A Social History of Family Life*, trans. Robert Baldick (New York: Knopf, 1962), 399.

28. Clark, *The American Family Home*, 58.

29. Elizabeth Chandler to Jane Howell, 23 Dec. 1830; 20 June 1832; Aug. 1832; 13 Dec. 1832; 9 Mar. 1834, all in *Remember the Distance That Divides Us: The Family Letters of Philadelphia Quaker Abolitionist and Michigan Pioneer Elizabeth Margaret Chandler,*

1830–1842, ed. Marcia J. Heringa Mason (East Lansing: Michigan State University Press, 2004), 34–35, 122, 130, 154, 233.

30. Jane Howell to Ruth Evans, 15 May 1834, in *Remember the Distance That Divides Us*, 238.

31. Grant McCracken, "Homey-ness: A Cultural Account of One Constellation of Consumer Goods and Meanings," in *Interpretive Consumer Research*, ed. Elizabeth Hirschman (Provo, Utah: Association for Consumer Research, 1989), 168–83.

32. This is consistent with David Lowenthal's observation that an interest in heritage and the things of the past developed in both Europe and the U.S. during the 1980s. David Lowenthal, *Possessed by the Past: The Heritage Crusade and the Spoils of History* (New York: Free Press, 1996), 4.

33. Steven Mintz and Susan Kellogg, *Domestic Revolutions: A Social History of the American Family* (New York: Free Press, 1988), 185.

34. William H. Whyte, *The Organization Man* (New York: Simon and Schuster, 1956), 288.

35. "Table A-1, Annual Geographical Mobility Rates, by Type of Movement: 1947–2003," *Current Population Survey, Historical Geographical Mobility Reports*, U.S. Census Bureau, http://www.census.gov/population/www/socdemo/migrate/past-migrate.html, accessed 22 June 2004; Jason Schacter, Rachel S. Franklin, and Marc J. Perry, *Migration and Geographic Mobility in Metropolitan and Nonmetropolitan America: 1995–2000, Census 2000 Special Reports* (Washington D.C.: U.S. Census Bureau, Aug. 2003), 1–2.

36. Mintz and Kellog, *Domestic Revolutions*, 203; Margaret Andersen, *Thinking About Women: Sociological Perspectives on Sex and Gender* (Boston: Allyn and Bacon, 1997), 145; *News: United States Department of Labor, Employment Characteristics of Families in 2001* (Washington D.C.: Bureau of Labor Statistics, 2002), 2.

37. Barbara Le Bay, "American Families Are Drifting Apart," *USA Today* 130, 1 Sept. 2001, 20–22.

38. Quoted in Heather Chaplin, "Past? Perfect!" *American Demographics* 21 (May 1999): 68–69.

39. Geoffrey Colvin, "What the Baby-Boomers Will Buy Next," *Fortune* 110 (5 Oct. 1984): 30.

40. Chaplin, "Past? Perfect!" 68–69.

41. J. Walker Smith and Ann Clurman, *Rocking the Ages: The Yankelovich Report on Generational Marketing* (New York: HarperBusiness, 1998), 270.

42. Marjorie Garber, *Sex and Real Estate: Why We Love Houses* (New York: Pantheon, 2000), 153.

43. Robert Steuteville, "The New Urbanism: An Alternative to Modern, Automobile-oriented Planning and Development," *New Urban News*, 28 June 2000, http://www.newurbannews.com/ (accessed 24 June 2004); Andrew Ross, *The Celebration Chronicles: Life, Liberty, and the Pursuit of Property Values in Disney's New Town* (New York: Ballantine Books, 1999), 331.

44. Sarah Boxer, "A Remedy for the Rootlessness of Modern Suburban Life?" *New York Times*, 1 Aug. 1998.

45. William L. Nolan, "Main Street Revisited," *Better Homes and Gardens* 78 (May 2000): 94.

46. Carl Hiaasen, *Team Rodent: How Disney Devours the World* (New York: Ballantine, 1998), 50–52; Russ Rymer, "Back to the Future: Disney Reinvents the Company Town," *Harper's Magazine* 293 (Oct. 1996): 68; Beth Dunlop, "In Florida, A New Emphasis on Design," *New York Times*, 9 Dec. 2001.

47. Dick Case, "New Urbanism Takes Root," *Post Standard*, 10 May 2001; Douglas Frantz and Catherine Collins, *Celebration, USA: Living in Disney's Brave New Town* (New York: Henry Holt, 1999), 24.

48. Joel Hirshhorn and Paul Souza, *New Community Design to the Rescue: Fulfilling Another American Dream* (Washington, D.C.: National Governors' Association, 2001), 5.

49. Philip Langdon, "Suburbanites Pick Favorite Home Styles," *New York Times*, 22 Apr. 1982.

50. American LIVES, *Community Preferences: What the Buyers Really Want in Design, Features and Amenities, A Follow-Up Study to the 1994 Shopper and Homeowner Study and the 1995 New Urbanism Study* (Oakland, Calif.: American LIVES, 1999), 38–39.

51. http://www.builderhouseplans.com/features/builder-favorites.hwx (accessed 24 June 2006).

52. Robert Lindsey, "A Renaissance of Victorian-Style Houses."

53. Debra Goldman, "Home Improvements," *Brandweek* 35 (7 Nov. 1994): 20–21.

54. Stephanie Gutmann, "Rusticated," *New Republic* 212 (3 Apr. 1995): 14–15.

55. "Are you a little bit country?" http://www.pioneerthinking.com/ara-country.html (accessed 15 July 2006).

56. Restorationhardware.com, http://www.restorationhardware.com/rh/catalog/product/product.jsp?productId = prod1166125&navCount = 37 (accessed 7 Apr. 2007).

57. Chaplin, "Past? Perfect!" 68–69.

58. Stephen Drucker, "Living Traditions," *Martha Stewart Living Magazine* (Sept. 1998): 29.

59. Txbugaboo, "How to decide my tastes?" 12 Jan. 2006, Message: [5768.1], http://dgroups.bhg.com/n/pfx/forum.aspx?nav = messages&tsn = 4&tid = 5768&webtag = bhgdecorating (accessed 23 June 2006).

60. suzieq775@msn.com, "How to decide my tastes?" 21 Feb. 2006, Message: [5768.4: 5768.1]; Mobarb2*, "How to decide my tastes?" 21 Feb. 2006 Message: [5768.6: 5768.1], at http://dgroups.bhg.com/n/pfx/forum.aspx?nav = messages&tsn = 4&tid = 5768&webtag = bhgdecoratng (accessed 23 June 2006).

61. SMLDesigns, "How to decide my tastes?" 22 Feb. 2006, Message: [5768.9: 5768.8] at http://dgroups.bhg.com/n/pfx/forum.aspx?nav = messages&tsn = 1&tid = 5971&webtag = bhgdecorating (accessed 23 June 2006); dpowell, "Photos of homes," 15 Mar. 2006, Message: [5971.1], http://dgroups.bhg.com/n/pfx/forum.aspx?nav = messages&tsn = 1&tid = 5971&webtag = bhgdecorating (accessed 23 June 2006).

62. Anakens, "What is your decorating style?" 19 Mar. 2004, Message [6230891], http://www.bhg.com/bhg/dgroups/viewForum.jhtml?forum = 33 (accessed 28 Mar. 2004);

gmjmon, "Why do you like the styles you do?" 26 Mar. 2004, Message [6272167]; breezie, "Why do you like the styles you do?" 27 Mar. 2004, Message [6276564]; deedlerock, "Why do you like the styles you do?" 25 Mar. 2004, Message [6265898] (accessed 28 Mar. 2004).

63. Sklar, *Catharine Beecher*, 151–67; Clark, *The American Family Home*, chap. 1.

CONTRIBUTORS

Ariel Beaujot is a Ph.D. candidate in the Department of History at the University of Toronto. Her dissertation, "Accessorize It: A Study of the Manufacture, Design, and Meaning of Victorian Women's Accessories," is an exploration of the ways fashionable objects reveal the beliefs, values, and prejudices of Victorians in England.

Regina Lee Blaszczyk is a visiting scholar and lecturer in the Department of the History and Sociology of Science at the University of Pennsylvania. She is the author of *Imagining Consumers: Design and Innovation from Wedgwood to Corning*, named Best Book in Business History for 2001, and *American Consumer Society: From Hearth to HDTV, 1865–2005* (forthcoming), and coeditor of *Major Problems in American Business History: Documents and Essays*. She is writing a book on color, commerce, and fashion in transnational perspective.

Elspeth Brown is Associate Professor of History at the University of Toronto. She is the author of *The Corporate Eye: Photography and the Rationalization of American Commercial Culture, 1884–1929* and coeditor of *Cultures of Commerce: Representation and American Business Culture, 1877–1960*. Her current research is an analysis of the commercial modeling industry in twentieth-century United States, exploring the complex relationship among visuality, identity formation, and the commodification of the self in modern American history and culture.

Heather Hess, a specialist in central European decorative arts, received her Ph.D. in Art History from Rutgers University in 2006. She is currently 2006–2008 Stefan Engelhorn Curatorial Fellow at the Busch-Reisinger Museum, Harvard University.

Susan J. Matt holds the Endowed Chair in the Social and Behavioral Sciences at Weber State University. She is the author *of Keeping Up with the Joneses: Envy in American Consumer Society, 1890–1930* (available from the University of Pennsylvania Press). She is currently writing a book on the history of homesickness in America, from the colonial era to the present.

Katalin Medvedev is a feminist dress scholar. A native of Hungary, she was a Professor at the Teacher Training College of Eötvös Loránd University in Budapest for twenty years before she came to the United States to get her Ph.D. at the University of Minnesota. She is an Assistant Professor at the University of Georgia where she teaches courses on dress and culture and the fundamentals of fashion industry. Her research focuses on the social and political aspects of material culture.

Elisabetta Merlo is Associate Professor at the Institute of Economic History at Bocconi University, Milan. She has been in charge of the cataloguing of the historical archives of the Camera Nazionale della Moda Italiana (Association of Italian Fashion Designers). She has published extensively on the history of the Italian fashion industry. Among her recent publications are *Moda italiana: storia di un'industria* and "Le origini del sistema moda," in *Storia d'Italia: Annali 19, La moda*, ed. Carlo Marco Belfanti and Fabio Giusberti.

Kaori O'Connor is a Research Fellow in the Department of Anthropology at University College London. She holds degrees in anthropology from Reed College in the United States and from Oxford University and University College London in the United Kingdom where she was an ESRC Ph.D. and Postdoctoral Fellow. She also worked at *Vogue*, was the founding editor of the annual *London Fashion Guide*, and has written widely on fashion, textiles, and material culture. Her most recent book is *The English Breakfast: The Biography of a National Meal, with Recipes*, and she is currently writing a cultural biography of Lycra.

Tomoko Okawa is a Ph.D. candidate in the Department of Social Science at Tokyo Metropolitan University in Japan. She has published "Investment and Launching of a Couture House: *Groupe Boussac* and Maison Christian Dior" in *Journal of Business and Institutions*, and "Development of a *Couture Maison* for the Cotton Conglomerate: Christian Dior and *Groupe Boussac*" in *Bulletin de la Société Franco-Japonaise de Gestion*. With extensive professional experience in the fashion industry, she works for the Institute of Fashion Industries, which is supported by the Japanese Ministry of Economy, Trade, and Industry (METI).

Francesca Polese is Assistant Professor at the Institute of Economic History at Bocconi University, Milan, where she conducts research in Italian business history and the history of the fashion business. Among her recent publications are "In Search of a New Industry: Giovanni Battista Pirelli and His Educational Journey Through Europe, 1870–71"; "Big Business Performance in the 20th Century: Italy," with C. Brambilla et al., in *Essays in European Business Performance in the 20th Century*, ed. C. Brautaset; and *Alla ricerca di un'industria nuova*.

Véronique Pouillard is a postdoctoral researcher at the Belgian National Scientific Research Fund at the University of Brussels; in 2006–2007, she was a BAEF Fellow in the Department of History at Columbia University. Her dissertation, "La publicité en Belgique (1850–1975): des courtiers aux agences internationales," bears on the rise of the advertising professions in Belgium. She is currently working on transatlantic relations in the fashion business.

Christine Ruane is Associate Professor and Director of Graduate Studies in the History Department at the University of Tulsa. She is the author of *Gender, Class, and the Professionalization of Russian City Teachers, 1860–1914* and coeditor of *Russian Studies in History*. She is currently completing a manuscript on the history of the Russian fashion industry, 1700–1917.

Marlis Schweitzer is Assistant Professor in the Department of Theatre at York University in Toronto. She received her Ph.D. from the University of Toronto in 2005 and spent the 2005–2006 academic year as an Andrew W. Mellon Postdoctoral Fellow with the University of Pennsylvania's Penn Humanities Forum. She is currently working on a book on theater, fashion, and American consumer culture, forthcoming with the University of Pennsylvania Press.

William R. Scott is Assistant Professor of History at the University of Delaware. His dissertation at the University of California, Berkeley, "Dressing Down: Modernism, Leisure, and the California Sportswear Industry, 1930–1960," links the changes in men's clothing over the last century to large currents in twentieth-century history: the rise of a consumerist masculinity, the transformation of labor, and the emergence of modernist aesthetics.

Steve Zdatny is Professor of History at West Virginia University. His books include *Hairstyles and Fashion: A Hairdresser's History of Paris*, *The Politics of Survival: Artisans in Twentieth-Century France*, and most recently *Fashion, Work, and Politics in Modern France*.

INDEX

ACKNOWLEDGMENTS

This book owes much to the exciting ideas and intellectual discourse generated at two conferences: "Producing Fashion," at the Hagley Museum and Library in Wilmington, Delaware, in October 2005, organized by Hagley's research arm, the Center for the History of Business, Technology, and Society; and "The Sixties," a public conference on 1960s fashion, held at the Georges Pompidou Center in Paris in December 2005. It also owes much to the diligence, patience, and imagination of the essayists. It has been a pleasure to work with so many scholars who are digging through the archives, conducting in-depth oral history interviews, and finding new historical materials that add much our knowledge about the business of fashion. I enjoyed working with young scholars who are bringing fresh approaches to a timeless topic as well as old hands whose insights stem from many years as journalists, professors, and executives in the global fashion business.

Most notable, however, are my debts to colleagues in Wilmington, Philadelphia, and Paris. In the United States, thanks go to Roger Horowitz, Philip B. Scranton, and Susan Strasser, coeditors of the Hagley Perspectives Series, for their ongoing support of my work; and to Theresa R. Snyder, Hagley's Deputy Director for Library Administration, for her continued investment in the Hagley Center for the History of Business, Technology and Society, and its annual fall conference. I am also indebted to Ruth Schwartz Cowan, chair of the Department of the History and Sociology of Science at the University of Pennsylvania, for providing me with access to a wonderful research institution and all of its resources. In France, special gratitude is extended to Patrick Fridenson, Michèle Ruffat, and Dominique Veillon for inviting me to spend time in Paris and speak at "The Sixties," where I met many new and established practitioners of fashion history, and to Diana Crane for continued inspiration. My greatest debt, however, is personal. This volume is dedicated to my muse and manager, Lee O'Neill, who supported this book, my latest project, with his unwavering faith and his enduringly elegant style.